The Teaching of Science in Primary Schools

5th edition

The new edition of this best-selling textbook provides an up-to-date discussion of the many aspects of teaching primary science, maintaining its strong focus on constructivist learning and the role of social interaction in learning. With emphasis on the child-centred approach, the book also promotes the importance of fostering motivation for learning through enjoyment and giving children some control of their activities.

The fifth edition has been updated to reflect:

- the move towards a cross-curricular approach in primary schools;

- recent developments in the use of ICT by teachers and pupils;

- how assessment and records can be used to help learning;

- what recent studies of the brain can tell us about learning;

- the widespread emphasis on teaching and learning through inquiry;

- the recognition of the importance of discussion, dialogue and argumentation;

- changes in curriculum management and planning.

The book opens with multiple case studies, four of which are new to this edition, offering cross-curricular examples of primary science in action. Each chapter is framed by an introduction and summary points. Suggestions for further reading are provided and there are numerous references to useful websites.

Combining theory and practice, *The Teaching of Science in Primary Schools* helps the reader to understand the rationale behind the practice. It continues to be essential reading for all trainee and practising primary school teachers, including students on PGCE Primary, BEd, BA Primary and Education Studies courses and those studying for further qualifications in education.

Wynne Harlen OBE has been involved in teaching and research in science education, evaluation and pupil assessment throughout her long career. She has been Sidney Jones Professor of Science Education at the University of Liverpool, UK, and Director of the Scottish Council for Research in Education and is now Visiting Professor at the University of Bristol, UK.

Anne Qualter has wide experience in research and professional development in science. She is Head of the Department of Education at the University of Liverpool, UK.

The Teaching of Science in Primary Schools

5th edition

**Wynne Harlen
and Anne Qualter**

Routledge
Taylor & Francis Group

LONDON AND NEW YORK

First edition published by David Fulton Publishers 1992

Second edition published 1996

Third edition published 2000

Fouth edition published 2004

This edition published 2009
by Routledge
2 Park Square, Milton Park, Abingdon, Oxon OX14 4RN

Simultaneously published in the USA and Canada
by Routledge
270 Madison Avenue, New York, NY 10016

Routledge is an imprint of the Taylor & Francis Group, an informa business

© 2009 Wynne Harlen and Anne Qualter

Typeset in Bembo by HWA Text and Data Management, London
Printed and bound in Great Britain by TJ International Ltd, Padstow, Cornwall

British Library Cataloguing in Publication Data
A catalogue record for this book is available from the British Library

Library of Congress Cataloging in Publication Data
Harlen, Wynne.
  The teaching of science in primary schools / Wynne Harlen and Anne Qualter. – 5th ed.
     p. cm.
  Rev. ed. of: Teaching, learning and assessing science 5-12. 2006.
  Includes bibliographical references and index.
  1. Science – Study and teaching (Elementary) I. Qualter, Anne, 1955- II. Harlen,
  Wynne.   Teaching, learning and assessing science 5-12. III. Title.
LB1585.H298 2009
372.35´044--dc22   2008038764

ISBN 10: 0-415-46527-3 (pbk)
ISBN 13: 978-0-415-46527-4 (pbk)

Contents

Acknowledgements

We would like to thank the many teachers in schools and other educators who have shared their time and expertise with us as we have tried to capture the developments in learning and teaching primary science since the previous edition. In particular thanks are due to Sue Andrews of Children Challenge Industry in the North West, David Leigh Evans of Sarn Associates and the industries supporting his work, including E.On, and BHP Bilton, Kathy Schofield of St Edward's Primary School Runcorn, Yvonne Niescier of Sacred Heart Catholic College, Crosby, Linda Davies and all the staff at Neston Primary School in Wiltshire, and Judith Salmon and her staff of Blackmoor Park Infants in Liverpool.

We would also like to express our gratitude to the following for permission to reproduce figures from their publications:

- The Association for Science Education for permission to reproduce material from various issues of *Primary Science Review* and from *Primary Science*;

- Paul Chapman Publishing to reproduce materials from *Assessing Science in the Primary Classroom, Written Tasks* by Schilling *et al.*,1990;

- Stuart Naylor and Brenda Keogh for permission to reproduce a concept cartoon from *Concept Cartoons in Science Education,* 2000;

- Taylor and Francis for permission to reproduce material from the *Making Progress in Primary Science Handbook* (Second Edition) by Harlen *et al.*, 2003;

- Liverpool University Press for permission to reproduce various drawings from SPACE Research Reports on *Growth* (1990), *Sound* (1990), *Processes of Life* (1992), and *Evaporation and Condensation* (1990);

- The Welsh Assembly for permission to reproduce a figure from 'Why develop thinking and assessment for learning in the classroom?'

Introduction

The pace of change in education, as in other parts of life, is ever-increasing. This is evident in the need we have found to replace about half of the material in this book only four years after the fourth edition. The most obvious innovations are in the area of ICT, where new technologies have opened up many different ways of enabling children to interact with ideas, objects, people and each other. There are equal, but less obvious, changes in how we see the aims of science education at the primary level and how to work towards them. Some of these are apparent in the reference to 'inquiry' throughout and in the discussion of the nature of scientific inquiry. We also note the emphasis on skills, not only science inquiry skills, but those relating more broadly to thinking, to learning how to learn and to self-assessment. These appear as goals in the revised science curricula of Scotland, Wales and Northern Ireland, whilst conceptual goals are expressed in broader terms than in the curricula created in the 1990s. (The new primary curriculum for England is expected in 2010.) These new curricula underline the view that the aims of primary school science are for children to use inquiry skills in developing understanding of the nature of scientific activity and the basic ideas of science as these apply to everyday experience.

Changes in the way the aims are to be achieved, urged in statements from governments and legislation in the UK, include greater integration of science with other curriculum areas, more learning outside the classroom and the use of assessment to help learning, as well as greater emphasis on skills. Those readers with memories of primary science 20 or so years ago may regard these more as a return to previous practice rather than as innovations. However, the differences from the 1980s to the 2000s are profound. Not only do we now have science taught – and by-and-large well taught – in all schools but we can learn from previous experience. It is important to avoid loose practices of the past, such as science disappearing within a broad topic, or visits being a fun day out rather than an important part of learning, or the collection of data taking precedence over its interpretation. We have taken care in this book to make sure that these aspects of practice are discussed so that earlier pitfalls are avoided.

An area where we can expect more change is that of assessment. Although in this book we focus on assessment for learning (formative assessment) more than assessment of learning (summative assessment) it is undeniable that the way in which summative assessment is carried out affects teachers and pupils, particularly when results are used to set targets and evaluate schools and teachers. Changes made to assessment legislation in Scotland, Wales and Northern Ireland, to avoid frequent testing and the high stakes use of results have already had a positive impact on science education. For instance, in Wales, following the end of national tests, teachers, particularly in Year 6, were giving more attention to skills rather than focusing rather narrowly on the content that was tested, using more group work and providing more opportunity for practical investigations.

At the same time as dealing with areas of change in primary science education, there are features that recent experience serves only to underscore. These include: the importance of finding out and building from the ideas that children bring to the classroom from what they have been told or have developed through their own thinking; the value of talk, dialogue and argumentation (using evidence to defend conclusions); using assessment to help learning; and the importance of good management and planning at school and class levels. We have attempted in this edition to enhance the discussion of these aspects of practice through use of examples, particularly drawing on six case studies throughout the book which form the first two chapters. These six case studies describe real events in real classrooms or out of school sites. All except one (which is taken from Teachers' TV) were created by observing and talking to the teachers involved. These were not 'super' teachers and not everything that happens is exemplary; the lessons are certainly not intended as models to follow. Indeed, they clearly have features specific to the classes, teachers and contexts involved which makes them difficult to transfer to other classrooms. But they also have features that are common to good practice in primary science and they provide us with real examples that help to communicate these features.

The structure of the book

The 26 short chapters are arranged in six parts: Primary science in action; Learning through inquiry; Teaching through inquiry; Assessment to help learning; Materials and ICT to support inquiry; and Managing science at the school level. These themes, helped by cross-referencing between chapters, make it possible to 'dip into' the book according to interest at a particular time.

Part 1 begins with two chapters presenting and discussing science activities in the primary school through case studies of children's activities. The focus in Chapter 1 is on learning experiences of children in the early primary years (5–8-year-olds) and in Chapter 2 on those of children in the later primary years (9–11-year-olds). In each of these chapters, three examples are followed by discussion of the features of the children's experiences that are particularly significant in enabling them to learn science. We then consider, in Chapter 3, what learning is required by the revised curricula in various parts of the UK. We look particularly at changes made to these curricula since the 1990s, giving greater emphasis to developing awareness of the relevance of science to environmental and social concerns and to the development of understanding of the nature, strengths and limitations of science and scientific activity. Then Chapter 4 reflects growing interest in what the study of the brain can add to our understanding of learning and how to bring it about. There we tentatively explore what neuroscience can provide in terms of explanations of why certain types of experience are important in learning.

Part 2 discusses different aspects of the process of learning through inquiry. Beginning with the reasons for taking children's ideas into account, we use examples of children's ideas from research to arrive at some characteristics, which are used in later discussion of how to help children develop more scientific ideas. A model of learning through inquiry helps to reveal the role of inquiry skills in the development of ideas from 'small' to 'bigger' ideas. This is followed by consideration of skills of different kinds and of how inquiry, thinking and learning to learn skills have different but complementary roles in learning. The section ends with a chapter on talk, its various forms and its importance in the development of children's understanding.

Part 3 complements the second by focusing on how to bring about learning through inquiry, but also pointing out that not all science is learnt this way. Although developed concurrently in practice, we discuss in separate chapters the strategies teachers can use to help children develop scientific ideas, inquiry skills, scientific attitudes and enjoyment of learning. We discuss motivation for learning and the importance of children finding satisfaction in making sense of the world around them. How teachers question children and how they handle the questions children ask are important aspects of teaching science discussed in this section. It concludes with consideration of lesson planning, essential to all teaching but particularly relevant to establishing the balance between giving children opportunities to think for themselves and ensuring that activities have purpose and relevance to learning goals.

Assessment of pupils is the topic of Part 4. It begins with general discussion of purposes, methods, properties and uses of assessment. We note that purposes should determine the appropriate methods used but that the use of the results of assessment determines whether or not the purpose is achieved. So, the difference between formative and summative assessment is determined by whether the results are used to help learning or to report and record it. The next three chapters deal with key aspects of using assessment for learning: methods of gathering and interpreting information; feedback that helps learning; and the role of children in assessing their work. The final chapter in this section concerns summative assessment. Here we discuss various ways of summarising achievement at certain points and compare the pros and cons of using teachers' judgements or using tests for this purpose. We note the adverse effects of using national test results for the 'high stakes' evaluation of schools and teachers.

Part 5 looks at how different materials, resources, locations and applications of computer technology help children's learning in science. It begins by discussing the value of practical work and direct interaction with objects and materials, whilst emphasising the role of debate and discussion in taking full advantage of active exploration and investigation. The selection, storing and maintenance of equipment are included in this chapter, as are matters of safety. The latter also apply in the next chapter, about learning outside the classroom. Examples of work in different locations add to those in the case studies in Chapters 1 and 2 to illustrate the learning opportunities provided by visits to natural locations, places of work and science centres and museums. Careful selection, planning and follow up enable children to benefit from the resources to which these provide access, which are not available in the classroom. The use of ICT provides many different ways of extending children's experience. The two chapters on the use of ICT by children and by teachers are those where content has changed almost entirely from the last edition of this book. We provide information that is as up-to-date as can be, but recognise that some will soon be overtaken by further developments.

Part 6 focuses on certain aspects of provision at the school level. We discuss here the planning and curriculum organisation for science that supports, for example, the involvement of parents, continuity and progression throughout the school and cross-curricular work. One aspect of the management of learning in science is keeping records of children's learning experiences and achievements and sometimes involving pupils in keeping records of their activities. These records are used not only for teachers' planning but also for self-evaluation of provision for science and suggest some standards for classroom practice and for school provision for science that teachers and senior management can use in this evaluation. We then discuss the responsibility of the science subject leader, or coordinator, to advise, support and ensure professional development of their colleagues. This leads to the final chapter, on teachers' continued learning, which describes a variety of opportunities for professional development in science.

Readers familiar with an earlier edition of this book may note an increase in the frequency of references to research and literature, often accessed through the Internet. This may seem odd in a book intended for use by teachers in training and practice, but it reflects two trends in education. One is an increase in the quantity of educational research that has been published in the 1990s and 2000s. This is itself a result of the second trend, which is for those involved to want evidence for the actions they are urged to take. Teachers ought to know when advice is, and is not, evidence-based and to be able to judge for themselves how firm any evidence is or how sound the arguments. This trend will no doubt increase as we move towards a profession qualified at Master's level and hopefully it will add to the satisfaction of enjoyment in teaching science in the primary school.

Wynne Harlen
August 2008

PART 1

Primary science in action

1

Primary science in action
The early years

Introduction

We begin by following some classes as the children explore, investigate and begin to develop their understanding of the scientific aspects of the world around. To do this it is important, particularly for the youngest children, to have direct experience of real things and phenomena in their environment. This will mean that, although for some activities the objects and equipment inside school will be sufficient, other activities ought to take children out of the classroom. In all cases, however, the engagement of the children will depend on whether the situation or problem they are investigating seems real and interesting to them.

The three cases in this chapter describe work with children aged between 5 and 8. We begin with Kathy and her class of 5- and 6-year-olds, working on a problem presented through a story about choosing a bouncy ball for a dog. Then we follow two small classes of children of similar age from a small primary school in North Wales as they visit their local beach and use classroom facilities provided there by a local industry. The third study is an account of how Chris transformed her classroom in order to provide her 6- and 7-year-olds with a real context for investigating the melting of ice. The chapter concludes with some discussion of significant features of these early years case studies. In later chapters it is often helpful to refer back to these examples.

Kathy's 5–6-year-olds and the dog's ball

Background

Kathy was starting a new topic with her class of 5- and 6-year-olds. The class had previously undertaken a topic focusing on materials, looking at the best materials for mopping up a spillage on the kitchen floor. This had been introduced through a DVD about a cartoon dog, 'Discovery Dog', projected onto the interactive white board (IWB). As a way of recording their project, they had produced a big, illustrated, book. Reviewing this book enabled them to revisit some of the things they had done and talked about, such as predicting, fair testing, and safety, reminding them of the language they has used as well as recalling what fun it was.

The lesson

The new project began with a short animation in which a naughty puppy had managed to burst the dog's favourite ball, had chewed another to a pulp, and had lost another over the garden fence. The children saw the different events depicted on the IWB and read the words, as well as hearing them. The teacher was able to pause as they went along the four pages of pictures and text to ask questions and respond to comments by the children. She let the children chip in with memories of balls that had popped after being bitten by a dog ('it was round and then it looked like a dish'), or what they knew of puppies and how they behave ('my Gran's got a dog and it chews the chairs').

The teacher focused the class on the problem of how they might find a good bouncy ball for the dog:

Teacher   If you went to a shop to buy a ball you wouldn't just pick one without trying it would you?

Children   Pick a really bouncy one out and then e-mail him to tell him.
Get him another football.

The children began to suggest particular balls and those used for play or sport. But before going further Kathy asked them to 'have a think', then to talk in pairs for a couple of minutes (thinking pairs was a common element of their lessons) to consider how they might help the dog find a really good bouncy ball. Bringing the children back together, Kathy asked them for their ideas:

Children   We could get a lot of balls and have a vote on them.
We could find which balls bounce and which don't, because Discovery Dog likes bouncy ones.
Yes we could have a vote on it.
We could get some balls and bounce them. But not in the classroom.

A brief discussion followed about the potential problems of bouncing balls all over the classroom. The teacher then showed the class the large box full of different balls that she had collected. How would they find which was the bounciest? The children began to settle on the idea of selecting out the relatively more bouncy balls and then focusing on these for further testing.

It was then play time, after which they reconvened in the school hall. With the children sat on the floor with the box of balls in the middle, Kathy reminded them of the problem and they recalled some of their discussion from before play time. She then passed some of the children a ball and encouraged them to describe it. The balls were passed around during the discussion and all the children had a chance to look at the balls and describe them.

The initial discussion was wide ranging, with children pointing to and describing balls. Kathy praised children for observing well and using good describing words:

Children   That looks like a dog's ball, that small pinky one.
This one is all rough and dull looking.
Oh look, this one is a mini rugby ball.

Kathy asked for more explanation:

Children	It's not a round.
	It's an oval shape.
Teacher	What makes them all balls?
Child	They are all round.
Teacher	But the rugby ball isn't.
Children	When it bounces it goes the other way.
	Some might be bigger.
	Some might be smaller.
	Some might be rough.
	Different colours and shapes.
	That one looks like the Earth (a map printed on the ball).
	Bumpy.
	Patterns.
Teacher	Do you think patterns on the ball would make a difference?
Children	No, it bounces the same.
	That one looks like a dog's ball. It is a dog's ball.
	Some are not sports balls, and some you kick and some you bat.
	That's different to all the others because it's got holes in it.
	Some are hard.
	There's a criminal [means 'chemical'] inside that one; it lights up.
	This has air inside it.
Teacher	How do we know?
Children	It can pop and go flat.
	That's a sponge all through.

The teacher then brought the children back to the issue of 'bounciness'.

Teacher	How are we going to find out, with all these different balls, which are the bounciest?
Children	Get a ball each and bounce it.
Teacher	Good idea. How many bounces?

The class settled on ten bounces from around waist height. The children were then asked to choose a ball they think might be a good bouncer. There were enough to go round. They spread out around the hall as they selected their ball, continuing to discuss and describe their selections:

Child	The green one.
Teacher	Why do you think that one?
Children	Because I think it will go high.
	The orange one; it's squashy.
	The red one. It looks like it's bouncy. The rubber might make it bouncy.
	The dog ball … it looks bouncy and dead hard.
	That one, because I have used it before and it's bouncy.

Once balls had been selected one of the children asked to change hers:

Teacher   Why do you want to change?
Child   It's too squashy to bounce much.
Teacher   Anyone else want to change?

There was further discussion as the children moved around.

Children   I chose this particular one because it's very tight full of air.
Because bigger balls bounce highest.
Teacher   Oh, so who chose a small ball?

To avoid the chaos of having too many balls being bounced at the same time, they agreed to having four children at a time bounce their balls ten times and the others to vote on the 'best'. The children were, in this way, encouraged to focus on observing the balls bounce.

The process was very swiftly carried out and the class identified the best ball in each of the groups:

Teacher   How could we find out which of these balls is the best bouncer?
Children   We could have a vote again?
We could measure it.
Teacher   How could we measure it?
Children   We could stick the balls together …
You could catch it and measure it with a ruler how high it is.
We could put Post-it notes on the board to see how high it is.
We could use blocks to see how high.
We could drop it down from a table and see if it goes back up to the table.
We could try which bounces quickest.

Trying this last idea allowed the children some further play and exploration, but was rejected as a good way to test the balls, because different children bounced them in different ways, and some children failed to catch them every time. So it really was not a fair test.

At this point the lesson was due to end. The teacher suggested that they take the selected balls back to the classroom and put them in the basket ready for the next day, when they would try some of their ideas for finding the best bouncer. A child pointed to one of the selected balls, and said:

Child   That ball doesn't bounce good in the wet.
Teacher   I'll make a note of that idea; we could test that out too.

Throughout the lesson the teacher took photographs of the children working – sitting discussing the balls, all bouncing balls, bouncing in fours and voting. This then provided the basis of the record of the investigation which would be used to create the big book. It meant that the children were not being distracted by having to write anything, which takes a long time for such young children. The big book and the selected balls provided the record of this lesson.

Class 1 and 2 visit a North Wales beach

Background

The trip was planned to take place towards the end of April, early in the summer term so that the 27 children of classes 1 and 2 of a school from a small, former mining community in North Wales could base their project work around the visit. Despite the proximity of the beach most of the children had seldom visited and some had never been there. The school badge depicts the lighthouse that still stands on the beach where some of the only remaining dunes on the North Wales coast still provide protection from the sea. There are many local industries, oil and gas refineries and a significant tourist industry based on large numbers of mostly static holiday caravans. The area of the dunes is designated as a site of special scientific interest. The large oil company in the area with a gas processing plant near the beach, funds some conservation work as well as school visits, especially for the children in local schools. The company provides a classroom, and supports its staff and rangers in working with schools in the area on a number of projects. In this case the focus was on the environment and conservation.

The weather on the morning of the visit was extremely wet. David, the project leader and teacher, had been down to the beach early to check that no dangers (such as items washed up on the beach, broken fences, sharp objects around the places where the class would be walking) had arisen since his last visit. One of the class teachers had also been out walking her dogs and worrying about the weather. An early morning phone call led to an agreement that the children would spend the first half of their visit in the environment classroom and would then go down to the beach just after noon when the weather promised to be at its best.

In the classroom near the beach

The children were sat around five tables, each with an adult (teacher or helper). David started the morning by showing the pupils some photographs of the area, the lighthouse, and some rather attractive sea- and beachscapes. The pupils were asked to discuss the differences between their village and the beach – things that they would see in the village that they wouldn't see at the beach, and then to think of things on the beach that they would not see in their village. In each group an adult acted as scribe, leaving the pupils free to think about differences. The tendency was to focus on the beach and to think about things that they would find there, so the adults helped to focus the children's attention on differences between the village and the beach. The discussions were lively and productive. After ten minutes the teacher drew the suggestions together completing a chart on the electronic whiteboard.

As each item was suggested, the teacher explored with the children why it might be found only in the village or only on the beach:

Teacher   The lighthouse. Did it grow or was it built?
Children   It was built.
             So the boats don't crash.

Teacher	Yes it was built a very long time ago after a big boat carrying lots of valuable cargo and lots of sailors sank in a bad storm because they hit rocks under the water. But now we have things called buoys. These are smaller and have lights on and they float in the sea. So we don't need the old lighthouse any more. Why don't we knock it down?
Child	No! *(quite shocked)*
Teacher	Why? Because it's a symbol. Who has a lighthouse symbol on their badge?
	(The pupils all know about the school badge, a lighthouse and they point to their sweaters with the badge.)
Teacher	Who else likes the lighthouse?
Child	Visitors.
Teacher	Yes we have lots of visitors in the caravans. Tourists, holiday makers, they like coming here. It's really nice that people like to come down to our beach.

After this discussion the teacher showed some slides of the beach and dunes that the school will be able to use in their topic. These included some showing damage – litter, dog mess, graffiti on 'you are here' map and warning signs – as well as more pleasant images of shells, seaweed, seagulls and sand dunes. Finally, there was a picture of a natterjack toad – which is very rare, and everyone is very proud to have it living on 'our' beach. These images were discussed in the context of helping children to realise that 'we really have got to look after our beach' and what to do if they find things damaged.

Two further activities for the children to carry out in groups were designed to stimulate thinking about seabirds and how different events could help or hinder their survival. Eventually, the weather cleared and the children were able to get to the beach.

Down on the beach

As the children walked towards the sea break of dunes with the project leader, he reminded them that the dunes were there to hold back the stormy seas and keep the land safe. Passing a beach shop he pointed to a nest in the gutter:

Teacher	Can you see up there? What is it? Who has made a home there?
Child	A bird.
Teacher	Yes it's a house sparrow. If you listen carefully you can hear him calling to his mate.

Village	Beach
Houses	Lighthouse
Trees	Sand
Stones	Shells
School	Windmills
Cars	Starfish
Garden	Fish
	Crabs
	Jellyfish

Figure 1.1 Children's views about things found in the village and on the beach

(He puts his hand behind his ear and the children fall silent.)

Teacher   There she is. Can you hear her answering? When we are out and about it's always good to observe carefully. What do I mean by 'observe'?

Children   Look.
           Listen.
           Keep quiet.

Teacher   Yes we need to keep quiet so we can hear things, and so that we don't frighten things away.

Child   Feel, smell.

Teacher   That's right; to 'observe' is what a scientist does so that they notice lots of things.

The leader stopped at a 'you are here' map. This is the one they saw in the photograph, and they all remembered seeing it. As the class walked up the rise to cross into the dunes the leader asked:

Teacher   Can you see that red flag? Do you know what it's for?

Child   Playing golf.

Teacher   No, not this flag.

Child   Watch out.

Teacher   That's right! A red flag is a warning. It's warning us that the tide is very fierce here and that it's dangerous.

As the children reached the top of the rise the leader asked:

Teacher   Who can see the lighthouse?

Child   Yes, yes.

Teacher   What do you notice? Is it straight?

Child   It's a bit sideways.

Teacher   Yes it's leaning over. Because it's built on sand.

Looking back a reed bed can be seen and the leader pointed out the place where natterjack toads can be found.

As they walked through the dunes the leader stepped off the duckboard walkway and focused the children on the marram grass:

Teacher   Look at this grass, can you see it? Feel it.

Child   It's dry and hard.

Teacher   Yes. Even though it's been raining and raining all morning. Why do you think that is?

Child   The sand is dry.

Teacher *(picking up some sand and running it through his fingers)*   It might have rained a lot but the rain has just run through it. So how does the grass survive?

Child   It doesn't need a drink.

Teacher   It does, it needs water badly and so has to grow very long roots.

He asked a child to walk about 3 metres away from him:

Teacher   See this grass, it's not very tall, but see how far he went. Well that's as long as the roots are; 1 metre of grass has 6 metres of roots, so the grass can find water. Also, the roots tend to criss-cross and weave in and out *(making a basket with his hands)* so they make a net to hold the sand in. That's how the grass helps to build the dunes.

A little further along the beach the leader reminded the class of the list of things they said they might find at the beach: the dunes, windmills, buoys (the children were not really familiar with buoys, and so needed to have them pointed out) and so on. Alerted to looking round them, the children noticed the tide line and all the things on it. They also spotted the special life saving rope store that they had previously seen in one of the photographs. They noticed that on the photograph the catch had been broken, but then it had been mended. This provided an opportunity to discuss the role of the ranger and the value of volunteers.

The various adults were asked to work with their groups to search the beach between two posts as markers, for any items of interest. Each adult had a carrier bag so that individuals were not burdened by their treasures. The children were extremely focused on finding objects. The beach is clean and the teacher had checked that section particularly that morning. A range of objects was found and a large circle drawn in the sand for them to be placed.

Among their treasures were various sorts of seaweed, razor shells, dog whelks, pieces of wood, and smooth stones. The children talked about how the stones were smoothed down by the sea, and indeed once sharp glass became smooth. They noticed the bladders on the seaweed and discussed how they help the weed float. They talked about the shells they had found and tried to match up halves, but were not very successful.

The children then walked back through the dunes a different way so that they could climb quite high and look back at the lighthouse. They could see where foxes had been and where rabbit holes were on the far side, and again discussed the fragility of the dunes.

The children and their teachers and helpers went back to the bus and back to school.

(Information about the location of this visit can be found at http://www.deeestuary.co.uk/swshore.htm)

Chris's class investigating ice

Background

Chris's class of 6- and 7-year-olds were working on a broad topic of changing materials. The children had made a collage using natural materials, had made cakes and animals out of clay, had developed appropriate language to describe materials and had experience of making predictions. They were now moving on to look at ice. Chris wanted the children to explore ice, describe it and, by thinking about how to slow down melting, to consider fair testing.

In the morning the children were told that there was something different about their classroom. A notice on the door read 'Penguins in Year 2, take care!' The children were encouraged to creep into the classroom, which was in semi darkness and rather cool. They found some footprints on the floor, a large 'iceberg' in the middle of the room, and two penguins sitting on it. The iceberg was constructed from the polystyrene packing materials around a new television, and some tinsel to make it glisten. Ice cubes were found in crevasses in the iceberg and around it, along with some small pebbles. The children's imaginations were fired and they were full of questions about icebergs, ice and the penguins. It transpired that the two penguins (puppets), Flapjack and Waddle, spent much of their time in the freezer department of the local supermarket but had been banned for leaving footprints in the ice cream. They had arrived with plenty of ice borrowed from the supermarket.

The children were given ice cubes on small dishes to explore and asked to look after them for the morning. The literacy lesson that morning involved the children in describing their ice, finding lots of 'icy' words and, after much discussion, writing some sentences about 'what I know about ice'.

The afternoon began with Chris calling the register, including Flapjack and Waddle, and some discussions with the two puppets. Chris asked where penguins came from and what sort of temperatures they were used to. The children knew they came from Antarctica and that this was a very cold place where it was difficult to keep warm. They talked about how people generally preferred warmer climates. The teacher showed the children a big book about penguins. They discussed how flocks of penguins keep warm, huddling together and taking turns to be in the centre of the group. Chris emphasised the fact that this meant that all the penguins had an equal chance of keeping warm, that they made it fair.

Chris reviewed with the children what they knew about ice, using their sheets from the literacy session: 'Ice melts in the sun', 'There are cold icebergs', 'Ice can build you a house', 'Ice is frozen water', 'Ice is see-through', 'Ice can be dangerous'. One child then told how he had swallowed an ice cube once. In discussion it was established that his warm body had melted the cube, although it had felt very cold and hard going down. Chris asked the children to describe their ice cubes:

Teacher   Who rubbed it on their forehead?
(*Many hands went up.*)
Teacher   How did it feel?
Child   Cold and wet.
Teacher   What happened to your ice cube?
Children   It's gone watery.
              Spread over the dish.
              Runny.
              Melted.

The penguins confided that, having borrowed the ice from the supermarket, they were keen to find the best place to store their ice so that it would not melt too quickly. Chris brought some more ice from the store cupboard. She had kept it in a freezer bag wrapped in layers of paper. Chris pointed out that the ice that was in the 'iceberg' crevasses had not melted away. She wondered why this was:

Child   Maybe the penguins cuddled it under their legs.
Teacher   But wouldn't that make it warmer?
Child   There was not just one block, but a lot of blocks together.

The class found this idea extremely difficult and Chris realised that, apart from this one child, they were not yet ready to consider it. She said that they would come back to this 'brilliant' idea later.

The children decided to put ice cubes in different places in the classroom and see how long they took to melt. Flapjack then selected an ice cube from the tray to test, and Waddle selected a large cube made in an ice cream tub. The children could immediately see that this was not fair. They discussed how to make their test fair.

Back at their tables, each group was given four ice cubes on small dishes and asked to think about where they might put them. The teacher gave them a simple worksheet for planning and recording, as in Figure 1.2.

Where it was	Prediction	Result
1.	I think	
2.	I think	
3.	I think	
4.	I think	

I think the ice changed because

Figure 1.2 What happens to ice?

The children began to discuss where they would place their ice cubes. Some children had asked to put their ice cubes in the freezer. Some wanted to put them in the school office (as it always seems cold in there). This caused a good deal of discussion about which was the coldest place, but for their investigation they had to stay in the classroom.

Many found the worksheet a challenge. However, they were seen to be moving around the room and some held out their hands to test the temperature of different locations. Chris circulated around the groups asking them to explain why they had chosen particular places. She was keen to find out their ideas about why the ice melts: 'Why do you think that might be a good place to keep the ice?' One thing that emerged was that a number of children seemed to believe that sunlight was a factor and that putting ice in the dark (as in the store cupboard or in the cardboard (Peter's) house) would slow down melting. However, when one child suggested wrapping the cube in plastic the other children rejected the idea because that would make it warmer.

The children went out for break and on returning looked at their ice cubes. Chris asked them to think about which was the best place to keep the ice cubes for longest.

At the end of the afternoon the children sat on the floor to discuss their findings with Chris, Flapjack, and Waddle. It was agreed that the coolest place in the classroom was on the window sill. The children thought that the cold wind coming in kept the cubes frozen for longer. Yet the cubes in the iceberg were still there. Paula, having thought about the problem, suggested that 'The polystyrene might have kept it cooler than the cups did'. Again other children struggled, finding this emerging idea of insulation a challenge.

The final part of the lesson considered the problem of how to get ice back for Flapjack and Waddle to take back to the supermarket. The children were asked to think about this overnight, as a follow up lesson would look at making ice from water.

In reviewing her lesson Chris felt that the children had enjoyed the lesson and that they had been able to explore ice and become aware that ice melts at different rates in places of different temperatures. During the practical activity she had focused her observations on a small number of children who she felt might have difficulty in setting up an investigation. As she discussed the work with the children she found that they had not really grasped the purpose of the activity. They were struggling with the notion of fair testing and had difficulty understanding what was meant by a prediction. Many of the children had trouble completing the worksheet. Although individual questioning revealed that they were able to make and support their predictions, their difficulties were in articulating this in writing. She felt that although some children were still at the stage of exploring and describing materials, others were at a point where they understood the idea of a fair test, could make predictions, and could describe and compare the properties of materials. However most were not able to record their ideas clearly in the table provided. She decided that, in the next lesson, she would focus more on fair testing and on prediction and perhaps find less demanding ways to record findings.

Key features of the case studies

First-hand experience

Although not presented as models of 'good practice', these case studies illustrate some important features of provision for learning science in the early primary years. First and foremost for these young children is the opportunity to observe and *investigate objects, materials and events at first-hand*. At this stage children have limited ability to deal with abstract ideas but this ability will develop through having plenty of experience of the kinds described here. In Kathy's and Chris's classes they dealt with familiar things – balls and ice – extending their ideas about them through investigation. On the sand dunes and at the beach the activities were less problem-oriented and more designed to extend the children's experience, encourage observation and learning about aspects of that environment from a knowledgeable resource in the form of David.

So that the children were involved in different kinds of inquiry in these classes. Kathy and Chris guided them into setting up 'which is best?' type investigations with familiar objects. This encouraged them to think about how to find things out by doing and changing things and eventually fair testing. David was helping them to build ideas about sand dunes, the sea shore and lighthouse, which were less familiar to them – even to those living quite near.

Talk

A second key point was the frequent opportunity for children to *talk*, to each other in groups and to the teacher, or an expert in the case of the expedition to the beach. Talk enables children to sort out their ideas, organise their thoughts and to find the right words with which to express them. It also allows them to hear others' ideas and to realise that there can be ideas different from their own. In all cases the teachers encouraged the children to talk about what they already knew from previous experience. Before visiting the beach the discussion in the classroom encouraged the children to think about the difference between what they find in their village and what they might find on the beach and possible reasons for the difference. This alerted them to paying attention to what they could see, both in the photographs and when they walked on the beach. Often the children offered comments or suggestions that seemed off the point ('everything I know about balls', for instance) but rather than discouraging their talk, the teachers took their ideas seriously and simply asked them to say more after thinking ('Do you think patterns on the balls would make a difference?', 'How do we know?').

Using and developing ideas

The talk also related to a third point, that the children were *expressing their existing ideas*, a starting point for developing them in the light of new information gathered either from their practical investigations, or their observation guided by the teacher or local expert. For Chris's young children the ideas of insulation was clearly a difficult one, which may be the reason why she decided not to follow up a child's idea that the penguins cuddling ice might keep it from melting.

On the dunes, direct observation enabled the children to expand their ideas about sand letting water through and about the roots of grass being important in keeping sand in the dunes.

In all cases the ideas being developed related to the relevant curriculum: in Kathy's lesson the properties of materials relating to hardness, elasticity and flexibility; for Chris 'that some materials are better thermal insulators than others'; and at the beach a contribution to several aspects of how to care for the environment.

Using and developing inquiry skills

A fourth feature concerns the *development of inquiry skills* (see Chapter 7), which was an aim for all the teachers. David was most direct about this, asking the children what it means to 'observe' and later encouraging them to feel, and smell as well as to look. In helping their pupils to investigate, both Chris and Kathy avoided telling the children what to do ('put one ice cube here and another here' or 'hold the balls at the same height and see which bounces higher when they are dropped'), but instead gave the children the opportunity to decide what to do. This not only gave them some ownership of their investigations, but provided the opportunity for them to use and develop process skills such as planning a fair test, making a prediction and communicating a result.

For Chris's class the development of these skills was only at the starting point and it was clear that in several cases the children needed more opportunities to develop them. Chris built into her planning the penguins' unfair suggestion to start the children thinking about fair testing. She found that the children were not as sure about what making a prediction meant as she had assumed on the basis of their previous experience of doing this. The difficulties the children had in using the worksheet that she provided led to her realising that communication on paper was more difficult for the children than talking about their ideas. Similarly Kathy allowed a good deal of time for exploration of the children's ideas of what to do. This might seem like 'messing about' but it meant that the children had reasons for what they did; seeing what didn't work well would enable them to go further towards more controlled investigation.

Careful planning

A fifth point that stands out from these lessons must surely be the amount of *planning* by the teacher. Visits always require a considerable effort and coordination of different kinds of support – from enlisting helpers to arranging transport, agreeing a programme and contingency plans, and of course asking for parents' consent and making sure that children are suitably dressed and shod. We say more about these preparations in Chapter 20. But there was also a good deal of work for Kathy and Chris, too, in preparing their lessons. There were alternatives which would have involved far less effort to prepare. Why not give the children explicit directions for what to do? Why go to the trouble of setting up a scene or a story to start from? The answers surely lie in the teachers' conceptions of how children learn best. We discuss this in Part 2 of this book. At this point it is enough to note that the teachers were convinced of the importance of implementing a 'constructivist' view of learning. This means starting from the children's ideas and skills but also recognises the importance of talk and discussion in supporting the development of ideas and inquiry skills through social interaction.

Although we have only described one lesson, in each case the work on the topic would continue. Kathy built in the opportunity to revisit parts of the children's work by taking photographs and creating a 'big book' for discussion later. This would enable the children to continue to learn from these activities. For Chris's class, too, there was a great deal of further discussion and investigation if the full value of the activities was to be exploited. And, of course, the visit to the beach led to a great deal of follow up work in the classroom, supported by the photographs that they were able to borrow and the stones, shells and other items from the beach that they collected for study before returning them to the beach. So it is by no means every lesson that would require the amount of preparation clearly necessary for the lessons we have glimpsed here. Indeed the effort would largely be wasted if the investigations were not followed by time for reflection and consolidation of the learning they provided.

Summary

Three case studies involving pupils aged 5 to 8 years have been presented briefly in this chapter. Each account provides some background information to the lesson. They all describe real events in real classes and are not intended as models although they reflect several features of effective practice in science education for young children. Some significant features have been discussed under the headings of:

- first-hand experience
- talk
- using and developing ideas
- using and developing inquiry skills
- careful planning.

These points are further discussed in later chapters of the book.

Further reading

Primary Science Review 92 (March/April 2006) includes a number of articles on using stories, poems and puppets to engage children in science, including:

'Involving young children through stories as starting points' by Jill Cavendish, Bev Stopps and Charly Ryan.

'Puppets bringing stories to life in science' by Brenda Keogh, Stuart Naylor, Brigid Downing, Jane Maloney and Shirley Simon.

'Goldilocks and the three variables' by Graham Lowe.

Case studies can be found on the teachernet website:

http://www.teachernet.gov.uk/CaseStudies/casestudy.cfm?id=509.

2

Primary science in action
The later years

Introduction

The three case studies in this chapter describe work of older primary children, aged between 8 and 11 years. As with the younger children, it is important for the work to be seen by the children to have relevance to understanding things in the world around them, but they are more able to perceive the link when the objects they investigate are representing real things rather than being the real things themselves. The first case is an account of work with 9- and 10-year-olds, where the connection to real life was made through an industry-linked project. In preparing for a visit to a power station, the children had been investigating 'problems' sent to them by the power station manager. Solving these problems involved controlled investigation and the development of understanding of materials.

The next case, also with 9- and 10-year-olds, was related to a key part of any curriculum, the nature of soil and the role its constituents play in the growth of plants. The content is nothing novel; the interest here is how the teacher engages the children in careful investigation of the properties of different soils and helps them to bring their findings together. Although classroom-based, the work was clearly linked to developing understanding of the world outside and so to the production of something of keen interest to children – food.

This is followed by a brief account of a 'science' week, organised for the oldest children in a primary school in England to take place after the children had taken their national tests. Although the activities had a considerable science focus, a good deal of the work was cross-curricular and enabled the children to use and develop skills of inquiry and use their knowledge in a range of subjects. In this case, we do not describe a specific lesson but rather give an overview of the range of activities. (The science week is the subject of an extended account, with video and examples of children's work, which can be viewed on the Teachers' TV website at http://www.teachers.tv/video/21978.) The chapter concluded with some discussion of key features of the case studies.

Anne's class using a link with industry

Background

The lesson was part of Children Challenging Industry, a project of the University of York, funded by the chemical industry. A small group of rural schools had collaborated in a topic about materials linked to the chemical industry. The children had very little real experience of industrial landscapes (other than farming), although some had parents who travelled some distance to work in such industries.

The series of lessons was based around letters from a senior manager at the power station asking the children to solve some real problems for them. In previous lessons the children had considered ways in which muddy water needed to be filtered as efficiently and cheaply as possible. A second project had been to look at ways in which hot water can be efficiently cooled down.

In the series of lessons, Anne, the teacher, had shown PowerPoint slides of the letters from the power station manager, images of the power station, including the river as the source of water, and the cooling towers and complicated pipe work around the site. She considered that the children were learning skills of working together, of analysing problems and of data analysis. They were also thinking about how their experiments could help to inform the industry and what additional factors might need to be taken into account when working on an industrial scale.

The lesson discussed here was the final science experiment before the children (aged 9 and 10) were to visit the power station, although with school holidays and other intervening factors, they were unlikely to be able to visit for some weeks.

The lesson

The power station manager had written to the children asking for their help. She explained in her letter the difficulties experienced in their large plant where pipes, often carrying hot water, would sometimes leak at the joints. Pictures of the power plant focusing on pipe work, and in particular on joints in pipe work, were shown to underline the problem. The children were challenged to think about different ways in which metal pipes could be joined together in a way that would seal in any liquid.

The children were given the opportunity to ask the teacher questions to clarify the problem and begin to consider ways forward. Questions such as 'Are the pipes metal?', 'Do the pipes corrode?', 'Are they bendy?', 'Is it just water in pipes or can it be other things?', 'Do people go round and check up on the pipes?' and 'Is the water really hot like steam?' helped the children to establish the kinds of properties that a sealant would need to have. In particular it needed to be waterproof and to be so at high temperatures and possibly at high pressures.

Questions moved on to the action they might take, such as 'Can you use stuff to wrap around the joints?' and Anne then showed the children the soup cans that she had prepared. These included some with the top and bottom removed, with edges made safe, and others where only the top had been removed. She explained that the idea she had for testing was to put two cans (one of each sort) together and to test out ways of sealing the join between the two. The children offered the suggestions that 'You could put water up to a certain point over the join' and 'You could see how much came out'.

Anne responded to factual questions and then, as the children began to formulate investigable questions, she moved on to developing plans. She gave the children some Post-it notes and asked them to jot down some ideas about ways in which pipes could be sealed. The children were sitting in groups of four or five with teaching assistants deployed to encourage discussion, focusing on the properties of the sealants.

When Anne looked at the Post-it notes she found that some groups had identified only one possible sealant while others had suggested up to four. The children's ideas, drawing on their experience, included the following:

- welding
- tape (like the tape you put on your bike to hold things on)
- sticking plaster (like when you have cut yourself)
- cement
- super glue
- sellotape
- wax
- grout
- insulation tape (that goes around wires)
- rubber bands
- silicone seal (like round our new double glazing)
- putty
- soldering
- duck tape
- clay
- rubber bands
- silicone seal
- nuts and bolts.

The teacher discussed the various suggestions with the class. She commented on the idea of welding and explained that a person needed a lot of equipment and long training to do welding, but that this was a very good idea, and that perhaps the children might see some welding when they visited the power station.

Anne then rummaged in a large container of different materials she had gathered and brought out items that had been suggested. The first was a fairly wide rubber band that would probably fit comfortably around a tin can:

Teacher	What do you think about this? *(Holding up two tin cans together as a reminder)*
Child	No.
Teacher	Why not, do you think?
Children	It's too stretchy.
	It will rot over time.
	The metal might rust.
Teacher	Yes, some of these might be a problem. Some people think it might work. If you want to you can try this, it's up to you.

She then showed a piece of dressmaker's elastic (a thick piece):

Children	No, it might be a really big pipe.
	It wears out and breaks.
	It's not waterproof.
Teacher	So we are thinking of the properties of the sealants. You are doing some good thinking. You could try this if you want to; it's up to you.

Blu-Tack was next:

Children	Hmmm, don't know.
	When it gets wet it loses its stick.

Then some insulation tape:

Children	Maybe, but it needs to be wider.
	You can wind it round lots.

Then Anne showed some plumber's tape:

Teacher	Nobody suggested this one. I don't know if you have seen it, it's called plumber's tape and they use it to join pipes together. *(She explained how it works, that it was quite tricky to use, but someone might like to try it.)*

Finally was sticking plaster tape:

Child	When my hose pipe got a thorn in it I used one of these tapes. When I put the water on, it just blew off.
Teacher	Yes, in industry there is often pressure from the water. That's why we have to be really clear about what we are testing and also to be sure that we don't make recommendations that are more than our tests really tell us.

The discussion moved on to setting up tests for the different sealants. Some of the equipment was given. Anne also gave them some instructions on a worksheet, one per table. The children were advised to use the two cans, to seal them together and stand them in a bowl, then to fill the cans up with 800 ml of warm (not hot) water. (Anne told them she had tried this part out earlier and knew this amount was about right.) They were asked to leave each container for a fixed amount of time, then measure the amount of water that had leaked out of the can.

They discussed how to ensure a fair test. Suggestions made were: temperature of the water, time the water is in the container, amount of water to start with. One child suggested 'it should be the same person', but the general conclusion was that while this might help, ensuring all other things are controlled was most important. Ideas for measuring the amount of water that had leaked were discussed. There was reference to measurement error – 'Jugs might not be accurate', 'We might spill some water when pouring'. They decided to use small syringes or measuring cylinders to measure what leaked out, or to measure what was left in the can and subtract it from the original.

Due to the rather cramped conditions, the teacher had left a bucket of water by each table before the lesson. Standard items were all together on trays that could be given out quickly. Children could then choose the particular sealants they wanted to test.

Some children needed a hand putting the cans together. The classroom assistants provided a good deal of support during this part of the lesson. There was much chat, but it was focused on the task in hand. Towards the end, children were asked to record their results on the class computer so that all the data could be viewed by the class at the end of the lesson.

Once the children had finished and the tables tidied up, the teacher asked for feedback on the results. She recorded these on a table on the whiteboard, asking the children to report their best sealant. The conclusions were discussed. Most children had found the rubber bands to be most effective, although one group had managed to use the plumber's tape effectively. This promoted discussion about further experiments. The possibility of the rubber corroding, mentioned earlier, was discussed. The children were happy with the idea that they had managed to rule out some sealants and realised that further work would be needed to determine which would be best for the job in hand.

In the last five minutes the teacher showed the children one way that pipes are joined in industry, demonstrating the use of bolts and gaskets to act as sealants with equipment provided by the project. Again, the pros and cons of this were discussed. The children recognised that the same solution might not be appropriate for all pipes. The next lesson would involve the children responding to the power station manager's letters, pulling together their findings from the series of experiments.

Graham's class investigating soil

Background

Graham was introducing science activities within an overall topic about growing food, to his class of 9- and 10-year-olds. He planned that the children should discuss and investigate the differences between types of soil. He had in mind that the children should undertake some investigations of sandy, loamy and clay soil, so he provided samples of each of these, to which some of the children contributed samples that they had brought from gardens at home. He wanted the investigations to advance the children's ideas, but felt it was important to start from their initial ideas and questions. It would have been easy to ask the children to find out, for example, 'Which soil holds most water?', 'Does water drain more quickly through some soils than through others?' etc. and to start the children's investigations from these questions. These are perfectly good questions for children to investigate and are likely to be among those the children would end up investigating, but he wanted to hold back his questions to find out what the children would ask and what ideas they had.

The lesson

The first part of the work was an exploratory phase of looking at the different soils. In groups, the children were given samples of the three main types, some hand lenses, sieves, disposable gloves and some very open instructions:

- separate the different parts that each of the soils contains;
- find out what is contained in all the soils;
- find out what is different in each soil;
- think about how these differences might affect how well plants grow in the soils.

This task required children to use their ideas about soil in making their observations. It encouraged them to look closely at the soil and to think about the differences they found. During this activity the teacher visited each group to listen in to what the children were saying about the types of soil. Many of their statements at this stage contained hypotheses and predictions. The children were quick to say which they thought would be best for plants to grow in (the darkest coloured one) and to identify the ability to hold water as a property that was needed.

There was then a whole-class discussion, pooling findings and ideas from different groups. Graham said that they would test their ideas about which was best for growing plants when they had found out more about the soils and the differences that might make one better than another. What would the plants need to grow? Water was the most popular answer. Some mentioned 'fertiliser' and there was a discussion of what this meant in terms of the soils they had looked at. It was eventually identified with the bits of leaves and decayed plant material they had found, particularly in the loam. Graham introduced the word 'humus' to describe this part of the soil.

No-one mentioned the presence of air in the soil until the teacher asked them to think about the difference between soil that was compressed and the same soil in a loose heap. He challenged them to think about whether there was the same amount of air between the particles in each soil and whether this was likely to make a difference to how well plants would grow in it.

The discussion identified four main differences to be investigated: the differences in the amount of water held in the soil; how quickly water drained through each one; the amount of humus in each and the amount of air. Each of the six groups of children chose one of these and set about planning how they would go about their investigation. Although having different foci, the investigations of all the groups were relevant to developing understanding of the nature and properties of soil so that, when they did the trial of which enabled plants to grow best, they might be able to explain and not just observe the result.

The investigations provided opportunities to help the children develop their inquiry skills, in order to carry out systematic and 'fair' tests through which they would arrive at findings useful in developing their ideas. He asked them first to plan what they would do and identify what they would need in terms of equipment. He probed their thinking about what variables to control and what to observe or measure by asking questions such as 'How will you be sure that the difference is only caused by the type of soil? How will you be able to show the difference?' He had ideas, gathered from various sources, about useful approaches but kept these 'up his sleeve' to be introduced only if the children did not produce ideas of their own. Graham encouraged the children to make notes of what they found as they went along and then use these to prepare a report from each group to the whole class. He told them that they should report what they did and what they found, but also say whether it was what they had expected and to try to explain the differences they found.

At the end of the practical work and after a period for bringing their ideas together in their groups, each group in turn presented a report, while other children were given opportunity to question. Graham refrained from making comments at this stage and asked questions only for clarification. When all the reports had been given he listed the findings for each soil and asked the children to decide which might be best for growing some seedlings. The choice was not as obvious as some children had initially thought, so they were very keen to try this next investigation and find out what really would happen.

Graham then turned to the samples of soil that the children had brought from home. In order to compare them with the three soils they had investigated he suggested mixing some of each with enough water to loosen the parts from each other and allow the constituents to separate as they settled to the bottom. They then used these observations on what they had found out about soil to predict which might be 'good growing' soils. These samples were then included in the seedling trials.

Before going on to set up the next investigations, Graham asked the children to reflect on which parts of the work just completed they had enjoyed most, which they would do differently if they could start again and what they now felt could be done better than before.

Science week for Year 6

Background

With the help of a colleague from the local science learning centre, some additional equipment borrowed from the local high school and college, and contributions from the local police, teachers in one large primary school in England planned a science week for their Year 6 (10–11-year-olds). The idea was to devise a cross-curricular theme with a science focus for pupils who had completed their national tests. The teachers wanted the children to experience science as it is applied in the real world and to raise the profile in investigative work, which they recognised had been neglected in the preparation for the tests. They agreed that they wanted greater emphasis on group work and discussion than on writing.

Working with an adviser from the science learning centre, three class teachers planned the week together. They decided on a forensic science topic as likely to fire the pupils' imaginations and provide the potential to use many aspects of science as well as other subjects. They decided to set up a 'crime' in school. The crime agreed was the theft of the two annual 'rounders trophies', for which children were to compete and were valued objects to them. The trophies were kept in a shed in the school grounds. They planned that the possible culprits could be one of the lunch time supervisors, the head teacher, the school caretaker or one of the class teachers. Although three teachers were involved in the lengthy planning, all the members of the school staff, including the non-teaching staff were in the picture. The planning also involved the local police, and the scene of crime officer (SOCO) agreed to participate.

In planning the week the science coordinator was very keen to ensure that the science was not lost in the role play, or other activities. She felt that the science had to be rigorous. However, the opportunities through the week for work on citizenship, drama, PSHE (personal, social and health education) and literacy skills were also clearly present.

The particular areas of science identified were:

■ materials and their properties – identifying fibres, chromatography;

■ characteristics of living things – fingerprints, DNA;

■ scientific inquiry – evidence, observation, hypothesising, recording.

The activities

On the Monday morning the pupils arrived to find a police car in the school yard, and a shed cordoned off with yellow striped tape. The Year 6 classes were gathered in a hall to be informed about the crime. The SOCO spoke to the children and told them that he would need their help. He asked for ideas about evidence to look for and immediately received suggestions for fingerprints, hair, and footprints. He emphasised the importance of not touching anything until photographs and notes had been taken. Then, in turn, groups, dressed in white overalls and hoods and given cameras, went with the SOCO to explore the scene of the crime.

The shed had a broken window and some 'blood' on the floor. A crowbar that had been used to prise open the lock. A ginger-beer can and a section of a shopping list lay on the floor. Also found were footprints in the mud outside and some pieces of fabric. The pupils noticed that the footprints leading away from the shed suddenly stopped. They hypothesised that the criminal had removed his or her shoes at this point.

They took photographs with a digital camera and collected evidence to take back to the classroom. There they worked together in groups to consider the evidence, with photographs from the scene printed out. They discussed and developed a list of suspects on the basis of the evidence they had about staff who had access to the shed, or who had some motive. They devised interview questions and went to interview each of the suspects, recording their responses to share with others. One group observed the lunch time supervisor had a tear in her blouse. This provided a reason to compare fibres from the fabric found at the scene of the crime. They used a digital microscope borrowed from the secondary school to look at the fibres found at the scene and to compare them with those of the lunch time supervisor's blouse.

The police fingerprint expert came to the school to show the pupils how to take fingerprints from the ginger-beer can. The pupils then collected sample fingerprints from all the suspects and compared them with the ones from the can using magnifying hand lenses. Moulds of prints, photographs and measurements were taken and the footprints were identified as those of the classroom teacher (who kept his bike in the shed). Meanwhile the head teacher was eliminated 'because his foot is in a plaster cast'.

The pupils wanted to analyse the handwriting on the shopping list found in the shed. They did this in two ways. First they asked each suspect to write something on similar paper. Then they collected the suspects' pens in order to analyse the ink and compare it with that used for the list, using chromatography. The teachers showed them how to do this, practising on coloured candy-coated chocolate beans (Smarties). They saw how the colours separated as the dye spread across the damp filter paper. They then used these skills to test small fragments of the shopping list found at the scene of the crime, comparing it with the pens used by the different suspects. In doing this, and using the handwriting analysis, they were able to identify the handwriting as that of the school secretary.

For the analysis of the 'blood' the children were told about DNA and about Professor Howard Jeffries who had developed a test for DNA. The equipment was borrowed from, and the requisite chemicals donated by, the local college so that the pupils could carry out their own DNA testing. This was done with the help of the advisor from the science learning centre (who also runs sessions for teachers on how to do DNA testing). The process was described as 'basically chromatography by putting 200 volts through DNA to split it up'.

When all the evidence was put together, the conclusion reached was that the class teacher was the culprit.

Although the main aim was not to emphasise conventional recording and writing, the pupils were keen to write articles for the school magazine. There were also many discussions about matters beyond the science of solving the crime, such as about safety, the role of the police, the nature of evidence. The pupils had really enjoyed the week and the teachers felt they had learnt a great deal in a really engaging way. The three teachers directly involved in the planning agreed that, although it had been very challenging, they would want to run a similar week the next year.

One teacher was worried about the ethics of being dishonest with the pupils by telling them that this was a real crime. Another argued that children had soon 'cottoned on' that it was not real but realised that joining in seriously enabled them to have fun and do lots of new things. Essentially the children were encouraged to join in the pretence and enjoy themselves.

Key features of the case studies

Relevance

The main key features of work with the older primary pupils are the same as for the younger children, discussed in Chapter 1. First-hand experience, talk, using and developing ideas and inquiry skills and careful planning are all important throughout the primary years but they take different forms as children progress in their ability to think in more abstract and theoretical ways. Relevance also remains of central concern so that pupils see a point in what they are asked to do. In the later primary years the relevance is closer to real life rather than the imaginative stories that often inspire the activities of the earlier years. Indeed some primary school pupils take an active part in making real decisions about, for instance, reducing the use of energy in the school through projects which include monitoring energy consumption and temperature to avoid waste through over-heating. Even though the setting for the pipe joining was 'set up', as was the crime investigated in the Year 6 science week, the situations were ones that genuinely reflected real life. The 'make-believe' was sufficiently close to reality for the children to take seriously the questions which they were investigating.

First-hand experience

In all three situations in this chapter the teachers not only provided the materials for first-hand experience but also the time to explore them – to look closely at the soils or to test the possible sealants for the pipe, rather than just being told about what would be best. Investigating the crime scene gave the Year 6 pupils a variety of first-hand experience, from using chromatography to using a digital microscope. Although not all primary science can involve first-hand manipulation of the objects being investigated (for example, Earth in space topics and some topics concerning the human body), where this is possible it helps understanding, since primary children need to see, feel and experience for themselves. However, the most important thing is that the children have information against which to judge the adequacy of their ideas in explaining things. Sometimes this information comes from secondary sources but where possible children should collect it through their own actions.

Talk

Children bring to new situations or events ideas derived from thinking about their individual experience. Finding out what others think is a key factor in developing more widely shared ideas. Douglas Barnes (1976) calls this 'co-constructing' ideas, helping each other to make sense of things. In simple terms it means 'putting our heads together', which we know so often leads to a better understanding than any-one working things out alone. Anne set up groups specifically to discuss and to jot down ideas on Post-it notes. The chat during the investigations was less structured but served to keep all the children in the group engaged on the task.

In both Graham's and Anne's classes, groups tried different things so combining the experiences of different groups was important to get an overall result. So reporting to each other had a definite purpose and was structured, with groups having time to prepare to report to the others. This was followed by whole-class discussion of their findings in which their data were combined to reach a shared result and understanding. In the crime investigation, too, the event was set up so that different kinds of data had to be brought together through argument and discussion.

Using and developing ideas

The beginning of both Anne's and Graham's lessons provided opportunities for children to reflect on what they already knew about the problems presented and to extend their experience of the materials being studied. Initial ideas about pipes were implicit in the questions that Anne's class asked (they might be metal, bendy, carry other things as well as water). They also used their experience of materials that could be used for sealing pipes in producing the ideas on the Post-it notes. Listening to ideas from other groups when these were brought together was itself a way of extending their knowledge of materials and their properties, further developed in the investigations. In Graham's class the children's ideas about the factors that made one soil better than another for growing plants were the starting point, but he also extended their first ideas so that a more complete set of variables, including air, were investigated. Developing a better understanding of the nature of soils and their role in plant growth was an important goal for Graham to be built up over several lessons, of which this was just the start.

The Year 6 crime scene was specifically set up to focus on investigative work, but since any investigation has to be about something, to have a subject, there is the opportunity to learn more about the subject. So children learnt about the change in materials in making a plaster cast of the footprint; about the composition of different colours in dyes in ink and in the sugar coating of sweets; and that a person's fingerprints are unique.

Using and developing inquiry skills

The goal of developing inquiry skills was prominent in all the cases, but particularly in the crime activities. These experiences were particularly rich in potential for developing systematic and careful collection of data, for recognising the importance of recording and understanding how to use data in arriving at conclusions. However, it does not require an elaborate set up (fun though it was) to develop these skills and understanding of scientific investigation. Graham asked his pupils to plan their investigation and expected them to keep notes to help them in reporting. He also encouraged their reflection on how they could have improved their investigations, thus focusing their attention on the process and not just the outcome of their investigations.

Anne gave more instructions than Graham possibly because of pressure of time or because the children would be unlikely to be able to create a 'mock-up' of a pipe joint without a good deal of guidance. However, the scene had been well set and the children had a good understanding of the problem, so the worksheet and directions saved them possible frustration in getting to the point where they could test the sealants. There was no sign that the children were merely following instructions without knowing the purpose, as can happen when worksheets are the starting point. She involved the children in some parts of the planning, considering how to make their tests fair and deciding how to measure any leaked water. With more time and less direction towards a particular way of answering the initial question, however, the children might have been able to use and develop more inquiry skills.

Careful planning

The particularly heavy load of planning was evident in the case of the 'crime scene'. This was exceptional and no doubt motivated by the filming of the week for Teachers' TV. It was not part of the school's long-term planning for science, although it might well become so given the evident enthusiasm for the event.

Whilst not as spectacular, there was, of course, a great deal of planning behind the scenes in both case studies – long-term, medium-term and short-term. The topics fitted into the long-term plans of each school's programme, devised to ensure progression in development of conceptual understanding and skills and to meet the requirement of the national guidelines. It is useful to recall, as noted in Chapter 1, that not every lesson has to be packed with 'hands-on' activity. To make the best use of such experiences, careful planning should include time for discussion and critical reflection on what was found, what it means, how it may have differed from expectations and how the process could, with hindsight, have been improved.

In his medium-term planning, Graham worked out how the work on soil fitted into the current term's work and built on what the children had done previously about what was needed for plant growth and how it would lead on to ideas about the formation of soil and how its fertility has to be preserved in order to grow food. In his short-term planning, he worked out what both he and the children would do, considered some questions he would pose and prepared himself with information about the ideas children might have and with suggestions for activities from sources such as the *Rocks, Soil and Weather* Teachers' Guide of Nuffield Primary Science. Anne's planning was supported by involvement in the Children Challenging Industry project and it was designed to meet the requirements of aspects of both Science and Design and Technology in the National Curriculum for England. In both cases the teachers used ideas from others, a published guide or project, so that planning did not need to begin from scratch. How they presented the activities to the children and the part they gave them in deciding how to investigate was their choice and, as we noted in Chapter 1, would depend on their view of how children learn best. These are matters we consider in detail in Part 2.

Summary

Three case studies involving pupils aged between 8 and 11 have been presented briefly in this chapter. The first two took place in the classroom but were linked to real events outside. The third, a week-long series of events for Year 6 (10–11-year-olds) brought the outside world into the school. The provision in each for learning science has been discussed under the headings of:

- relevance;
- first-hand experience;
- talk;
- using and developing ideas;
- using and developing inquiry skills;
- careful planning.

All these are further discussed in later chapters of the book.

Further reading

Primary Science Review, 90 (Nov/Dec 2005) includes the following articles on the theme of Forensic Science:

'The baker did it!' by Ian Richardson (on how forensic science activities can engage children in developing their inquiry skills).

'Murder' by Ivor Hickey, Colette Murphy, Jim Beggs and Karen Carlisle (describing how children can carry out DNA fingerprinting).

'Fibres, blood and broken glass' (Bob Tomlinson talking to Alan Peacock about the work of scene-of-crime investigators).

Aims and outcomes of primary science education

Introduction

It is universally accepted that learning science is important for the future lives of all citizens and because of this it is a required part of primary and secondary education in practically all countries. Nevertheless it is important to be aware of the reasons why we consider that all children should learn science from an early age so that we can ensure that what is taught, and how, matches intentions. For these reasons we review, in the first part of this chapter, the evidence and arguments that support the role of science in the primary curriculum. These reasons changed, or rather evolved, during the second part of the twentieth century as a result of research about children's learning and review of the goals of science education as a whole. Recognition of the importance for all young people, not just for future scientists, of the development of understanding of key concepts, inquiry skills and appreciation of the nature of science – encapsulated in the notion of scientific literacy – has been accompanied by realisation that this learning cannot be achieved unless it begins in the primary school.

Having looked at what the primary school curriculum should provide, we then, in the second part of the chapter, consider some strengths and weaknesses of the science curricula in the UK developed in the 1990s. Responses to the need for revision made in the curricula for England (at Key Stage 3 only at the time of writing), Wales, Scotland and Northern Ireland are briefly summarised.

The rise of science in the primary curriculum

It was in 1989 that the National Curriculum in England and Wales set out what was to be taught in science and nine other subjects apart from religious education. At the same time, the Northern Ireland Curriculum was established and the non-statutory 5/14 Guidelines in Scotland. In England and Wales, science was identified as part of the primary curriculum 'core', together with English and mathematics (and Welsh in Wales). Core status meant that these subjects were given priority in the development of the programmes of study and attainment targets, which were set out in more detail than for other subjects, and that they were the focus of national testing – a mixed blessing (see Chapter 14).

Building the case for science: a little history

Support for giving science a key role in primary education began to grow in the 1960s. Indeed a leading educator had urged that science in the primary school should be seen as 'part of the very ABC of education' (Isaacs 1962: 6). The reasons he gave were:

- the need for everyone to be able to relate to the rapid changes that science and technology were making to the world around;

- the ability to share in understanding and celebrating science as an important human achievement;

- the need for more scientists;

- the generation of a scientific approach to human problems through seeking relevant information and basing decisions on evidence.

Since that time, further strong reasons have been added to the case through increasing attention of research into children's learning. Despite the disappointing impact of early curriculum projects, Science 5/13 and the Nuffield Junior Science Project, the importance of science at the primary level was underlined by its inclusion in the Assessment of Performance (APU) surveys. These were carried out annually in English (from 1978 to 1983), mathematics (1979 to 1984) and science (1980 to 1985), involving small samples of pupils at ages 11, 13 (science only) and 15 (Foxman *et al.* 1991).

Apart from the trends in pupils' performance provided by the results, the APU surveys added to our understanding of the nature of inquiry (or process) skills and their interaction with content knowledge. They also led directly to the research on children's ideas at the secondary level which revealed that pupils had ideas about scientific phenomena that quite often were not consistent with the scientific view. These ideas, sometimes held despite science teaching, are ones which seem to make more sense to the pupils than abstract scientific explanations.

Research into the ideas of younger children began with studies in New Zealand (Osborne and Freyberg 1985). In the UK, the Science Processes and Concepts Exploration (SPACE) project revealed a range of ideas about the scientific aspects of their surroundings that children had developed from their limited experience and ways of thinking (SPACE Research Reports, 1990–1998). It was clear that these ideas could not be ignored; children believed them, had worked them out for themselves, and indeed they had to be the starting point from which more scientific ideas could be developed (see Chapter 5).

Thus a further argument was added to the case for science in the primary curriculum, that children's ideas about the world are developing throughout the primary years whether or not they are taught science. Without intervention to introduce a scientific approach in their exploration, many of the ideas they develop are non-scientific and may obstruct later learning.

Since then other research has added to the importance of starting science early:

- Attitudes towards science develop in the pre-secondary years, earlier than attitudes to some other school subjects. This was first reported by Ormerod and Duckworth in 1975, but more recently research evidence from the Royal Society (2006) shows that most children develop interests and attitudes towards science well before the age of 14 and many before the age of 11.

■ Gender differences in academic performance, which continue to be of concern in science education at higher levels, have not appeared at the primary stage (Haworth *et al.* 2007).

■ At the primary level there is no correlation between attitudes to science and science achievement, so primary pupils can feel positive about science regardless of their level of achievement.

The contribution of primary science to scientific literacy

The aims of school science education as a whole are now commonly expressed in terms of developing 'scientific literacy'. Scientific literacy is the term used for the essential understanding that should be part of everyone's education, rather than a detailed knowledge of facts and theories as required by scientists. Just as the term 'literacy' on its own denotes competence in using language at the level needed for functioning effectively in society, so scientific literacy indicates a competence in relation to science:

■ being able to function with confidence in relation to the scientific aspects of the world around;

■ being able to look at something 'in a scientific way', seeing, for example, whether or not evidence has been taken into account in the explanation of an event or phenomenon, whether it makes sense in terms of related events or phenomena, and so on;

■ being aware of the nature (and limitations) of scientific knowledge and the role of values in its generation.

The term 'scientific literacy' is used in statements about the aim of science education in various countries and in statements of international bodies such as UNESCO and the OECD. Box 3.1 gives the definition used in the OECD Programme for International Student Achievement (PISA).

In the UK, an influential report (*Beyond 2000: Science Education for the Future*) on the aims of the science curriculum for all pupils from age 5 to 16 recommended that 'The science curriculum for 5 to 16 should be seen primarily as a course to enhance general scientific literacy' (Millar and Osborne 1998: 9). What this means is set out in Box 3.2.

The aims of developing scientific literacy, as described here, may seem remote from primary science, but they are in essence easily identified as developing ideas ('understanding of important ideas and explanatory frameworks'), developing process skills ('the procedures of scientific inquiry') and developing attitudes ('a sense of wonder, enthusiasm and interest'). Primary science

---

Box 3.1 The PISA definition of scientific literacy

The capacity to use scientific knowledge, to identify questions and to draw evidence-based conclusions in order to understand and help make decisions about the natural world and the changes made to it through human activity.

(OECD 2003: 133)

Box 3.2 A curriculum for developing scientific literacy for age 5–16

The science curriculum should:

- sustain and develop the curiosity of young people about the natural world around them, and build up their confidence in their ability to enquire into its behaviour. It should seek to foster a sense of wonder, enthusiasm and interest in science so that young people feel confident and competent to engage with scientific and technical matters;

- help young people acquire a broad, general understanding of the important ideas and explanatory frameworks of science, and of the procedures of scientific inquiry, which have had a major impact on our material environment and on our culture in general, so that they can:

  - appreciate why these ideas are valued;

  - appreciate the underlying rationale for decisions (for example, about diet, or medical treatment, or energy use) which they may wish, or be advised, to take in everyday contexts, both now and in later life;

  - be able to understand, and respond critically to, media reports of issues with a science component;

  - feel empowered to hold and express a personal point of view on issues with a science component which enter the arena of public debate, and perhaps to become actively involved in some of these;

  - acquire further knowledge when required, either for interest or for vocational purposes.

(Millar and Osborne 1998: 12)

has a contribution to make to all of these. We just have to remember that in all cases we are talking about *development*, starting from the simple foundations which are needed for later more abstract ideas and advanced thinking.

Developing ideas

Development of understanding starts from making sense of particular events that we encounter. We might call the ideas found useful for this 'small' ideas, because they are specific to the events studied and have limited application beyond these. As experience extends it becomes possible to link events which are explained in similar ways to form ideas which have wider application and so can be described as 'bigger' ideas.

The ultimate aim of developing scientific literacy is to develop the 'big', widely applicable, ideas that enable us to grasp what is going on in situations which are new to us. But clearly the 'big' ideas are too abstract and too remote from everyday experience to be a starting point for this learning. Learning has to start from the 'small' ideas and build upwards so that at each point the ideas are understood in terms of real experience. The role of primary science is, therefore, to build a foundation of small ideas that help children to understand things in their immediate environment but, most importantly, at the same time to begin to make links between different experiences, and ideas to build bigger ideas.

Developing skills and attitudes

The overall aim of scientific literacy in relation to the development of skills and attitudes is the ability and willingness to recognise and use evidence in making decisions as informed citizens. Again the starting point is to become familiar with the ways of identifying, collecting and interpreting evidence in relation to answering questions about things around. Being able to do this is an essential starting point to reflecting on the kinds of questions that science can, and cannot, answer and the kinds of conclusions that can, and cannot, be drawn from certain kinds of evidence.

Making links with the world around

The achievement of scientific literacy depends on, but is more than, the acquisition of scientific knowledge, skills, values and attitudes. It does not automatically result from learning science; it has to be a conscious goal even at the primary level, by giving attention to linking together ideas from a range of experiences of real phenomena, problems and events both within the classroom and outside it. Indeed, extending first-hand experience beyond what the school can supply, in the way that museums and science centres can do (see Chapter 20), is essential to the development of scientific literacy.

A curriculum fit for purpose

As we have seen, research evidence and thinking about what we want to achieve through primary science education have changed somewhat from the late 1980s when the curricula in the UK were designed. So we now have to ask the following question: 'Do the curricula for the twentieth century still match the aims of the twenty-first century?' We begin to address this question by looking at evidence of how successful the primary science curricula have been, first in terms of measured learning outcomes and then through the eyes of teachers.

Trends in pupil performance

The data we have about pupils' performance in science relates to England only and comes from the national tests given to pupils at ages 7 and 11 and from international surveys of 9–10-year-olds in the Trends in International Mathematics and Science Survey (TIMSS) 2003. Both of these sources need to be treated with caution. The national tests are weighted in favour of facts that can be recalled; and teaching to the test means that even the items intended to assess process skills are influenced by coaching, which leads to children giving answers without going through the intended thinking. Moreover an investigation of the equivalence of tests over the years 1996 to 2001 concluded that the standard of the tests had declined over that time (Massey *et al.* 2003). International surveys favour multiple choice items, largely focused on recall, and are subject to a number of criticisms of their procedures (e.g. Winter 1998).

With these caveats, the results for the national tests in England show a steep increase in percentages of 11-year-olds reaching the expected level from 1995 to 2000, followed by a levelling off, with very little real change from 2001. The results for 7-year-olds follow a similar pattern but with a much smaller initial rise. However, data from other sources show much less change over the same periods. Tymms (2004) suggested several technical reasons for the standards of the tests having changed over the years. Further, since tests were new to the age 11 pupils in 1995, the effect of teaching test technique and of teaching to the content of the tests could have accounted for a good deal of the initial change. However there remains some evidence of increase in achievement, which is perhaps to be expected since, for the first time, all pupils in state primary schools were being taught science. Similarly the results of international surveys provided an optimistic picture of a rise in performance of 9–10-year-olds over the period 1995 to 2003. Between 2005 and 2008 there was little change in national test levels at Key Stage 2 in England, which remained above the target level of 85 per cent of pupils reaching level 4 or above. These results show that at least the pupils were taught the science that was tested. So we are left with the question as to whether this is what is needed for the twenty-first century.

Teachers' views of the curricula of the 1990s

During the 1990s, the National Curriculum for England and Wales was revised twice, as were the age 5–14 guidelines for environmental studies in Scotland. The reason for the changes was to simplify the structure and to reduce the content. Nevertheless the main complaint of teachers was of an overloaded and over-specified curriculum. In England the problem of 'covering' content was exacerbated by the introduction of the national frameworks for teaching literacy and numeracy, with revised frameworks provided in 2006. The time and even the methods to be used in teaching English and mathematics were specified and, although not statutory, schools were strongly advised to follow the frameworks and to show that they were giving priority to government targets in numeracy and literacy. The effect was not only to elevate the status of these subjects and to separate them from other subjects, but to downgrade others, including science. An ASE survey (ASE 1999) confirmed that the time for science had declined for 1997 to 1998, that it had been put 'on the back-burner' at Key Stage 1 and that much professional development in science had been postponed. In addition the publication of national test results in England and the inevitable creation of 'league tables' put further pressure on teachers to teach the knowledge tested. For many this left little time to make science interesting and relevant to the pupils.

Key findings from a study of primary science across the UK conducted in 2004 show that, far outweighing other factors, teachers considered that giving greater relevance to real life was the most important change needed to improve the quality of children's science education and their interest in science. As the report (Wellcome Trust 2005) noted, there are various ways of making science relevant. Creative approaches to presenting problems or topics, as in the case studies in

Box 3.3 A teacher's perception of the effect of pressure to cover content

I want to teach through investigations – that is how I was taught in my teacher training but it's time … we will set it aside and we will just talk about it or I will do it [as a demonstration] at the front – the time is just not available.

(Wellcome Trust 2005: 19)

Chapters 1 and 2, can link children's activities to the world outside school. But whilst teachers may not find enough good ideas for developing such activities, even when ideas are available many are deterred from implementing them by lack of funding, time and classroom assistance – all also mentioned in the research.

The content of the curriculum also plays a large part in each of these inhibiting factors. Time for setting a relevant scene for science work is limited by both the amount and type of content that teachers have to cover. For instance the requirement that 'pupils should be taught to make and use keys' (Key Stage 2 National Curriculum for England 1999) could be met as part of investigation of creatures and plants found locally, but it is all too frequently taught directly for lack of time. In Box 3.3 a teacher expresses the frustration brought on by this pressure.

Relevance can be in the form of connections to other curriculum subjects as well as to real life. Cross-curricular topics help this relevance. They were encouraged in the 1960s and 1970s but criticised in the 1980s (DES 1989) for fragmentation of the subject and activities that did not justify the label of 'science activities'. However, the reaction in moving to discrete science lesson led to isolation of science and to the resounding call for relevance.

Moreover the detailed specification of items 'to be taught' loses sight of the 'big ideas' that are the eventual aims of science education for all pupils. Progression in developing these ideas is not clear; each small idea becomes an aim in itself rather than building to a broader understanding of scientific aspects of the world around.

Curriculum reviews and revisions

The criticisms just noted were felt throughout the countries of the UK and led to reviews of existing curriculum statements and to the production of new draft programmes of study and outcomes. Political changes in Northern Ireland and the establishment of the Welsh Assembly mean that separate institutions deal with the curriculum and its assessment in each country. We therefore look at each one in turn.

England

Attention was turned initially to revising the curriculum for the secondary school – Key Stages 3 and 4 (11–14-year-olds and 14–16-year-olds). Revision of the primary curriculum began in 2008, with the revised programme of study to be published in March 2009. Thus, at the time of writing, the nature and extent of any changes are not known, but some idea of change can be anticipated from the content of the letter from the Secretary of State to Sir Jim Rose who leads the revision. The letter makes clear that the review concerns only the curriculum and does not include assessment and testing. It makes reference to some of the major shortcomings of the 1999 curriculum in teachers' criticisms and points to some other aspects to be considered, the main ones being:

- the amount of prescription of the curriculum;
- the number of subjects at the primary level, whilst at the same time maintaining a broad range and adding languages;
- whether all subjects should be introduced from Year 1, having in mind continuity with the early years foundation stage;
- the transition from primary to secondary school;
- the opportunity for meeting pupils' individual needs and strengths and narrowing the gap between the higher and lower achieving pupils.

Assuming there will be some continuity with the new secondary curriculum, which was implemented for Year 7 (first year of the secondary school) from 2008, it is useful to consider briefly the structure of the science programme of study for Key Stage 3 and the attainment targets for level 4, which is the target level for 11-year-olds in the primary school.

The programme of study for Key Stage 3 has two components:

1. Key concepts
   1.1 Scientific thinking
   1.2 Applications and implications of science
   1.3 Cultural understanding
   1.4 Collaboration

2. Key processes
   2.1 Practical and inquiry skills
   2.2 Critical understanding of evidence
   2.3 Communication

In developing these key concepts and processes, the range and content of the subject matter to be included is specified under four headings:

- energy, electricity and forces;
- chemical and material behaviour;
- organisms, behaviour and health;
- the environment, Earth and universe.

Under each of these content headings there are the main or 'big' ideas to be developed. For example, under 'Chemical and material behaviour' these are:

- the particle model provides explanations for the different physical properties and behaviour of matter;
- elements consist of atoms that combine together in chemical reactions to form compounds;

Box 3.4 How science works: level 4 (KS 3 National Curriculum for England)

Pupils decide on an appropriate approach, including using a fair test to answer a question, and select suitable equipment and information from that provided. They select and use methods that are adequate for the task. Following instructions, they take action to control obvious risks to themselves. They make a series of observations and measurements and vary one factor while keeping others the same. They record their observations, comparisons and measurements using tables and bar charts and begin to plot points to form simple graphs. They interpret data containing positive and negative numbers. They begin to relate their conclusions to patterns in data, including graphs, and to scientific knowledge and understanding. They communicate their conclusions using appropriate scientific language. They suggest improvements in their work, giving reasons.

- elements and compounds show characteristic chemical properties and patterns in their behaviour.

(QCA 2007a)

There are considerable differences here from the 1999 curriculum, which spells out details (for instance at Key Stage 3 'mixtures are composed of constituents that are not combined'). The attainment targets in the new curriculum are expressed in narrative style under four headings which are not the same as the four setting out the 'range and content'. The one most closely relating to attainment target 1 of the 1999 curriculum (scientific inquiry) is called 'How science works'. The description of level 4 attainment for this is given in Box 3.4.

Scotland

In Scotland the curriculum revision is set within a wider programme of work entitled 'Curriculum for Excellence'. While guidance on the curriculum content is central, the programme has implications for teachers and other staff, curriculum organisation and the qualifications system. Its overall aims are to provide:

- more freedom for teachers;
- greater choice and opportunity for pupils;
- a single coherent curriculum for all children and young people aged 3–18.

(Curriculum for Excellence website)

In the draft curriculum the pre-school and primary years (designated as P1 to P7, ages 5–12) have been divided into three stages: Early (pre-school and P1); First (P2 to P4); and Second (P5 to P7). As in the case of the *5 to 14 Curriculum Guidelines* introduced in the early 1990s, the curriculum is advisory and non-statutory. However, science is no longer combined with social subjects and technology in environmental studies but identified as a distinct subject.

The draft curriculum guidance for science (being trialled in 2008) is expressed in terms of 'experiences and outcomes', statements in which the learning process and skill, knowledge and understanding outcomes are combined. Thus the outcomes have suggested learning and teaching strategies embedded within them. Box 3.5 gives examples of these statements for the Early, First and Second levels in relation to the area 'sustainability', a sub-area of 'planet Earth'.

The experience and outcomes have been identified within seven areas and sub-areas (not all of which apply in the primary levels):

- planet Earth (sustainability, biodiversity, climate and earth science, astronomy);
- energy in the environment (energy transfer, energy sources, energy in food, electricity, (electronics));
- forces and motion (forces and motion);
- communications (communications systems, light, (using the electromagnetic spectrum), sound);
- life and cells (keeping my body healthy, (cells), biotechnology, reproduction, genetics, using my senses);
- materials (properties and uses, (elements), chemical reactions, forensic science);
- topical science.

Progression within each of these areas is identified by the statements of experiences and outcomes across the primary stages and into the secondary years, although there is not an entry for each sub-area at every one of the levels. The 'topical science' area is for consideration of matters such as those that relate to ethics, how the media report science and aspects of science in the news at various times. There are frequent cross-links to other areas of the curriculum, particularly to social science and health and wellbeing studies. Final versions are expected in 2009.

Box 3.5 Examples of draft experiences and outcomes for science in Scotland's Curriculum for Excellence

Planet Earth: sustainability

EARLY STAGE (PRE-SCHOOL AND P1)
I have investigated materials around me and I can sort them for reuse or recycling.

FIRST (P2 TO P4)
Through my experience of different materials which I use, I can talk about the need to conserve the Earth's resources at home and in school and what I can do to help.

SECOND (P5 TO P7)
I can assess the sustainability of my school environment and by helping to create and carry out an action plan to make improvements I can record how my responsible actions make a difference over time.

I can research a major environmental or sustainability issue of national or global importance and report on my findings.

Wales

As in Scotland, the new Welsh curriculum covers the age range 3 to 18 and is part of a wider programme of change. The new curriculum is being implemented from September 2008. The primary years have been divided into the Foundation Phase, which covers the pre-school years plus Key Stage 1 (children aged 3 to 7) and Key Stage 2 (for children aged 8 to 11). This enables advantage to be taken of the successful introduction of a Foundation Stage Curriculum and meets some of the concerns that formal subject studies are beginning too early in some parts of the UK.

A non-statutory skills framework has been developed across the full age range 3 to 18, giving guidance about continuity and progression in developing thinking, communication, ICT and number. The revised assessment arrangements include optional skills assessment materials for use, initially, in Year 5. The special attention to Year 5 aims to enable teachers to identify and support progression in these skills a year before pupils leave primary school.

In the Foundation Phase the skills are to be developed across seven statutory areas of learning, one of which is 'knowledge and understanding of the world' where the opportunities indicated include those relating to science concepts. For example, under 'myself and other living things' are included the opportunities to:

- learn the names and uses of the main external parts of the human body and plants;

- observe differences between animals and plants, in order to group them;

Under 'myself and non-living things' are included the opportunities to:

- experiment with different everyday objects and use their senses to sort them into groups according to simple features;

- develop an awareness of, and be able to distinguish between, made and natural materials.

(DCELLS 2008)

Box 3.6 Welsh National Curriculum for Science: Key Stage 2 'How things work'

Pupils should use and develop their skills, knowledge and understanding by investigating the science behind everyday things e.g. toys, musical instruments and electrical devices, the way they are constructed and work.

They should be given opportunities to study:

1. The uses of electricity and its control in simple circuits.

2. Forces of different kinds, e.g. gravity, magnetic and friction, including air resistance.

3. The ways in which forces can affect movement and how forces can be compared.

4. How different sounds are produced and the way that sound travels.

5. How light travels and how this can be used.

(DCELLS 2008)

The curriculum for science at Key Stage 2 is set out separately. It states explicitly that learners should be given the opportunity to build on the skills, knowledge and understanding acquired during the Foundation Phase and should be taught to relate their learning in science to everyday life, including current issues. The science skills at Key Stage 2 are identified under three headings: communication, inquiry and planning. As in the Foundation Phase, these skills are to be developed through a defined range of subject matter. At Key Stage 2 this is identified under 'Interdependence of organisms', 'The sustainable Earth', and 'How things work'. Box 3.6 indicates the range for 'How things work'.

Level descriptions for use in statutory assessment and reporting by teachers (tests having been made optional from 2005) have been revised to reflect the changes in the programme of study and to clarify the path of progress between levels.

Northern Ireland

Primary education in Northern Ireland has three phases:

- Foundation (Years 1 and 2, ages 5 and 6)
- Key stage 1 (Years 3 and 4, ages 7 and 8)
- Key stage 2 (Years 5, 6 and 7, ages 9–12)

The new Northern Ireland Curriculum for the primary school is set out in the same way for each of these three phases; statements describe a progression through the seven primary years. It was phased in from 2007, when it became statutory for Years 1 and 5. In each phase there are six areas of learning (plus Religious Education as required by the Northern Ireland Department of Education):

- Language and literacy
- Mathematics and numeracy
- The arts
- The world around us
- Personal development and mutual understanding
- Physical development and movement.

Specified outcomes include cross-curricular skills (communication, using mathematics and ICT) and thinking skills and capabilities (managing information, being creative, thinking, problem solving and decision making, working with others, and self-management).

Science, history, geography and technology contribute to learning in 'The world around us'. The statutory requirements are that pupils should have opportunities to develop knowledge, understanding and skills in relation to subject matter set out under four themes: 'Interdependence', 'Place', 'Movement and energy' and 'Change over time'. There are suggestions for the contributions of science, history, and so on, to these themes. Box 3.7 gives these suggestions for science and technology at Key Stage 1.

The curriculum document provides suggestions for teaching approaches and for building each phase on earlier experiences. A spiral curriculum is recommended and the nature of progression

Box 3.7 Northern Ireland Curriculum Key Stage 1: science and technology suggestions for 'The World Around Us'

Interdependence

- How we grow, move and use our senses, including similarities and differences between ourselves and other children.
- The variety of living things in the world and how we can take care of them.
- Some living things that are now extinct.

Place

- The range of materials used in my area.
- Sound in the local environment.
- How animals use colour to adapt to the natural environment.
- Animals that hibernate and the materials they use.

Movement and energy

- The use of electricity as an energy source and the importance of using it safely.
- Animals that migrate.
- The importance of light in our everyday lives.
- Different sources of light, such as traffic lights, candles or stars.
- Devices that push, pull and make things move.
- Design and make simple models.

Change over time

- The effect of heating and cooling some everyday substances.
- Changes in the local natural environment, including how they can affect living things.

(The Northern Ireland Curriculum for Key Stages 1 and 2 can be found at www.nicurriculum.org.uk/key_stages_1_and_2/areas_of_learning/the_world_around_us/index.asp).

through stages 1 and 2 is made explicit in a series of statements such as: '(to progress) from recognising a fair test to designing and carrying out fair tests', 'from using everyday language to increasingly precise use of subject specific vocabulary, notation and symbols'.

Comment

Perhaps the main message from this brief look at the new curricula developed in the four countries of the UK is that there are very many ways of setting out the intended learning experiences in science! In some ways there seem to be moves in opposite directions in the structure of the curriculum. For instance, while Scotland has removed science from the remit of environmental studies, the new Northern Ireland curriculum has science as part of 'the world around us' to which history, geography and technology also contribute. The place of science in the first two years of school also differs, although we have yet to see what will happen in England.

However, despite appearances of form, there is much in common in the aims of the revisions in the different countries; just different ways of achieving these aims. In particular there is a general intention to:

- provide for greater relevance to real life and other learning;
- make a place for current issues of concern, such as sustainability;
- reduce content to allow greater attention to skills and processes;
- give teachers more freedom by less prescription;
- identify progress in skills and ideas;
- improve continuity from pre-school to school and from primary to secondary.

Of course there are possible dangers in some changes. For instance, less prescription could be taken as a signal to spend less time on science. Relevance could mean cross-curricular topics that risk returning to a superficial treatment of science. Avoiding such pitfalls depends on teachers seizing the opportunities offered by revised curricula to provide for their pupils the kind of processes and outcomes of learning we describe in this book. The next chapter makes a start on this.

Summary

This chapter has considered how the aims of primary science education have evolved from the 1960s to the present day. Modern aims are summed up as being to lay a foundation for the development of scientific literacy. It has identified the meaning of scientific literacy and what is required of a primary science programme to contribute to it. Some impacts of the curricula developed in the 1990s in the countries of the UK have been discussed. Whilst there is some evidence that requiring science as part of the core curriculum in England and Wales has led to some improvement in achievement, as measured by tests, there was also a growing discontent with some aspects of the programmes of study. As a result the curricula for England, Wales, Scotland and Northern Ireland have been subject to review and revision, the results of which, where known, have been summarised. While differing in structure and detail, these four countries have produced curricula which aim to make science more relevant to children's everyday lives and reduce prescription of content to allow more emphasis on the development of skills and attitudes.

Further reading

Harlen, W. (2008) *Science as a Key Component of the Primary Curriculum: A Rationale with Policy Implications*, London: Wellcome Trust.

PSR Editorial Board (2007) All change or small change? *Primary Science Review* 100: 9–13.

4

Experiences that promote learning in science

Introduction

Having looked at what we want children to learn in the last chapter we need to consider how to help this learning, which is indeed what this book is about. Classroom events, such as those described in the case studies, supported by systematic research, suggest some key features of experiences that promote learning in science, discussed at the end of Chapters 1 and 2. Many of these are, of course, required for learning in any subject area; conversely, science is so much part of everyday life that what promotes learning in general will have relevance for learning in science. In everyday work with children we identify learning with change in behaviour – in what they show they know and can do. But learning must have something to do with what happens inside the brain. So in this chapter we begin by looking at what is needed to help learning from a different perspective than the classroom – what is known about the changes inside our heads when learning takes place.

After this brief foray into events at the micro-level, we return to the large scale level of behaviour that we can more easily observe. Drawing on information at these two levels, we identify the characteristics of experience that are most likely to be effective in promoting learning in science. Finally, we illustrate how these can be used as criteria in evaluating activities and in deciding how to adapt or elaborate activities to increase their value for learning.

What do we learn about learning from neuroscience?

There is rapidly increasing interest in neuroscience – the study of the brain – made possible largely because of the development of non-intrusive techniques for finding out about links between external behaviour and internal brain activity. This means that it is no longer necessary to depend on investigations with non-human animals or humans with brain disorders. Studies show that learning definitely changes the brain both in structure and size. So, even though the available knowledge is at present limited, it is useful to know what neuroscience can say about learning.

Trying to relate the ideas and behaviours of a person to the function of cells in the brain is one of the great challenges facing neuroscience. This is partly because understanding of the brain is still at an early stage, but also because there are estimated to be 15 to 32 billion cells in the brain (OECD 2007: 36–7) and a large number of these will be involved even in the simplest actions, such as decoding a word. It makes sense that there should be some relationship between what happens inside the brain and response to the world around, but a great deal has yet to be worked out about the nature of the connections. Meanwhile, what can we learn about learning from what is already known about the brain?

The brain

Our brains are composed of neurons, cells which are made up of a main part, called the cell body, with dendrites and an axon attached. Dendrites are thread-like, branching structures which grow out of the cell body, whilst the axon is in most cases a single fibre, thinner than a dendrite thread and much longer than the cell body. An axon running down the spinal cord (which is an extension of the brain) can be up to a metre long.

The activity of the brain depends on communication between neurons. There are other nerve cells in the brain, called glial cells, but these do not transmit messages. The communication is through electric signals which are the result of movement of ions (atoms that have a positive or negative charge) within and surrounding the neuron. Without going into detail of how charges move into and out of a neuron, it is enough for our purposes to know that these electric signals are transmitted by one neuron to another by axons and received from another neuron by dendrites. There is a small gap (synapse) between the terminal of an axon of the cell sending a message and the dendrite of a receiving neuron. If several signals are received in a cell body this can 'excite' the cell body and send a signal across the gap to another neuron. To communicate with the target cell, the axon has to release chemical signals across the gap. Communication between neurons is increased by an insulating layer of myelin which forms a fatty sheath around the axon (see Figure 4.1).

Each neuron can communicate with a large number of others, forming networks. It is these networks of communications that enable the brain to carry out its functions. At birth, the human brain has most of the neurons it will ever have; the brain development from there onwards comprises growth of communication among the neurons (Box 4.1).

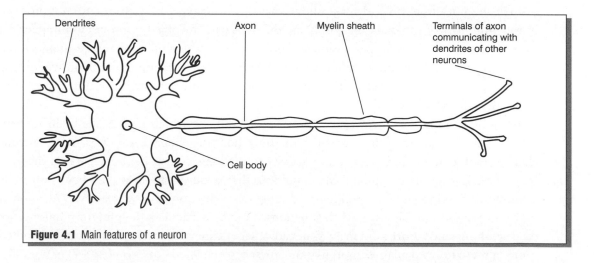

Figure 4.1 Main features of a neuron

Box 4.1 Growth of the brain

> Much of the spectacular increase in brain size after birth is actually attributable to the development of these processes acting as lines of communication between neurons, rather than simply to the addition of more neurons.
>
> (Greenfield 1997: 141)

At the same time, lines of communication between neurons that are no longer used are 'pruned'. Thus there is enormous potential for different connections to be made in response to changing environmental stimuli. The relationship between the internal changes in the brain and the external environment, which is under the influence of education, is of particular interest in improving the effectiveness of learning and teaching.

Memory

Memory is described by Greenfield (1997) as 'the cornerstone of the mind', for it is the basis of our adaptation to experience, which of course means learning. The difference between short-term and long-term memory is well known, but this is not the only difference within the overall concept of memory. Short-term memory, also known as working memory, used in the recall of series or numbers such as a telephone number or a series of actions, requires constant repetition. Otherwise the memory will fail in about 30 minutes, or sooner if there is distraction by other things happening. But when something is rehearsed and remembered for more than this time the memory will probably last for a few days (Greenfield 1997: 159) and then may be held in the long-term memory.

There are several types of long-term memory, for each of which there is a different type of short-term memory. Information such as a telephone number, which has to be consciously recalled, is described as explicit long-term memory. Another type is described as implicit, because it is more automatic, like riding a bicycle. Evidence from the study of people who have lost some of their memory from brain damage shows that these two types of memory are not processed in the same part of the brain. Not only are different parts involved in processing implicit and explicit memory, but these processing locations are also different from where memories are stored. Experimental studies have shown that there is no one location in the brain where long-term memories are held. Rather they appear to be distributed through the outer layer of the brain (the cortex).

By using various non-intrusive techniques for identifying which areas of the brain are being activated during learning, it is possible to show how dependence on short-term memory changes with practice and gives rise to activity in the longer-term memory parts of the brain. Such investigations have explored the conditions that favour memorisation. They confirm, for example, that writing down a problem and some representation of how it was solved, improves the ability to solve problems. 'In such situations, it can be particularly helpful for pupils to show their working, since, apart from many other advantages, external representations can help offload some of these heavy demands upon working memory' (Howard-Jones *et al.* 2007: 17).

| Box 4.2 | Critical times in early development of the senses |

Greenfield (1997) recounts the story of a boy who, as a baby, had one eye bandaged for two weeks to help treat an infection. Later he was found to be blind in this eye even though the eye itself was completely normal. The explanation was that this happened at a critical time for the establishment of connections between eye and brain. The brain, not receiving signals from the eye treated it as if it were not there and the neurons were not connected to this eye, but instead had been taken over by the other eye. Had the bandaging taken place later, after the normal connections had been established, it would not have had the same impact on the brain. In general, during the time when most connections are being made, up to the age of 16, a neuron that is insufficiently stimulated to make contact with other neurons will die.

(Greenfield 1997)

Critical periods for learning

Can neuroscience tell us about the best time for certain experiences? The question of whether there are certain critical times for learning particular things is not as certain as it was once thought to be. For one thing, it depends on what is being learnt. The main distinction is between those functions which are developed naturally in a normal environment – relating to the operation of the senses and to movement, for instance – and those which depend on particular experiences such as provided in education. Whilst there is some evidence of critical periods during the early years for the development of the function of those parts of the brain dealing with the senses (see Box 4.2), this is less so for learning that is dependent on specific inputs. Although it is easier to learn certain things earlier in life than later, this is because greater changes occur in the brain in childhood. But changes continue to some extent throughout life.

There are periods when the brain seems to be developing particularly significantly. The first three years are one of these, relating particularly to language development. Another is adolescence, when the main changes are in the increase in the myelin insulating the axons and in 'pruning' of synapses. Until these changes have taken place, adolescents do not show the same abilities as adults in respect of processes such as 'directing attention, planning future tasks, inhibiting in appropriate behaviour, multitasking, and a variety of socially-oriented tasks' (Howard-Jones *et al.* 2007: 9).

The brain continues to change and develop beyond adolescence and is well-designed for lifelong learning and adaptation to new situations and experiences. These changes are shown in the structure and size of the brain, as illustrated in Box 4.3.

Emotions

The chemicals in our bodies that relate to emotions have a modifying effect on the working of the networks of neural connections (Zull 2004). The main ones relevant to learning are adrenalin, which affects the heart rate in preparation for unusual action (fighting or fleeing), and dopamine, which is related to feeling pleasure and satisfaction. The close relationship of feeling

> **Box 4.3** Physical change associated with learning
>
> In a study of juggling, the brain areas activated at the beginning of a three-month training period increased in size by the end of it. After three months of rest, these areas had shrunk back and were closer to their original size. This graphic example of 'if you don't use it, you lose it' demonstrates the potential importance of education in mediating brain development throughout our lives.
>
> (Howard-Jones *et al.* 2007: 21)

> **Box 4.4** The importance of feeling good about learning
>
> As part of the teacher's art, we must find ways to make learning intrinsically rewarding. Learning should feel good, and the student should become aware of those feelings. To achieve this goal, we need to make two things happen. First, classes and assignments should lead to some progress for students, some sense of mastery and success. Second, students should work on topics and activities that naturally appeal to them.
>
> (Zull 2004: 70)

and thinking shows in the pleasure we feel from solving a difficult problem and in frustration from not being able to understand something. The pleasure is not only a reward for completing a task successfully but is a motivation for tackling further tasks. We all know how the response of other people to our suggestions or ideas can affect our feelings about ourselves and our willingness to offer further ideas. Recognising this relationship means taking the emotions into account in helping learners to use and change their brains. Some implications are identified in Box 4.4, and others are discussed in Chapter 11.

Implications for learning in general

Considerable words of caution are needed before we make claims that link the insights from neuroscience about what is going on inside the brain to the external environment. Probably the best we can say is that evidence supports, but does not prove, the value of:

- practice – repeating an action increases the growth and strength of links between neurons;
- motivation – through the experience of success in meeting a challenge;
- externalising thinking – in the way mentioned earlier, by making some concrete representation, by writing, drawing, talking, or using a computer, so that not everything has to be held in memory;
- engaging several parts of the brain, particularly those concerned with the senses, with action, reflection and abstracting meaning;

■ linking to existing knowledge – there is an area of the brain activated when we try to make something meaningful by relating it to what we already know. Once meaning is created through these associations the new information becomes more memorable.

There are also some more general conditions for learning that are supported, and others that are not supported, by evidence relating to the brain. Among those that are known to help learning are:

■ having breakfast (studies show that missing breakfast interferes with learning and that a cereal-rich breakfast improves memory);

■ having enough sleep;

■ avoiding caffeine (in cola drinks, for instance);

■ avoiding dehydration (although there is no evidence for the value of drinking large amounts of water when not dehydrated).

Research studies supporting these points can be found in the OECD publication (2007) mentioned at the end of this chapter.

There is little evidence to support the notion that the left- and right sides of the brain work in different ways and that some people are left-brained and others right-brained. In normal children, most functions require brain activity in both hemispheres. Nor is there support for different 'learning styles' (Goswami and Bryant 2007). An activity such as talking requires several different areas of the brain to be working. However, the remarkable ability of parts of the brain to take over functions from other parts that are damaged shows that areas can become active in quite different processes (see Box 4.5).

Box 4.5 The boy with half a brain

The story of Nico, as told by Battro (2000), is about a boy who developed severe epilepsy after his first year. The seizures became so bad that at the age of 3 years 7 months, half his brain (the right hand side) was completely removed. This not only cured the epilepsy but he very soon became able to operate at a normal level for his age in language, mathematics, arts and music, which are often thought of as being under the dominance of different halves of the brain. Indeed his only limitation was in writing things down and in drawing. However, given access to a computer, he made good drawings and his writing was normal when using a word processor. Thus it was only in the physical aspects of performing these tasks where he was deficient; the cognitive aspects were not deficient. The importance of the computer should not be underestimated, since it helped him to compensate for a deficiency (he had a disabled left hand) that could have impeded learning in several areas. Battro describes the computer as an 'intellectual prosthesis'. As might be expected, such was the interest in Nico that his development across a range of abilities was tested frequently and it was found to be completely normal. Of course it is not yet known how he will develop in later life, but his story so far is a remarkable testimony to how half a brain can take over the functions of a whole brain, at least in a young child.

Implications for learning science

All that we have said so far applies to all learning and so to learning in science. Is there anything more that is specific to science? From brain investigations perhaps the most relevant is that 'a concept in science may depend on neurons being simultaneously active in visual, spatial, memory, deductive and kinaesthetic regions, in both brain hemispheres' (Goswami and Bryant 2007). This indicates the need for a wide variety of different kinds of experience: being able to touch and manipulate objects; using language; linking to previous experience; reasoning; and reflection.

Beyond this we must move from the microscopic level of brain cells to the level of macroscopic observable behaviour of an individual. At this level the brain is treated as a 'black box' and the evidence of effectiveness comes from how the child responds to the environment and shows learning through change in behaviour.

Bringing together what we know about learning in general and what we know about learning in science from experience and research, leads to the following as important characteristics of learning experiences. They should:

1. be interesting, relevant and appealing to the children;

2. build on their previous experience and promote progress;

3. involve use of the senses, action, reflection and making meaning;

4. encourage talk, dialogue and the representation and communication of ideas and events in various forms;

5. help to develop scientific concepts, inquiry skills and attitudes of and towards science;

6. provide opportunities for working cooperatively and sharing ideas with others.

We now look at these in a little more detail and show how they can be used as criteria to evaluate and adapt activities from curriculum materials, or to develop broad suggestions for activities, such as in the DfEE (1998) scheme of work, into rich learning experiences.

Interesting and relevant

This must be considered in relation to all the children, both boys and girls, and those of different social and ethnic backgrounds, so that activities are accessible to all. Interest is not always spontaneous and can be encouraged by, for instance, displaying materials in the class prior to a new topic, with questions to stimulate curiosity, or in other ways suggested in Box 4.6.

Box 4.6 Engaging children's interest

Children's interest can also be stimulated by making science more relevant to their lives, integrating with other subjects, and using creative contexts such as role-plays and stories.

(Wellcome Trust 2005)

As noted in Chapter 3, one of the themes that emerge from seeking pupils' views of school science is that they often do not see it as relevant. Lack of perceived relevance is likely to be an important reason why attitudes to science become less positive in the later primary years (Murphy and Beggs 2003). So it is important to address this aspect of classroom activities, but doing so is not always easy. Real-life events are often complex and involve several ideas, so there is a dilemma as to whether they should be 'tidied up' to demonstrate certain relationships or principles. In doing this, the essential links to real life – the 'relevance' – can be lost. Some degree of extraction from real events is generally necessary, but it should always be possible to see a link between what is learnt and real events.

Linked to previous experience and to progress

For activities to be meaningful and engaging, they should help children to understand and find out more about the things that they have encountered directly or indirectly and to develop further the ideas and skills they have previously used. It should be possible for children to make a link between new experience and previous experience. At the same time they need challenges to move forward, so, in the enduring words of the Plowden Report, over 40 years ago:

> The teacher's task is to provide an environment and opportunities which are sufficiently challenging for children and yet not so difficult as to be outside their reach. There has to be the right mixture of the familiar and the novel … (CACE 1967: para 533)

As we have seen, there is evidence from studies of the brain that support the importance of making links and requiring learners to make conscious efforts to make sense of new experience in terms of what they already know. We will see, in Chapter 6, how this process involves inquiry skills in generating 'bigger' ideas from 'smaller' ones. There is also evidence to support the importance of experiencing success for motivating learning. But children need to experience successively more complex ideas and sophisticated ways of thinking to support their learning in order to experience satisfaction. Thus a sense of progression is needed.

When they enter school, children will start from the ideas they bring with them, and during their time in the primary years will develop ideas and skills that are a foundation for secondary school science. It is easier to see progression over this large span of years (for instance in the national curricula or guidelines discussed in Chapter 3) than it is from month to month or even from year to year. Nevertheless it must be there and be built into the school's overall plan for science (see Chapter 23). One of the criticisms of primary school practice before the advent of the national curricula in the countries of the UK was that children often repeated activities from year to year. With the reduction in the detail of the curricula and the number of topics studied, it is important that this situation does not recur. This means teachers should be clear about the aims of activities and how they fit into the overall progression from age 5 to 12.

Using the senses, first-hand action, reflection and making meaning

We have seen that activity in different parts of the brain is important for learning, and science has the special value of enabling direct interaction with materials in which sight, sound, smell, touch

Box 4.7 Active learning

Science education begins for children when they realize that they can find things out for themselves by their own actions: by sifting through a handful of sand, by blowing bubbles, by putting salt in water, by comparing different materials, by regular observation of the moon and stars.

(Harlen (ed.) 2001: 4)

and, when safe, taste, can be involved. Encouraging these interactions is therefore extremely important for learning science. Through first-hand manipulation, children learn that in this way they can find answers to some of their questions, just like scientists (see Box 4.7). As children get older they become more able to manipulate some things in their heads and to learn from secondary sources, such as books, films, CDs, television and computer programs, but the link to reality is essential for understanding (see Chapter 21).

Reflection and extracting meaning

Reflection, like practice, means going over actions, but in the mind, rather than physically. Revisiting something by visualising it – seeing it in the mind – is known to activate most of the brain areas associated with actually seeing it. It can help in relation to strengthening networks of neurons and memory. Thus time used in reviewing activities before going on to the next, is time well spent on learning. Reflection about how things were done can improve skills. Reflection about what was found that was not known before can produce new meaning and develop ideas.

Encouraging talk, dialogue and representation in various forms

We will be considering the value to learning of various forms of verbal interactions in Chapter 8. Here all that needs to be emphasised is that we know that learning is encouraged by 'thinking aloud', when learners make clear for themselves and others how they are making sense of things and what they understand and do not understand. It is the main way for teachers to have access to children's thinking, particularly in the early years, when children are not skilled enough in writing and drawing to express their ideas.

Evidence from studies of memory indicates that holding ideas or facts in short-term memory long enough for them to be taken into long-term memory is helped by using some external prop. Representing their developing ideas in some way, perhaps through drawing, modelling, role-playing and actions that demonstrate relationships or changes in the world around, requires children to make some external representation of their knowledge. Finding a way of representing in actions an event such as water evaporating into the air and then condensing to form clouds and rain, forces thinking about 'Is it like this ... or that?' 'What comes first, the rain or the cloud?' So these opportunities are not just useful for adding fun to science but also help children to rehearse their ideas, to go over and refresh what they know.

They help children to reflect on what they understand and whether it makes sense when put in a different form.

Developing scientific concepts, inquiry skills and attitudes

The potential for the development of science concepts depends to a greater extent on the content of the activities than in the case of the other characteristics of activities. Developing understanding of science concepts is a central purpose of science education, so the content of activities should involve relevant scientific ideas. Even when the main aim of an activity is the development of inquiry skills, it may scarcely be described as a 'science activity' unless the skills are used in relation to content that involves scientific ideas (see Chapter 10).

Inquiry skills are sometimes referred to as process skills, since they are involved in the processes of interacting with materials and in the 'processing' of information so gained, but inquiry (or enquiry) is the term now more widely used. They include physical skills of manipulation, and mental skills that are central to reasoning and to the development of understanding. Developing inquiry skills means using them. So what is important is that children have opportunity, for example, to raise questions, to suggest ways of answering them, to make predictions, to propose explanations (hypotheses) to collect evidence and to interpret it in relation to the question being investigated (see Chapter 7).

In relation to attitudes, it is useful to distinguish between attitudes towards science and the attitudes that are part of engaging in scientific activity. We are concerned with the latter here, meaning willingness to act in certain ways that promote scientific understanding. These are attitudes such as open mindedness, willingness to consider evidence, flexibility in taking new evidence into account (see Chapter 11). It is the decline in attitudes of the first kind, shown in children's liking for science or willingness to continue studying it that has raised concern about the impact of science education in some countries. There is little evidence about change in children's willingness to think scientifically, since this has not been assessed except insofar as it is involved in understanding the nature of science.

Working cooperatively and sharing ideas with others

The process of learning science involves the development and change in the ideas that individuals hold. The direction of change is from children's own ideas, which may be unscientific (as we will see in Chapter 5), towards ideas that are more widely shared because they explain a range of phenomena. Expressing ideas and listening to others is an important part of this process. But sharing and changing ideas can be risky and it is important for teachers to take steps to avoid a classroom atmosphere that would inhibit children airing and sharing ideas, perhaps by being too competitive or anxious to get 'the right answer'. So it is important, for example, for teachers to show genuine interest in what the children think, by phrasing questions carefully and allowing time for children to give considered answers (see Chapters 8 and 12 for more discussion).

Criteria for evaluating and adapting activities

The characteristics of activities that are learning opportunities listed earlier can be turned into criteria to evaluate already planned activities for their learning potential, to help in planning new activities and to adapt existing activities to enrich their learning potential. All this can be done whilst adhering to content requirements; for in most cases, it is the way the children interact with the materials, with each other and with the teacher, not the content of the activity, which makes the difference between a richer and a poorer learning opportunity.

Evaluating activities

The criteria can be expressed as questions to apply to activities. Box 4.8 shows how they can be used in evaluating the lessons in one of the case studies, the activities that Graham carried out with soil.

Reviewing Graham's lesson using this framework also reveals certain aspects where opportunities for learning could have been increased. For instance, he might have been more explicit in encouraging children to exchange views and reasons for their views about the soil samples in small groups; he could have also discussed with the children what to include in their reports. Of course, these things may well have been done, but just not recorded in the case study. However, such analysis, whilst useful for teachers' reflection on their lessons, is most useful at the stage of planning activities.

Box 4.8 Evaluating Graham's lessons about soil

Were the activities interesting and relevant to the children?

Interest was created by the prospect of growing seedlings and using soil samples from their own gardens. Since the work was within an overall topic of food, the prospect of growing something that they could eat would have increased the relevance. The activities allowed for a range of different kinds of interaction with the materials which would cater for different needs. Children with learning difficulties may have only gone so far as to feel, smell and look at the soils to appreciate their differences.

Did they build on previous experience and promote progress?

The children had previously planted seeds and had experience of seeing them grow into seedlings. So they were aware that there were roots in the soil which were important in determining the health of the plant. The children's idea of soil as a single, and not very interesting, substance was developed into one that recognised different types and constituents. Further development into understanding how soil is formed might follow from these observations of what it contained. Their inquiry skills and attitudes were also advanced through conducting careful comparisons and seeking for explanations, not just describing them.

Were the children able to use a range of senses and learn actively?

The children used sight, smell and touch in the free exploration of the soils, when they handled the soils and looked carefully using magnifying lenses, and in the controlled investigation of specific questions. The opportunities of this activity were well exploited; other senses might be more appropriately used in other activities. The children were active mentally and physically in planning and then carrying out their tests.

Did the children reflect and make meaning from their activities?

Graham set aside time at the end of the investigations for the children to reflect on what they had found and how they had found it.

Did the children talk and represent their ideas in other ways?

The initial group work in the exploratory phase involved talk in small groups, and the whole-class discussion gave opportunities for more formal reporting from each group, and structured exchanges. We do not know whether the children made drawings of the differences they found in soils during their group investigations.

In some investigations, drawing would help to focus observation, requiring children to move between the representation and the real things, refining their identification of differences.

Could they develop scientific ideas, use inquiry skills and demonstrate scientific attitudes?

Ideas about important differences between soils were developed; for example, their ideas advanced from the initial one that dark soils were more fertile. There were many opportunities to use and develop observational, planning, interpretation and communication skills. They were encouraged to compare their expectations with their findings and to reflect on how to improve their investigations. The careful collection of evidence and use of it to decide the best soil encouraged willingness to change their ideas on the basis of evidence.

Could they work cooperatively and share ideas with each other?

The reporting to and questioning by each other suggests an atmosphere in which ideas are shared.

Box 4.9 Parachute workcard

- Cut 4 pieces of string 14 inches long

- Cut a 14-inch square from sturdy plastic

- Securely tape or tie a string to each corner of the plastic

- Tie the free ends of the 4 strings together in a knot. Be sure the strings are all the same length

- tie a single string about 6 inches long to the knot

- Add a weight, such as a washer, to the free end of the string

- Pull the parachute up in the centre. Squeeze the plastic to make it as flat as possible

- Fold the parachute twice

- Wrap the string loosely around the plastic

- Throw the parachute up into the air

Results The parachute opens and slowly carries the weight to the ground.

Why? The weight falls first, unwinding the string because the parachute, being larger, is held back by the air. The air fills the plastic, slowing down the rate of descent. If the weight falls quickly a smaller object needs to be used.

Adapting or elaborating activities

Take the example of the activity presented to children on the workcard in Box 4.9. There are some obvious reasons why this is limited as a learning experience although it is certainly an activity most children would enjoy.

It is perhaps useful to recognise what is valuable about the activity before considering its deficiencies. It is capable of relating to children's interests across a broad spectrum, with no obvious gender or cultural bias. Thus it meets the first criterion. It uses simple and safe materials, which are familiar and cheap and it would be an easy activity for teachers to manage. It also meets the criterion of children using their senses directly and being active. However, they have no invitation to be reflective, nor to develop their own ideas about what happens. They manipulate materials, but only according to instructions. This can be a good start when particular techniques have to be learnt, but they would learn more about what is going on by interacting with the materials more independently. There are many other ways in which the activity could be changed to meet the criteria. For example:

Building on children's experience and promoting progress

Children's experiences of air resistance are many and not restricted to parachutes. Children could relate them to more everyday events, such as riding a bicycle in a strong wind, and the 'helicopter' wings of sycamore seeds seen drifting gently down to the ground. They should be encouraged to think about air resistance in relation to horizontal movement, in yachts and sailing ships as well as in slowing aircraft in landing on short runways and aircraft carriers. They can be challenged to think about the kind of materials and construction which is needed in each case.

Work cards can have a useful role as part of a topic in which there is a progression in ideas, but for this they need to provide incentive for children to question and find ways of answering their own questions. In this case the instructions could provide an initial experience and encourage children to raise questions which this material could so easily be used to answer: 'What happens if there is no weight on the string?', 'More weight?', 'A bigger/smaller canopy?', 'A different shape?' Alternatively the activity might begin with the experience of throwing several parachutes, of different sizes and even shapes, and noticing how they fall. This would provide the context for expressing their initial ideas about what is happening and opportunity for comparing them with evidence.

Encouraging talk and representation of events

When children have to follow instructions, their talk is focused on the details of what they have to do rather than on the purpose of doing it or what they are learning from it: 'Where do you tie the strings?', 'Don't put the weight there; it has to go here', 'You need to throw it like this.' This might be necessary at the start but after the initial experience, there is room for much more educationally useful talk focused on 'why' rather than 'what'. The directions could ask the children to explain what is happening, to discuss in groups how to make the parachute fall more/less quickly, to agree on how to test their ideas and then to do it. Other questions would no doubt arise, about the effect of the suspended load, which could be discussed in groups or with the whole class.

This is a good example of an activity where children could be asked to make an annotated drawing of what they think is happening and why changing certain things changes the way the parachute falls. Children could be encouraged to work in groups to add labels and arrows to show their ideas about the forces acting on the parachute.

Developing ideas and inquiry skills

A main point of the activity is to enable children to recognise the role of air in slowing down the fall of the parachute. With this in mind it would be useful for children to observe how quickly the parachute falls when it is not allowed to open. Exploration of larger and smaller parachutes might further children's ideas about the effect of air. The question of why the parachute falls at all could also be discussed leading to recognition of the main forces acting on the parachute when it is falling. Giving the 'answer' to why the parachute moves slowly is not allowing the children to use and explore their own ideas. Rarely does the explanation of an event by others lead to understanding; the children have to work it out for themselves.

The provision of precise instructions removes the opportunity for children to investigate and think out for themselves how to make a parachute. Opportunities for children to develop their inquiry skills are further limited by the lack of any investigation once the parachute is constructed. There are many variables which affect the fall of the parachute, such as shape, area, length of strings, which children could explore in a controlled way as they test out various ideas and try to find answers to questions they raise for themselves. More investigations planned by the children would give them the chance to review their work critically and to improve their future inquiries.

Working cooperatively and sharing ideas

Even within the context of a work sheet, there could be instructions for pooling ideas within a group, planning how to find out 'what happens if … 'and preparing a group report to others when they meet together as a class to listen to reports of each other's progress and share ideas. Different groups might investigate different variables and so ideas about explanations could be tested in different ways: 'Does the explanation for the effect of changing the size of the canopy also explain what happens when the shape is changed? or when there is a hole in the canopy?'

Implications of creating richer opportunities for learning

There are three main consequences of modifying activities in these kinds of ways:

- First, it will depend more on the teacher than on the content of the activity. In the case of the workcard, although careful wording can go a long way in encouraging children to use their own ideas and think things out for themselves, there is less room for the children to make their own links and pursue their own questions.

- Second, it will undoubtedly take up more time. This has to be balanced by the much greater learning which takes place. Even if the same time as required for a modified parachute activity were to be used for several activities of the original kind, there would still be no opportunity for developing real understanding. Fewer activities, with more opportunity for different kinds of learning, for discussion, for reflection and for developing skills will be a greater contribution to learning with understanding.

- Third, it requires a different kind of lesson planning. Planning to allow children to use and develop their own ideas requires more, not less, planning than preparing prescribed activities. It means thinking about the teacher's and the children's role in the activities. This is taken up in Chapter 13.

Summary

This chapter has considered the characteristics of classroom activities that optimise opportunities for learning science. The characteristics were drawn from what is known about learning in general from studies of the brain, as well as from examples of effective classroom practice and research. The characteristics identified related to the potential of activities:

- to be interesting and relevant to children;

- to build on their previous experience and promote progression in learning;

- to require use of the senses and physical and mental activity;

- to encourage reflection and the extraction of meaning;

- to involve talk and representation of experience in different forms;

- to foster the development of science concepts, inquiry skills, scientific attitudes and cooperative working.

By turning the characteristics into questions they become useful criteria for evaluating and adapting ideas with respect to the opportunities for developing scientific understanding, skills and attitudes.

Some implications of providing activities meeting these criteria emphasise the role of the teacher, the need to spend more time on fewer activities rather than less time and less thought on more activities, and the importance of planning.

Further reading

Greenfield, S. (1997) *The Human Brain: A Guided Tour*, London: Phoenix.

Hall, J. (2005) *Neuroscience and Education: What Can Brain Science Contribute to Teaching and Learning?* Spotlight 92. Glasgow: The SCRE Centre, University of Glasgow.

Murphy, C. and Beggs, J. (2003) Children's perceptions of school science, *School Science Review* 84 (308): 109–16.

Organization for Economic Cooperation and Development (OECD) (2007) *Understanding the Brain: The Birth of a Learning Science*, Paris: OECD.

Zull, J.E. (2004) The art of changing the brain, *Educational Leadership* 62(1): 68–72.

Learning through inquiry

Children's own ideas

Introduction

In the 1980s and 1990s there was a burgeoning of interest in the ideas that children develop about the world around them from their own experience and thinking, without school science activities. This followed the initial research that showed the existence of these ideas and the role they play in children's learning. Systematic research into children's ideas in science began in the late 1970s with work mainly at the secondary level. The main work of this kind at the primary level began with ground-breaking studies in New Zealand in the 1980s (Osborne and Freyberg 1985) and the SPACE (Science Processes and Concepts Exploration) in the UK (1987–1992). The SPACE project studied children's ideas across the full range of the curriculum for children aged 5 to 11 years.

Topics across the curriculum have also been studied by researchers in various parts of the world and, while there is still interest in uncovering more of children's ideas, the fact that these ideas exist is no longer a surprise. Indeed, some of the ideas described in this chapter are well known. This does not, however, diminish their importance as starting points. The arguments for this remain as firm as ever. We therefore begin this chapter with a brief review of these reasons and then look at some examples of children's ideas. The chapter concludes with a list of characteristics of children's ideas which give clues to helping children to develop more scientific ideas. We return to these later, in Chapter 9.

Reasons for taking children's ideas seriously

There are several reasons why we should start, in developing children scientific ideas, from their initial ideas, rather than just 'telling them the correct ideas'. There are theoretical reasons, related to how children learn, which will be explored in Chapter 6. There are also practical reasons: 'telling' children just does not work. If you insist on children 'learning' the correct idea when they still have their own ideas, they will possibly memorise the correct one, but without really believing it, and will hold on to their own ideas to make sense of real phenomena around them.

But the strongest reason of all comes from looking at what the children's ideas are. This reveals that the ideas are the product of thinking about experience (necessarily limited experience) and are not childish fantasy. The children have reasons for what they think and unless they are helped to have even better reasons for thinking differently and more scientifically, they will retain their own ideas. So this is why we now look at some examples of children's ideas, mostly from the Science Processes and Concepts Exploration (SPACE) research.

Some examples of children's ideas

Ideas about growth inside eggs

Research in the SPACE project studied the ideas of children about what was happening inside hens' eggs that were being incubated in the classroom. The most popular idea was that there was a miniature but mainly complete animal inside the egg, feeding on what was there. This is evident in the drawings made by the children when asked to depict what they thought was inside an egg while it was incubating.

An alternative was that the complete animal was inside simply waiting to hatch. This is perhaps not surprising, given that children may have seen TV nature programmes showing birds hatching from eggs.

There was also the view that the body parts were complete but needed to come together.

The more scientific view that transformation was going on inside the egg was evident in some children's ideas. It was also clear that the children used knowledge derived from experience

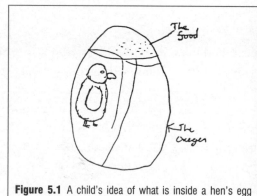

Figure 5.1 A child's idea of what is inside a hen's egg when incubating (Russell and Watt 1990, p. 31)

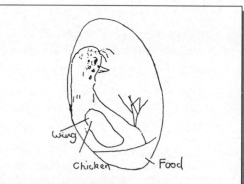

Figure 5.2 A child's idea of what is inside a hen's egg when incubating (Russell and Watt 1990, p. 10)

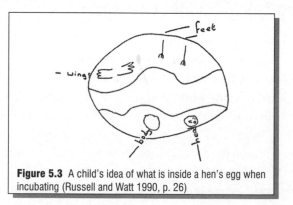

Figure 5.3 A child's idea of what is inside a hen's egg when incubating (Russell and Watt 1990, p. 26)

of reproduction of pets and observations of human babies when trying to understand what was going on inside the eggs.

Ideas about growth in plants

When asked 'What do you think plants need to help them grow?' infant (5–7-year-old) children generally mentioned one external factor. For example, Figure 5.4 suggests that light in necessary.

Other young children mentioned soil or water or sun, but rarely all three. Characteristically the younger children made no attempt to explain why these conditions were needed or by what mechanism they worked. Junior children, however, made efforts to give explanations, as in Figure 5.5.

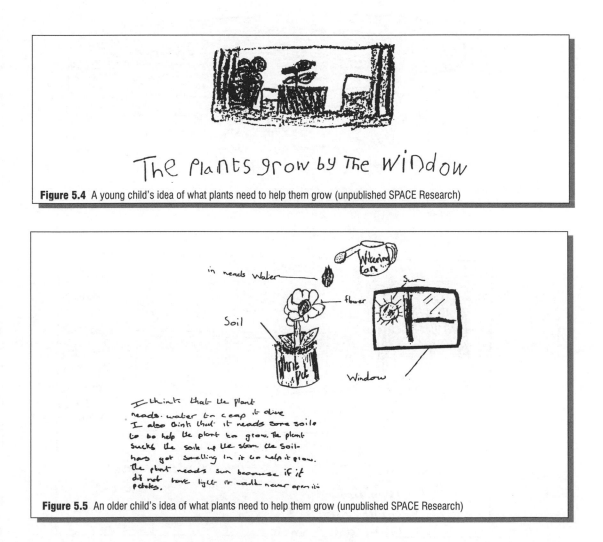

Figure 5.4 A young child's idea of what plants need to help them grow (unpublished SPACE Research)

Figure 5.5 An older child's idea of what plants need to help them grow (unpublished SPACE Research)

Ideas about how sounds are made and heard

Children's ideas about sound were explored after they had opportunity to make sound with a variety of instruments. The instance in Figure 5.6 suggests no mechanism for sound being produced by a drum or for it being heard; it is as if being 'very loud' and 'listening hard' are properties which require no explanation.

The simplest mechanism suggested is that the impact of hitting produces 'sound'. In contrast, Figure 5.7 explains the sound in terms of vibration. But notice that the vibration comes out of the drum through 'the hole'. A very common understanding of children was that sound travelled through air, or at least through holes in solid objects and not through the solid itself.

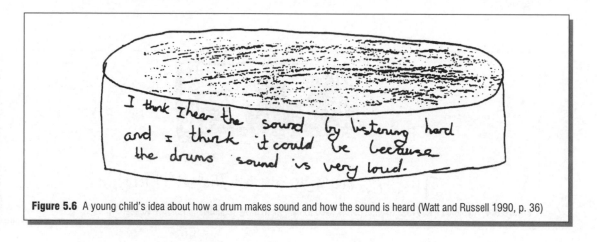

Figure 5.6 A young child's idea about how a drum makes sound and how the sound is heard (Watt and Russell 1990, p. 36)

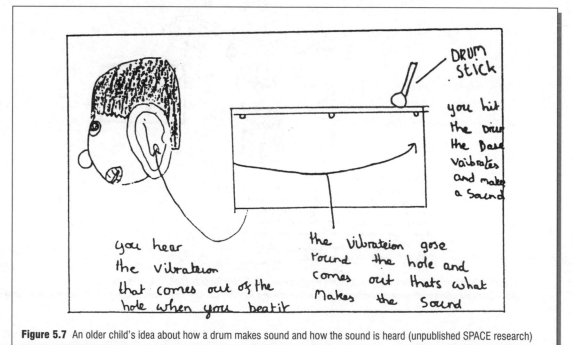

Figure 5.7 An older child's idea about how a drum makes sound and how the sound is heard (unpublished SPACE research)

The notion of 'vibration' was associated with sound in ambiguous ways, sometimes sound being the same as vibration and sometimes having some cause and effect relationship to it. Figure 5.8 illustrates this struggle to connect the two.

Ideas about forces

Children's ideas about how things are made to move and what makes them stop were explored in various contexts including the 'cotton reel tank' which is propelled by the energy put into twisting a rubber band. Again the younger children found no need to explain more than 'it works because you're turning it round' and 'it stops because it wants to.' Another 6-year-old could see that the pencil (used to twist the rubber band) was important but the idea of why went no further than its presence:

> When we wind it up it goes because of the pencil. When the pencil goes to the tip it stops.

Energy was mentioned in the ideas of older children (Figure 5.9) but the meaning the word was given is not entirely consistent.

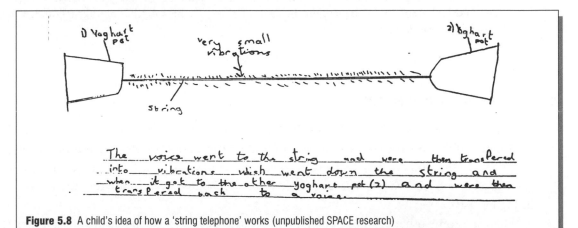

Figure 5.8 A child's idea of how a 'string telephone' works (unpublished SPACE research)

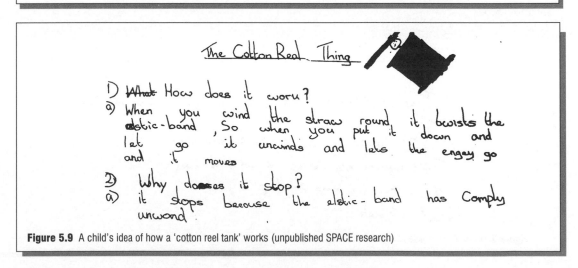

Figure 5.9 A child's idea of how a 'cotton reel tank' works (unpublished SPACE research)

Ideas about solids, liquids and gases

The idea that air is all around, including inside 'empty' containers, was expressed in some way by most junior age children but by a much smaller proportion of 5–7-year-olds. This statement by an 8-year-old shows a child who has not yet acquired an idea of air as a substance although its presence is accepted:

> You can't see the air, but sometimes you think there is nothing in there 'cos you can't see anything, but it isn't a matter of seeing, it's a matter of knowing.

Even young children have relatively little difficulty in identifying something hard, such as steel, as solid, and something watery as a liquid. A 5-year-old, after activities with liquids, managed to give a general definition:

> Liquids are all kinds of things that don't stay where you put them. They just run. If you put them on the table it runs along the table.

But where does talcum powder fit? One explanation was:

> It's something like a kind of liquid, but it isn't a liquid, its talcum powder. It goes fast like vinegar and it's not a solid because you can put your finger through it. It's a bit solid, but not like a liquid. A liquid feels wet and this doesn't.

> (quoted in Russell *et al.* 1991)

Ideas about change in materials

In relation to changes in materials, too, there is a stage in which there seems to be no need for explanation. Children use their experience of finding rust under bubbles of paint on metal gates or bicycle frames to conclude that rust is already there under the surface of metal, hence there is no need to explain what causes it to form. For example, an 8-year-old wrote the explanation in Figure 5.10.

There are some other examples of children's ideas about materials in Chapter 15, Figures 15.2 and 15.3.

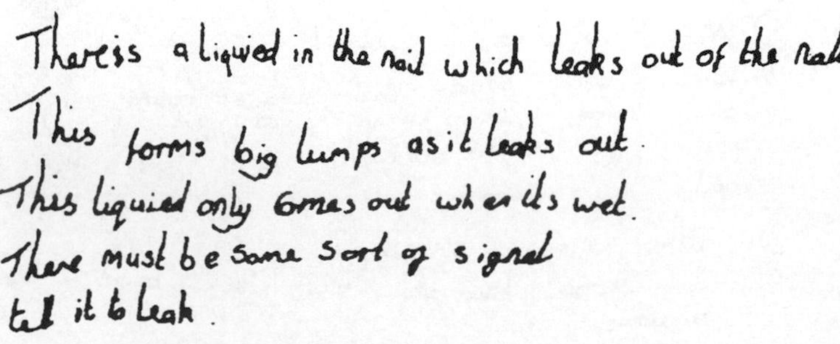

Figure 5.10 An 8-year-old's idea about rust (ASE, 1998)

Characteristics of children's ideas

It is not difficult to see that there is some reasoning, albeit limited, behind these ideas and that they may well make sense to the children themselves. It is precisely because of this that we must take these ideas seriously. If we just ignore them, the children may well hold onto them, since non-scientific explanations often seem more rational to children than scientific ones. (For instance, it makes more sense to conclude that puddles dry up because water seeps away through the ground, than that water particles fly off the surface into the air.)

Looking through these examples, it is evident that the ideas have certain characteristics. In many cases it is easy to see why children might come to hold these ideas. After all, they reflect what the children have experienced and clearly indicate effort to make sense of their experience. Would anyone know what is inside an incubating egg unless they had seen it? But clearly this does not stop children thinking about it and forming their own ideas.

Children's drawings are particularly useful in conveying their ideas since they try to represent what they know, or think they know. For example, young children's drawings of vehicles with wheels often show all the wheels on one side although these are not in fact all visible, or animals with four legs equally spaced along the body (Figure 5.11). They know cars have four wheels and dogs four legs and represent this idea rather than what a car or dog looks like.

Even with the article in front of them, young children will draw something that is more like a symbol than a representation of the object. For instance trees are frequently drawn as in Figure 5.12.

When some children were asked to draw some leaves they included a stem that was not actually there (Harlen 2001). Similar findings were reported by Tunnicliffe and Litson (2002) in a study of children's drawing of apples. They found that children added a stalk and leaves that were not present on the apple they were asked to draw, but were typical of drawings of apples found in books. It seems that children have developed a mental model of common objects such as a tree or a car which over-rides observation of the real things. There are implications here for both art and science, where children are often asked to draw what they have seen.

Figure 5.11 A 6-year-old's drawing of herself with her dog

Figure 5.12 A 5-year-old's tree

There are several general features of the children's ideas which it is helpful to bring together since they begin to point to how they can be developed into more scientific ones. This is attempted in Box 5.1.

We shall return to these characteristics in Chapter 9, for they give important clues as to how to help children develop more scientific ideas. When we do so we need to start from their ideas and help them, through scientific reasoning and use of inquiry skills, to change them or replace them with ideas which fit the evidence better than their own.

Box 5.1 Some general characteristics of children's own ideas

- Generally children's ideas *are* based on experience but this is necessarily limited and therefore the evidence is partial. So children may well consider rust to be within metals if they have only noticed it when it appears under paint or flaking chromium plating.

- They may hold on to earlier ideas even though contrary evidence is available because they have no access to an alternative view that makes sense to them. In such cases they may adjust their idea to fit new evidence rather than give it up, as in the idea that 'light turns the eye on'.

- Children pay attention to what they perceive through their senses rather than the logic which may suggest a different interpretation. So if the sun appears to move around and follow them, then they think it *does* move in this way.

- Younger children particularly focus on one feature as cause for a particular effect rather than the possibility of several factors. For example, children of 6 or 7 might mention water or light or soil as needed by plants to grow, but not all of these.

- Although it may satisfy them, the reasoning children use may not stand comparison with scientific reasoning. For example, if they were to make genuine predictions based on their ideas, these ideas would be disproved. But instead they may 'predict' what they know to fit their idea.

- They often hold different ideas about the same phenomenon when it is encountered in different contexts. For example, while they may realise that exposure to air helps washing to dry outside, they often consider that puddles on the road dry up only because the water leaks through the ground.

- Children may use words without a grasp of their meaning. We have seen that this can happen with 'floating', 'vibration' and 'evaporation' but many more examples could be cited.

- Their representations of common objects often reflect a mental image influenced by illustrations in books, rather than details of real object that are there to observe.

Summary

This chapter has been concerned with the reasons for taking children's ideas into account in science education. The main points have been:

- the reasons are related to the nature of the ideas, indicating that they have arisen from experience and thinking, both necessarily being limited, and the role they play in children's learning (taken further in Chapter 6);

- the examples of children's ideas show that they are the product of reasoning, and so make sense to the children. It follows that these ideas have to be taken seriously and addressed in helping children to come to hold more scientific ideas;

- the characteristics of children's ideas help in indicating how more scientific ideas can be developed (taken further in Chapter 9).

Further reading

Harlen, W. (2000) *Primary Science: Taking the Plunge* Second Edition, Portsmouth, NH: Heinemann.

Harlen, W. (2007a) The SPACE legacy, *Primary Science Review* 97: 13–15.

6

Developing understanding in science

Introduction

This chapter considers how children's ideas are modified by scientific inquiry and what factors and conditions are important in developing children's understanding in science. In the first part examples are used to suggest a framework, or model, of how different parts of classroom activities come together to help children develop their understanding through inquiry. In the context of cross-curricular topics it is particularly important that the potential for developing scientific understanding is recognised and exploited. The framework is based on the observation that learners bring ideas from earlier experience to try to make sense of new experience or answer new questions. It identifies the role of inquiry skills in developing 'bigger' ideas. This is one of the three dimensions of progression in ideas that are suggested, the others being development from description to explanation, and from personal to shared ideas.

Analysing inquiry-based learning in the case-study classrooms

Kathy's lesson

Kathy's lesson (pp. 7–10) starts with a question, stimulated by a story, and made real by a collection of different balls. Which ball is best for a dog? is the initial question, which through discussion is turned into an investigable question (discussed later, p. 85, and in Chapter 10): 'Which is the bounciest ball?' The children make lots of predictions and claims based on their previous experience of balls ('The red one. It looks like it's bouncy. The rubber might make it bouncy.'). Their predictions are then challenged by the teacher's question: 'How do you know?' The teacher asks for the children's ideas on how to collect data that can provide evidence of 'bounciness'. Through discussion of many different suggestions they agree the procedure, which is in two parts.

In the first part they carry out an investigation in four groups and as a result find four balls which they judge to be the bounciest. The second part, not described in the case study, comprised a further round of planning and data gathering. Then the final result was compared with their predictions. The record of the whole inquiry enabled the children to look back and reflect on what they had done and learnt, not just about balls but how to answer a question through scientific investigation.

So we can identify several stages in the inquiry: the initial question; discussion that refines the question; the exploration and observation of the materials that leads to predictions; planning how to test the predictions (to see which is the best bouncer); collecting data (two parts); interpreting the result (deciding the bounciest); recording and reflecting.

In the context of the subject of this chapter it is also important to ask: 'What science ideas did this activity help to develop?' These young children brought to the activity ideas about particular balls in their experience. They certainly extended their knowledge of different balls, but they also learnt more about the materials of which balls are made. Through the activity there was therefore opportunity to develop understanding of the range of material used in everyday objects.

Graham's lesson

Looking back at the description of Graham's lessons on soil (pp. 26–28) we can identify stages similar to those in Kathy's lesson. The stages in the children's activities and thinking are set out in Figure 6.1.

The children were given a new experience in the form of the soils to observe and a question about how the differences between the soils might affect how well plants would grow in them. In exploring and making a prediction about which soil would be best, they used their existing ideas (dark, damp soils). Further discussion and prompting by the teacher led to the identification of four properties that might be relevant. Thus four investigable questions were identified: 'Which soil holds most water?', ' Which lets water through most easily?', ' Which has most air?' and 'Which contains most humus?' Different groups investigated these questions, so there were four parallel plans and investigations carried out to test their predictions about which was best.

The evidence collected by each group was interpreted to answer that group's particular question and then the data from various groups were combined and interpreted. What they predicted initially was not supported by the evidence, so the ideas on which the prediction was based were not confirmed. As a result the ideas were modified – dark soil is not necessarily the most fertile. They had learnt not only that their initial ideas were limited, but they had reasons for changing them and reached a better understanding of the properties of soil.

In their subsequent work with the soils, they would go through the cycle of thinking again – this time with a more informed idea as a basis for predictions.

Science in the 'crime' investigation

It is particularly important to be able to identify the science learning in considering cross-curricular topics such as the Year 6 science week (pp. 28–30). By definition not all activities in a cross-curricular theme are focused on learning in science, but it is important to ensure that opportunities for developing understanding in science are not missed. In this example, the overall question of who committed the crime was broken down into a number of questions for investigation. It is in answering the investigable questions that the opportunities for learning in science are to be found.

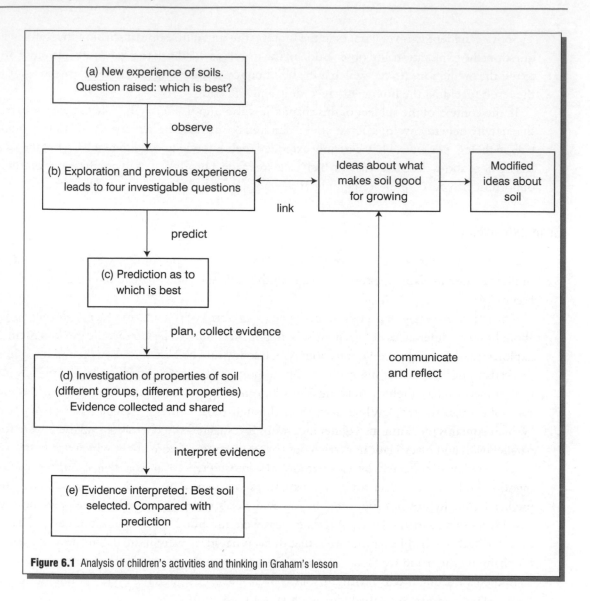

Figure 6.1 Analysis of children's activities and thinking in Graham's lesson

The science week was full of activities with the potential for developing science concepts. However, it would have been easy for the search for the 'culprit' to have overshadowed the science learning. For instance, there were predictions as to who might have committed the crime but the predictions that led to developing scientific ideas were different ones, related to the various investigations. In the chromatography the prediction was that it would be possible to match colours in the ink on the shopping list with the ink in the pens of the suspects. Testing this and finding it possibly strengthened their understanding of the properties of these materials. Similarly their predictions about fingerprint patterns were tested and the results increased their ideas about human characteristics as well as helping them to solve the crime.

A general framework for inquiry-based learning in science

We could identify in all the activities of the science week the sequence of thinking and actions set out in Figure 6.1 for Graham's class. Similar patterns can be seen in other classrooms where inquiry-based science is in action. This suggests a general framework, as in Figure 6.2.

Starting with an experience to be explained, or a question that has been raised, the first two stages, (a) and (b) relate to making a link with something similar encountered in previous experience. The link may be made because of some physical property or something else that calls it to mind, such as a word or situation. Pooling different ideas in a group discussion is particularly useful here; it means that the experience used is greater than that of any one individual. Creativity and imagination also have a part. Indeed, in the case of the scientist faced with an unexpected phenomenon, it is the ability to try ideas outside the immediately obvious that may be the start

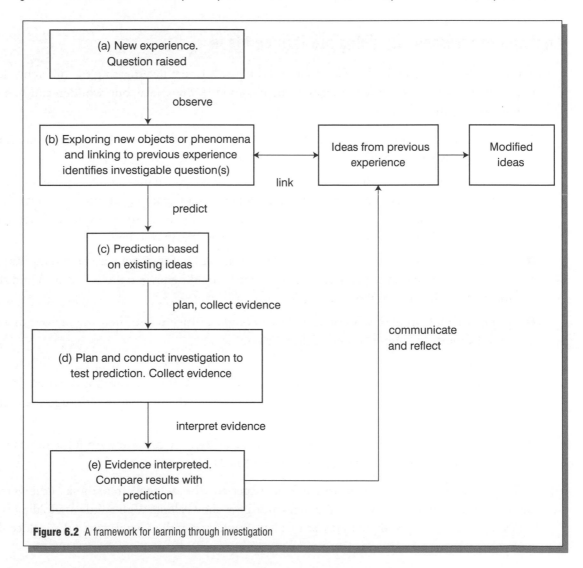

Figure 6.2 A framework for learning through investigation

of a 'breakthrough'. If the initial question needs to be refined, it is at this stage that it is turned into one or more investigable questions.

The stages (c) and (d) are concerned with testing the idea by making a prediction and gathering evidence to see if the idea 'works' in terms of predicting something that actually happens. When the evidence is interpreted (e), if it does not support the prediction it is probably necessary to think of another link that might provide a better idea, looping back to (b). If what is predicted *is* actually found, however, then we might cautiously accept that the idea helps to explain the new experience or to confirm the predicted answer to the question. The idea is modified by becoming one of wider application than before; just a little 'bigger'. Thus 'small' ideas, so described because they relate to particular individual situations, gradually become bigger because they relate to several situations and eventually become generalised to a set of conceptually related properties or phenomena.

Applying the framework: using alternative ideas

These stages can be seen in the case of some children who were investigating the difference felt in placing their hands on three surfaces in the classroom – one metal, one wooden and one of polystyrene foam:

- The metal felt considerably colder than the other two surfaces, which raised the question: why? This was stage (a).

- They immediately said that the metal was indeed at a lower temperature, because that was usually the case when something felt cold, as when touching an object just taken out of the fridge or touching things out of doors on a cold day (b). The investigable question was then identified as 'Does the metal feel colder because its temperature is lower?'

- Their teacher asked them what they would expect to find if they measured the temperature of the surfaces and they predicted that the metal would be lowest, the wood next and the foam about the same as their hands (c).

- Using a temperature sensor connected to a computer, they tested their prediction (d) and found almost no difference among the three surfaces.

- They were so surprised by this (e) that they wanted to repeat it and to try it in different places. In particular they wanted to take the surfaces out of the classroom to where it was colder. The result was the same, no difference in measured temperature, although the metal still felt much cooler than the other surfaces.

- It was clear that their idea that the metal was at a different temperature from the others was not explaining what they found. An alternative had to be found.

The teacher helped them to link to a different experience by asking them to think of things that had made their hands cold. Among the suggestions was snowballing. With a little scaffolding (see p. 118) the teacher helped them to realise that heat was lost from their hands when they felt cold:

- Could this account for the hand on the metal getting cold (back to (b))?
- If so, then the hand would really be colder after touching the metal than after touching the other surfaces (c).
- A fair test of this was devised by the children to test this (d).
- This idea seemed to be confirmed (e).

To see whether they could apply this idea, the teacher challenged them to predict what would happen if the surfaces were all warmer than their hands rather than colder. For safety's sake their predictions were not tested, but various experiences were collected that helped to provide supporting evidence – the handles of cooking pans being wooden or plastic rather than metal, the kinds of gloves that keep our hands warm, and so on.

What if there are no alternative ideas?
Children may ignore contradictory evidence in interpreting findings and hold on to their initial ideas even though these do not fit the evidence. The example in Box 6.1 illustrates a common way in which children deal with the situation of lacking experience to give them alternative ideas. It is to modify the idea they do have in order to accommodate the conflicting evidence. It seems characteristic of human beings to try to explain things and if ideas that really fit are not available then less satisfactory ideas will be used. It is more comfortable to modify an idea than to abandon it, especially if it is your only way of making any sense of an observation.

In such circumstances teachers have to decide what alternative ideas are within the reach of the children and support them in trying out ideas that can explain the phenomenon. This is described as scaffolding and we shall investigate more what it means, with examples, in Chapter 9.

When is an idea scientific and when is it not?
The answer according to modern philosophers of science (e.g. Popper 1988) is 'when it can be disproved'. This is a simple but profound statement that, in straightforward language means that:

Box 6.1 Children holding on to ideas because there is no alternative accessible to them

Faced with the evidence that smooth varnished cubes of wood stick to each other when wet, several groups of 11-year-olds concluded that the blocks became magnetic when wet (Harlen 2006a: 20). The resemblance of a block sticking to the underside of another, without anything to hold them together, to a magnet picking up another magnet or a piece of iron was clearly very strong. An equally good alternative explanation was not available to them and so they held onto their view of magnetism, modifying it to accommodate the observation that the blocks only stuck together when wet by concluding that 'they're only magnetic when they're wet'. Had they had experience, say, of 'suction cups' being held to a surface when air is forced out from under the cup, they might have used a different linking idea – that air pressure can 'stick' things together.

Box 6.2 Science as falsifiable

Any physical theory is always provisional, in the sense that it is only a hypothesis: you can never prove it. No matter how many times the results of experiments agree with some theory, you can never be sure that the next time the result will not contradict the theory. On the other hand, you can disprove theory by finding even a single observation that disagreed with the predictions of the theory.

(Hawking 1988: 10)

- if there is no possibility of evidence being used to contradict an idea or theory, then it is not scientific;

- but if the theory or idea can be used to make a prediction that can be checked against evidence, which could either agree or disagree with it, then it is scientific.

Thus the test for whether an idea or theory is or is not scientific is not whether the evidence does or does not confirm it, but whether it is possible to find evidence to disprove it. Often, in science, technological development enables evidence to be found that disproves a theory, for which there had previously only been confirmatory evidence. This is how Newton's theories were overtaken by those of Einstein, but this did not mean that his ideas were unscientific. The very fact that they could be disproved by evidence meant that they *were* scientific. This is because even if the evidence agrees with the prediction, that does not prove the theory to be 'correct', for there is always the possibility of finding further evidence that might not agree with the prediction. This is explained by Stephen Hawking in Box 6.2.

Are children's ideas scientific?

This may seem a long way from the primary classroom, but it explains why we want children to express their ideas and question in terms that are testable. The ideas children create can be scientific if they are testable and falsifiable and the fact that they are often disproved by the evidence makes them no less scientific. *Learning* science and *doing* science proceed in the same way. Indeed we find many parallels between the development of ideas by the scientific community and the development of children's ideas. For example, both are influenced, and to some extent formed, by the reactions and alternative views of peers. The ideas of both are provisional at any time and may have to be changed to be consistent with new experience or evidence not previously available. Children also have non-scientific ideas, which they hold on to by ignoring contrary evidence or adjusting their ideas to accommodate it bit by bit (see the example in Box 6.1).

Young children may base their predictions on unscientific ideas, as in the cases in Box 6.3.

The role of inquiry skills in the development of ideas

Using the framework to reflect on learning enables us to identify the role that inquiry skills play in developing more scientific ideas.

Box 6.3 Children with untestable ideas

Luis had an idea about what made snow melt, which was that it was caused by the presence of air; he did not consider heat. He wanted to preserve some snow and said that it would not melt if it were put in a jar with a lid on to keep out air. His first attempt led to the snow melting when the jar was brought into a warm room. He said that there was still some air there and that if the jar were to be packed with snow it would not melt. But however much snow was put into the jar he still said that there was room for air. He had, therefore, turned his claim into one which was irrefutable since on his assertion it would never be possible to have only snow in his jar.

Emma was convinced that something that did not float would do so if the water was deeper. To try to test this, more water was added. But it was never enough and all the time she maintained her claim that it would float in very, very deep water. Again, the idea had become untestable.

Suppose that the tests that the children in Graham's class carried out were not 'fair', because the soils were not compared equally. Or suppose that the children testing the surfaces did not use the temperature probe correctly and came up with findings that supported their sensations. In such cases the results of their investigations would not lead to changes in ideas. We can see that development of the children's idea is dependent on the extent to which inquiry skills have really been used.

If the observing, predicting, testing, etc. is rigorous and systematic, in the way associated with scientific investigation, then ideas which do not fit the evidence will be rejected and those which do fit will be accepted and strengthened. But it may not be the case that the testing has this quality. The skills of young children – and those of some adults – may not have developed to the appropriate degree.

Thus the extent to which ideas become more scientific and 'bigger' (by fitting more phenomena) depends both on the way ideas from previous experience are linked to new experience and on how the testing of possible explanatory ideas is carried out, that is, on the use of the inquiry skills. So inquiry skills involved at all stages have a crucial part to play in the development of ideas. This is one important reason for giving attention to helping children to develop their inquiry skills and to become more conscious of using them with appropriate rigour. The other reason, of course, is that these skills are needed for making sense of new experiences in the future and for learning throughout life. We return to these points in Chapter 7.

Development of 'bigger' ideas

A major aim of science education is to help children develop 'big' ideas. These are ideas that help us to make sense of a number of related events or phenomena. They contrast with 'small' ideas that apply only to specific situations. We can see how the model describes the gradual enlargement of ideas.

Using an idea from previous experience immediately links two experiences and if the idea is found to explain both, it becomes 'bigger'. Often several other related events can be linked when a teacher asks children to apply their newly modified ideas to other situations. In the investigation of the temperature of different surfaces, for example, the teacher took the opportunity to see if the children could extend the idea of metals conducting heat to give a reason for metal pans often having wooden or plastic handles.

Progression in scientific ideas

What are the main differences between the ideas of younger children with less experience and those of older children with more experience? One dimension we have already identified is from 'small' to 'bigger' ideas. Others come from considering the different levels of explanation that we can have for a particular phenomenon. For instance consider the views which younger and older children might hold about adaptation of living things to their environment:

Younger	*Older*
There are different kinds of living things in different places and each kind likes a certain kind of place. Some animals would not be able to live where other ones live because they would be too hot or too cold.	In a particular place some things will be able to live and some things will not. The reason for this is that each living thing needs food, water, air, shelter and protection for its offspring, but different ones obtain these in different ways. What suits one will not suit others because of differences in their bodies and structures.

When we look at the difference in these ideas we find the three main types of change set out in Box 6.4.

These overall dimensions of progress are the kind of changes that it is helpful to have in mind and to encourage in children whatever the content of their activities. However, the extent to which children progress during the primary years does vary between different concepts. The more abstract the ideas, the more difficult they are to grasp. In some cases, for instance in the case of 'force', it is assumed that the children understand the words used, whereas in reality this is not the case. For example, in an investigation of children's understanding of forces, it was found that 'Few young children knew the word force and where they had identified pushes and pulls, could not name these as forces' (Simon *et al.* 1994). Clearly knowing what the word means is basic to being able to think about forces acting in various situations, particularly when they are in equilibrium and not causing any movement or distortion. This suggests that what it means to 'understanding something' changes with ideas progress.

Understanding is not, then, something that a learner either has or has not. Its meaning constantly changes. At certain points all of us may have had the experience of thinking that we understand something, then something comes along to challenge this and we have to develop a new understanding. So it is with children: they understand to the extent that the ideas they have fit their experience and help them to explain things around them. But when their experience is extended, as it will be through experiences in daily life as well as through planned experiences at school, understanding may require change in their ideas of how things work or what they are. So we should try to ensure that their ideas keep pace with the change in experience. We will look at ways of encouraging development of ideas in Chapter 9.

Box 6.4 Dimensions of progression in ideas about adaptation of living things

From description to explanation

The ideas of the younger children are closely related to gathering information, finding out what is there and what is happening, as opposed to explaining why. There is the beginning of explanation in terms of what the habitat provides for the living things in it. The ideas of the older children are clearly much more related to explanation.

From 'small' to 'big' ideas

Each experience leads to a small idea that helps to make sense of specific observations. 'Worms can live in soil because they can slither through small spaces and can eat things that are in the soil' is an idea that applies to worms only. It is transformed to a bigger idea when it is linked to other ideas, such as 'fish can live in water because they can breathe through their gills and find food there', to form an idea that can apply to all animals. Eventually this idea may be linked to ideas about the habitats of plants, to become an even bigger idea about living organisms in general.

This is an important dimension of progress since the formation of widely applicable ideas, or concepts, is essential if we are to make sense of new experience.

From personal to shared ideas

It is characteristic of young children to look at things from one point of view, their own, and this is reflected in their ideas. These are based on their personal experience and their interpretation of it. As children become older and willing to share how they see and how they explain things, their ideas are influenced by those of others, including their teacher and other adults and other children. Thus ideas are constructed on the basis of social and educational interactions as well as their own thinking.

Through becoming aware of others' ideas and sharing their own, children negotiate meaning for their experiences and for the words that are used to communicate them (such as 'habitat'). In this way children derive assurance that their understanding is shared by others. It is central to learning in science that children have access to the views of others and to the scientific view, but at the same time retain ownership of their own developing understanding.

Summary

This chapter has provided an overview of learning in science, as a process in which ideas are developed through the use of inquiry skills.

Through reflection on some of the cases presented in Chapters 1 and 2, a framework for describing inquiry-based learning has been developed. This framework has been used to:

- identify the role in learning science of different parts of classroom activities;

- recognise the central role that their inquiry skills have in developing children's scientific ideas;

- argue that if inquiry skills are not developed to the point of being scientific, then ideas will not be properly tested and may be retained when there is no real evidence to support them.

Progression in scientific ideas can be described in terms of change from description to explanation, from 'small' to 'bigger' ideas that explain more phenomena, and from personal to shared ideas. Understanding has been discussed as something that changes and hopefully keeps pace with children's expanding experience.

Further reading

Kibble, B. (2006) Teaching for progression in conceptual understanding, in W. Harlen (ed.), *ASE Guide to Primary Science Education*, Hatfield: Association for Science Education.

7

Skills used in developing understanding

Introduction

As indicated in Chapter 3, skills feature prominently in revised curricula in the UK. The familiar list of inquiry, or enquiry, skills has been joined by other skills, expressed variously as thinking skills, interpersonal skills and learning skills as well as communication and use of ICT, all of which are relevant and developed across the curriculum and thus in science. In this chapter we discuss the meaning of these skills, their rationale and what is known or claimed about progress in their development in the primary years.

We begin with the skills particularly relevant to learning in science: inquiry skills. We saw in Chapter 6 how the use of these skills influences the development of scientific concepts by determining whether new experiences are used effectively in forming 'big' ideas.

Inquiry skills

The varied nature of inquiry

The skills required for scientific inquiry are implied in the various definitions of the processes of inquiry. A typical definition is quoted in Box 7.1. From this we can see that there are many different forms that inquiry can take. For instance, some examples of different types are identified in the new National Curriculum for Wales as: pattern-seeking, exploring, classifying and identifying, making things, fair testing, using and applying models.

Box 7.1 A definition of inquiry

Inquiry is a multifaceted activity that involves: making observations; posing questions; examining books and other sources of information to see what is already known; planning investigations; reviewing what is already known in light of experimental evidence; using tools to gather, analyze, and interpret data; proposing answers, explanations, and predictions; and communicating the results. Inquiry requires identification of assumptions, use of critical and logical thinking, and consideration of alternative explanations. (NRC 1996: 23)

Before we go further we should be clear about two important points: that not all learning in science involves inquiry and not all inquiry is scientific inquiry. It is not expected that all science learning will involve inquiry. There are some things, such as conventions, names and the basic skills of using equipment, that are more efficiently learnt by direct instruction, as and when they are needed. But if we are talking about the development of understanding and ideas that depend on gathering and interpreting data, then inquiry is the appropriate activity and ought to be used.

Inquiry has relevance to learning in other subject domains as well as science. What is it, then, that makes inquiry scientific and different from inquiry in mathematics, geography or history education? One answer must surely lie in the type of evidence that is sought and how it is used. Scientific inquiry is the deployment of inquiry skills in striving to make sense of events and phenomena in the natural and made world around us. We have suggested in the framework set out in Chapter 6 that this endeavour is stimulated by questioning, and the investigation of possible answers based on initial ideas. This may involve experiment or careful observations or consulting secondary sources or discussion about the problem or event.

But even when the subject matter of the activity is a phenomenon or event in the natural or made world, the inquiry may not justify the label of 'scientific inquiry'. This may well be the case when, despite being active, the children are not developing ideas from evidence, but are being told the answers to what happens and why. In other words there may be lots of action, with observation and recording, even predicting, but not much of the other skills that mean that their minds are engaged and they are developing their own understanding. This brings us, then, to consider what children will be doing when engaged in genuine science inquiry.

The range of science inquiry skills

There is no definitive list of inquiry skills. Each science curriculum spells them out in different words and detail. A useful list of what children may be doing when undertaking inquiry, proposed by an international group including scientists and science educators, is given in Box 7.2.

It is not expected, and indeed rarely feasible, for children to be undertaking all these activities in any one inquiry. There are different types of inquiry which require greater emphasis on some skills more than others. However there are four main groups of skills which ought to be represented in any activity that is described as 'science inquiry':

- gathering information by observing and using secondary sources;
- questioning, predicting and planning;
- interpreting information and drawing conclusions;
- communicating and reflecting.

In Chapter 10 we discuss the nature of progression and how to help development in these groups of skills.

Box 7.2 Inquiry in action as identified in an international project on IBSE (inquiry-based science education)

Students will be:

- gathering evidence by observing real events or using other sources;

- pursuing questions which they have identified as their own even if introduced by the teacher;

- raising further questions which can lead to investigations;

- making predictions based on what they think or find out;

- talking to each other or to the teacher about what they are observing or investigating;

- expressing themselves using appropriate scientific terms and representations with understanding both in writing and talk;

- suggesting ways of testing their own or others' ideas to see if there is evidence to support these ideas;

- taking part in planning investigations with appropriate controls to answer specific questions;

- using measuring instruments and other equipment appropriately and with confidence;

- attempting to solve problems for themselves;

- using a variety of sources of information for facts that they need for their investigation;

- assessing the validity and usefulness of different ideas in relation to evidence;

- considering ideas other than their own;

- reflecting self-critically about the processes and outcomes of their inquiry.

(IAP 2006: 26)

Thinking skills

Thinking in science

Thinking skills are widely taken to be those concerned with identifying patterns, finding order and relationships that help in making sense of things around. The idea that thinking skills can be enhanced by special teaching was tested and confirmed by the Cognitive Acceleration in Science (CASE) project developed over many years by Adey and Shayer (1994). Their work was initially with secondary school pupils but programmes for children aged 5–7, 7–8 and 8–9 years have now been produced.

The materials for the youngest children provide activities in which children work in groups with specially designed materials which involve them in sorting and sequencing, classifying in different ways and considering situations from different points of view. Group working is a key part of the programmes and teachers have a key role in stimulating children to help each other. Research during the trials of the materials showed that they 'work best when children work in groups with a range of abilities and differences. It is advised that teachers choose groups of mixed gender, ethnicity, language, ability and personality' (Robertson 2004: 6).

For older children various key features of dealing with a problem form the core of the experiences for each situation. As an example, Serret (2004) described how the topic of making sandwiches can be exploited to develop thinking. The children start by discussing their favourite sandwiches and the different ingredients that can go into a sandwich (different types of bread, fillings and dressings, such as mayonnaise). This ensures familiarity with the content. Then they are challenged to work out how many different sandwiches can be made with a given range of ingredients. The next stage is for the teacher to ask them how they came to their answer, what they discussed and how they tackled the task. This leads to questions about what they had to think about and what was important in solving the problem. Finally they are asked to link what they have learnt to other areas, such as how they could use the same methods to solve other problems and whether a sandwich could be part of a healthy diet.

Experiences of this kind encourage both teacher and pupils to change their ideas about what it is to be a good learner, that is, not someone who knows all the right answers and doesn't need help or give help to others but someone who works things out carefully together with others. They also challenge established notions about intelligence and the extent to which it can be changed and developed by practice. Tests of the children's cognitive development showed that those involved in the programme made greater gains than others not involved and that the gains extended to other aspects of thinking, in particular, conservation, which were not part of the programme.

Thinking across the curriculum

One of the ways in which greater attention to teaching methods is made evident is the emphasis on developing thinking. McGuinness (1999) reviewed approaches to developing thinking skills as well as reviewing the evidence of their effectiveness. She makes a distinction between three kinds of approach: those which target general thinking skills (and are usually timetabled separately); those that are related to a specific subject (for example the CASE projects); and a cross–curricular approach in which thinking skills are 'infused' across all lessons (McGuinness 1999: 2).

The Activating Children's Thinking Skills (ACTS) (McGuinness 2000) is an example of the third, infusion, approach. The ACTS project, originating in Northern Ireland from where it has spread throughout the UK and beyond, was developed in collaboration with teachers of 8–12-year-olds but has been adapted for older pupils. Essentially it identifies a framework of clusters of thinking processes and strategies (see Box 7.3) which are used in analysing the curriculum to target contexts where there is potential for developing some of the kind of thinking in the framework. For instance, sequencing can occur in history (sequencing events

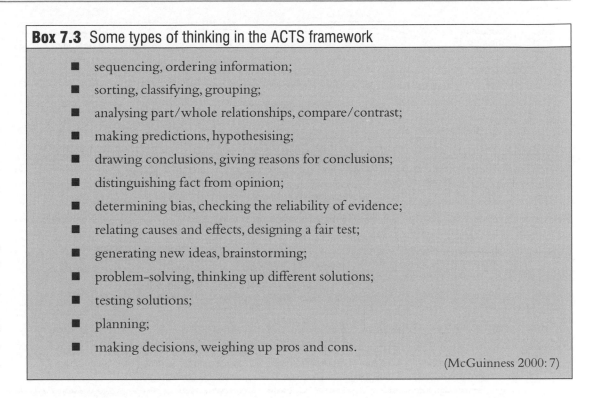

Box 7.3 Some types of thinking in the ACTS framework

- sequencing, ordering information;
- sorting, classifying, grouping;
- analysing part/whole relationships, compare/contrast;
- making predictions, hypothesising;
- drawing conclusions, giving reasons for conclusions;
- distinguishing fact from opinion;
- determining bias, checking the reliability of evidence;
- relating causes and effects, designing a fair test;
- generating new ideas, brainstorming;
- problem-solving, thinking up different solutions;
- testing solutions;
- planning;
- making decisions, weighing up pros and cons.

(McGuinness 2000: 7)

and changes in a period being studied, constructing a time line) as well as in science (sequencing the stages of development in the life cycle of a frog or butterfly).

Thinking skills in the UK curricula

The new curricula in Northern Ireland, Wales and Scotland have all been influenced by the attention given to development of thinking. In Scotland, skills are embedded in the 'I can do' statements of experiences and outcomes (see p. 44) and are not set out separately. By contrast, in Wales cross-curricular thinking skills are identified separately from the subject-based programmes of study and there are also subject-specific skills within the programmes of study (communication and inquiry skills in the case of science). The Welsh curriculum makes an interesting connection between the changes in teaching required to foster thinking skills, and the development of the use of assessment for learning. Figure 7.1 shows how the features of developing thinking and of using assessment for learning overlap and complement one another.

Skills of learning how to learn

Another closely related set of skills being widely advocated, although not required by mandatory curricula, are about learning how to learn. Since learning requires thinking, it is not surprising that some of the skills are the same as those just discussed, particularly when thinking skills are identified as broadly as in Box 7.3. There is also similarity in the close relationship of both

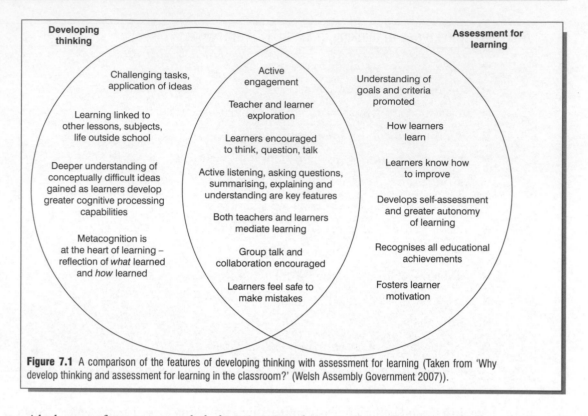

Figure 7.1 A comparison of the features of developing thinking with assessment for learning (Taken from 'Why develop thinking and assessment for learning in the classroom?' (Welsh Assembly Government 2007)).

with the use of assessment to help learning. But there are also differences, both in rationale and practice, which make it important to consider separately the skills of learning how to learn.

The meaning and importance of learning how to learn

First it might be necessary to explain why these skills are being called 'learning how to learn' skills and not just plain 'learning skills' or 'learning to learn'. The main reason is that the latter phrases suggest that there is something to be learnt in the same way as 'language skills' or 'learning to play a musical instrument'. Rather, what is to be learnt is the practice, or a set of practices, that leads to learning. These skills are not about learning particular subject matter but about the process of learning itself. The aim of developing learning how to learn skills is that someone with these skills will in theory be able to go about learning without help. That is, they become autonomous learners. Indeed autonomy is seen as a key aim in education, often used interchangeably with phrases such as 'independent learning', 'taking responsibility for one's own learning', 'self-determination' and 'self-regulation' (Boud 1988, quoted in James *et al.* 2007).

The importance of learning how to learn follows from the widely recognised expansion of knowledge and the accelerating change in daily life, largely resulting from scientific and technological advances. (Just consider the impact of the mobile phone and the i-pod and the complex electronics of the modern car.) Future citizens need to be able to adapt to the many changes that will be a constant feature of their lives. The consequences for education are described by the OECD in Box 7.4.

> **Box 7.4** Need for adaptation to constantly changing circumstances
>
> Students cannot learn in school everything they will need to know in adult life. What they must acquire are the prerequisites for successful learning in future life. … Students must become able to organise and regulate their own learning, to learn independently and in groups, and to overcome difficulties in the learning process. This requires them to be aware of their own thinking processes and learning strategies and methods.
>
> (OECD 1999: 9)

In the process of learning how to learn, pupils become able to use strategies for learning new things, not just at school but in other contexts, and develop the attitudes that motivate continued learning.

Learning how to learn in the primary school

All this talk of reflection, and learning autonomy might seem more relevant at later stages of school than in the primary years. But, like many goals which seem too complex for young children, there are essential foundations to be laid in the primary school. The first step in reflecting on learning is to become aware of what one is actually learning. We can help this process ensuring that children know what they are learning and why. Then by reflecting on what has been learnt, and how, children gradually become able to take more conscious control of their learning, and able to pursue learning independently.

Some strategies for doing this are similar to those of using assessment for learning; for instance the communication of goals to children, the type of feedback given by the teacher and the encouragement of self-assessment. These were the starting points for teachers involved in a project aimed at helping teachers develop their pupils' learning how to learn skills described by James *et al.* (2007). Their account of three case studies of primary teachers shows that the teachers found it necessary to adapt these strategies (of which we will say more in Chapter 17) when their focus was on helping children to become independent learners. For example one teacher found the notion of giving children explicit learning goals for a lesson was 'too simplistic'. She describes how she modifies it in her own words in Box 7.5.

> **Box 7.5** Helping primary children to think about their learning
>
> Sharing the 'big picture' with the children, involving them through the use of mind maps to clarify what they already know *but also* recognising that it can also be diverse and unexpected, helping children talk about the language of learning, and to recognise what kind of thinking is required for different activities – enabling children to pose questions so they can make sense of the world in which they live.
>
> (James *et al.* 2007: 118)

Scientific attitudes at the primary level

It is useful to make a distinction between two kinds of attitudes:

- attitudes towards science as an enterprise;
- attitudes towards the objects and events which are studied in science, and the use of evidence in making sense of them.

To develop an informed attitude towards science it is necessary to have an idea of what 'science' is. Without this, attitudes will be formed on the basis of the many myths about science and about scientists which persist in popular belief, and the caricatures which are perpetuated in the media and in some literature. Typically these portray scientists as male, bespectacled, absent minded and narrowly concerned with nothing but their work (see, for example, Jannikos 1995 and Johnston 2005). Science as a subject may be portrayed as the villain, the origin of devastating weapons and technology which causes environmental damage or as the wonder of the modern world in providing medical advances, expanding human horizons beyond the Earth and being responsible for the discoveries which led to computers and information technology.

At the primary level the concern is to give children experience of scientific activity as a basis for a thorough understanding, which will only come much later, of what science is and is not and of the responsibility we all share for applying it humanely. So the main concern here is with attitudes which we might call the attitudes *of* science, those which support scientific activity and learning.

Although development of scientific attitudes is not identified explicitly as an aim in national curricula, it is widely acknowledged as an important outcome of science education. Most make some reference in non-statutory statements to helping children to develop 'care, responsibility, concern and respect for all living things and the environment' (DCELLS 2008) and make reference to valuing others' opinions, being sensitive to others' feelings, and fostering curiosity. These fall into the category of attitudes *of* science and would also support learning in several subject areas. The generalised nature of attitudes is such that no clear line can be drawn between 'scientific' and other attitudes; and in Chapter 11 we consider what is needed to foster positive attitudes in general as well as the ones particularly relevant to developing ideas through exploration of the world around such as willingness to consider evidence and to change ideas.

Summary

In addition to the skills of inquiry directly related to the development of understanding in science, this chapter has discussed thinking skills, skills of learning how to learn and attitudes. We have noted that not all learning in science involves inquiry and not all inquiry leads to learning in science. Skills of thinking and learning how to learn are recognised as important goals of education if this is to prepare children for their further lives where change will be the norm. Being able to adapt to changing circumstances will be as important as developing subject knowledge. These skills also have much in common with abilities of self-assessment engendered by the use of assessment to help learning. However, they make particular contributions to learning which are worth noting:

- inquiry skills feature the use of evidence in developing understanding;

- thinking skills are particularly concerned with the development of links and finding patterns in objects and phenomena that assist concept development;

- learning how to learn skills focus on recognition of what has been learnt and the conscious consideration of how it has been learnt.

Related to all three are attitudes which support engagement in the activities that develop these skills and which also apply to learning across the curriculum as well as to learning in science.

Further reading

James, M. *et al.* (2007) *Improving Learning How to Learn*, London: Routledge, Chapter 6.

Useful websites

The Standards site provides a short history of thinking skills development and some case studies of how teachers have infused thinking into their lessons at http://www.standards.dfes.gov.uk/thinkingskills/guidance/567257

8

Talking to learn

Introduction

This chapter presents evidence and arguments for the value of children's talk in developing their understanding in science as well as in communicating ideas and information to others. It begins by considering talk that involves reflection, described as 'dialogic talk', where thinking is made explicit and different views can be combined in coming to a shared understanding of observations or findings. We consider the meaning in theory and in practice of 'dialogic teaching', in which the teacher encourages children to express their reflective thinking. The extent to which primary pupils can engage in argumentation is also considered.

In relation to more formal reporting we discuss the need for a classroom climate in which children listen and respond positively to each other and make an effort to communicate effectively. The organisation of group and class discussions is considered, and in the final section questions relating to the use of scientific words are addressed.

The importance of talk

Douglas Barnes was one of the first educators to focus on the importance of talk in the classroom and to distinguish between speech as communication and speech as reflection. Throughout this book there are many references to the value of children discussing with each other, exchanging ideas and developing their own views through trying to express them and to explain them to others. This involves both communication and reflection. The reflective part is sorting out their own ideas aloud, indeed 'thinking aloud'. The communication is sharing with others and involves listening as well as presenting in a way which is coherent and understandable by others. Barnes claims that both are needed and that it does not serve learning to focus only on the more formal communication since 'if a teacher is too concerned for neat, well-shaped utterances from pupils this may discourage the thinking aloud' (Barnes 1976: 28).

More recently Robin Alexander has taken further the discussion of oracy in the classroom, presenting it, as in Box 8.1, as essential to learning.

In his publication *Towards Dialogic Teaching* Alexander (2004) brings together evidence from international studies and from projects such as the ORACLE project (Galton *et al.* 1980), which involved intense observation of primary classroom interactions, to show 'the relative scarcity in English classrooms of talk which really challenges children to think for themselves' (Alexander

Box 8.1 Talk as the foundation of learning

Talk has always been one of the essential tools of teaching, and the best teachers use it with precision and flair. But talk is much more that an aid to effective teaching. Children, we now know, need to talk, and to experience a rich diet of spoken language, in order to think and to learn. Reading, writing and number may be the acknowledged curriculum 'basics', but talk is arguably the true foundation of learning.

(Alexander 2004: 5)

2004: 10). Research conducted after the introduction of the national curriculum and assessment (for instance, Galton *et al.* 1999b) shows that little had changed in 20 years. Yet the theoretical arguments and research evidence continue to build up a firm case for the importance of children thinking for themselves and for the key role of talk in enabling them to do so.

It is clear from this that we are concerned with a particular kind of talk; not the chatter of the playground, but talk in which children are engaged in thinking and initiating as well as responding. The context for this is the interaction with the teacher and with other pupils that Alexander describes as 'dialogic' teaching.

Dialogue or dialogic talk?

Dialogue is defined as a conversation between people but in the context of classroom interchange it has a rather more precise meaning. To signal this, the term 'dialogic talk' has been adopted to describe the kind of interchange where there is an aim of exploring in depth a situation, problem or possible answer. Box 8.2 gives an example of dialogic talk among two girls and their teacher.

The teacher does little here except to encourage the girls in their struggle to work out their answer and to explain their reasoning. Just the occasional 'Why do you think that?', the acknowledgement 'I see', and reinforcement 'A little raw', encourages their exploratory talk.

We can see from this interchange about the eggs how the girls use evidence to check their ideas. This comes through most clearly in Allyson's 'if we work on the principle that …' where she relates what she predicts on the basis of her judgement to the observation of how quickly the egg floats up in the salty water, but it also occurs throughout. It is worth noting in passing that the origin of her idea is previous knowledge about how to distinguish 'good' from 'bad' eggs.

Contrast the dialogic talk in Box 8.2 with that in Box 8.3, where June and David are working on the same problem. In the absence of the teacher at this particular time, they seem to regard the task as one where giving an answer is more important than having a reason for the answer. June, particularly, seems keen to move to early closure.

Even here, though, there are signs that they are close to becoming more involved. David's 'How do you know?' could have sparked June into explaining her ideas, had she been less defensive. Later on, when an egg which she declares 'sinks' begins to rise up again, there is potential for questioning, but it goes no further. How could this potential have been exploited? How, more generally, can we encourage interchanges which involve reflective thinking? Clearly the teacher's role is important, even though it seems very low key in Box 8.2.

Box 8.2 Dialogic talk with the teacher present

Deirdre and Allyson were investigating the way in which three whole hens' eggs, labelled A, B and C behaved in tap water and in salty water. They knew that one was hard-boiled, one soft-boiled and one raw. They had to find out which was which.

This is how the eggs landed up just after being placed in the salty water. The transcript begins with the teacher approaching them after they had been working alone for some time.

Deirdre	...hard-boiled.
Allyson	I know.
Teacher	(*coming up to them*) Can you tell me how you're getting on?
Deirdre	I think that C is raw.
Allyson	We both think that C is raw.
Teacher	Do you?
Deirdre	B is ...
Teacher	(*to Allyson*) Why do you think that?
Allyson	Because when you put eggs in water bad ones rise to the top.
Deirdre	(*at the same time*) Because it ... we put them all in ...
Teacher	Bad?
Allyson	Yes, I think so – or it is the good ones? ... well, I don't know.
Teacher	Yes?
Allyson	... they rose to the top, so ...
	(*Deirdre is putting the eggs into the salty water.*)
Deirdre	... that's the bottom (pointing to C).
Allyson	... if it's raw it should stay at the bottom.
Teacher	I see.
Deirdre	So that's what we think. C is raw and B is medium and A is hard-boiled.
	(*Allyson starts speaking before she finishes.*)
Allyson	... and I think that B is hard-boiled and she thinks that B is medium.
Teacher	Ah, I see. (*to Deirdre*) Can you explain, then, why you think that?
Deirdre	If we put ... er ... take C out (*takes C out, puts it on the table, then lifts A and B out*) and put these in, one after the other. Put A in – no, B first. That's what ... Allyson thinks is hard-boiled, I think it's medium. If you put that in ... (*she puts B into the salty water.*)
Allyson	... 'cos it comes up quicker.
Deirdre	It comes up quick. And if you put that in ...
	(*She puts A into the salty water. It goes to the bottom and rises very slowly.*)
Allyson	And that one comes up slower.
Deirdre	So, I think that one (*pointing to A*) is hard-boiled because it's ... well ...

Allyson	I don't. I think if we work on the principle of that one (*pointing to B*). Then that one comes up quicker because it's, you know, not really boiled. It's like a bit raw.
Teacher	A little bit raw.
Allyson	So, therefore, it'll come up quicker.
Deirdre	Yes, but it's not bad.
Teacher	What'll it be like inside?
Allyson	Runny.
Teacher	It'll be runny still, I see.

Having agreed that C is the raw egg, Deirdre and Allyson disagree about the identity of the other two eggs. Allyson has a reason for considering B is hard-boiled on the basis that 'bad ones rise to the top', so she considers that B behaves as if it had had something done to it. But she does not articulate the consequences of this until Deirdre attempts to give her reason. Then it is as if Deirdre's reason, which she interrupts, sparks off her own thinking.

Box 8.3 Group discussion without the teacher

David	Look at that one, this one, look, June.
June	That one's the one that's not boiled.
David	How do you know?
June	Oh, I'm not stupid.
David	Shall I put them in there, or in there? (*On the table or in the container where they were first.*)
June	Put them in there. (*David puts the one he took out in the container and June brings out the other two eggs.*)
June	There's B ... (*as she passes them to David who places them carefully*). Now put them in the salty water. (*David picks up A and puts it in the jar of salty water.*)
David	A floats. A.
June	B (*She puts B in. It sinks.*) Sinks.
David	C. (*He puts it in the salty water. It goes to the bottom and slowly begins to rise again.*)
June	Sinks.
David	Yea, look ... no, it doesn't.
June	No ... that one (*she points to C. Pauses, uncertain for a moment.*) No, how are we going to tell ...
David	That one's ...
June	Hard-boiled. The one at the bottom's hard-boiled. Put C hard-boiled. (*She instructs David to write. But it isn't C which is at the bottom.*)

101

The teacher's role: dialogic teaching

The importance of the teacher's role in setting the context for the exchanges that lead to learning is emphasised by Barnes:

> The quality of the discussion – and therefore the quality of the learning – is not determined solely by the ability of the pupils. The nature of the task, their familiarity with the subject matter, their confidence in themselves, their sense of what is expected of them, all these affect the quality of the discussion, and these are all open to influence by the teacher.
>
> (Barnes 1976: 71)

The role taken by Deirdre and Allyson's teacher gives several clues to positive encouragement of reflective thinking:

- joining in as part of the group, without dominating the discussion;
- listening to the children's answers and encouraging them to go on ('I see', 'Yes?');
- asking the children to explain their thinking;
- probing to clarify meaning ('what'll it be like inside?').

Not all aspects of the teacher's role can be illustrated in one short interchange and indeed much of it is in setting a context and a classroom climate which encourages exploratory thinking and talk. Important in this respect are:

- expecting children to explain things, which involves valuing their ideas even if these are unformed and highly conjectural;
- avoiding giving an impression that only the 'right' answer is acceptable and that children should be making a guess at it;
- judging the time to intervene and the time when it is better to leave a children-only discussion to proceed.

The presence of the teacher changes a discussion quite dramatically, for it is difficult for him or her not to be seen as an authority (see also Chapter 15). Left alone, children are thrown on to their own thinking and use of evidence. But, as we see with June and David, the absence of a teacher does not always lead to a productive interchange and it is not difficult to imagine how a question from a teacher could have supported the move towards inquiry which David seemed to be making. The teacher needs to monitor group discussions, listening in without intervening, before deciding whether 'thinking aloud' is going on usefully or whether it needs to be encouraged.

Whole-class dialogic teaching

Although it is easier to illustrate the teacher's role in establishing dialogic talk in the context of small group work, the features listed above apply equally to whole-class discussions. The key feature of such whole-class activity is to engage in 'joint inquiry' in which pupils bring their different ideas to the shared learning task (Barnes and Todd 1995). The collection of findings from the different groups by Graham in his class (p. 26) is an example of such a context. Although we don't have details of the oral exchanges, it seems that he asked questions for clarification and may have asked groups to explain how they came to their conclusions as well as giving the pupils the chance to query and challenge so that they understood what each group had done and found. Bringing the findings together was an opportunity for all to be involved in the thinking that led to the eventual decision about the different soils.

A whole-class discussion is the obvious context for this kind of discussion. It can also be the context for rather different exchanges, where teachers are more authoritative and controlling not just the interactions but the content of the talk as well. In such cases, instead of sharing in the creation of understanding, children become recipients of someone else's understanding. Alexander (2004) makes a point of clearly distinguishing between the whole-class context and the kind of interactions and thinking that takes place within it. It is important that good examples of whole-class dialogic teaching are not interpreted as reasons for wholesale use of whole-class teaching where most children are passive receivers.

Encouraging argumentation

We should not be put off by technical terms, nor use them unnecessarily, but it is often useful to use a special word to make an important distinction. Using 'dialogic talk' rather than 'discussion' is one example; 'argumentation' is another. It means arguing about evidence, particularly when that evidence can be interpreted in different ways. To call it plain 'argument' suggests that it is little different from the exchange of opinion that characterises everyday disputes (who should be first, for instance). To call it 'discussion' – although it is one type of discussion – leaves out its particular function in developing reasoning about whether evidence supports one or another conclusion or hypothesis.

Young children find it difficult to entertain different interpretations of evidence, but they make a start when helped to identify alternative reasons for observations. For example, the children who visited the beach (p. 12) identified different meanings for the red flag, and Chris's class (p. 14) mentioned different reasons for some ice cubes melting more quickly than others. Older primary children can begin to argue more thoughtfully about the interpretation of evidence as, for example, when Deirdre and Allyson contested their views on which eggs had been boiled.

Speech as communication

This is the more formal side of using talk, where shared conventions and expectations have to be observed if others are to be able to make sense of what is said. It is part of socialisation to be able to describe in a way comprehensible to others what has been done or thought about and to be able to listen to others, attending not only to the words but to the implicit messages conveyed by tone of voice and manner. Giving attention in this way is not an automatic response of children, as teachers know all too well; it is a behaviour that has to be taught. Box 8.4 sets out some ways of providing the classroom climate in which children have opportunity for reporting orally to

Box 8.4 Creating an atmosphere for productive oral reporting

- Providing guidelines for preparing presentations and a structure for ensuring that each report can be heard and given attention.

- Giving an example in the teacher's own response, of showing interest, asking questions for clarification, making positive comments, etc.

- Making use of children's ideas in comments, thus encouraging children to do the same ('That's an interesting idea you have about …' 'Tell us how you think it explains …').

- Encouraging children to respond to each other and not just to make statements of their own ideas.

- Listening attentively and expecting the children to do so.

- Setting up expectations that children will put effort into their presentations to each other and try to make them interesting, and giving time for and help in preparation with this in mind.

others in a setting where they know that others will be listening and where they have to convey their information clearly.

These things have to become part of the general way of working, since expectations that children will respond to what their classmates say are set by the pattern of previous lessons as well as by the response on a particular occasion. Then the telling and listening can have a role in the development of children's ideas as well as in their communication skills. It means that they go back over their activities and make sense of them for themselves so that they can make sense of them for others.

Organising class and group discussions

In setting up discussion the (perhaps obvious) point is to ensure the attention of all involved. For a whole-class discussion the location of the children is significant in avoiding distractions. Occasionally it may be necessary to hold a brief discussion during the course of practical activities, for the purpose of bringing together observations which have been made, reporting progress, or sharing information which will help everyone (including instructions about safety if unexpected hazards have arisen). On these occasions it may be advisable to move the children away from the materials they are working on in order to ensure their attention. The discussion will only last a few minutes and it will be no hardship for the children if they are cramped in a small space for this time. It is intended to help them with their work when they return to it; otherwise interruption should be avoided until the time for warning of the impending end of the time for group work.

Apart from these infrequent interruptions, whole-class discussion will be at the beginning and end of the group work, with group discussion in between.

Whole-class discussion at the start of the lesson

The initial discussion is the key to setting up group work which is sufficiently clear and motivating to ensure that children begin work promptly and with enthusiasm. Some motivating starting activities are discussed in Chapter 11. Whether the purpose is for children to continue work already begun or to start on fresh activity, the essential function of the initial discussion is to ensure that children know the purpose of their work (see Chapter 17) and what role is expected of them.

Group discussion during the lesson

Group discussions are important parts of practical work; children should be encouraged to talk freely among themselves. The teacher will visit each group for various purposes – to monitor progress, to encourage exchange of views, to offer suggestions, to assess. It may be only necessary to ensure that the talk is productive (as in Box 8.2) but other groups may need more input. Since it is almost impossible for teachers to 'hover' without their presence affecting the children, it is best to make clear what is intended. 'I'm not going to interrupt; just carry on' or 'Tell me what you've been doing up to now'. During a teacher-led group discussion, the teacher should show an example of how to listen and make sure that everyone has a chance to speak. The group might also be left with the expectation that they should continue to discuss, 'Try that idea, then, and see if you can put together some more suggestions.'

The noise, which discussion inevitably generates, is part of the working atmosphere. If the noise level becomes unacceptable it should be possible to spot the reason:

- too much excitement about certain activities?
- children waiting for equipment and not 'on task'?
- 'messing about'?

Once diagnosed, appropriate action can be taken – for example, diluting the excitement by staggering work on certain activities, organising equipment for easier access, checking the match between the demand of an activity and the children's readiness to respond.

Whole-class discussion at the end of the lesson

Holding a whole-class discussion at the end of a practical session, whether or not the work is completed, should be the normal practice. The reasons for this strong recommendation have been well articulated by Barnes in Box 8.5.

It is important to warn the children in good time for them to bring their activity to a stage where equipment can be put away and to allow five or ten minutes for reviewing and reporting ongoing work. At the end of the activities on a particular topic, a longer time for whole-class discussion should be organised and children given time beforehand to prepare to report, perhaps with a demonstration, to others.

Box 8.5 The value of discussing activities that have been completed

Learning of this kind (from experience of manipulating objects, visits or group discussions) may never progress beyond manual skills accompanied by slippery intuitions, unless the learners themselves have an opportunity to go back over such experiences and represent them to themselves. There seems every reason for group practical work in science, for example, normally to be followed by discussion of the implications of what has been done and observed, since without this what has been half understood may soon slip away.

(Barnes 1976: 30–1)

Introducing scientific words

The importance of introducing children to scientific vocabulary is made clear in both new and 'old' curriculum requirements and guidelines. For example, the National Curriculum (DfEE 1999) states that, at Key Stage 1, pupils should be taught to 'use simple scientific language to communicate ideas and to name and describe living things, materials, phenomena and processes.' At Key Stage 2, the requirement is to 'use appropriate scientific languages and terms, including SI units of measurement, to communicate ideas and explain the behaviour of living things, materials, phenomena and processes.'

Teachers have to decide the answers to the difficult questions of when and how new words should be introduced. Should they use the correct word from the moment children become involved in an activity in which they might use it and insist on them using the word? Or should they allow children to 'pick up' words as they go along? We know that children pick up and use scientific words quite readily; they often enjoy collecting them and trying them out as if they were new possessions. At first one of these words may have rather a 'loose fit' to the idea which it is intended to convey. Does it matter if children use scientific words without knowing their full meaning?

Before trying to answer some of these questions, it is useful to reflect on the notion of the 'full meaning' of scientific words.

Different levels of meaning

Most scientific words (such as evaporation, dissolving, power, reflection) label concepts which can be understood at varying levels of complexity. A scientist understands energy in a far broader and more abstract way than the 'person in the street'. Even an apparently simple idea of 'melting' is one which can be grasped in different degrees of complexity: a change which happens to certain substances when they are heated or an increase in energy of molecules to a point which overcomes the binding forces between them. This means that the word 'melting' may evoke quite a different set of ideas and events for one person than for another. Now, to use the word 'melting' in a restricted sense is not 'wrong' and we do not insist that it is only used when its full meaning is implied. Indeed the restricted meaning is an essential step to greater elaboration of the concept. We should, perhaps, accept children's 'loose' use of words as a starting point to development of a more refined and scientific understanding of the word.

For example, take the child's writing in Figure 5.8 (p. 73) where, in describing how the sound is transmitted in a yoghurt-pot string telephone, he explains how vibrations go down the string. The word 'vibration' is certainly used in a manner here which suggests that the child understands sound as vibration, until we notice that he writes that the voice is 'transferred into vibrations' at one end and 'transferred back to a voice' at the other. It seems that the sound we hear is not understood as vibration, but only its transmission along the string. It may be that ideas both of sound and of vibration have to be extended, so that vibration is something which can take place in air and occurs wherever sound occurs, which will take time and wider experience, but he has made a start. And he is not wrong in using 'vibration' in the way he has done.

When to introduce new words

Teachers seem to be caught between, on the one hand, giving new words too soon (and so encouraging a verbal facility which conceals misunderstanding) and, on the other, withholding a means of adding precision to thinking and communication (and perhaps letting children continue to make use of words which are less than helpful).

The value of introducing the correct word at a particular time will depend on whether:

- the child has had experience of the event or phenomenon which it covers;
- the word is needed at that time;
- the word is going to help the child to link related things to each other (since words often give clues to these links).

In other words, *if a word will fill a gap, a clear need to describe something which has been experienced and is real to the children, then the time is right to introduce it.* With young children, one of the conditions for the 'right time' is the physical presence or signs of the phenomenon which the word refers to. Only then can we hope to fit the word to an idea, even loosely.

How to introduce new words

The above argument suggests that until the moment for introducing the word is right, the teacher should use the language adopted by the children in discussing their experiences. Then, once the word is introduced the teacher should take care to use it correctly. For example if children have been exploring vibrations in a string, drum skin, a tissue paper against a comb, and wanting to talk about what is happening to all these things, it may well be useful to say 'what all these are doing is called "vibrating"'. Before this the children and teacher may have called it by descriptive names: trembling, jumping, moving, going up and down, etc. A useful way of ensuring that the new word and the children's words are connected to the same thing, suggested by Feasey (1999), is to use them together ('the thing that's trembling or vibrating') until the new becomes as familiar as the old.

Much more experience of a concept has to follow so that the word becomes attached to the characteristic or property rather than to the particular things present when it was first encountered. But there is no short cut through verbal definitions in abstract terms.

Words describing inquiry skills

It is not only 'concept' words that children need to learn to use correctly. Edmonds (2002) makes the point, in the context of teaching children for whom English is an alternative language, that: 'Children are unsure what is required of them when they are asked to predict, hypothesise or interpret' (p. 5). This applies to all children, however, as do the suggestions in Box 8.6, for alternatives to giving verbal definitions of processes.

Box 8.6 Suggestions for conveying the meaning of processes

Some of the most effective strategies appear to be:

- teacher modelling the procedures with a group or the whole-class; demonstrating the whole procedures of planning parts or the whole of an investigation;

- providing examples of the kind of procedures the teacher has asked for;

- identifying and sharing clear criteria for what the procedure would look like if completed successfully;

- looking through pieces of other children's work where they have carried out the procedure or skill and making a running commentary on what the child has done;

- detailed feedback and discussion on the child's work.

(Edmonds 2002: 5)

Summary

This chapter has considered various aspects of oral communication in the classroom. The main points have been:

- children's talk can take an important role in the development of their understanding when it takes the form of 'dialogic talk', which is characterised by 'thinking aloud' about a situation or problem;

- the teacher's role in this is one of taking part as an equal member of the group, encouraging explanations and helping to clarify meanings;

- primary children can be encouraged to consider alternative explanations and to use evidence to argue the pros and cons;

- more formal talk for reporting requires a classroom climate in which children listen and respond positively to each other and make an effort to communicate effectively;

- whole-class discussion is needed at the start of a lesson to motivate engagement and at the end to reflect on what has been learnt and discuss its implications;

- scientific words for processes as well as concepts are best introduced when the children have experienced the event or phenomenon that they represent.

Further reading

Asoko, H. and Scott, P. (2006) Talk in science classrooms, in W. Harlen (ed.) *ASE Guide to Primary Science Education,* Hatfield: ASE.

Dawes, L. (2004) Talk and reasoning in classroom science, *International Journal of Science Education* 26 (6): 677–95.

Teaching through inquiry

Helping development of scientific ideas

Introduction

This chapter is concerned with the action that teachers can take to help children's progress in developing scientific ideas. In Chapter 6 we described this progress as: moving from limited 'small' and sometimes unscientific ideas towards 'bigger' ideas that help understanding of the world around; moving from description to explanation; and moving from personal ideas to ones shared by others. By the time they come to the classroom children have already formed ideas about the things they have encountered and it is important to take these as the starting point. The characteristics of these ideas, identified in Chapter 5, suggest strategies teachers can use for helping children to develop more scientific, widely accepted ideas. Since the process of forming 'bigger' and more scientific ideas, as argued in Chapter 6, depends on the use of inquiry skills, the development of these skills is a key factor. This is discussed in Chapter 10. Other strategies for developing more scientific ways of thinking are considered here, with particular emphasis on introducing and scaffolding alternative ideas.

Starting from children's ideas

In Chapter 5 we looked at some examples from research into children's ideas. Although these ideas are different from the scientific ways of thinking about the phenomena involved, it is not difficult to see why children come to hold them. They result from children trying to make sense of events and phenomena using their own limited experience and thinking. We also referred to research that indicates that these ideas should not be ignored. Ideas that children have worked out for themselves make sense to them and will not be replaced by simply giving them the scientific view. A child has to realise that the scientific ideas are more useful than his or her own for helping understanding of what is going on.

Some characteristics of children's ideas were set out in Box 5.1 (p. 76). We now take up the matter of how to help children to use more scientific ideas in the way they understand the world around – 'more scientific' meaning ideas that fit a wider range of experiences. Each of the characteristics of children's ideas, briefly identified in the left-hand column of Box 9.1, indicates some action that could help children to change their thinking. In the right-hand column are some suggestions for action.

Box 9.1 Strategies matched to the characteristics of children's own ideas

	Characteristic	Strategies for development
1	Ideas are based on (inevitably) limited experience.	Give experience selected to show that things can behave contrary to the child's idea, e.g. that heavy things can float, seeds can germinate without soil.
2	Children may hold on to their ideas despite contrary evidence if they have no access to an alternative view that makes sense to them.	Scaffold the introduction of alternative ideas. Ask children to consider evidence in relation to other ideas than their own – from information sources or other children. Encourage application of new ideas.
3	Children base their ideas on how things appear to change rather than on the whole process.	Encourage attention to what happens during a change and not just at the start and end, e.g. to observe closely whether anything has been added or taken away when a quantity appears to change.
4	Younger children, particularly, focus on one feature as an explanation	Encourage observation of other factors that might also explain why something happens, e.g. that plants need light (and sometimes heat) as well as water.
5	Their reasoning may not be scientific.	Help them to develop the inquiry skills to find and use relevant evidence (see Chapter 10).
6	Their ideas are tied to particular instances and not connected to other contexts where they could apply.	Refer to other contexts in which the same idea is applicable. For example, is there something vibrating in a wind instrument that produces sound just as the vibration of a drum skin?
7	They may use words without a grasp of their meaning.	Find out what they mean by a word through asking for examples; give examples and non-examples of what words mean and introduce scientific words along with children's own expressions (see Chapter 8).
8	Their representations reflect a generalised idea of an object rather than observed details.	Help children to identify differences between, for instance, trees, flowers, boats, or other vehicles of different kinds.

Not surprisingly, given the interdependence of ideas and inquiry skills, some of the strategies involve development of inquiry skills, linking to Chapter 10. Some are actions that can be taken in the course of children's work without introducing new experiences (for instance, the discussion of the words the children are using). Others require more planning to provide new experiences as the subject for children's inquiry. We now consider the strategies in Box 9.1 that are not covered in other chapters.

Extending children's experience

Extending the range of types of material, living things, and events in children's experience is a central purpose of primary science activities. Sometimes this new experience is enough in itself to challenge existing ideas and prompts children to be more cautious in their generalisations. It can change generalisations to more guarded statements:

- almost all wood floats (not ebony or lignum vitae);
- most conifers are evergreen (but not all);
- sound travels through the air (and through solids and liquids as well).

These are not only matters of definition but also matters of explanation, when used, for example, to 'explain' that something floats because it is made of wood.

Often children's ideas indicate the experience that is lacking. For example, the quite common idea that rust forms inside metals and leaks out on to the surface (see Figure 5.10, p. 74) can be challenged by cutting through a rusty nail. More difficult to provide is more experience of things that cannot be directly seen by the children; the insides of living things and of themselves, for instance. This is where visits outside the classroom can play a really special part in children's learning.

Interactive museums or science centres often have curriculum-related exhibits that are designed to take into account children's ideas and find intriguing ways of challenging and advancing them. For example, in a science centre for 3–12-year-olds, the staff designed an exhibit about the human skeleton which takes into account research about young children's ideas of the bones in their body. This shows that children may view their body as a 'bag of bones' or as having strings of many small bones which could not provide support (see Figure 9.1). The interactive exhibit that was produced enabled a child to sit on and pedal a stationary bicycle which was next to a large sheet of glass that acted as a mirror. When the child begins to pedal and looks at the image of his or her legs in the glass, a skeleton is superimposed on this image, showing the moving bones in the legs. This experience was found to have a much greater impact on children's ideas about bones in the body than classroom lessons about the human skeleton (Guichard 1995).

Information from other sources can also be found from the websites that museums and various industries and organisations set up to help education, and from CD-ROMs. The children's ideas about what is inside the egg (p. 70) will no doubt be changed by access to photographs of the development of egg embryos and discussion of other evidence of the changes in form and in size

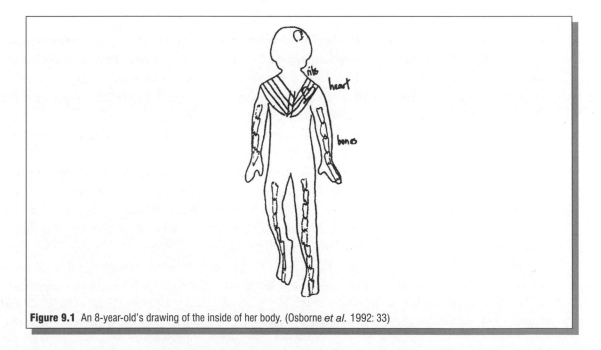

Figure 9.1 An 8-year-old's drawing of the inside of her body. (Osborne *et al.* 1992: 33)

that take place in the reproduction of all living things, to be found in books or CD-ROMs. More and more industries and commercial organisations have education sections which give children learning opportunities that cannot be provided in the classroom, as in case studies in Chapters 1 and 2. Ideas about the origins and processing of food can be developed by visits to a farm or dairy or a supermarket. (*Primary Science Review* 62 (2000) describes a number of such opportunities.)

Experiences of these kinds become the 'new experience' leading to the development of ideas, as represented in Figure 6.2 (p. 81). As children use their initial ideas in investigating them they find these ideas inconsistent with the evidence from the new experience. They need to be able to consider different ideas, leading us to the next strategy in Box 9.1.

Introducing new ideas

While we can often see how to challenge children's unscientific ideas, it is not always clear how they find more scientific ones to replace them. There is an important role for the teacher here; one which has, perhaps, been underplayed in discussing constructivist approaches to learning (which sometimes give the impression that children will arrive at new ideas through thinking about new experience for themselves). It is also a subtle role, since we must avoid giving the 'right' answer that children have to accept whether or not it makes sense to them. We have to ensure that the new ideas are taken into the children's own thinking. In order to do this, children need:

- access to ideas different from their own;
- support in trying out the new ideas in relation to their existing experience;
- opportunities to apply them to new experiences.

Access to different ideas

New ideas need not necessarily be introduced by the teacher. They can also come from books, the Internet, CD-ROMs, videos and from people who visit the classroom or places that are visited by the children. Other children are often a source of different ideas and these may include ideas that are closer to the scientific view than the ideas of a particular child. Whatever the source, children are likely to need encouragement and support while trying out new ideas.

Analogies may provide the new idea that children need in order to understand something. Analogies can provide a link between one situation (A, which a child wants to understand) and another (B, more familiar) which is thought to illustrate the idea or process in action in A. For instance it is common to illustrate the water cycle (A) using a boiling kettle and condensing the water vapour on a cold surface (B). The problem for the children is making the link between the pieces of equipment in A and B. As a consequence, the kettle often ends up in a child's representation of how rain is formed from clouds in the sky!

Often the models which adults think up to represent difficult concepts, such as water flow in pipes as an analogy of the flow of electricity in a circuit, can cause more problems in understanding the analogous situation in the first place. A small-scale research project (Jabin and Smith 1994) which involved trying different analogies for electric circuits, seemed to show that it was the effort made to create a link with something already familiar to the children which had an effect rather than the nature of any particular analogy. Asoko and de Bóo (2001), presenting a collection of analogies used in primary science, warn that analogies can introduce irrelevant or misleading features and may be as difficult to understand as the phenomenon they are supposed to explain.

Support in trying new ideas

This is where 'scaffolding' new ideas comes in (see Box 9.2).

Scaffolding is particularly important in relation to ideas which cannot be tested out in practice. It is difficult, for example, for children to understand that if a moving object stops, there must be a force acting to stop it. Many children accept or offer the reason as being 'friction' but don't go

---

Box 9.2 Scaffolding children's ideas and skills

Scaffolding means supporting children in considering an idea or a way of testing an idea that they have not proposed themselves but are capable of making 'their own'. The judgement of when this is likely to be possible has to be made by the teacher, taking into account the existing ideas or skills of the children and how far they are from taking the next step. It often means the teacher making links for the children between experiences and understanding they already have, but have not linked up for themselves.

In theoretical terms, it means finding what Vygotsky (1962) introduced as the 'zone of potential development'. This is the point just beyond existing ideas, where the learner is likely to be able to use new ideas with help. What the teacher does in scaffolding is to suggest the new idea and provide support for the children while they use it and, finding it helps to make sense, begin to incorporate it into their thinking. The teacher might ask children to 'Try this idea' or 'Try looking at it this way' or 'Suppose …' An example might be 'Suppose the water that disappears from the puddle goes into the air?' or 'Suppose the sun is not moving but the Earth is turning round …' Each of the 'supposed' ideas can be used to make a prediction that can be tested and as a result children can see that they do help to explain experience.

Scaffolding can be used to develop skills, too. It is indeed familiar in teaching new skills such as using a microscope or a calculator. In these cases the learner needs first to be told what to do, may need a reminder later and eventually uses the skill confidently.

It is important to underline that scaffolding ideas is not the same as telling children the 'right answer'. It is essentially enabling children to take a further step in progress that is within their reach. It depends on teachers having a good knowledge of their children's ideas and skills and using this in deciding the next steps and helping children to advance their thinking.

as far as realising that without friction the object would not stop moving. Scaffolding is necessary here, just as it is in relation to ideas about the Earth in space, the causes of day and night, the seasons, and phases of the moon. These are cases where the teacher may have to lead children to take a few steps without their realising why until they can look back. For example, children are unlikely to decide on their own to make a model of the sun, moon and Earth to explain why we see the moon in different phases. So the teacher takes the initiative and sets up the situation that enables the children to 'see' a spherical object looking like a half-moon and then they can make the connection.

Opportunities to try out new ideas in different situations

Given that the new idea is a scientific one, it should help children make sense of further experience. Helping children to do this will secure the new idea in their thinking as well as expanding their understanding of things around. It also gives the teacher the opportunity to see how secure the new idea really is. It may be necessary to stop and return to familiar ground if the signs are that the new idea is still a little wobbly. However, if new ideas can be successfully applied this brings a feeling of enjoyment and satisfaction in learning. For example:

- Can eclipses be explained in terms of the movement of the moon around the Earth and the Earth around the sun?

- Can the ideas about reducing friction be used to explain why ice skates have knife-edged blades?

Developing reasoning about changes in appearance

Some of the well-known, and often replicated, results of Piaget's investigations with children showed that young children may judge by appearance rather than reasoning about when a quantity of a material has changed. A child might claim that, for example, there is more in a lump of plasticine after it has been squashed out than when it is in a ball. Learning that things are not always what they seem to be is important in science. Reasoning often has to overcome appearance, as for instance when salt or sugar dissolves in water and appears to have vanished. The action that the teacher can take is to draw attention to the whole process of change, to reverse it where possible (as with the plasticine) and provide some evidence that will overcome the visual sensation of change.

Encouraging attention to more than one factor

Another feature of young children's thinking, related to the one just discussed, is that it is uni-dimensional. One view of things, or one factor, is considered when there are others that need to be considered to explain particular phenomena. This shows, for instance, in children saying that plants need water or light to grow, but not both, and rarely adding air or heat. There are very many ideas in science that involve a combination of factors (such as the meaning of something being 'alive') so it is important to encourage children to think in terms of all possible factors and not just the first that comes to mind. Having children brainstorm in groups about, for example, what we need to maintain good health, will not only gather more ideas but help them to realise that a combination of factors is involved.

Creating links between events with a common explanation

Children develop ideas about events in terms of the particular features of those events. These are 'small' ideas and probably don't apply to other situations that actually share common explanation. For example, children commonly explain the disappearance of water from puddles only in terms of draining away through the ground, while they may explain the drying of damp clothes on a washing line in terms of some action of the air. The children could be helped to link these two: could the air have something to do with the puddle drying up, too? Some investigations, testing this idea in relation to puddles could make this a useful idea in both situations. Further examples of water disappearing could then be drawn into the range of things explained in this way. The idea has then become one that applies more widely, that is, has become a bigger one.

In other cases the small ideas are ones that refer to different aspects of a phenomenon, and need to be brought together. For instance understanding why things don't fall off the side of the Earth means bringing together these ideas that:

- things fall downwards;
- the Earth is spherical;
- 'down' means towards the centre of the Earth.

Another example is putting together ideas about light and how we see to understand the formation of images in mirrors or lenses. This depends on understanding that:

- we see an object when light enters our eyes from it;
- putting a mirror or lens between the object and our eyes changes the path of the light;
- we interpret the path of the light as a straight line from the object to the eye.

If all these ideas are understood it may be possible to bring them together to realise that the eye does not 'see' the change in direction that the mirror or lens has caused and so interprets it as if it came in a straight line, so the object is interpreted as in a different place than it really is.

Discussing children's drawings

It is significant that we learn a great deal about children's ideas from their drawing. It is no accident that much of the evidence collected in the SPACE project and the examples in Chapter 5 take the form of drawings which express their ideas. Part of children's development in representation is drawing something that is more like a generic symbol for an object than an attempt to produce a picture of a particular object. Drawing a lollipop tree (Figure 5.12) is an example, but it may also indicate the conception of a tree as a trunk with leaves. To develop the concept of a tree as something more than this requires more experience and discussion of real objects and the help of a teacher in developing the skills needed to represent observed details (Morgan nd). Computer programs that enable children to draw (and change their drawings more easily than on paper) can also help (Williamson 2006).

Selecting strategies for helping progression in ideas

It is not until teachers take steps to find out children's ideas (in ways discussed in Chapter 14) that they can decide what is the appropriate action to take. The appropriate action can be decided by diagnosing the shortcomings of the children's ideas and selecting from the kinds of strategies that we have discussed. This requires, of course, that we pay attention to children's ideas and take them seriously.

Summary

This chapter has suggested some strategies for helping children to develop scientific ideas, matched to the particular characteristics of the ideas that children initially hold. The main points have been:

■ it is important to start from the ideas that children have in trying to help their progress towards more scientific ones;

■ there are many sources of alternative ideas for children to test, including other children as well as information sources;

■ when alternative ideas are introduced, the teacher's role should be to scaffold their use and give opportunity for application in a variety of contexts;

■ a range of different strategies can be used to help development, the selection depending on the nature of the ideas that children hold.

Further reading

Asoko, H. and de Bóo, M. (2001) *Analogies and Illustrations. Representing Ideas in Primary Science*, Hatfield: ASE.

10

Helping development of inquiry skills

Summary

In Chapter 6 we showed that process skills have a central role in the development of scientific understanding. We noted that if these skills are not well developed, relevant evidence may not be gathered, or some evidence may be disregarded. As a result, preconceptions may be confirmed when they should be challenged. So the question of how to help development of skills, which we take up in this chapter, is an important one. After suggesting some different types of inquiry, we consider what is meant by the development of inquiry skills and suggest three indicators of progress that apply across the skills. Then we consider the action that teachers can take to help progress in development of different groups of skills and some strategies that can apply across all inquiry skills.

Inquiry skills and the development of understanding

In the case studies in Chapters 1 and 2 the teachers collected materials (ice, balls, soil samples, sealants) or took children to an environment (or created it in school) for children to explore and observe. Their observations were focused by a question – often starting with a 'which is best' question or a 'what is going on here' question and leading to a 'how do we find out' question. The children's ideas based on earlier experience led them to suggest answers and the teachers encouraged them to gather more information which enabled the children to test their ideas. This was followed by interpreting and drawing conclusions from what they found and by communicating and reflecting on what they found. What understanding emerges from the inquiry, as noted in Chapter 6, depends on what and how information is gathered and used, in other words on the skills of observation, hypothesising, questioning, predicting, planning, interpreting, drawing conclusions, communicating and reflecting.

The process of inquiry was described as a rather linear series of stages, which is perhaps rather different from what happens in real classrooms. Indeed, as noted in Chapter 7, there are different kinds of inquiries and not all include all the skills listed here. However, children should have experience across a range of different kinds of inquiry, so that they have opportunity to use and develop these key skills. Before we look at the development of inquiry skills, we look at some of the types of inquiry.

Types of inquiry

'Which is best' inquiries

Finding out which is the best floor covering for the kitchen or which wind-up car goes furthest are probably the type of inquiry most familiar to many primary teachers. They involve the manipulation and control of variables to make tests 'fair'. The first step is for children to engage with the following question. We need a new carpet for the class to sit on. Which of the ones available is the best? Once the question is a real one the next step is to consider what we mean by 'best'. In this situation there could be more than one 'best' – children might suggest the least irritating on their legs, the most easily cleaned of the mud brought in on shoes, and many more. By starting with a real and important question pupils gain ownership of the problem; and a formulaic approach, perhaps with a workcard offering a 'recipe' for finding the answer, can be avoided.

Pattern-finding inquiries

These apply where there is a relationship to be found between variables associated with the behaviour of a thing or substance. Examples are: the note produced by blowing across the top of a bottle with different amounts of water in it; the direction of a shadow cast by the sun and the time of day; the number of turns given to a wind-up toy and how far it will go. These inquiries involve the same skills as 'which is best' inquiries since the effect of changes in one variable have to be tested fairly, with other variables or conditions kept the same. However, there is additional emphasis here on the interpretation of findings. They also provide valuable opportunities for developing the skills of presenting data in the form of graphs, tables or charts.

In some cases the relationship leads to an explanation of one variable in terms of another. For instance, after finding that a higher note is the product of a tighter string, it is reasonable to conclude that tightening is the cause of higher notes. But there is need for caution here. In other cases there may be another factor causing one thing to vary with another. For example, the fact that trees of the same kind with more growth rings tend to be taller does not mean that one causes the other; there is another factor that links the two. So these inquiries can provide experiences that help children to distinguish between an association between things and a cause and effect relationship.

Information-seeking inquiries

These are inquiries carried out to see what happens, either as a natural process unfolds or when some action is taken. Examples are seeing eggs hatch, raising butterflies or silk worms, observing the expansion of water on freezing, seeing what things dissolve in water. Usually these concern the behaviour of particular living things or substances, not with comparison between things. For example, the use of technology, such as the bird-box camera in Box 10.1, provides opportunities for children to understand the needs and processes of living things.

Box 10.1 A bird box in the classroom

Despite their rural location the 5–7-year-old children in Sally Buckle's class were unfamiliar with the diversity of life around them. Raising their awareness, sensitivity and care for living things was a key aim. With the help of a grant, a solution was found by setting up a bird box in the school grounds with a micro camera placed in it linked to a monitor in the classroom showing the blue tits who set up home in the box in real time. The monitor was constantly switched on and became like another window in the classroom. Children were able to record the nest building, egg laying and hatching, and feeding the fledglings. Although the death of the adult male meant that most of the fledglings did not survive, the whole community was by that time enthralled by the experience.

(Based on Barker and Buckle 2002: 8–10)

The fact that the whole school and wider community were fascinated by the nesting birds demonstrates clearly that information seeking is relevant at all ages, building up a stock of personal experiences that are needed to make sense of later experiences. In this case information seeking was an end in itself, but in other situations it might be a forerunner for hypothesis-generating inquiries.

Hypothesis-generating inquiries

These inquiries can often begin with 'I wonder why?' questions where the first step is to consider possible reasons why and then to test them out: 'I wonder why footsteps echo in some places on the path', 'I wonder why the mirror in the bathroom steams up when I have a shower'. Suggestions could lead to observations as to which surfaces become 'steamed up' and which do not. Further discussion can lead to suggestions, such as that the mirror and the bathroom tiles feel cold and this has something to do with why the 'steam' turns back to water on contact with them. This hypothesis can then be tested out in a pattern-finding inquiry.

How-to-do-it inquiries

These are inquiries where the end product may be an artefact or a construction that meets particular requirements – a model bridge that will support a certain load, for example. These are problems of a technological nature though involving many scientific inquiry skills and ideas. It is not necessary to make a clean distinction in children's activities between science and technology, but it is important for the teacher to be aware of the difference and of the particular learning that can be developed through these activities. In making decisions about organising the practical work it is important to keep in mind the features that enhance the value of first-hand experience: the physical interaction with materials, the discussion and social interaction (see Chapter 19).

Box 10.2 Dimensions of progression in inquiry skills

1 *From simple to more elaborated skills*

This is the most obvious dimension, comprising the development of ability to perform more aspects of a skill. A parallel in another field, is the development from just being able to move round an ice-rink on skates to being able to jump, twist and dance and still land on your feet. Both might be called 'ice skating' but one is much simpler and less elaborated than the other. In the case of science inquiry skills it is the difference between observing main features and observing details, between predicting what might happen in vague terms and being more specific, between concluding that a change in one variable does affect another, and identifying the direction and nature of the relationship.

2 *From effective use in familiar situations to effective use in unfamiliar situations*

All inquiry skills have to be used in relation to some content and it is not difficult to appreciate that what the content is will influence the way children engage with it. Some children who may be able to make a reasonable prediction or plan an inquiry about, say, how far paper darts will fly may be less likely to do these things effectively in relation to the effect of resistance in an electric circuit. The reason is that some scientific knowledge is always involved in using inquiry skills because the skills have to be used on some science content. Whether or not knowledge of this content is the main obstacle in a particular case depends on familiarity with it. A consequence of this is that the extent to which young children can conduct scientific inquiries can only be assessed when they are engaged on inquiries about things familiar to them or ones they have thoroughly explored.

3 *From unconscious to conscious action*

Unconscious action here means doing something without recognising just what one is doing. For example, noticing something without making a conscious effort to observe it, or finding an answer to a question by inquiry without recognising the kind of question that is being answered in this way. The kind of thinking that is at the conscious end of this dimension is meta-cognition, being aware of one's thinking and reasoning processes. It is often considered that primary children are not able to stand back from their inquiries or problems and reflect on how they tackled them and so opportunities to do this are not offered. Involving children in such thinking (as in the AKSIS and CASE projects) has, however, provided evidence of some positive effects (see, for example, Robertson 2004; Serret 2004). Giving children more opportunity of this kind may well advance the development of their inquiry skills and thus their ability to make sense of the world around them.

Indicators of development in inquiry skills

If we want to help development we need some idea of what changes signify progress in inquiry skills. One of the differences between experts and novices in any field is that experts are able to function at a more general level than novices. One of the aims of education has been expressed as releasing thought from particular contexts (Hodson 1998). Children at the primary level are functioning as novices, who learn particular skills in particular contexts and are not able to transfer skills from one subject to another, which can happen even within science subjects, much to the frustration of secondary science teachers. This is why we have identified, as one dimension of progression in process skills, the ability to use them effectively in unfamiliar as well as in familiar contexts. There is a development in each skill, but also a pattern across all the skills in which there are three main dimensions, as suggested in Box 10.2.

With these overall changes in mind, we now consider what teachers can do to help development in the four groups of skills proposed in Chapter 7.

Helping development of observation and use of information sources

Box 10.3 summarises some actions that teachers can take to encourage these skills. In the case of observation, the first essential is something to observe. As children will spend most time in the classroom it is important for this to be rich in opportunities for observation – displays of objects related to a theme, posters, photographs, living things, etc., with sources of further information nearby, should be regular features.

Providing time is significant in encouraging observation, perhaps more than for other inquiry skills. Children need time to go back to things they may have observed only superficially or when a question has occurred to them about something they want to check. A display enables children to use odd moments as well as science activity time for observing and so increases an important commodity in the development of this skill.

Not all observations are made in the classroom, of course, and careful preparation for expeditions outside is important if things are not to be missed. There is less opportunity to revisit objects and so it is essential for the teacher to explore in advance the place to be visited, keeping the capabilities and knowledge of the children in mind (see also Chapter 20).

Invitations to observe

Some children need encouragement to observe and to do this carefully, with attention to detail. Question cards should be placed by displayed objects. For example, 'Try to make this bottle make a high and a low sound' can be placed next to a bottle three-quarters full of water to encourage interaction. 'How many different kinds of grass are there here?' placed next to a bunch of dried grasses encourages careful observation. Or a card could be placed next to a 'Cartesian diver', made from a dropper floating in water inside a large plastic bottle, asking 'What happens when you squeeze the sides of the bottle?' In this case there are several things to observe including how the level of the water inside the dropper's tube rises when the bottle is squeezed, which helps to explain why the dropper sinks. So the card could ask 'What do you notice that could explain what happens?'

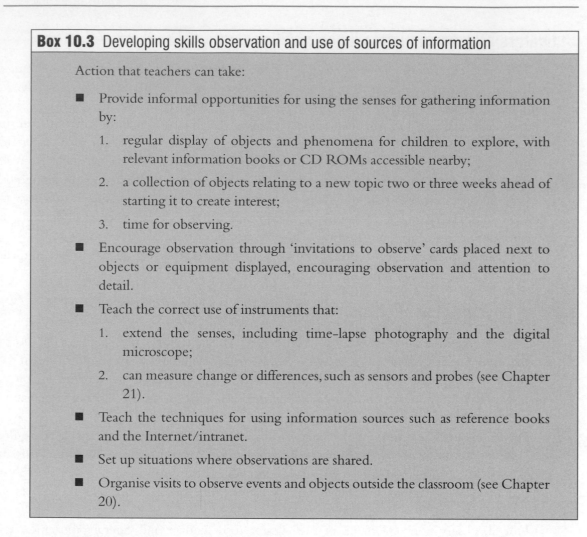

Box 10.3 Developing skills observation and use of sources of information

Action that teachers can take:

■ Provide informal opportunities for using the senses for gathering information by:

1. regular display of objects and phenomena for children to explore, with relevant information books or CD ROMs accessible nearby;

2. a collection of objects relating to a new topic two or three weeks ahead of starting it to create interest;

3. time for observing.

■ Encourage observation through 'invitations to observe' cards placed next to objects or equipment displayed, encouraging observation and attention to detail.

■ Teach the correct use of instruments that:

1. extend the senses, including time–lapse photography and the digital microscope;

2. can measure change or differences, such as sensors and probes (see Chapter 21).

■ Teach the techniques for using information sources such as reference books and the Internet/intranet.

■ Set up situations where observations are shared.

■ Organise visits to observe events and objects outside the classroom (see Chapter 20).

Using aids to observation

Observing is the basis of all means of collecting data in a practical situation. Where attention to detail or to small differences is necessary it will be appropriate to extend senses by using an instrument such as a hand lens or stethoscope and to use measuring instruments to quantify observations. Data can also be obtained from secondary sources, of course, from books, displays, film, television and computer-based sources, and children will need to know how to use these sources properly. Observation aids, such as the use of a hand lens can be taught through a card with a drawing, placed next to some lenses and selected objects in the classroom display. Older children with the required manipulative skill can learn to use a microscope through similar informal opportunities. Other techniques, such as the use of sensors involving computers, need more formal instruction.

Reporting and discussing observations

Sharing observations helps children to become aware of what can be found by careful observation and so be more conscious of this skill. Making a point of spending a few minutes, as a whole class, discussing what has been noticed about things on display, for example, may draw the attention of some children to things they have missed. Asking questions about details during this discussion will help children to pay attention to them in further observation.

Helping development of questioning, predicting and planning skills

Box 10.4 sets out some key ways of helping children to develop these skills. The importance of children asking questions, and the kinds of response to different kinds of questions is taken up in Chapter 12. Here we are concerned with encouraging the kinds of questions that lead to inquiries.

Identifying investigable questions

We have mentioned on several occasions the significance in science of being able to put questions in an investigable form. One of the actions that teachers can take is to make time to discuss with children explicitly what this means and how to do it, using some examples. The AKSIS project (Goldsworthy *et al.* 2000) produced lists of questions for discussion with children in structured activities designed to make children aware of the need to clarify questions. The idea is to help children realise that questions such as 'Does toothpaste make a difference to your teeth?' 'Is margarine better for you than butter?' can only be answered when the meaning of 'making a difference' and 'better for you' have been clarified. There has to be some indication of the kind of evidence that could be collected to answer the question (even if, in these cases, the children might not be able to collect it themselves). One of the AKSIS activities is to ask

---

Box 10.4 Developing skills of questioning, predicting and planning

Action that teachers can take:

- stimulate curiosity through classroom displays, posters, and inviting questions through a question board or box;

- help children to refine their questions and put them into investigable form;

- ask children to use their suggested explanations for something to make predictions: 'What do you think will happen if your idea is correct?'

- provide opportunities for planning by starting from a question to be answered by inquiry without giving instructions;

- scaffold plan a fair test using a planning board (see Figure 10.1);

- talk through an inquiry that has been completed to identify how it could have been better planned.

---

children to decide whether in certain questions it is clear what would have to be changed and what measured to answer the question. The children can then be asked to reflect on their own questions and reword them to make clear how they could be investigated.

Using ideas to make predictions

Children's predictions are often implicit, and helping to make them explicit and conscious enables them to see the connection between an idea and the prediction from it that is tested. For example, children may explain the moisture on the outside of a can of drink just taken out of the refrigerator as having come from the drink inside the can. Asking 'What do you think will happen if you put an empty can in the fridge and then take it out?' will make them use this idea to predict something that can be tested. If children are helped to make predictions in simple cases and to think about the way in which they do this, the process will become more conscious and more easily applied in other contexts.

Opportunity to plan how to answer a question by inquiry

Too often children's experience of what is required in planning an inquiry is by-passed because they are given written instructions to follow, as in the parachute activity in Box 4.9 (p. 62). It also happens when their teachers guide their activities too strongly, as in the following classroom observation of a teacher introducing an activity to find out if ice melts more quickly in air or in water at room temperature:

> You'll need to use the same sized ice-cubes. Make sure you have everything ready before you take the ice cubes out of the tray. Put one cube in the water and one close to it in the air. Then start the clock.

Here the children will have no problem in doing what is required, but they may have little idea of why they are doing it. If they did, they might challenge the need for a clock in this activity!

In the early years, children's experience should include simple problems such that they can easily respond to 'How will you do this?' For example, 'How can you find out if the light from the torch will shine through this fabric, this piece of plastic, this jar of water, this coat sleeve?' Often young children will respond by showing rather than describing what to do. With greater experience and ability to 'think through actions' before doing them they can be encouraged to think ahead more and more, which is one of the values of planning.

Supporting (scaffolding) planning

If children are to develop the ability to plan there must be opportunities for them to start from a question and work out how to answer it, or to make a prediction and to think out and carry out their own procedures for testing it. To take these steps by themselves is asking a great deal of young children and of older ones unused to devising inquiries. They will need help, which subsequently can be gradually withdrawn.

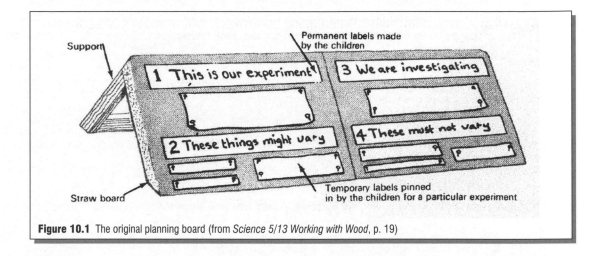

Figure 10.1 The original planning board (from *Science 5/13 Working with Wood*, p. 19)

Planning a fair test can be scaffolded (see Box 9.2) by using a planning board. The original planning board was developed in 1972 as part of a Science 5/13 unit on Working with Wood. Several variants on it have been devised since, but the main features remain much as in the original description shown in Figure 10.1.

Reviewing a complete inquiry

For older children, help in planning can begin, paradoxically, from reviewing an inquiry which has been completed (whether or not the children planned it themselves), helping them to go through what was done and identifying the structure of the activity through questions such as:

■ What were they trying to find out?

■ What things did they compare (identifying the independent variable)?

■ How did they make sure that it was fair (identifying the variables which should be kept the same)?

■ How did they find the result (identifying the dependent variable)?

Planning continues throughout an inquiry and indeed the initial plan may change as the work progresses and unforeseen practical obstacles emerge. However, it is important for children to recognise when they make a change to their plans and to review the whole plan when a change is made. Writing plans down is a useful activity because it requires forward thinking, actions carried out in the mind.

Helping development of interpretation and drawing conclusions

Interpreting results means going further than collecting individual observations and recording them. It means trying to find patterns and to relate various pieces of information to each other and to the ideas being tested. As with other inquiry skills, children need the opportunity and encouragement to do these things if they are to develop these abilities. Some of the ways teachers can help are summarised in Box 10.5.

Box 10.5 Developing skills of interpreting information and drawing conclusions

Actions that teachers can take:

■ make sure that the thinking does not stop when data have been collected or observations made and recorded;

■ provide time and opportunities for children to identify simple patterns or relationships which bring their results together;

■ ensure that results are used to decide whether a prediction was confirmed or whether a question was answered;

■ talk about what has been learnt about the phenomenon investigated, not just the observed effects;

■ encourage identification of overall statements that bring all observations together.

Linking results to the question under investigation

This is a vital aspect of interpretation which can make all the difference in ensuring that inquiry leads to the development of understanding. The main thrust is to ensure that children use the results of their inquiries to advance their ideas. Asking 'How does this compare with what you expected/predicted?' brings the children back to the reason for their enquiry and to be thinking about the ideas they were testing.

As an example, consider children measuring the length of the shadow of a stick at different times of the day. They must go beyond just collecting the measurements if the activity is to have value for developing ideas. Important outcomes from this activity include:

■ seeing that there is pattern in the decreasing and then increasing length of the shadow;

■ realising the possibility of using this pattern to make predictions about the length at times when the shadow was not measured, or the time of day from the measurement of the shadow;

■ developing ideas about how shadows are formed.

All depend on *using* the results the children obtain, so the development of the skills required is important. The central part of the teacher's role is to ensure that results are used and children don't rush from one activity to another without talking about and thinking through what their results mean.

Identifying patterns in results or observations

Sometimes children implicitly use patterns in their findings without recognising that they are in fact doing so. Teachers can help to foster greater consciousness of the process by discussing simple patterns, such as the relationship between the position of the sun and the length of the shadow (or the equivalent in a classroom simulation using a torch and a stick). The starting point must be the various ways in which children express their conclusions. For instance there are several ways of describing the relationship between the length of the shadow and the position of the sun:

- The shadow is shortest when the sun is highest.

- The shortest one is when the sun is high and the longest when it is low.

- Its length depends on where the sun is.

- The higher the sun the shorter the shadow.

All of these require thinking about the set of information about the position of the sun, or other source of light, and the length of the shadow but the first three are incomplete expressions of it. The last one refers to all the data in one statement and says not just that there is a relationship, but what this is. Discussion will help children to realise this, but it is quite an advanced skill and should not be short-circuited by teaching a formula for 'the great/small -er X, the short/long -er Y.'

Helping development of communication and reflection skills

Communication by children plays an important part in their learning. Some actions that teachers can take to encourage communication and reflection are summarised in Box 10.6. In Chapter 8 we noted how thinking and speaking are connected; how we 'talk ourselves into our own understanding'. So regular class discussion of what children have found in group activities is important for development of understanding and for recognising how the skills of collecting and interpreting information were used in arriving at this understanding. Such exchanges are particularly useful if they are conducted so that children question each other, ask for explanations as well as descriptions and suggest improvements in what was done.

Using a notebook

The same arguments apply to writing as to talking, but children need more help to develop the skills of using personal writing to support their thinking. Providing children with a personal notebook is a start. However, they also need to recognise its function not just as an aid to memory, but also as a means of organising their thinking, through writing rough notes and recording observations.

It is important for personal notebooks to be seen as informal, a place where words do not have to be marshalled into sentences. This can liberate children from seeing writing as a chore – one that deters some from activities, even ones they enjoy, 'because we will have to write about it afterwards'. Just as informal talk helps reflection so does informal writing. Teachers can help this by suggesting making notes – 'you might want to think about this and write down some ideas in your notebook before starting' – and by showing an example of using a notebook themselves. Children should begin using notebooks as soon as writing becomes fluent. It is probably best to introduce them to the whole class, encouraging those less able to write to draw and use what words they can.

> **Box 10.6** Developing skills of communication and reflection
>
> Actions that teachers can take:
>
> - provide opportunities for oral reporting and time for preparing so that procedures and ideas are shared;
>
> - provide children with a personal note-book for recording and reflection;
>
> - discuss with children how they might use their notebook and set aside time for them to use it;
>
> - provide ideas about how to record certain kinds of information, using tables, or drawings with labels and symbols;
>
> - discuss criteria for evaluating reports and provide time for peer and self-assessment (see Chapter 17). gGive time to review activities and reflect on, for instance, whether questions could have been better expressed, other variables controlled, measurements repeated, etc;
>
> - discuss ways of communicating particular information to particular audiences.

Time for discussing what and how to report

Children will need to draw upon their notes in preparing for reporting on what they have done when the class gets together at the end of an activity or topic. This is an opportunity for them to realise the value of making notes. It is also the occasion for thinking about what is needed for formal reporting. Different occasions may require different forms of report. Not every activity needs to be written up formally and displayed. (We saw that Kathy was content to have the selected balls as the record of the children's activity (p. 8).) But the occasional preparation of a report that could be displayed to other classes, parents or at a science fair is an opportunity for children to think about the audience when deciding what words, diagrams or other illustrations to use for effective communication.

Some general strategies for developing inquiry skills

When we look across the action suggested for helping development of these groups of skills we find some common themes. Frequent mention has been made of certain points which appear to be key strategies that can be applied to all inquiry skills. These are:

- providing opportunity to use inquiry skills in the exploration of materials and phenomena at first-hand;

- providing opportunity for discussion in small groups and as a whole class;

- encouraging critical review of how activities have been carried out;

- providing access to the techniques needed for advancing skills;

- involving children in communicating in various forms and reflecting on their thinking.

Summary

This chapter has identified different types of inquiry, described as 'which is best?', pattern–finding, information–seeking, hypothesis–generating, and how–to–do–it inquiries. Between them they provide opportunities for use and development of the skills of observation, hypothesising, questioning, predicting, planning, interpreting, drawing conclusions, communicating and reflecting. We have suggested three main changes that indicate development of inquiry skills:

- from simple to more elaborate skills;
- from effective use in familiar situations to effective use in unfamiliar situations;
- from unconscious to conscious action.

Actions that teachers can take in helping developing four groups of skills have been discussed and summarised in Boxes 10.3 to 10.6. Finally, general strategies that apply to helping all inquiry skills have been brought together.

Further reading

Harlen, W. (ed.) (2001) *Primary Science. Taking the Plunge,* 2nd edn, Portsmouth, NH: Heinemann, Chapters 6, 7 and 8.

Teaching for enjoyment, motivation and scientific attitudes

Introduction

We are concerned in this chapter with the classroom conditions which have direct impact on children's response to their activities and thus on their learning outcomes. These are not features of the learning environment that are easily measured and consequently attract less attention than they merit, yet they are critical to the achievement of some of the more important aims education. A good deal depends, not on the materials and physical resources, but on teachers' actions, language and behaviour.

We discuss first the features of a classroom that supports learning for all pupils through taking account of their emotional response to particular tasks. We also acknowledge the importance of how children see themselves as learners. In the second part we look at the role of different kinds of rewards on children's motivation for learning and discuss how to encourage intrinsic, as opposed to extrinsic, motivation. The third section, on attitudes, begins by considering attitudes to learning in general and the teacher's role in developing positive attitudes. Finally we propose ways of helping children's development of attitudes specifically relevant to learning science.

The importance of affect

How children feel about themselves and the ideas that they encounter in the classroom influences their learning. 'Feelings of wonder, delight, amusement, interest, disinterest, boredom and disgust will clearly impact in different ways on the learning task – sometimes favourably, sometimes unfavourably' (Hodson 1998: 54). Children's feelings about learning tasks are affected by many different factors including ones in their personal background which are beyond the influence of the school. But the school can have a role in relation to the impact of other factors, relating to their previous experience of similar tasks, the response of others to what they have done, and how their ideas are received. For instance:

- previous success in a task similar to the one to be undertaken is likely to encourage children to try hard; constant failure will most likely create reluctance;

- if others have responded well to a child's contribution, (s)he is more likely to join in with others and offer ideas than if these contributions have been ignored or the child made to feel 'silly';

- the non-scientific ideas that children have created for themselves and which have worked in everyday contexts may be so firmly held that they become part of their sense of themselves, which is challenged when the ideas are challenged (Abelson 1988).

So sensitivity to children's feelings is as important in interaction with and among children as it is for adults. It is shown primarily as interest in children's feelings about their learning. But this interest has to be sincere. Children are not taken in by the superficial interest of their teacher, for it will be revealed by manner and tone of voice as well as by whether anything happens as a result. A genuine interest creates an atmosphere in which children's own ideas are encouraged and taken as a starting point; where effort is praised rather than only achievement; where value is attached to each child's endeavours. In this atmosphere, a child who does not achieve as well as others will not be ridiculed or feel inferior. Box 11.1 summarises some other actions that teachers can take to make children feel comfortable, in the emotional sense, in the classroom.

Children's self-image as learners

An important part of the emotional context of learning is how children see themselves as learners and how they attribute their success or failure. Those who attribute their successes to their ability and hard work recognise that their learning is within their own control. When they are challenged by difficulty they try hard, and when they fail they consider that they could succeed if they try hard enough. So failure does not damage their self-esteem. The reverse is the case for those who attribute their success to circumstances outside themselves: to chance, to luck

---

Box 11.1 Creating a classroom climate for learning

- Find out about individual children's interests, likes and dislikes, as well as their previous experiences and home background.

- Respect differences in ideas, resisting making judgemental comments.

- Seek to understand how children come to form their ideas.

- Use language, particularly in relation to learning in science, that children understand.

- Check that children have understood the aims of learning tasks in the way intended.

- Provide an example of respecting children's feelings and expect them to do the same for each other.

---

or to their teachers. For these learners, experience of failure leads to loss of confidence, for they do not feel to be in control of whether they succeed or fail. Such learners try to protect their self-esteem by avoiding the risk of failure through selecting tasks well within their grasp.

Motivation for learning

Creating a supportive atmosphere by caring for children's emotional response is basic to motivating learning. But there is more than this in motivation for learning – which we can describe as the willingness to make the effort that learning often requires. There has to be something in it for the learner, some reward that makes that effort worthwhile.

There is an important distinction to be made between different types of reward: rewards that are unrelated (extrinsic) to what has or has not been learnt and those that relate (or are intrinsic) to the learning. The idea of motivating learning through extrinsic rewards and punishments is the basis for the approach to learning known as 'behaviourism' (Skinner 1974). The underlying theory is that behaviours that are regularly rewarded will be reinforced and those that are repeatedly punished will disappear. The assumption here is that learning is under some control that is external to the learner. By contrast, the view that learning depends on the active participation of the learner means that it is under internal control and the reward is in the satisfaction in what has been achieved.

Extrinsic and intrinsic motivation

Motivating learning by rewards and punishments, described as extrinsic motivation, is widely criticised and indeed there is evidence from research studies (Kohn 1993) to suggest that the use of rewards is associated with reduction in the quality of children's work. When the achievement of an extrinsic reward is the aim, it leads to short cuts and less thoughtful work. If the reward is in the doing or the learning that results, on the other hand, and the motivation is intrinsic, then this reward will be achieved by more thoughtful and careful work. To anticipate the discussion of feedback in Chapter 16, intrinsic motivation is more likely to be encouraged by comments on children's work identifying what is good about it and giving suggestions for improvement, rather than grades or marks.

Some psychologists identify other forms of motivation; for example, McMeniman (1989) adds achievement motivation, but it is generally agreed that the chief distinctions to be made are between intrinsic and extrinsic. Intrinsic motivation means that someone engages in an activity because of the satisfaction that is derived from doing it. When there is extrinsic motivation the satisfaction comes from a result that has little to do with the activity – a new bicycle for passing an examination or an ice-cream for finishing the homework. Some characteristics of extrinsically and intrinsically motivated learners are given in Box 11.2. From this we can see that intrinsic motivation is clearly desirable, since it leads to self-motivated and sustained learning. It is particularly relevant to learning to make sense of things around and not being satisfied until they are understood.

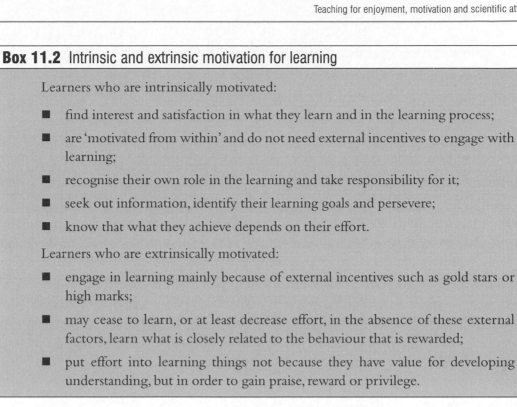

Box 11.2 Intrinsic and extrinsic motivation for learning

Learners who are intrinsically motivated:

■ find interest and satisfaction in what they learn and in the learning process;

■ are 'motivated from within' and do not need external incentives to engage with learning;

■ recognise their own role in the learning and take responsibility for it;

■ seek out information, identify their learning goals and persevere;

■ know that what they achieve depends on their effort.

Learners who are extrinsically motivated:

■ engage in learning mainly because of external incentives such as gold stars or high marks;

■ may cease to learn, or at least decrease effort, in the absence of these external factors, learn what is closely related to the behaviour that is rewarded;

■ put effort into learning things not because they have value for developing understanding, but in order to gain praise, reward or privilege.

Encouraging intrinsic motivation

We must recognise, of course, that in practice it is difficult to work on the principle that all children will find satisfaction in learning all the time. The occasional bribe or threat relating to privileges will do no harm, providing that the regular expectation is to find satisfaction and enjoyment in working to the best of their ability. Celebrating this is an important intrinsic reward. In what other ways, then, can intrinsic motivation be encouraged? Experience from a range of studies of learning across the curriculum suggests that there are things that a teacher can do and things to avoid in aiming to create the climate to foster intrinsic motivation.

Positive action to take includes:

■ Providing some choice of activities. This does not mean a free choice to do anything but a choice from among carefully devised alternatives, all seen by the children as having some relevance to them. The act of choosing gives the children some ownership of the activity and transfers some responsibility to them to undertake it seriously and complete it to the best of their ability.

■ Involving children in identifying some reasonable objectives for the activity and some ways of achieving these objectives.

■ Helping them to assess their own progress, using approaches such as the ones suggested in Chapter 17.

■ Setting up activities in a way that requires genuine collaboration in pairs or small groups, so that the effort of all those involved matters and all are obliged to pull their weight.

- Showing confidence that children will do well; having high expectations.
- Encouraging pride in having tried and made a good effort.

Such actions set up a 'virtuous' circle, where children try harder and as a result succeed, which raises their self-esteem. By the same reasoning, it is important to avoid the vicious circle or self-fulfilling prophesy whereby children see themselves as failing even before they begin a task and therefore make little effort, leading to failure which confirms their judgement of themselves. Again, we can identify actions that should be avoided.

Things to avoid include:

- Labelling children either as groups or individuals. This can happen consciously, as when children are streamed or grouped by ability and are referred to by a label, or unconsciously. It is difficult to imagine that being labelled 'the B stream', reinforced by the uniformly low level of work expected, does not transfer to the children's self image. Children are acutely sensitive to being treated in different ways from others and are not deceived by being described as the 'green' group when this means that they are the 'slow' ones.
- Making comparisons between children. This encourages competition and detracts from each child working towards his or her own objectives.

Attitudes and learning

General approaches to development of attitudes

Attitudes show not in what children can do or know but in their willingness to use their knowledge or skills where appropriate. They are outcomes of learning that result from a range of experiences across which there is some pattern. For instance, an attitude of willingness to take account of evidence does not result from a single activity or even several activities around a topic. Instead it may result from extended experience in which the value of using evidence has been clear or from the example over a period of time of someone who showed this attitude in their behaviour. In other words, attitudes are picked up from a range of experiences; they are 'caught' rather than 'taught', particularly from influential adults. Thus showing an example of the behaviour in practice is a key action that teachers can take. Others are: providing opportunity for children to make the choices that enable them to develop attitudes; reinforcing positive attitudes; and discussing attitude-related behaviour. We now look at these in a little more detail.

Showing an example
Given that attitudes are 'caught', showing an example is probably the most important of the positive things that teachers can do. To make a point of revealing that his or her own ideas have changed, for instance, can have a significant impact on children's willingness to change their ideas. 'I used to think that trees died after dropping their leaves, until …', 'I didn't realise that there were different kinds of woodlice', 'I thought that it was easier to float in deep water than in shallow water but the investigations showed that it didn't make any difference.' The old adage that 'actions speak louder than words' means that such comments will not be convincing by

themselves. It is important for teachers to show attitudes in what they do, not just what they say, for example by:

■ showing interest in new things (which the children may have brought in) by giving them attention, if not immediately, then at some planned time later, and displaying them for others to see, if appropriate;

■ helping to find out about new or unusual things by searching books, the Internet or using other information sources with the children;

■ being self-critical, admitting mistakes and taking steps to make amends.

In a classroom where useful ideas are pursued as they arise and activities extended beyond well-beaten tracks, there are bound to be opportunities for these teacher behaviours to be displayed. Situations in which the teacher just doesn't know, or which bring surprises or something completely new, should be looked upon, not as problems, but as opportunities for transmitting attitudes through example.

Providing opportunity

Since attitudes show in willingness to act in certain ways, there has to be opportunity for children to have the choice of doing so. If their actions are closely controlled by rules or highly structured lesson procedures, then there is little opportunity to develop and show certain attitudes (except perhaps willingness to conform). Providing new and unusual objects in the classroom gives children opportunity to show and satisfy – and so develop – curiosity. Discussing activities while they are in progress or after they have been completed, gives encouragement to reflect critically, but unless such occasions are provided, the attitudes cannot be fostered.

Reinforcing positive attitudes

Children pick up attitudes not only from example but from how others respond to their own behaviour. When children show indications of positive attitudes, it is important to reinforce these behaviours by approval of the *behaviour*. There is an important distinction here between praising the individual and reinforcing the behaviour. It's important not to adopt a behaviourist approach of giving general praise of the person as a reward for behaving in a certain way, which can reinforce the behaviour without the understanding of why it is desirable. As in the case of feedback to children about their work, which we discuss in Chapter 16, feedback about attitude-related behaviour should avoid judgement of the person.

For example, if critical reflection leads to children realising that they did not make fair comparisons in their experiment, the teacher's reaction could be 'well you should have thought of that before' or, alternatively, 'you've learnt something important about this kind of investigation'. The latter is clearly more likely to encourage reflection and the admission of fault on future occasions. Moreover, if this approval is consistent it eventually becomes part of the classroom climate and children will begin to reinforce the attitudes for themselves and for each other. Those who have not developed positive attitudes will be able to recognise what these are from the approval given to others.

Discussing attitude-related behaviour

Attitudes can only be said to exist when they are aspects of a wide range of behaviour. In this regard they are highly abstract and intangible. Identifying them involves a degree of abstract thinking which makes them difficult to discuss, particularly with young children. However, as children become more mature they are more able to reflect on their own behaviour and motivations. It then becomes possible to discuss examples of attitudes in action and to help them identify the way they affect behaviour explicitly. When some 10-year-olds read in a book that snails eat strawberries, they tested this out and came to the conclusion that 'as far as our snails are concerned, the book is wrong'. Their teacher discussed with them how the author of the book might have come to a different conclusion from them and whether both the author and the children might gather more evidence before arriving at their conclusions. The children not only recognised that what was concluded depended on the attitudes to evidence but also that the conclusions were open to challenge from further evidence, thus developing their own 'respect for evidence'.

Ways of helping the development of scientific attitudes

The attitudes of science that we identified in Chapter 7 (p. 96), that is, willingness to consider evidence and change ideas, sensitivity towards living things and the environment, are a subset of attitudes that apply to learning more widely (such as curiosity, perseverance, flexibility). The general points discussed above can readily be applied to these specifically scientific points, leading to action suggested in Boxes 11.3 and 11.4.

Box 11.3 Developing willingness to consider evidence and change ideas

Actions that teachers can take:

- protect time for discussing and interpreting evidence, thus conveying how important this is;

- pay attention to the evidence children gather and make sure that none is ignored, thus setting the expectation of taking note of evidence;

- provide an example, by talking about how the teacher's own ideas have been changed by evidence;

- acknowledge when evidence does require a change of ideas ('we need to think again about this');

- reinforce the importance of not rushing to conclusions with inadequate evidence by approval when children suggest that more evidence is needed before they can come to a conclusion.

Box 11.4 Developing sensitivity to living things and the environment

Actions that teachers can take:

- provide an example of responsibility for living things by checking on the health of animals and plants in the classroom, even if children have been assigned to look after them;

- give opportunities for children to care for living things temporarily brought into the classroom (but check on their welfare, as suggested above);

- discuss the care that should taken when exploring the natural environment, such as replacing stones to preserve habitat;

- show approval of thoughtful behaviour to living things;

- ensure that, where possible, living things taken into the classroom for study are returned afterwards;

- provide bins for recycling that are used by staff and children.

Summary

In this chapter we have noted the importance of creating a classroom climate that takes account of children's emotional reactions that can affect their learning. Chief among actions to be taken are to take real interest in children's feelings and their different ideas, and value their efforts as well as achievements. We have also considered how teachers can help the development of motivation and positive attitudes towards learning. The main points have been:

- teachers should try to encourage children to enjoy learning and find satisfaction in making sense of the world around, that is, intrinsic motivation;

- ways of doing this include giving children some choice and responsibility for their learning, leading to ownership, involving children in identifying and working towards clear goals and assessing their own progress, setting up situations for genuinely collaborative work, raising children's expectations of themselves, and celebrating effort as well as achievement;

- attitudes are ways of describing a willingness or preference to behave in certain ways;

- attitudes in general and scientific attitudes in particular can be encouraged by teachers providing examples through their own behaviour, ensuring opportunities for children to make decisions and form their own ideas, reinforcing relevant behaviours and discussing the value of behaviours that lead to self-motivated learning.

Further reading

Keogh, B. and Naylor, S. (2006) Access and engagement for all, in W. Harlen (ed.) *ASE Guide to Primary Science Education*, Hatfield: Association for Science Education.

McCrory, P. (2007) Getting them emotional about science, *Education in Science* 229: 26–7.

12

Teachers' and children's questions

Introduction

Teachers' questioning practice is one of the most important factors in determining children's opportunities for developing their understanding and their inquiry skills. Three aspects of this practice are discussed in this chapter. First we look at the kinds of questions that teachers can ask to encourage children's active inquiry, and at the importance of giving sufficient time for children to answer questions. The second part deals with encouraging children to ask questions. However, when children ask questions, they have to be answered, or at least addressed in some way. This is often a worry to teachers who feel that their knowledge of science is not adequate. So in the third part we look at ways of dealing with the different kinds of questions that children ask.

Teachers' questions

Questioning is frequently mentioned in discussing the teacher's role and is perhaps the main means of finding out their ideas and of encouraging children's thinking and use of inquiry skills. In the detailed study of primary classroom interactions conducted by Galton *et al.* (1980) in the ORACLE study of 1976, questions formed 12 per cent of all the teacher behaviours observed. When the study, involving children in England at Key Stage 2 (8–11-year-olds), was repeated 20 years later, the proportion overall was 16.2 per cent. But there were significant changes in the types of questions asked. The proportion of all questions that were 'closed' increased in that time from 18.3 per cent to 34.6 per cent, which Galton *et al.* (1999b) suggested was due to the larger incidence of whole class teaching. The researchers' summary of the findings in 1998 is given in Box 12.1.

The findings reported in Box 12.1 are confirmed by other research analysing classroom discourse such as that by Alexander (1995). Occasional questioning of what the children know is expected, but it seems that far too many questions are of this type. The change that is needed is not in the number of questions asked but in their form and content. This is particularly important in a constructivist approach to learning science, where questions have an important role in finding out children's ideas and encouraging their active learning through inquiry.

Box 12.1 Summary of types of questions asked by teachers

In summary, teaching in today's primary schools at Key Stage 2 is very much a matter of teachers talking and children listening. Of this talk by far the largest amount consists of teachers making statements. When questions are asked of children, these questions require them either to recall facts or to solve a problem for which their teachers expect a correct answer. Open or speculative or challenging questions, where children are required to offer more than one answer are still comparatively rare. Even in science, where the highest percentage of open questions was recorded, teachers were three times more likely to require a single correct answer than they were to invite speculation.

(Galton *et al.* 1999: 33)

The form of questions

In relation to form, the important distinctions are between open and closed questions (Box 12.2) and between person–centred and subject–centred questions (Box 12.3).

When the purpose of the question is to explore children's reasons and ideas behind them, or to encourage their inquiry-based thinking, person–centred questions are clearly essential. At other times, too, they are a more effective, and a more friendly, way of involving children in discussions which help them in making sense of their work.

Box 12.2 Open and closed questions

Open questions give access to children's views about things, their feelings and their ideas, and promote inquiry by the children. Closed questions, while still inviting thought about the learning task, require the child to respond to ideas or comments of the teacher. For example these open questions:

■ What do you notice about these crystals?

■ What has happened to your bean since you planted it?

are more likely to lead to answers useful to both teacher and children than their closed versions are as follows:

■ Are all the crystals the same size?

■ How much has your bean grown since you planted it?

Closed questions suggest that there is a right answer and children may not attempt an answer if they are afraid of being wrong.

> ## Box 12.3 Person-centred and subject-centred questions
>
> A *subject-centred* question asks directly about the subject matter; a *person-centred* question asks for the child's ideas about the subject matter.
>
> Subject-centred questions are such as:
>
> - Why do heavy lorries take longer to stop than lighter ones?
> - Why did your plant grow more quickly in the cupboard?
>
> cannot be answered unless you know, or at least think you know, the reasons. By contrast the person-centred versions:
>
> - Why do you think heavy lorries take longer to stop than lighter ones?
> - Why do you think your plant grew more quickly when it was in the cupboard?
>
> can be attempted by anyone who has been thinking about these and has some ideas about them, whether or not correct.

The content of questions

Elstgeest (2001) distinguished between 'productive' and 'unproductive' teachers' questions. The latter are questions that ask directly for facts or reasons where there is clearly a right answer. The former are far more useful in helping children's investigation and thinking. There are different kinds of productive question, set out in Box 12.4, which serve different purposes in encouraging inquiry.

Questions for different purposes

It is evident from what has just been said that questions should be framed so that their form matches their purpose. Here are some examples of questions for different purposes.

Questions for finding out children's ideas

The following questions were among those designed to be used by teachers to find out children's ideas in the SPACE project. They are the kind of questions that led to the children's work presented in Chapter 5. These particular questions were used when children had been involved in handling, observing and drawing sprouting and non-sprouting potatoes:

What do you think is coming out of the potato?
What do you think is happening inside the potato?
Why do you think this is happening to the potato?
Do you think the potato plant will go on growing?
Can you think of anything else that this happens to?

(Russell and Watt 1990: A-10)

Box 12.4 Elstgeest's types of productive questions

Attention-focusing questions have the purpose of drawing children's attention to features which might otherwise be missed: 'Have you noticed …?', 'What do you think of that?' These questions are ones which children often supply for themselves and the teacher may have to raise them only if observation is superficial and attention fleeting.

Comparison questions: 'In what ways are these leaves different?' and 'What is the same about these two pieces of rock?' draw attention to patterns and lay the foundation for using keys and categorising objects and events.

Measuring and counting questions: 'How much?' and 'How long?' are particular kinds of comparison questions which take observation into the quantitative.

Action questions: 'What happens if you shine light from a torch onto a worm?' 'What happens when you put an ice cube into warm water?' and 'What happens if … ', are the kind of question which leads to investigations.

Problem-posing questions give children a challenge and leave them to work out how to meet it. Questions such as 'Can you find a way to make your string telephone sound clearer?' and 'How can you make a coloured shadow?' require children to have experience or knowledge which they can apply in tackling them. Without such knowledge the question may not even make sense to the children.

They can readily be seen to be open, person-centred questions. They encourage children to express their thoughts before starting investigations, giving teachers information about the kinds of ideas the children were bringing to their activities.

Questions for developing ideas

According to the kinds of ideas the children start from, activities to develop them may take various forms as discussed in Chapter 9. Questions can be used to initiate children's investigation of their ideas.

For example, questions of the kind:

- What evidence would you need to show that your idea works?
- What would show that it …was better than … ?
- What could you do to make it even better?

require children to think through the implications of an idea and extend its application.

When the development of children's ideas seems to require further experience and comparisons between things, then attention-focusing, measuring and counting, and comparison questions are the most useful. For applying ideas, the problem-posing questions are appropriate. For discussing the meaning of words, it is best to ask for examples rather than abstract definitions, through questions such as: 'Show me what you do to "dissolve" the butter', 'How will you know if the sugar has dissolved?' and other ways of introducing scientific words discussed in Chapter 8.

Questions for encouraging inquiry skills

Questions can be framed so that children have to use inquiry skills to answer them, giving the teacher the opportunity to find out how far their skills have been developed. Examples of questions relating to some inquiry skills, set in the context of children investigating a collection of different seeds, are given in Box 12.5.

Box 12.5 Questions encouraging particular inquiry skills

Observing

- What do you notice that is the same about these seeds?
- What differences do you notice between seeds of the same kind?
- Could you tell the difference between them with your eyes closed?
- What difference do you see when you look as them using the lens?

Predicting

- What do you think the seeds will grow into?
- What do you think would make them grow faster?
- What do you think will happen if they have water without soil?
- What do you think will happen if we give them more (or less) water/light/warmth?

Planning

- What will you need to do to find out …(if the seeds need soil to grow)?
- How will you make it fair (to be sure that it is the soil and not something else which is making the seeds grow)?
- What equipment will you need?
- What will you look for to find out the result?

Interpreting

- Did you find any connection between …(how fast the plant grew and the amount of water/light/warmth it had)?
- Is there any connection between the size of the seed planted and the size of the plant?
- What made a difference to how fast the seeds began to grow?

Box 12.6 'Wait time'

In 1974 Mary Budd Rowe published significant research on teachers' questions in elementary science classes in the USA. She reported that teachers waited on average less than one second after asking a question before intervening again if no answer was forthcoming. Teachers tended to rephrase the question or ask a different one that the children could answer more quickly – invariably making the question more closed and fact-related. Research in the UK confirmed that this situation was far from being confined to American classrooms.

Budd Rowe found that when teachers were advised to increase the 'wait time' after asking questions requiring explanations, the children's answers were longer and more confident. Also:

- the failure to answer decreased;
- children challenged, added to or modified each others' answers;
- children offered more alternative explanations.

Giving time for answering

Allied to the careful selection and framing of questions to promote thinking and action is the need to allow time for children to answer and to listen to their answers. Questions that ask children to think require time to answer. Teachers often expect an answer too quickly and in doing so deter children from thinking. Research shows that extending the time that a teacher waits for children to answer increases markedly the quality of the answers (Budd Rowe, 1974). This is a case where patience is rewarded and time saved overall by spending a little more in allowing children to think about their answers before turning to someone else, or rephrasing the question. The time given for answering has become known as 'wait time' (see Box 12.6).

Later research with teachers (Black *et al.* 2003) has found that increasing wait time for answering, without feeling the need to 'fill the silence' has led to

> more students being involved in question-and-answer discussions and to an increase in the length of their replies. One particular way to increase participation is to ask students to brainstorm ideas, perhaps in pairs, for two or three minutes before the teacher asks for contributions. This allows the students to voice their ideas, hear other ideas and articulate a considered answer rather than jumping in to utter the first thing that comes into their head in the hope that it is what the teacher is seeking.
> (Black *et al.* 2003: 35)

Children's questions

Asking questions is an important means for both adults and children to try to understand the things around them. When engrossed in the study of something new we use our existing knowledge to make sense of it and try out the ideas we already have to see if they fit. When we find a gap between what we already know and making sense of something new, one way of trying to bridge it is to ask questions. We might do this immediately by asking a question if there is an authority present, as might happen at an exhibition, on a guided tour, or in a class or lecture. At other times the question may remain unspoken but guides us to a source of information which is then more efficiently used because we know what ideas or information we are looking for.

But all of us, adults and children alike, ask a number of different kinds of question as well as those seeking information or ideas. Some questions are rhetorical and some just show interest; neither of these expects an answer. Some questions are asked to establish a relationship with someone, or to gain a response; some to attract attention; some even to irritate or harass (as in Parliaments).

Children's questions that arise from curiosity and the desire to understand have a key part to play in learning science. However, it is important not to discourage any questions by implying that only some are worth answering. At the same time, while we recognise the value to children of encouraging the expression of their questions, including the vague and unspoken ones, it is helpful to their learning if they begin to recognise the kinds of questions which can be addressed through scientific activity. Children who realise that they can find out answers to 'what, how and why' questions by their own interaction with things around have made the best start they can in scientific development. They realise that the answer to 'Why do daisies spread out their leaves?' 'Why do paper tissues have three thin layers rather than one thick one?' 'What happens when you turn a mirror upside-down?' are to be found directly from observations and actions on the daisies, the tissues, the mirror.

Encouraging children's questions

The importance of stimulating questions means that the classroom should foster the curiosity from which they arise. Here are some ways of doing this:

- provide plenty of interesting materials for children to explore;

- make provision for children to bring into the classroom, material and objects, for these have built in interest that is likely to be shared by other children;

- set up a 'question corner' or a 'question of the week' activity where there are materials to stimulate inquiry that might be incorporated into class work;

- while introducing new or unusual things to stimulate curiosity, provide familiar materials as well (see Box 12.7);

- encourage children to question as well as to report what they have done and say what they don't understand;

- more generally, and importantly, regularly extend the invitation 'what question would you like to ask about …' either orally or in writing on workcards or work sheets;

- and resist the temptation, as a teacher, to do all the question raising.

Box 12.7 A stimulating display of familiar things

A display of different tools, nuts and bolts and screws was set up with a 'question box' enabling children to post their questions on small pieces of paper. The apparently gender-biased subject matter in fact produced no bias in the interest and questions the display stimulated. When the box was opened and each question considered, girls were as ready as boys to come up with reasons for different sizes and shapes of heads of screws, why screws had threads but nails did not or whether the length of the handle of a screwdriver made any difference. They followed up some suggestions through practical investigations and other questions were left pinned to the display board awaiting information from an 'expert'. The work added considerably to their experience of materials and their properties as well as showing that questions were valued.

Handling children's questions

Despite the value to children's learning of encouraging their questions, many teachers are worried about answering children's questions and, perhaps unconsciously, adopt classroom strategies that reduce opportunities for children to ask questions. So if questioning is to be encouraged, being able to handle the questions that children raise has high priority.

Fortunately handling questions is a skill which can readily be developed. It requires thought about the kind of question being asked, about the likely motive for asking it and knowledge of how to turn a question into one which can be a useful starting point for investigation. The word 'handle', rather than 'answer', is used deliberately here. One of the first things to realise – perhaps with some relief – is that at times it is better not to answer children's questions directly (even if the teacher does know the answer). But it depends on the question which is asked and so we look now at what is appropriate for different types of question.

Responding to different types of question

Most questions that children ask fall into five groups:

■ comments that are expressed as questions but which require a response that is not an answer;

■ philosophical questions that have no answer that scientific inquiry can provide;

■ requests for simple facts such as names or definitions;

■ requests for explanations that would be too complex for children to understand;

■ requests for explanations that children could find through inquiry.

Some suggestions of how to handle these different types now follows. The first step, however, is to identify the type of question and if this is not clear ask the children to clarify or rephrase what they want to know.

Comments expressed as questions

These are questions which children ask when they are intrigued or excited. The questions don't really need to be answered but there has to be some response which acknowledges the stimulus which gave rise to the question. For example, here is how an infants' teacher handled a question from a 6-year-old when she and a group of children were examining a birds' nest:

Child	How do they weave it?
Teacher	They're very clever …
Child	Birds are very clever with their beaks.
Child	Nobody would ever think they were because they're so small.
Teacher	Yes, it's wonderful isn't it? If we turn this right round and let you have a look at this side …

The child's question was used to maintain the close observation of the nest and a sense of wonder. She might have replied 'Look carefully and see if you can tell how it is done,' but perhaps she judged that this was too early a stage in the exploration for focusing on one aspect, but her response leaves open the possibility of returning to the subject in this vein if the children's interest is still there. Another way of putting this is that she judged the question to be a way of expressing wonder rather than a genuine query. The child might just as easily have said 'Look at how it's woven!'

Philosophical questions

This is another category of questions to which the response has to be of the 'yes, isn't it interesting/intriguing' kind, sharing the wondering behind the question. 'Why do we have birds and all different things like that?' is such a question. Taken at face value the only answer is to say that there is no answer. However, we should not read too much into the exact words children use. They often phrase questions as 'why' questions, making them sound philosophical when the answer they are wanting is much more related to 'What makes it happen?' rather than 'Why does it happen?' When children's questions seem philosophical the initial step is to ask them to explain their question. It may well then turn into a question in a different category, but if not it should be treated as an interesting question but one to which no-one can give a definite answer.

Requests for simple facts

These are questions which satisfy the urge to name, to know, to identify. These are questions to which there are simple factual answers which may help the children to give a context to their experience and their ideas, as for example, in Box 12.8, about the birds' eggs. The teacher may know the answers and if so there is no point in withholding them.

Requests for names of things fall into this category, as do definitions which arise in questions such as 'Is coal a kind of rock?' While names can be supplied if they are known, undue attention should not be given to them. Often children simply want to know that things do have a name and, knowing this, they are satisfied. If work requires something to be named and no-one knows the proper name at that moment then children can be invited to make up a name to use. 'Shiny cracked rock', 'long thin stem with umbrella', 'speedy short brown creature' will actually be more

---

Box 12.8 Questions about nests and eggs

The children looking at the bird's nest asked 'Where did it come from?', 'What kind of stuff is this that it's made of?', 'How long do the eggs take to hatch?' In this case, the teacher knew where the nest had come from and helped the children identify the 'stuff' as hair. But for the length of hatching she did not have the knowledge and the conversation ran on as follows:

Teacher   Well, you've asked me a question that I can't answer – how many days it would take – but there's a way that you could find out, do you know how?

Child   Watch it …

Child   A bird watcher …

Child   A book.

Teacher   Yes, this is something you can look up in a book and when you've found out …

Child   *(who had rushed to pick up the book by the display of the nest)* … I've got one here, somewhere.

Child   … here, here's a page about them.

Teacher   There we are …

The children were engrossed in the stages of development of a chick inside an egg for some time. The question was answered and more was learnt besides. Had the book not been so readily available the teacher could have suggested that either she or the children could look for the information and report back another day.

---

useful in talking about things observed in the field than their scientific or common names. Later the 'real' names can be gradually substituted.

Some requests for simple facts cannot be answered. Young children often have a view of their teacher as knowing everything and it is necessary to help them to realise that this is not the case. When the children asked 'Where are the birds now, the ones who built the nest?' they were expecting a simple question to have a simple answer. In this case the teacher judged that the kind of answer they wanted was 'They've probably made their home in another shed, but I really don't know for sure' rather than an account of all the possibilities, including migration and whether or not birds tend to stay in the same neighbourhood. A straight 'I don't know' answer helps children to realise the kinds of questions that cannot have answers as well as that their teacher is a human and not a superhuman being.

Questions requiring complex answers

Apart from the brief requests for facts, most questions children ask can be answered at a variety of levels of complexity. Take 'Why is the sky blue?' for example. There are many levels of 'explanation' from those based on the scattering of light of different wavelengths to those

> ## Box 12.9 'Turning' complex questions to find related investigable ones
>
> The teaching skill involved is the ability to 'turn' the questions. Consider, for example, a situation in which children are exploring the properties of fabrics. They have dropped water on different types and become fascinated by the fact that water stays 'like a little ball' on felt. They tilt the felt, rolling the ball around, and someone asks 'Why is it like a ball?' How might the question be turned by applying the 'doing more to understand' approach? We need to analyse the situation quickly and use what I call a 'variables scan'. The explanation must relate to something 'going on' between the water and the felt surface, so causing the ball. That being so, ideas for children's activities will come if we consider ways in which the situation could be varied to better understand the making of the ball. We could explore surfaces, keeping the drop the same, and explore drops, keeping the surface the same. These thoughts can prompt others that bring ideas nearer to what children might do.
>
> (Jelly 2001: 44–5)

relating to the absence of clouds. Questions such as 'Why is soil brown?', 'Why do some birds build nests in trees and others on the ground?' and 'How do aeroplanes stay up in the air?' fall into this category.

They seem the most difficult for teachers to answer. The difficulty lies in the fact that many teachers do not know the answers and those who do will realise that children could not understand them. There is no need to be concerned, whichever group you fall into, because the worst thing to do in either case is to attempt to answer these questions!

It is sometimes more difficult for the teacher who does know the scientific explanation to resist the temptation to give it than to persuade the teacher who does not know not to feel guilty about not being able to answer. Giving complex answers to children who cannot understand them is underlining for them that science is a subject of facts to memorise that you don't expect to understand. If their questions are repeatedly met by answers which they do not understand the children will cease to ask questions. This would be damaging, for these questions particularly drive their learning. So what can be done instead of answering them? A good answer is given by Sheila Jelly in Box 12.9.

Turning questions in this way enables teachers to treat difficult questions seriously but without providing answers beyond children's understanding. It also indicates to children that they can go a long way to finding answers through their own investigation, thus underlining the implicit messages about the nature of scientific activity and their ability to answer questions by inquiry.

Questions which can lead to investigation by children
Teachers looking for opportunities for children to explore and investigate will find these are the easiest questions to deal with. The main problems are: resisting the urge to give the answer because it may seem so evident (to the teacher but not the child); and storing such questions when they pop up at an inconvenient time.

Questions which can be profitably investigated by children will come up at various times, often times which are inconvenient for embarking on investigations. Although they can't be taken up at that moment, the question should be discussed enough to turn them into investigations and then, depending on the age of the children, picked up some time later. Some kind of note has to be made and this can usefully be kept publicly as a list of 'things to investigate' on the classroom wall, or just kept privately by the teacher. For younger children the time delay in taking up the investigations has to be kept short – a matter of days – but the investigations are also likely to be short and so can be fitted into a programme more easily. Older children can retain interest over a longer period – a week or two – during which the required time and materials can be built into the planned programme.

The five categories of questions and ways of handling them are summarised in Figure 12.1.

Type (i) (Comments as question)	Type (ii) (Philosophical)	Type (iii) (Facts, names)	Type (iv) (Complex)	Type (v) (Investigable)
Express interest, share wonder	Ask for more explanation of what the question is	Could the question be answered from reference material by the children? If not	Explain that the answer is complex, but we can find out something to help	Discuss how to find answer
↓	↓	↓	↓	↓
Can I ask a question about it that would lead to inquiry?	Does it become a different kind of question? If not	Give answer (if known) or say you will find out	Focus on the part which involves things familiar to children	Can we do this now? If not
↓	↓		↓	↓
Type (v)	Explain that there is no answer to it		Consider variables, the effects of which can be investigated	Store and take up later
			↓	
			Turn into type (v)	

Figure 12.1 Flow diagram for handling questions

Summary

This chapter has concerned issues relating to questions: questions asked by teachers, ways of encouraging children's questions and ways of handling the questions that children ask. The main points have been:

- research in England shows that teachers ask many more closed than open questions and the difference has increased coinciding with an increase in the amount of whole class teaching from 1976 to 1996;

- the form and content of questions should match their purpose and the kind of response that the teacher is seeking from the child (attention, action, problem-solving, etc.);

- when teachers ask questions that require thoughtful answers, children need time to think about their answers;

- children's questions are valuable for a number of reasons: they show the gaps that the children feel they need to fill in their understanding; they can provide the basis for children's investigations; and they give children the opportunity to realise that they can find things out for themselves and satisfy their curiosity;

- teachers can encourage children to raise questions by providing interesting and thought-provoking materials in the classroom, mechanisms for inviting questions, such as a question box, and an atmosphere that welcomes and encourages questioning;

- children will ask all kinds of questions and not just those which can lead to investigations; in order not to deter questioning, teachers need to be able to handle these different kinds – the first step in doing this is to recognise the type of question so that the appropriate response can be given.

Further reading

Elstgeest, J. (2001) The right question at the right time, in W. Harlen (ed.) *Primary Science: Taking the Plunge,* 2nd edn, Portsmouth, NH, USA: Heinemann.

Galton, M., Hargreaves, L., Comber, C., Wall, D., and Pell, T. (1999b) Changes in patterns of teacher interaction in the primary classroom: 1976–96, *British Educational Research Journal* 25 (1): 23–37.

Jelly, S.J. (2001) Helping children raise questions – and answering them, in W. Harlen (ed.) *Primary Science: Taking the Plunge,* 2nd edn, Portsmouth, NH, USA: Heinemann.

13

Planning lessons

Introduction

In discussing the goals of primary science we have set our sights high. The development of scientific literacy and an enthusiasm for continued learning, that is so essential in the modern world, requires creative and inspirational teaching. After several years of rather narrow focus on content and prescription of how science teaching should be planned, a more flexible and open approach is being encouraged in the new curricula being developed and implemented in the countries of the UK. This greater freedom for teachers probably requires more planning rather than less, but the planning might be of a somewhat different kind from following a prescribed scheme. Teachers can plan more imaginative science lessons.

In this chapter we begin by thinking about the ways in which policy changes are having an impact on the ways in which teachers can operate at the class level. Being more free to consider the curriculum in a more holistic way and to think more broadly about what it is that is valuable in the science we are teaching leads to planning richer and more enjoyable lessons. After considering approaches to planning with goals in mind we delve deeper into thinking about the ways in which lessons can be enriched through the questions we ask children and the interactions we have with them. Being creative as teachers is an important pre-requisite for encouraging creativity in pupils; so next we consider creativity and sources of creative ideas. Of course creative ideas cannot all be thought up from scratch, so in the final section we consider the ways in which published materials can provide interesting ideas as starting points on which to build.

Changes in the work of teachers

Since 2000, there has been increasing concern over the extent to which, in England and some other countries, the tightly prescribed curriculum and associated assessment and accountability systems have restricted the development of creativity and flexibility in young people. There have been associated concerns, born out in a study of teacher workload (PricewaterhouseCoopers 2001) that teachers were spending significant amounts of time on paperwork including planning to meet these requirements. We have already discussed the recent changes in the various national curricula in the UK and the reduction in prescription of context. There has also been an attempt to support teachers by reducing their workload and providing protected planning, preparation and assessment time. Teachers have welcomed the extra time, although in primary schools this has meant an increase in the numbers of teaching assistants with more responsibility for teaching. Hence teachers need to plan the work of assistants in order to ensure high quality learning even when away from the classroom. These developments mean a change in approaches towards more collaborative planning where possible. Planning with a broader focus rather than towards specific learning outcomes is being encouraged across the UK.

Planning with goals in mind

Considering broader goals in the context of the less prescriptive curriculum can facilitate a more creative approach to planning. Dabell *et al.* (2006) argue that 'planning is about more than "coverage"; its purpose is to translate goals into practice and to make the teaching and learning experience as effective as possible' (p. 135). Goals need to be established for the whole school, and within that at the level of the class. National curricula and commercial or other locally developed schemes of work can provide the basis for consideration of these goals. We discuss the use of commercial schemes later in this chapter and whole-school programmes in Chapter 23. The focus in this section is on short-term lesson planning.

At the level of the lesson, or group of lessons, planning should take account of the children's needs. Ensuring clear, broadly based goals for a lesson or series of lessons is essential if a truly rich experience is to be achieved. This is demonstrated by Dabell *et al.* (2006: 138–9) where they compare the stated goals of two lessons on the same topic. In Figure 13.1 we adopt the same approach, first looking at a lesson with narrowly defined learning goals (lesson A). This is a typical lesson that might be taken from an Internet site or from schemes of work such as QCA (DfEE 1998).

In the revised approach starting with broader goals (lesson B) the original lesson A can be developed to enable more discussion and sharing of ideas, a greater involvement of the children in setting the learning agenda and improved links in terms of progression and scientific attitudes. It also has the effect of extending the topic, but adding in the prior experience of a walk around the school, and results in the prospect of a wider variety of questions to be generated and potentially addressed in future lessons. If we consider the framework for learning through investigations as described in Chapter 6 (Figure 6.2) it is clear that both lessons involve all parts of the framework, but lesson A does not give time to the very first part of the process (new experience, questions raised), so the second step, (exploring new objects or phenomena, and linking to previous experience, identifies investigable questions), is less rich, requiring more teacher direction in order to get to the investigation planned by the teacher.

Moving from lesson A to lesson B

As noted in Chapter 4, richer opportunities for learning undoubtedly take up more time, but this is balanced by the greater learning that is taking place. We can use the questions from Chapter

	LESSON A	LESSON B
Learning goal	To know that woodlice prefer dark damp places. To observe carefully. To ask questions.	To begin to recognise that living things have different needs and specific habitats. To raise interesting questions about woodlice. To see that woodlice have their place in the environment, and to learn to treat them with care. To really enjoy being out of doors and exploring nature.
Introduction	PowerPoint image of a woodlouse with some useful facts about them – ie where they live and what they eat. Ask children if they have seen woodlice before. Learning objective on board. Where do woodlice live? Ask children to suggest what conditions woodlice might prefer to live in. Group these on the board. Group ideas on board and use slides on IWB to show images of woodlice habitats. Children draw a woodlouse on worksheet.	Remind children of their walk around the school the previous week (it was fun even 'though it rained really hard') and all the living things they found. Ask them to think about the different places animals and plants live in. Recap. Project list of places identified in previous lesson and the descriptions of flora and fauna and habitats. Admire drawings done since. Questions – what did we notice about the places where the bluebells were growing? What did we find under stones? If I were to say, 'Go out and find me a woodlouse.' Would you know where to go? Why do you think you would find them there? (paired talk before sharing). Write a list of places on flip chart – including differences of opinion (under wood, under stones, in the shed). What do you notice about all these places? Discuss with class the learning goals. 'What I thought we would do today is to find out some more about where woodlice live and then to ask some questions about these interesting creatures.'
Setting up whole-class work	Discuss with class their ideas about finding out preferred places for woodlice. Light or dark, damp or dry.	Provide children with trays and brushes to pick up woodlice. Explain that they can look at a number of possibilities, but collect some woodlice from one site (otherwise once disturbed they might be more difficult to find). A child in each group to be charged with taking a picture of the place the woodlice were found. CA/teacher to hold cameras until needed.
Class activity	In groups design a plan to find out which conditions woodlice prefer to live in. (choice chamber)	In groups, children move around school grounds looking for good places. Staff to encourage them to think about the places: 'What do you notice under the stone? (smell?, feel?)' Once children have explored the area and picked up about 10 woodlice per group, reconvene at the picnic tables (if dry). Children write down brief description of place where they found their woodlice on large Post-it notes and place on flip chart. Brief discussion (to be followed up later). Close observation of woodlice. Children look (hand lens available) and talk to one another about what they see. Make sketches on paper on clipboards. Using laminated question cards (Do …? , Who …?, What if …?, Can…?, Where…?) children encouraged as groups to discuss questions they would like to ask and to write them down on Post-it notes to stick onto their clipboard for later sorting. Children return woodlice to place found, wash hands.
Plenary	Groups present plans for choice chamber experiment for next lesson. Discussion of good plans – collectively decide on ideal plan for next time.	Discussion about woodlice habitat (introduce word if appropriate). Class work together to discuss questions raised and to consider ways in which they might be answered (from a book, ask an expert, set up an investigation, etc.). Discuss who will take charge of different questions and when experiments might be set up.
Resources	PowerPoint slides, woodlice, worksheets.	Digital cameras Metal dishes, soft brushes, laminated question words, flip chart

Figure 13.1 Planning different approaches to the same topic

4 to interrogate the original lesson plan A and move it towards more open goals and enjoyable activities.

Are the activities interesting and relevant to the children?
Looking at the original plan A the class teacher and teaching assistant thought it would be better if the children had the chance to see different habitats around school, so they decided that the class should have a walk at the start of the lesson to give all children the chance to know what woodlice are.

Do the activities build on previous experience and promote progression?
They planned an experience to precede the woodlice hunts, to look at habitats more generally, on a walk in the previous week. They would also make sure that books and other resources were on the shelves in the classroom in the week between the walk and the woodlice hunt. Then the children could discuss the fact that different creatures need different conditions.

Will the children be able to use a range of senses and learn actively?
If the children go outside to look for woodlice they can see where they live and will feel the damp places and smell the detritus.

Will the children reflect and make meaning out of their activities?
Children would be encouraged to discuss observations, and given plenty of time to talk in groups. If possible they would do this outside so that they can point to places and return to them if they want to check things out.

Will the children talk and represent their ideas in different ways?
In lesson A the children can make drawings and use their ideas to design the experiment, but they would have a less rich basis on which to share ideas. In lesson B children would be invited to discuss ideas and observations, raise any questions they like about woodlice and to do it in situ.

Will they develop scientific ideas, use inquiry skills and demonstrate scientific attitudes?
While children are looking around the grounds they will be making predictions about where to look and testing these out. They will begin to formulate questions and in discussion consider which questions can be pursued (What do they eat? Can they make a noise?).

Can they work cooperatively and share ideas with each other?
Children will need to work collaboratively to plan a test in lesson A. In lesson B the children will need to discuss ideas, share materials, and make decisions about what questions to write down.

Managing lesson B

The process of interrogating an initial lesson plan will also involve questions about health and safety, resources, timing, staffing and the types of questions teachers and teaching assistants or other helpers might usefully ask.

Staffing
Teaching assistant and learning support for individuals.

Resources needed before the lesson
Lidded containers lined with damp paper towels, soft brushes for picking up woodlice, flip chart, clipboards, Post-it notes, laminated words, etc.

Health and safety
Ensure school grounds are gated. Check area before children go out. Wipe picnic tables. Remind children to wash hands.

Timing
Just after play time, but if wet move to afternoon

Organising the timing and resources for the lesson is important, especially if responsibility for different elements is to be shared. However, in terms of the learning goals, discussion amongst the staff who will be involved in the lesson is probably more important than writing everything down in detail. The key is for all to be clear about the questions they might ask to encourage thinking, for example, to encourage inquiry skills. It is also important to be clear about the ways in which adults can encourage the children to ask their own questions (in the case of this lesson, with the help of prompt words). Part of the lesson resulting from this plan is described in Box 20.3.

Questions to stimulate children's thinking

As we discussed in Chapter 12 the form and content of teachers' questions should match the purpose and the kind of response the teacher is seeking. It is therefore important to take the time to consider how key questions might be phrased ensuring that questions are generally open and person centred. It is particularly important to consider this issue where classroom assistants are taking a group or the whole class as without appropriate questions a well-planned lesson can become rather wooden and so result in far less learning. It is no simple matter to formulate the best questions for finding out children's ideas and for developing them. So some 'starting' questions need to be thought out. The questions will match the stages of the lesson. For instance:

■ questions to elicit the children's current knowledge and understanding will include questions such as 'Have you noticed…?' and 'Do you remember when we…?' These are followed by questions which ask for children's ideas about the phenomena e.g. 'Tell me what you think happens …?';

■ questions to encourage exploration of materials will include attention-focusing questions, such as 'What do you notice about your ice cube now?';

■ during investigations, questions will encourage the children to think about what they are trying to find out with the observations and measurements they are making, e.g. 'What does this tell you about how the sound gets from here to there?';

■ in the reporting and discussing stage, questions will help children to link their findings to what they were initially trying to discover, e.g. 'So what have we learned about the kind of soil that helps seedlings to grow best?';

■ for reflecting on how the investigation was done: 'If you were to do this again, what would you change to make the investigation better?'.

During the lesson more questions will arise, and it is not possible to anticipate exactly what ideas and questions the children will contribute. Indeed being able to react to and work with children's responses to questions, and to the ideas and questions that they pose is much more likely when lessons are well planned. One teacher wrote 'Being open and flexible, and willing to allow the children to follow their own thinking was an integral part of my planning' (Boctor and Rowell 2004).

Creative learning requires creative teaching

In previous chapters we have argued that science learning involves children developing their own ideas, building on experiences and making sense of the world and so gaining a sense of satisfaction and enjoyment of learning. This requires young people to be free to be creative; that is, to be involved in 'imaginative activity fashioned so as to produce outcomes that are both original and of value' (NACCCE 1999: 6). The teacher's role in supporting learning in science needs to be seen in light of the notion of what it is to learn in science. Teachers must provide the conditions in which to maximise learning. 'Creative learning requires creative teaching' (NACCCE 1999: 6). In 2003 Feasey found that many primary teachers did not believe that the encouragement of creative thinking is central to the process. Since then a good deal has been written and talked about creativity in the primary curriculum so teachers now are likely to be far more open to letting their imaginations free. The lesson described in Box 13.1 is an example of teachers being creative and as a result we can see how very young children were encouraged to think creatively.

In this example the teachers' creative approach to the topic led to a creative and enthusiastic response from the children. Although the description in Box 13.1 is fairly brief it is still possible to evaluate the lesson as planned and experienced against the evaluation criteria we used to develop lesson B in Figure 13.1.

Box 13.1 Young children thinking creatively in science

Dawn McFall and Chris Macro (2004) report on some exciting work with nursery classes. They were inspired by a visit by the head teacher to a school in Reggio Emilia, Italy, where early years' education is based on 'a respect for children's natural curiosity and creativity and their ability to produce powerful theories about the world and how it works (Thornton and Brunton 2003). Having reviewed children's previous work the practitioners decided to focus on colour, camouflage and shadow. They wanted to develop the sense of wonder the children had shown when mixing colours as they painted model birds (after a visit to a local botanic garden) and noticed the shadows that were made.

The whole class sat on the carpet in front of an overhead projector and a blue shadow puppet. They were asked to predict what they would see on the screen when the puppet was placed on the OHP. Most thought he would be blue. Some made links with their experience of shadows and suggested grey or black. They tried this out, along with some stiff green foam in the shape of a tree, and one of a house (all part of the story they knew). The children began to modify their ideas as they noticed each time that the shadow was black. Then Mr Red was introduced. He had a shape but no eyes or mouth. The children were asked how these could be produced on the shadow. Initially many suggested drawing a face on the puppet, but this did not work. Finally, after lots of thought some children suggested cutting out eye and mouth shapes. They were given plenty of time and appropriate equipment to try out their ideas. In this way they built up their ideas of light being blocked by a solid shape, and went on to observe that they could change the size and shape of the shadows by moving the puppets closer to and further away from the light. They then went on to explore coloured cellophane, experiencing with their own eyes how light passes through certain materials.

Were the activities interesting and relevant to the children?
Most adults with any knowledge of young children must almost be able to hear the squeals of pleasure as the children engaged with the shadow puppets. For this age group play and story is clearly relevant.

Did the activities build on previous experience and promote progression?
The sessions built on prior experience of painting and observing of model birds and the shadows formed by them. There is also here a recognition on the part of the children of the common ideas children hold about light and shadows and so an explicit attempt to address these through additional experiences and challenges.

Were the children able to use a range of senses and learn actively?
Although they all started off sitting and watching the 'show' the children were actively involved and then continued as they moved into cutting out shapes and exploring cellophane.

Did the children reflect and make meaning out of their activities?
This is more difficult to establish, although in the case of young children, having plenty of time to do and think suggests opportunities for reflection as well as activity.

Did the children talk and represent their ideas in different ways?
Although it is not explicitly stated, the children do seem to have had the opportunity to talk; but whether they represented their ideas in drawings or through 'showing' what they did is not clear.

Could they develop scientific ideas, use inquiry skills and demonstrate scientific attitudes?
The children built up their ideas through testing out different puppets, and went on to explore the way light passes through certain materials and not others. This would not look so much like the careful collection of evidence that we might expect in older pupils, but testing and refining ideas with the puppets themselves provided a concrete way to develop inquiry skills and to begin to develop scientific attitudes.

Could they work cooperatively and share ideas with each other?
It is not clear that the children were working in groups, or sharing their ideas with each other, although they were sharing ideas together as a class with their teachers.

In the example of Chris and Dawn's class it is interesting that they expressed their original intentions not as specific intended learning outcomes such as 'to know that light passes through some objects and not others' and 'that when light is blocked, shadows form'. Rather they chose to express their intentions in terms of the broader goal of 'developing the sense of wonder the children had shown'. But it is not just a matter of 'going with the flow' of the children's ideas; it is also about knowing where the children are and finding interesting and imaginative ways to seize the opportunities to help children develop concepts, skills and attitudes.

Sources of creative ideas

It is not always easy to pluck a good idea out of the air. Thus a team approach to planning can be valuable (see Chapter 25) and in the same way that we aim to encourage children to take risks, there also needs to be a willingness on the part of teachers to take risks and to try out new ideas. Teachers need to be alert to possibilities and be keen to learn from the expertise and experience of others. Indeed one of the arguments for introducing planning and preparation time in England was that teachers were losing their creative spark because their work–life balance had tilted too far in the direction of work. Creative ideas come from many sources. Journals, the Internet, discussion among teachers from different schools, and attendance at courses can be most helpful. It is important to continue to learn from others and to gather ideas along the way. We discuss opportunities for teachers' continued learning in more detail in Chapter 26. Here we focus briefly on the use of published curriculum materials, which many teachers have found to be a useful way to get practical advice and interesting ideas, although too heavy a reliance on these has been blamed for lack of creative teaching.

The use of published resources is also becoming more commonplace: these can be helpful but can also lead to a lack of creative teaching if they are followed rigidly.

(Ofsted 2004: 6)

The key to ensuring creative teaching is not to rely entirely on inspiration (which would be exhausting), but to take a flexible approach to using all the ideas and opportunities available, including published materials of all sorts. It is for this reason that we now turn to look at the use of published resources.

Using published curriculum materials and schemes

The best schemes provide ideas for activities, background knowledge for teachers, insights into progression, possibilities for assessment and often interesting materials for children and teachers. Although the distinctions are not always clear it is useful to recognise the difference between published curriculum materials, published schemes and the Programmes of Study which are the required elements in the National Curriculum or other prescribed curricula.

Curriculum materials can have several elements:

- a teacher's guide in which there is a statement about the views of teaching and learning and of primary science on which the materials are based, and explanations as to the how the structure of the materials is intended to support progression, how the materials can be used to meet the learning needs of the children and possibly, the approach taken to assessment and suggested cross-curricular links;

- suggested activities arranged under topics, such as forces, living things, houses or homes, keeping clean;

- indications of resources needs;

- background science knowledge for the teacher;

- pupil materials such as worksheets or pupil books.

Not all curriculum materials have all of these elements, but they all include suggested activities around particular topics.

Schemes of Work (SOW) present a clear structure and order in which suggested activities might be used to ensure progression and coverage of the prescribed curriculum. They represent one interpretation of a required programme of study. They can include indications of the time that might be allocated for sections of the scheme. They can include suggestions for differentiation, and for assessment opportunities. They can, because they are so structured, give a clear idea of the resource needs. They tend not to include pupil books.

Programmes of study (POS) are neither schemes nor curriculum materials. They are simply an indication of the concepts and skills that are required by the school, district or country. They tend to be laid out according to the phases of education and to be subject specific.

The scheme published by QCA (DFEE 1998) was widely taken up in England perhaps because it had the government seal of approval. Its use has declined as many schools have freed themselves from the constraints it seemed to impose, and have adapted it to meet the needs of their pupils. This is as a result of the relaxation of the curriculum that we described in Chapter 3. For example, in Northern Ireland, since the revision of the curriculum, materials have been developed entitled 'Ideas for connected learning' (ICLs), to provide advice, ideas and materials to support a cross–curricular approach. This is more akin to curriculum materials than a scheme of work, as it is set out as topics that teachers can adapt for their own use.

> The ICLs provide a range of active learning experiences that assist teachers in making the revised Northern Ireland Curriculum come alive. They are a means of developing the overall aim and objectives of the curriculum and the principles that underpin it: Connected Learning, Cross-Curricular Skills Development and Assessment for Learning.
>
> (Northern Ireland Curriculum 2008)

There is no intention that these materials will be followed slavishly, but they are offered as an opportunity for teachers to pick and choose, and so hopefully not have the negative effects that the QCA scheme had in some schools. The risk, as teachers may see it, is that there will be gaps in coverage that could put their pupils at a disadvantage. We discuss this further in Chapter 23, 'Aspects of whole-school planning'.

If we believe that we need to start from children's ideas and interests, then no scheme can replace the teacher's insights into what will interest and excite the children, and

what approach is most likely to build on their ideas and help them to develop knowledge and understanding, skills and attitudes. However, there are significant advantages as well as some disadvantages to using published schemes and curriculum materials. Some of these are listed in Box 13.2.

What we need is to be open minded about the use of schemes and curriculum materials. In this way schools and teachers can make the most of their advantages, whilst avoiding the disadvantages. The key is to ensure that, in developing a scheme of work, the needs and interests of the children are central to the planning process at all levels.

Box 13.2 Some advantages and disadvantages of using published materials

Advantages of using published materials	*Disadvantages of using published materials*
• Helps to ensure coverage. • Saves a lot of planning time. • Helps to identify resources. • Can offer useful background knowledge for teachers. • Can provide useful support as a teacher develops in confidence and knowledge. • Curriculum materials can provide exciting resources for children and teachers to use.	• May limit the extent to which teachers use children's initial ideas as a starting point. • May reduce the use made of the school's own environment and context. • May limit the opportunities for cross-curricular links. • May limit opportunities to plan for the differing needs of children (by implying that they all move on at the same pace). • May become boring for the children (and the teacher).

Using lesson plans from the Internet

Since about 2000 there has been an explosion of materials to support primary teaching on the Internet. Some of this is from government-funded bodies such as Teachernet, or local authority developed sites. Others, from non-profit organisations, including environmental or nature groups, are supported by advertising or require a subscription. In a study of teachers in mid-America who were registered on an online programme, Archambault and Crippen (2007) found that, of the various sites visited by teachers, those offering teaching resources such as worksheets and lesson plans were by far the most visited; although looking more deeply, some of these visits were for inspiration, information, pupil resources and ideas rather than simply tailor-made plans.

Such sites offer a wealth of support, information and ideas. For example English Nature (http://www.english-nature.org.uk/science/nature_for_schools/) provides lesson plans around habitats. In one they include the idea of a 'habitat address' to help pupils describe a particular habitat; an idea easy to pick up and use. However, the lesson plan could not be used 'off the shelf' because it is far too general. This is generally the case with all such lesson plans, because planning is what happens in your head and not what is written down. Making use of such lesson plans can be helpful, but a process such as that illustrated in Figure 13.1 would need to be conducted in order to ensure that the lesson fits with your own goals and with the wider goals of the schools programme.

Summary

This chapter has been concerned with the detailed planning for lessons, but with the need to be creative and responsive firmly in mind. The main points have been:

- creativity in learning in science is essential and this requires creative teaching;

- teachers need to be flexible in their planning, which means more careful advance preparation rather than less;

- planning which is directed by broad goals rather than narrow objectives is likely to be richer and more rewarding for both the teacher and the pupil;

- a crucial element of and a key challenge in lesson planning is to be clear about the purpose of the lesson, to link questions to this but adapt them to the needs of the pupils and the stage in the lesson;

- creative ideas to support lesson planning can come from a range of sources; one such is published schemes of work and Internet sites – these are a valuable addition but cannot replace planning for individual classes and pupils within them.

Further reading

Dabell, J., Keogh, B. and Naylor, S. (2006) Planning with goals in mind, in W. Harlen (ed.) *ASE Guide to primary Science Education*, Hatfield: ASE, pp. 135–41.

McFall, D. and Macro, C. (2004) Creativity and science in the nursery, *Primary Science Review* 81: 17–19.

Assessment to help learning

14

Assessment for different purposes

Introduction

This first of five chapters on assessment clears some ground for later discussion of key aspects of assessment in the primary school. We begin by defining terms and considering the purposes of assessment, chiefly for helping learning and for summarising learning. We then tackle questions of when and how to assess, involving decisions about what is relevant information, how to collect and interpret it and communicate the result. We discuss the meaning of reliability and validity in relation to assessment and how these two concepts interact. Finally we summarise the characteristics of formative and summative assessment.

The meaning of assessment

Assessment in education is generally taken to be a process in which information is gathered about learners' achievements, interpreted and used for some purpose. It is in this sense that we use the term in this book, that is, as a process rather than a product. There are many decisions involved in assessment concerning:

- the range of information that is required to serve the purpose of the assessment;
- how best to gather the information so that it is suited to the purpose;
- how to interpret the information;
- how to report and communicate the result to those who need to know what children are achieving.

Combining various ways in which evidence is collected and the various ways of interpreting and reporting it creates different methods of assessment. These range from standardised tests where information is gathered while children are tackling carefully devised tasks, under controlled conditions, to assessment carried out almost imperceptibly during normal interchange between teacher and children. The most appropriate form for it to take should be decided by purpose of the assessment.

Clarifying related terms

While it is important to avoid jargon, it is necessary to be clear about the meaning of various terms connected with assessment and to use them consistently. For instance, the distinction between tests and assessment is central to current discussions about national testing and alternatives; to treat them as interchangeable would make nonsense of some important issues. Tests are one way of conducting assessment which is particularly suited to certain purposes. Tests are specially devised activities designed to assess knowledge and/or skills by giving precisely the same tasks to children who have to respond to the tasks under similar conditions. Tests are not necessarily externally devised; teachers prepare tests (of spelling, arithmetic, for example) and some 'tests' can be embedded in classroom work and look very much like normal classroom work as far as the children are concerned. It is therefore more helpful to characterise assessment differences in terms of purposes rather than in terms of methods.

Other words used in this context are 'examinations' and 'evaluation'. Examinations are commonly combinations of tests or tasks and other forms of assessment used for qualifications, entry into certain kinds of education or professions. Educational evaluation is the term used in some countries interchangeably with assessment and referring to the achievements of individuals; while in the UK, evaluation is the term normally used in relation to teaching and materials for teaching and, in the context of accountability, to teachers, schools and systems.

Why do we assess?

There are two main reasons for assessing individual pupils in the primary school:

■ to use the information to help learning;

■ to find out and report on what has been learnt at a particular time.

The first of these is described as formative assessment or assessment *for* learning (AfL). The second is described as summative assessment or assessment *of* learning. These are not different *kinds* of assessment but different purposes. Whether they serve their purpose depends on how the information is used. Formative assessment is, by definition, used to make decisions about how to advance learning while it is taking place. Summative assessment has several uses including reporting to parents, other teachers, tracking progress and sometimes for grouping and selection. At the secondary level its uses include choosing courses of study, certification, and selection for further or higher education. In principle, summative assessment should also help learning but in the longer term through the decisions based on it, in a less direct way than in the case of formative assessment.

However, there are other ways in which information from assessment is used which have a considerable impact on teachers and schools and which cannot be ignored, although the main focus in this book is on assessment that helps learning and learning science in particular. We refer to the use in the system in England of the results of assessment of individual pupils for evaluation of schools and the monitoring of national standards of achievement and for setting targets at school and national levels. These uses are highly controversial and we cannot go into

> ## Box 14.1 High stakes use of assessment results
>
> The practice in England in 2008 is to use the percentages of pupils reaching level 2 at the end of Key Stage 1 in mathematics and English and level 4 at the end of Key Stage 2 in all three core subjects in the evaluation of primary schools. The information used in deciding levels reached is obtained from national tests only. The consequences of pupils not achieving in the tests at the target levels can be severe, including the school being described as having 'serious weaknesses', being placed in 'special measures' or even closed. This is what is meant by the results having 'high stakes' attached. The publication of 'league tables' comparing schools with each other on the basis of results adds to the high stakes of the tests. To avoid these consequences, inevitably teacher place emphasis on making sure that pupils' test results are maximised, with all that this implies for teaching to the test and giving practice tests (ARG, 2002). Since the range and number of items in the tests is limited to what can be included in short written tests, the effect is to narrow the curriculum and the teaching methods. Other well-documented consequences include teachers' focusing on children just below the target levels, spending a great deal of time in practising tests and reducing the use of assessment to help learning.
>
> In other parts of the UK, in recognition of the problems just outlined, assessment arrangements have been changed to place greater emphasis in summative assessment on the use of teachers' judgements and avoid the creation of league tables.

the complex and sometimes technical arguments involved. These can be found, for example, in Gardner (2006) and Harlen (2007b). However, a brief overview of the impact of high stakes use of assessment results is given in Box 14.1.

When do we assess?

It may seem ominous to answer this question by saying 'all the time', or even 'at any time'. That reaction would indicate a view of assessment as something that causes anxiety – something we have to do but do not enjoy. Instead we should think of assessment as helping learning and therefore relevant at any point. Viewed in this way, it becomes part of the teaching. Take the case study of Chris's class, for instance (p. 14). At first reading it would be easy to assume that there was no assessment going on. There was no test at the end of the lesson, not even a quiz to find out what they had learnt. But Chris 'circulated the groups asking them to explain why they had chosen particular places'. She could then understand their ideas and help them to try them out. She was able to respond within the lesson and ensured that the children knew the purpose of their activities.

Of course teachers have to plan and prepare lessons. However, not everything can be pre-determined if challenges are to keep in step with children's development. There must always be room to adjust the pace – and even the direction – of the lesson to respond to children's ideas and skills. We can see that Graham (p. 26) did this when eavesdropping on the groups exploring soils. He introduced the notion of humus and the need for air in the soil, ideas prepared but used only when they were found to be necessary. He also helped them to recognise what was needed in a group report on their work. Formative assessment means taking action as appropriate but equally refraining from spending time on things the children already know or can do for themselves.

How do we assess?

We noted at the start of this chapter that assessment involves decisions about what information to gather, how to gather it, how to interpret it and how to report it. We deal in brief outline with these here, taking up points about how they apply specifically to science education in later chapters.

Deciding what information to gather

Formative assessment is close to learning, so the information required is everything that is relevant to learning at a particular time. The lesson goals, which will be communicated in some form to the children as discussed in Chapter 17, will be the main determinant of the information needed about cognitive development. So, Chris was finding out what her 6- and 7-year-olds knew about ice, what caused it to melt and what might prevent it from melting, and about their emerging ideas about a fair test. In the teacher's mind these lesson goals will be related to the broader concepts of change of state and development of inquiry and thinking skills identified as key concepts and processes in the curriculum. For helping learning information about the children's physical, emotional and motivational states will also be relevant. Children who are upset, anxious or unwell are unlikely to make the effort that learning often requires.

A teacher may review children's work five or six times a year in order to monitor progress but make a formal summative report only twice a year. The information required is much more general than what has been learnt in specific lessons and will relate to the broader statements of the curriculum, such as about 'the effects of heating and cooling on some everyday substances' (Box 3.7).

Deciding how to collect information

The main methods for collecting information for assessment are:

- observing children during regular work (this includes listening, questioning and discussing with them);
- studying the products of their regular work (including writing, drawings, artefacts and actions);
- observing children and/or studying the products of embedding special activities into the class work (such as concept-mapping, diagnostic tasks);
- giving tests (teacher-made or externally produced).

For formative assessment, regular work is a rich source of information about children's abilities and understanding which can be gathered through observation. But it is important to know what to look for in order to help progress. We give some ideas about this in Chapter 15.

Interpreting the information

Once the information is gathered it is interpreted in terms of what it means in relation to progress or achievement to date. This can be done in three main ways:

- by reference to a description of what it means to be able to do something or to explain something that indicates ideas at a certain level (criterion-referenced);

- by reference to what is usual for children of the same age and/or ability (norm-referenced);

- by reference to what each child was previously able to do (child-referenced or ipsative).

Box 14.2. illustrates what these mean in terms of an example, which is unlikely in practice but illustrates the principles.

Box 14.2 The bases of judgements in assessment

Suppose that a teacher wants to assess a child's ability in knocking nails into wood. This can be described in different ways:

- The teacher may have some expectation of the level of performance (knocking the nail in straight, using the hammer correctly, taking necessary safety precautions) and judge the child's performance in relation to these. The judgement is made in terms of the extent to which the child's performance meets the criteria; that is, it is criterion-referenced.

- Alternatively, the teacher may judge in terms of how the child performs at knocking in nails compared with other children of the same age and stage. If this is the case there will be a norm or average performance known for the age/stage group and any child can be described in relation to this as average, above average or below average, or more precisely identified if some quantitative measure has been obtained. (The result could be expressed as a 'knocking nails age' or a 'hammer manipulation' quotient!) The judgement arrived at in this way is called a norm-referenced assessment.

- A third possibility is that the teacher compares the child's present performance with what the same child could do on a previous occasion – in which case the assessment is child-referenced, or ipsative.

How is the information communicated?

When the purpose of the assessment is formative, to help learning, then the information will be used by those involved in the learning – the teacher and the child – to decide about what are the next steps to take and how to take them. The way in which information is communicated from teacher to pupil is discussed in Chapter 16, and the role that pupils can take in Chapter 17.

If the purpose is summative (to summarise learning), then the judgement of what has been achieved will be used for reporting this to those who need this information in addition to the child and his or her teacher: other teachers, including the head teacher, the parents, and others with an interest in the progress of the children. This can be done in various ways, such as by scores from tests, grades, marks, levels and discursive accounts. Tests scores give very little information about what children can and cannot do, being a summation over a diverse set of questions where the same total can be made up in different ways. A score also gives the impression of accuracy, which is far from being justified in consideration of the reliability and validity of tests (see later). Converting scores to levels or grades avoids this to a certain extent, and also serves to equalise the meaning of a level from year to year in the case of national tests in England, where new items are created each year.

In theory, reporting in terms of criteria which describe levels or grades can say something about what children have learnt, but when a single overall grade or level has to combine so many different domains it becomes almost meaningless. A profile giving information about different aspects is more meaningful. But expressing learning in terms of levels is only useful to those who know what they mean. For reporting to parents and pupils, the levels need to be explained or replaced by accounts of which the student can do (see Chapter 24).

How good is the assessment?

The reliability and validity of the results of assessment are key factors in deciding how effectively they serve their purpose. Box 14.3 summarises some points about these concepts.

For formative assessment, validity is paramount; the assessment must provide information about all relevant goals and attributes related to learning. Reliability is less important because of the ongoing nature of the process. The information is used to inform teaching in the situations in which it is gathered. Thus there is always quick feedback for the teacher and any misjudged intervention can be corrected. Thus considerations of reliability do not need to impact on validity. This is not to say that teachers do not need to consider how they gather and interpret information, but they do not need to be concerned about accuracy in judging it in terms of levels. Such accuracy is needed for summative teacher assessment, but formative assessment is concerned with the future, not with judgements about the past.

For summative assessment, however, reliability is important since its purpose is to provide information about where children have reached in their learning that parents and other teachers can depend upon. So attention has to be given to increasing reliability as far as possible without endangering validity.

Box 14.3 The concepts of reliability and validity

Reliability and validity

Reliability refers to how much you can depend on the result of an assessment; that is, how likely it would be that the same result would be obtained if the assessment were to be repeated. Reliability depends on the procedure that is used. Thus tests where children choose between fixed alternative answers, that can be machine marked, are more reliable than ones that ask children to provide answers which then require some judgement in the marking. However the latter may be a more valid test if the purpose is to find out what answers children can construct. *Validity* refers to the match between what is actually assessed and what it is intended should be assessed.

The interaction between reliability and validity

These aspects of an assessment are not independent of one another, since if reliability is low this means that various unintended factors are influencing the result and therefore what is being assessed is uncertain. However there is a limit to the extent that both reliability and validity can be high. To raise the reliability it is necessary to reduce the error by increasing the control of what is assessed and how. This often means focusing on outcomes that can be more accurately assessed, such as factual knowledge, where there is a clear right answer. But if the purpose is to assess skills and understanding, where we need children to generate rather than select answers, this would reduce the validity. Similarly to increase validity by including more open-ended tasks would reduce reliability because the marking would be less clear cut. There has to be a compromise and what this is depends on the purpose of the assessment.

The characteristics of formative and summative assessment

We now bring together the points about assessment for the two main purposes considered in this chapter – formative assessment and summative assessment.

Formative assessment

Formative assessment helps the process of learning. This statement is supported by both theories of learning and research into practice, as summarised in Box 14.4.

Formative assessment has to take account of all the aspects of children which affect their learning – not only the progress being made in knowledge and skills, but the effort put in and the other aspects of learning which are unspecified in the curriculum. It must be positive, indicating the next steps to take, not pointing out what is missing without identifying what to do about it. The teacher will have in mind the progression which (s)he intends for the child,

Box 14.4 Empirical and theoretical support for formative assessment

The best known of several reviews of research studies on classroom assessment was carried out by Paul Black and Dylan Wiliam (1998a). They found a considerable positive impact of assessment on children's learning when certain conditions were in place. The main conditions were that it:

- involved sharing goals of learning with pupils;

- helped pupils to know the standards to aim for;

- provided feedback to help pupils know how to improve or move on;

- involved pupils in the process of assessment and reflection of the information gained.

They also reported that 'improved formative assessment helps the (so-called) low attainers more than the rest, and so reduces the spread of attainment whilst also raising it overall' (Black and Wiliam, 1998b).

The theoretical reasons follow from the widely accepted theories of learning that emphasise the role of learners in constructing their own understanding. Formative assessment involves children recognising where they are in progress towards goals and participating in decisions about their next steps in learning. The feedback provided through formative assessment has a role in regulating learning so that the pace of moving forward is adjusted to ensure the active participation of the learners. As in other regulated processes, feedback into the system is the important mechanism for ensuring effective operation. Just as feedback from a thermostat allows the temperature of a room to be maintained within a particular range, so feedback about learning helps to ensure that new experiences are neither too difficult nor too easy for learners.

(Harlen 2006b)

and this will be the basis of the action taken. Thus formative assessment is not a pure criterion-referenced assessment; it is more ipsative or child-referenced. The teacher will be looking across several instances in which a particular skill or idea is being used and will see variations and possibly patterns in behaviour. It is these variations (which would be seen as sources of 'error' if the purpose of the assessment were summative) that, in the formative context, provide diagnostic information.

A further characteristic of formative assessment, which is increasingly recognised as central to it, is the involvement of children. The developing theory of educational assessment, and various models within it, emphasises the important role that children have to play in their own assessment as they come to understand the process, learn to work towards explicit standards and modify what they do in relation to constructive task-related feedback from teachers (Gipps 1994). We pick up these matters in Chapter 17.

So, to summarise, the characteristics of formative assessment are that it:

- takes place as an integral part of teaching;

- relates to progression in learning;

- depends on judgements which can be child-referenced or criterion-referenced;

- provides feedback that leads to action supporting further learning;

- uses methods which protect validity rather than reliability;

- uses information from children's performance in a variety of contexts;

- involves children in assessing their performance and deciding their next steps.

There is a good deal of common ground between formative assessment and learning through inquiry – both serve to develop learning with understanding and to enable pupils to take responsibility for identifying what they need to do to achieve the goals of their activities. It could almost be said that inquiry requires formative assessment. The additional features of formative assessment – the provision of formative feedback and the involvement of pupils in self- and peer assessment – all support active engagement in learning and encourage pupils to take ownership of their learning and progress.

Summative assessment

Summative assessment has an important but different role in children's education. Its purpose is to give a summary of achievement at various times, as required. As noted in Chapter 18, it can be achieved by summing up (summarising evidence already used for formative purposes) or checking up (giving a test or special task) or a combination of these. Since its purpose is to report achievement to parents, other teachers, children, school governors, etc., then reliability of the judgements is important and the criteria have to be used uniformly. Thus, if the summary is based on a review of information gathered during teaching, some form of moderation, or procedure for quality assurance, is required. So the characteristics of summative assessment are that it:

- takes place at certain intervals when achievement has to be reported;

- relates to progression in learning against public criteria;

- enables results for different children to be combined for various purposes because they are based on the same criteria;

- requires methods which are as reliable as possible without endangering validity;

- involves some quality assurance procedures;

- should be based on evidence relating to the full range of learning goals.

The difference between assessment for these two purposes should be kept very clearly in mind, especially when both are carried out by teachers. It is too often assumed that all assessment by teachers is formative or that assessment carried out frequently in whatever way is formative. Unless the assessment is used to help the ongoing learning, this is not the case. Where this happens the true value of formative assessment will not be realised.

Summary

This chapter has defined assessment as the process of deciding, collecting and interpreting information about children's learning and skills. It has considered the why, when and how of assessment and the characteristics of assessment for formative and summative purposes. The main points have been:

- how assessment is best carried out depends on its purpose;

- the purposes considered in this book are assessment for a formative purpose (assessment *for* learning) and assessment for a summative purpose (assessment *of* learning);

- testing is one way of conducting assessment; it is not the same as assessment;

- information about children's achievements can be interpreted by comparing it with norms, criteria of performance or the child's previous achievement;

- depending on the purpose of the assessment, different emphasis is laid on reliability (dependability of the assessment result) and validity (how well what is assessed reflects what is needed to serve the purpose of the assessment).

Further reading

Harlen, W. (2005) Teachers' summative practices and assessment for learning – tensions and synergies, *The Curriculum Journal* 16 (2): 207–23.

Wiliam, D. (2008) Quality in assessment, in S. Swaffield (ed.) *Unlocking Assessment,* London: David Fulton, Chapter 8.

15

Gathering information to help learning

Introduction

As we noted at the end of the last chapter, formative assessment is a continuing cyclic process which informs ongoing teaching and helps learners' active engagement in learning. The cycle involves the collection of evidence about learning, the interpretation of that evidence in terms of progress towards the goals of the work, the identification of appropriate next steps and decisions about how to take them. This chapter makes a start on discussing how to put formative assessment into practice by discussing how to gather information about the children's ideas and inquiry skills in order to use this to help them achieve the goals and move on.

Setting the scene

This chapter is about gaining information about children's thinking – their scientific ideas, inquiry skills and attitudes. Before we discuss particular strategies and techniques for doing this it is important to consider two prerequisites: clarity about goals and establishing a classroom climate in which children feel comfortable about expressing their thoughts without fear that they will be 'wrong'.

Having goals in mind

Clarity of goals is a pivotal requirement for all assessment; the difficulty that this often presents to primary teachers, in science, accounts for a good deal of poor practice in assessment in this area. Teachers need to know what ideas and skills the children should be developing before they can find out about what relevant ideas and skills they already have. But sometimes the focus is so much on what the children will be *doing* that what they are intended to *learn* from it is left a little hazy. Science learning goals can be expressed with different degrees of specificity and while 'attainment targets' or other ways of specifying intended learning in national curricula have helped to communicate overall goals it is still up to the teacher to identify the specific lesson goals. These must be clear if assessment is to be used to help learning.

Broad aims such as 'ability to plan and conduct a scientific investigation' or 'understanding the diversity and adaptation of organisms' are too general to be achieved in a single lesson or even a set of lessons on a particular topic. The goals of a specific lesson might include the understanding of how the structure of particular plants or animals is suited to the places where they are found. This will contribute to a broader goal of understanding how living organisms in general are suited to their habitats, but achieving this understanding will depend on looking at a variety of organisms, which will be the subject of other lessons with their own specific goals. Similarly, skills such as planning a scientific investigation are developed not in one lesson, but in different contexts in different lessons and topics.

The learning environment

Everything that happens in the classroom takes place within the ethos or social climate created by the teacher. Before a teacher can have any chance of gaining access to children's ideas and skills, it is necessary to establish a classroom climate in which children feel that is it 'safe' to express the ideas they have and in which these ideas are valued and taken seriously, not disregarded or ridiculed.

The point is well made by Keogh and Naylor (2004):

> As adults we realize how close the connection is between self-esteem and having our ideas accepted and valued. Children are no different. If we want children to 'think out loud', to be creative in their thinking and to argue about alternative possibilities, then we need to provide the kind of learning environment in which they feel comfortable to do that. They need to know that they can make mistakes or give wrong answers and still feel good about themselves.
>
> (Keogh and Naylor 2004: 18)

Such an atmosphere cannot be created overnight. It results from teachers showing by example how to respect others' ideas, how to be sensitive to others' feelings and to value effort and attitudes of perseverance, responsibility, and openness (see Box 11.1). An environment that lays the foundation for continued learning should not only accept, but also motivate, change in ideas and ways of thinking. Above all we need to create a desire to learn, to understand things around, and to make this enjoyable.

Gaining access to children's ideas and inquiry skills

Against this general background of a supporting classroom climate, there are various strategies that teachers can use for eliciting pupils' ideas and finding out about their inquiry skills. These are listed in Box 15.1 and each illustrated in the following sections. Some of these methods are useful for collecting information about either skills or ideas. For instance, concept mapping has great potential for finding out children's ideas, whilst observing actions provided rich information about skills and attitudes. However, most are capable of providing information about both, and since inquiry-based leaning will involve children in developing their understanding through using inquiry skills, it makes sense to consider what can be learnt about both in the same situation where this applies.

Box 15.1 Ways of gaining access to children's ideas and inquiry skills

- Questioning – using open and person-centred questions.
- Observing – focusing on significant indicators of development.
- Asking for writing or drawings that communicate what pupils think.
- Involving children in concept mapping.
- Initiating debate with concept cartoons.
- Eavesdropping and discussing words.
- Using technology to discuss specific activities with children.

Questioning

We discussed the form and content of teachers' questions in Chapter 12. Here we are particularly interested in those questions that reveal children's ideas and inquiry skills. Consider, for instance, a situation in which a teacher has provided lots of home-made and other musical instruments for children to explore as a preliminary to more structured activities aimed at the idea that sound is caused by objects vibrating. To find out the ideas the children already have, the teacher might ask questions such as:

1. What is happening when you pluck the string and hear the sound?
2. What causes the guitar to make a sound?
3. Why does the sound change when you shorten the string?
4. Explain why you are able to make the bottle make a sound by blowing across the top.

Or the teacher might ask:

5. What do you think makes the sound when you pluck the string?
6. What are your ideas about how the guitar makes a sound?
7. What do you think is the reason for the bottle making a sound when you blow across the top?
8. What are your ideas about why you get different sounds when you shorten the string?

Or perhaps:

9. What difference do you see in the drum when it makes a sound?
10. What do you think will happen if you make the string even shorter?
11. How can you show me what makes a difference to the note you get by blowing across the top of the bottle?
12. What could you do to find out if the way you pluck the string makes a difference?

In the first set (1–4) the questions are open ones (see Box 12.2), but they ask directly for *the* answer, not the children's ideas about what is happening. These are subject-centred questions (see Box 12.3) and do not specifically ask the children to express their ideas. By contrast, the second set (5–8) are expressed so as to ask for the children's own ideas, with no suggestion that there is a right answer. They are person-centred open questions. All the children should be able to answer the second set, while only those who feel that they can give the right answer will attempt to answer the first set. Thus the open, person-centred questions are preferred for eliciting children's ideas.

The questions in the third set (9–14) are also expressed as open, person-centred questions, but they are more likely to lead to action and to the use of process skills. To answer them, children have to use or describe how they would use inquiry skills – observation, prediction, planning. Although the actions taken would imply some ideas about the cause of the effects, these questions are more useful for finding out about children's ways of observing or investigating than for eliciting their ideas.

A further point about questioning that should be recalled in this context is the importance of giving children time to answer. The 'wait time' (see Box 12.6) is necessary not only to allow for the children to think and to formulate their answer but to convey the message that the teacher is really interested in their ideas and will listen to them carefully. It also slows down the discussion, giving the teacher time to phrase thoughtful questions and the children time to think before answering. The whole exchange is then more productive in terms of giving teachers access to children's real understanding and not just their first superficial thoughts.

Observing

There is a great deal of information to be gained, particularly about children's inquiry skills from observing how they go about their investigations or seek evidence from secondary sources. The main problem is one of logistics – how to observe each and every child in relation to a range of skills and attitudes. This is an impossible task and is not to be expected. It is made manageable by planning and focusing. Not all skills will be used in every inquiry and so the focus can be on the particular skills that are the goals of the lesson. Moreover, while in theory everything a child does can give some evidence of his or her thinking, some things are more useful than others. So it helps to be able to pick out the behaviours of most significance. This can be done with the help of 'indicators', which describe aspects of behaviour that can be taken as evidence of certain skills being used. Indicators can be even more useful if they describe different levels of development of the skills.

The starting point in developing such indicators, say in relation to skills of observation, is to ask the question: 'What kinds of actions would indicate that a child is observing?' The first thought might be that the child seems to be paying attention to details, which might show through noticing similarities and differences between things, perhaps using senses other than sight. Then the question: 'How would this be different for younger than for older children?' For the younger child the similarities and differences might be just the obvious ones, while

Box 15.2 Indicators of development of skill in gathering evidence by observing and using information sources

Things children do that indicate gathering evidence by observing and using information sources:

1. Identify obvious differences and similarities between objects and materials.

2. Make use of several senses in exploring objects or materials.

3. Identify relevant differences of detail between objects or materials and identify points of similarity between objects where differences are more obvious than similarities.

4. Use their senses appropriately and extend the range of sight using a hand lens or microscope as necessary.

5. Take an adequate series of observations to answer the question or test the prediction being investigated.

6. Take steps to ensure that the results obtained are as accurate as they can reasonably be and repeat observations.

7. Regularly and spontaneously use printed and electronic information sources to check or supplement their investigations.

Box 15.3 Indicators of development of skill in questioning, predicting and planning

Things children do that indicate questioning, predicting and planning:

1. Readily ask a variety of questions and participate effectively in discussing how their questions can be answered.

2. Attempt to make a prediction relating to a problem or question even if it is based on pre-conceived ideas.

3. Suggest a useful approach to answering a question or testing a prediction by investigation, even if details are lacking or need further thought.

4. Identify the variable that has to be changed and the things which should be kept the same for a fair test.

5. Succeed in planning a fair test using the support of a framework of questions.

6. Identify what to look for or measure to obtain a result in an investigation.

7. Distinguish from many observations those which are relevant to the problem in hand and explain the reason.

Box 15.4 Indicators of development of skill in interpreting evidence and drawing conclusions

Things children do that indicate interpreting evidence and drawing conclusions:

1. Discuss what they find in relation to their initial questions or compare their findings with their earlier predictions/expectations.

2. Notice associations between changes in one variable and another.

3. Identify patterns or trends in their observations or measurements.

4. Try to explain simple patterns in their observations or measurements.

5. Use patterns to draw conclusions and attempt to explain them.

6. Use scientific concepts in drawing or evaluating conclusions.

7. Recognise that there may be more than one explanation which fits the evidence and that any conclusions are tentative and may have to be changed in the light of new evidence.

Box 15.5 Indicators of development of skills in communicating and reflecting

Things children do that indicate communicating and reflecting:

1. Talk freely about their activities and the ideas they have, with or without making a written record.

2. Listen to others' ideas and look at their results.

3. Use drawings, writing, models, paintings to present their ideas and findings.

4. Use tables, graphs and charts when these are suggested to record and organise results.

5. Use appropriate scientific language in reporting and show understanding of the terms used.

6. Choose a form for recording or presenting results which is both considered and justified in relation to the type of information and the audience.

7. Compare their actual procedures after the event with what was planned and make suggestions for improving their ways of investigating.

for the older child we would expect more detail, more accuracy in observation, through using measurement and checking results.

Given more information about the development of skill in observation, these statements could be refined into a list of indicators arranged as far as possible in the sequence of development. 'As far as possible' is a necessary qualification because there is not likely to be an exact and invariable sequence the same for all children, but it is helpful to have a rough idea. As a result of this kind

Box 15.6 Indicators of development in willingness to consider evidence in relation to ideas

Things children do that indicate the scientific attitude of willingness to consider evidence in relation to ideas:

1. Recognise when the evidence does not fit a conclusion based on expectations.
2. Modify ideas enough to incorporate new evidence or arguments but resist relinquishing them.
3. Check parts of the evidence which do not fit an overall pattern or conclusion.
4. Show willingness to consider alternative ideas which may fit the evidence.
5. Relinquish or change ideas after considering the evidence.
6. Spontaneously seek other ideas which may fit the evidence rather than accepting the first which seems to fit.
7. Recognise that ideas can be changed by thinking and reflecting about different ways of making sense of the same evidence.

Box 15.7 Indicators of development in sensitivity to living things and the environment

Things children do that indicate the scientific attitude of sensitivity to living things and the environment:

1. Take part in caring for living things in the classroom or around the school, with supervision.
2. Provide care for living things in the classroom or around the school with minimum supervision.
3. Show care for the local environment by behaviour which protects it from litter, damage and disturbance.
4. Adhere to a code of behaviour which avoids damage to the environment on visits outside the school; replacing disturbed stones, not collecting plants, and returning animals caught for study to where they were found where possible.
5. Take responsibility, and initiative where necessary, for ensuring that living things in and around the classroom are cared for.
6. Take part in developing a code of care for the environment, with reasons for the actions identified.
7. Help in ensuring that others know about and observe such a code of care.

of thinking and using shared experience of how children's skills develop, the set of statements of 'indicators of gathering evidence by observing and using secondary sources' given in Box 15.2 was created. Boxes 15.3–15.7 give the result of similar exercises for the other groups of inquiry skills and attitudes identified in Chapter 7.

Using developmental indicators

In all these lists the earlier statements indicate skills or attitudes that are *likely* to be developed before the ones later in the list. However, as mentioned, this will not necessarily be the case for every child. It should also be noted that there are no 'levels', grades or stages suggested: just a sequence expected for children in the primary, and perhaps early secondary, years. For formative assessment it is not necessary to tie indicators to grades or levels; all that is required is to see where children are and what further progress they can make. The numbers against the statements here are for convenience and do not signify levels in the same way as, for instance, the levels of the National Curriculum.

The function of the indicators is quite different from the level descriptions of attainment targets. They provide more detail of what to look for than the level descriptions of attainment targets in order to serve two important functions. First, they focus attention on particular aspects of behaviour that signify a skill or attitude in action. Knowing what to look for makes observing much easier. Second, because they are arranged in a rough sequence of progressive development, they give an indication of where a child has reached. To make progress the child is likely to need to consolidate these behaviours and begin to develop the ones later in the list. This use of the indicators is further considered in Chapter 16.

Children's writing and drawings

In the discussion of questioning it was implicit that the questions and answers were oral. Alternatively in some circumstances children may write or produce a drawing, or set of drawings to express their ideas and inquiry skills. This can give the teacher a view of the full range of ideas in the class and a permanent record for each child which can be perused at a later time. The same points made about oral questions apply, however, to the form of the questions that the teacher asks in setting children's written work and drawings in order to find out their ideas and skills; open, person-centred questions are necessary.

Examples of children's drawings which reveal their ideas have been given in Chapter 5. It is not easy for anyone to draw abstract things such as ideas about melting, force or evaporation. The use of labels and annotation as a commentary on what is happening is necessary, but the drawing is essential for conveying the image that the child has in mind. For example, the drawing in Figure 15.1 by a 7-year-old shows very clearly that the child considered the direct action of the sun as important in causing the disappearance (by evaporation) of water from a tank.

In this example we see that the value for opening access to children's ideas depends on how the drawing task is set. Merely asking for a drawing to show the water levels in the tank would not necessarily be useful in this respect. A request for a drawing of 'what you think makes the water level change' is more fruitful.

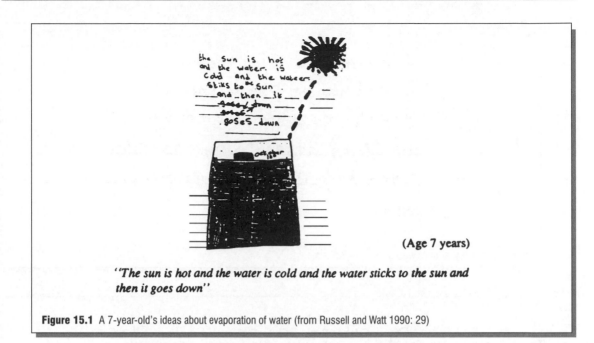

"The sun is hot and the water is cold and the water sticks to the sun and then it goes down"

Figure 15.1 A 7-year-old's ideas about evaporation of water (from Russell and Watt 1990: 29)

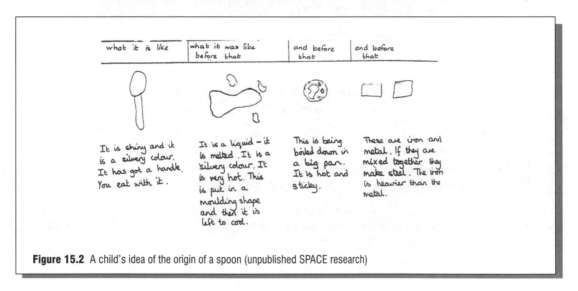

Figure 15.2 A child's idea of the origin of a spoon (unpublished SPACE research)

Another kind of drawing that helps children to show their ideas is to create a 'strip cartoon' or a series of drawings across time, as in the example of the representation of the stages in the manufacture of a spoon in Figure 15.2. In this case the teacher asked the children to draw what they thought the object was like just before it was in its present form, then what it was like just before that, and so on.

While drawings can usually be made by even the youngest children, writing is most helpful when children become at ease in doing it. Figure 15.3 was written by a 6-year-old to explain why the condensation from her breath on a cold window went away.

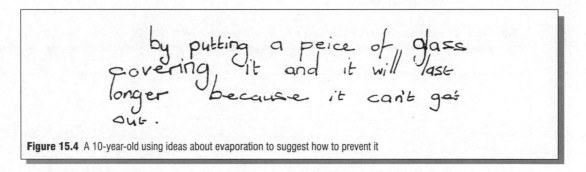

I went out side and I
breathed on the windows
and My cold breath comes out
and if you look at it you can see it
algo a way it goes when it gets so
warm.

Figure 15.3 A 6-year-old's writing about condensation

by putting a peice of glass
covering it and it will last
longer because it can't gas
out.

Figure 15.4 A 10-year-old using ideas about evaporation to suggest how to prevent it

In Figure 15.4, a 10-year-old's answer to how to slow down evaporation of water from a tank indicates the value of not just asking for writing about what has been observed but posing problems where ideas have to be used.

Children's written work also provides information about their inquiry skills, particularly in the case of older children. Again, it is important for the task to be set so that the children are required to describe what they have done, or plan to do. The examples in Figures 15.5 to 15.7 illustrate the value of the products. They all come from Paterson (1987: 17–20).

In Figure 15.5 two predictions are made, both of which can be tested by investigation. The first prediction is based on the everyday experience that it is easier to see things which are closer than when they are far away. However, the basis of the second prediction, about people wearing glasses, is less easy to follow and deserves discussion.

Figure 15.6 shows a child's reflection on an investigation of how far away the sound of a coin being dropped can be heard. Not only does she identify the deficiencies of the investigation carried out, but shows some aspects of planning, including the ingenious use of an instrument to measure the sound level.

Figure 15.7 shows very detailed observation, using four senses, carefully and vibrantly described so that the reader can almost share the experience.

> Our prediction is that people will be able to complete the test when they are much closer to the chart and the chart will be not so clear as the first test when they are further away from the chart. We also think that people with glasses will see better than other people because they have more focus in their glass lenses.

Figure 15.5 An 11-year-old's prediction as part of planning an investigation

> If I did this again I would try to think of a way to test the sound and not just guess and try to think of more surfaces and try with different coins at different heights. On the sound I have got two ideas, one, see how far away you can here it drop, and two, get a tape recorder with a sound level indicator.

Figure 15.6 A 9-year-old's reflection on her investigation

> When we examined a lychee we found out that the skin or peel had tiny hairs on it. When we held it quite far away the whole fruit looked like a hard and over grown rasberry. When we tasted the peel it was like an advocardo. The peel was all either red or yellow as I just said the red tasted like an advocardo but the yellow was reaily diausting this ment that the fruit is ripe when it is red or yellow. Then when we took the peel of totltaly we found that there was another skin but this was transparent. When we took that skin of we found that the juice was in some sort of segments like an orange. Then we tasted the flesh and it was lovely. After that we found a stone or seed in the middle so we cut it open and it
>
> went brown after a few seconds then we smelt it and it smelt like a conker (or Horse Chessnut)

Figure 15.7 Observation recorded by two 10-year-olds

Concept maps

Concept maps are another kind of drawing that is particularly useful for finding out children's ideas. Concept maps are diagrammatic ways of representing conceptual links between words. There are certain rules to apply which are very simple and readily grasped by children of 5 or 6. If we take the words 'ice' and 'water' we can relate them to each other in this way by connecting them with an arrow to signify a relationship between them. If we write 'melts to give' on the

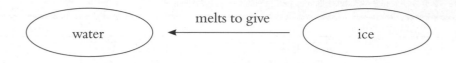

arrow, we have a way of representing the proposition that ice melts to give water, but not vice versa:

We can add to this by linking other words and so forming a map.

Asking children to draw their ideas about how things are linked up provides insight into the way they envisage how one thing causes another. The starting point is to list words about the topic the children are working on and then ask them to draw arrows and to write 'joining' words on them. Figure 15.8 shows the list and the map which a 6-year-old, Lennie, drew after some activities about heat and its effect on various things. It is possible to spot from this that Lennie has not yet distinguished heat from temperature but that he has some useful ideas about what heat can do. As with all diagrams, it is advisable to discuss them with the child to be sure of the meaning intended.

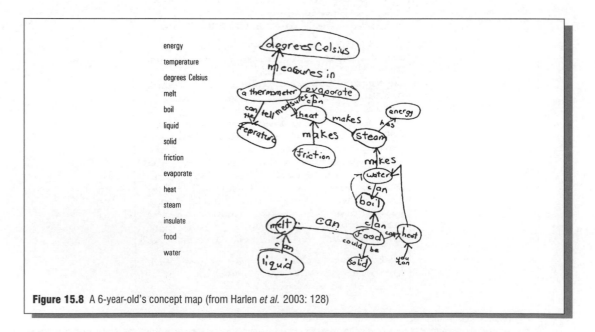

Figure 15.8 A 6-year-old's concept map (from Harlen *et al.* 2003: 128)

Concept cartoons

Concept Cartoons were devised by Naylor and Keogh (2000). One example is given in Figure 15.9, but a wide range of cartoons have been published and used both with trainee teachers and primary children. Their key features include:

- representing scientific ideas in everyday situations wherever possible, so that connections are made between scientific ideas and everyday life;

- using minimal amount of text, in order to make the ideas accessible to learners with limited literacy skills;

- using simple cartoon-style presentation which is visually appealing and which empowers teachers and learners to create their own concept cartoons;

- using published research to identify common areas of misunderstanding, which then provide a focus for the concept cartoon.

(Keogh and Naylor 1998: 14)

Concept cartoons have various uses including finding out children's ideas and skills. For this purpose, children can discuss the ideas suggested by the cartoon characters either in small groups or as a whole class and talk about why they may agree or disagree with the suggestions, or give

Figure 15.9 Concept cartoons: ideas about germinating seeds (from Keogh and Naylor 2000: 30)

their own ideas. In many cases the situations have no 'right' answer and in all cases the discussion of pros and cons of the suggestions made requires some explanation of why one or another view could be supported. The situations and speech bubbles can refer to how to conduct an investigation, such as 'How are we going to find out if sunshine makes any difference to how quickly these ice cubes melt?' with different suggested ways of doing this.

Eavesdropping and discussing words

Concept cartoons provide a very useful way of setting up small group discussions that allow the teacher to listen in to the conversation without taking part. Setting groups to work on a combined concept map serves a similar purpose. Children-only discussions are valuable in freeing children to express their ideas in their own words. To quote Douglas Barnes:

> The teacher's absence removes from their work the usual source of authority; they cannot turn to him [sic] to solve dilemmas. Thus … the children not only formulate hypotheses, but are compelled to evaluate them for themselves. This they can do in only two ways: by testing them against their existing views of 'how things go in the world', and by going back to 'the evidence'.
>
> (Barnes 1976: 29)

So 'listening in' can help the teacher to find out how children are reasoning and using evidence in their arguments as well as about the words they use. When the children are talking directly to each other they use words that they and their peers understand. These, as well as the explanations and reasons that they give to each other can give clues as to their ideas. For example, in their discussions of melting, children often appear to confuse it with dissolving. Being alerted to this, the teacher can take some action to find out whether the children have not distinguished between the processes of melting and dissolving or just not realised which is called melting and which is dissolving. In such cases it is important to explore the children's meaning for the words in order to know what their ideas are. It is useful to ask them to give an example of melting or to say how they would try, for instance, to make sugar melt. This would indicate whether melting is different in their mind from dissolving. (Other points about using scientific words are discussed in Chapter 8.)

Using technology to discuss specific activities with children

The ready availability of digital cameras has opened up a new set of opportunities for exploring children's thinking. The speed with which the photographs can be displayed on a computer screen or an interactive white board means that teachers can study images of children within a short time of the event, discuss with the children their thinking at the time, or preserve the images for perusal later. An example was described by Lias and Thomas (2003) in Primary Science Review working with 8-year-olds:

> During the activity (making a 'circuits game' for practising multiplication tables) we took several digital photographs of the children making and testing their circuits to display later. Because there was a PC, an LCD projector and an interactive whiteboard in the room, we decided to show the photographs to the children at the end of the activity … The captured images of particular events

helped children to recall what they were doing at a particular time and prevented confusion over which event was being discussed. They also helped to keep the children's minds focused and provided a visual scaffold to support their descriptions and explanations. Compared with previous occasions, the children answered questions far more confidently and fluently, needed far less prompting and support, and their responses were far more detailed and complete.

(Lias and Thomas 2003: 18)

Summary

This chapter has discussed ways of gathering information about children's scientific ideas and inquiry skills to use in helping learning. All the methods are ones that teachers can use during regular science activities in the classroom or elsewhere. The main points have been:

- it is important to be clear about the specific goals of the children's activities in order to focus the information gathering;

- also important is a classroom ethos in which children feel comfortable in expressing their ideas;

- the main strategies that are useful in gathering information from regular activities are questioning, observation, testing writing or drawing tasks that reveal their ideas and skills, concept mapping, discussing concept cartoons, eavesdropping and discussing words and using technology to reflect on particular activities;

- most useful questions for gaining access to children's ideas and skills are open and person-centred;

- indicators of development help both in identifying significant aspects of behaviour relating to skills and attitudes and in suggesting what action might be taken.

Further reading

Goldsworthy, A. (2003) *Raising Attainment in Primary Science: Assessment, Monitoring and Evaluation,* Oxford: GHPD.

16

Formative feedback

Introduction

The use of assessment to help learning depends on information being fed back into the processes of teaching and learning. This chapter is about who is involved, what to feed back and how best to do it. We begin with a model of formative assessment which represents the various actions that are involved for teacher and pupils. Having considered the goals and collection of information in Chapter 15 we take up here the matters of how to interpret the information and use it to identify action to take in relation to adapting teaching or deciding the next steps for children. We consider the use of developmental indicators in guiding decisions about next steps for children and how to provide feedback that has a positive impact on their learning.

Feedback in the context of formative assessment

In Chapter 14 we described formative assessment as an ongoing process in which information is gathered and used by teacher and pupils to regulate teaching and learning and ensure children's active engagement in learning. It can be represented as a cyclic process, as in Figure 16.1 where A, B and C represent activities through which pupils work towards the goals. If we break into the continuing cycle of events at activity A, information gathered there is interpreted in terms of progress towards the goals of the work. Following the outer arrows round the cycle clockwise, this facilitates the identification of appropriate next steps and decisions about how to take them (leading to activity B). The cycle is repeated and the effects of decisions at one time are assessed at a later time as part of the ongoing process.

In Chapter 15 we considered the importance of goals and ways of gathering information. In this chapter, continuing round the second part of cycle, we consider the interpretation of the information, the decision about next steps and how to take them.

Describing the process in this way makes it appear far more formal and teacher-directed than is the case in reality. The actions indicated by the boxes in Figure 16.1 are not 'stages' in a lesson or necessarily conscious decisions made by the teacher. They represent a framework for thinking about what is involved in focusing on what and how children are learning and using this to help further learning. But of course it is the children who have to take the action; only they can do the learning. For this reason they are at the centre of the process and the two–headed arrows indicate

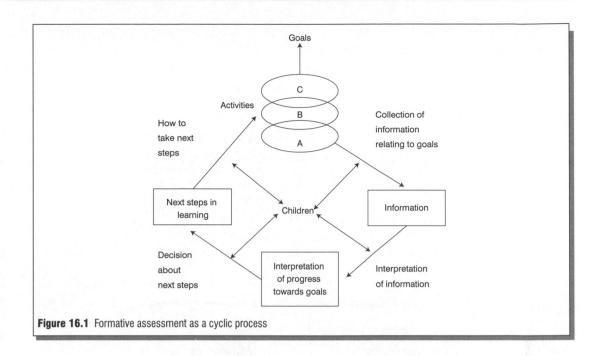

Figure 16.1 Formative assessment as a cyclic process

their role as both providers and receivers of information. We look at various aspects of pupils' roles in self- and peer assessment in Chapter 17.

Here we start from the point where information has been gathered, perhaps in one of the ways suggested in Chapter 15. Now it needs to be interpreted in terms of where the pupils are in relation to achieving the goals and what next steps are appropriate to improve or move on.

Interpreting information about inquiry skills

The indicators of development in inquiry skills, introduced in Chapter 15 (Boxes 15.2 to 15.7), provide the opportunity to decide where children have reached in development of the skills that are the goals of the activity. A useful way of using these indicators in deciding next steps is to regard them as questions to be put to the evidence gathered by observation or from written work. So we could ask, in relation to 'observing and using information sources' for instance, what information is there that the children:

- identify obvious difference and similarities between objects and materials?
- make use of several senses in exploring objects or materials and so on?

To identify next steps, the information about the observations the children are making in their work is scanned in relation to each question in the list. Probably the answer to the first few question will be 'yes' and there will be a point where the answers turn into 'no'. It is this point that suggests where development has reached and so where the next steps are required. Where answers are a qualified 'yes' (it happens sometimes, but not always) it is useful to consider situations where the indicator has and has not been met, leading to identifying the kind of help needed. These are in fact the most useful answers since they identify the points where the development is fluid. A 'no' answer signals where future help is needed, focusing first on using the skills in more familiar situations.

Although it is not advisable to judge from one event, for the purpose of illustrating the approach we can use the example shown in Figure 16.2.

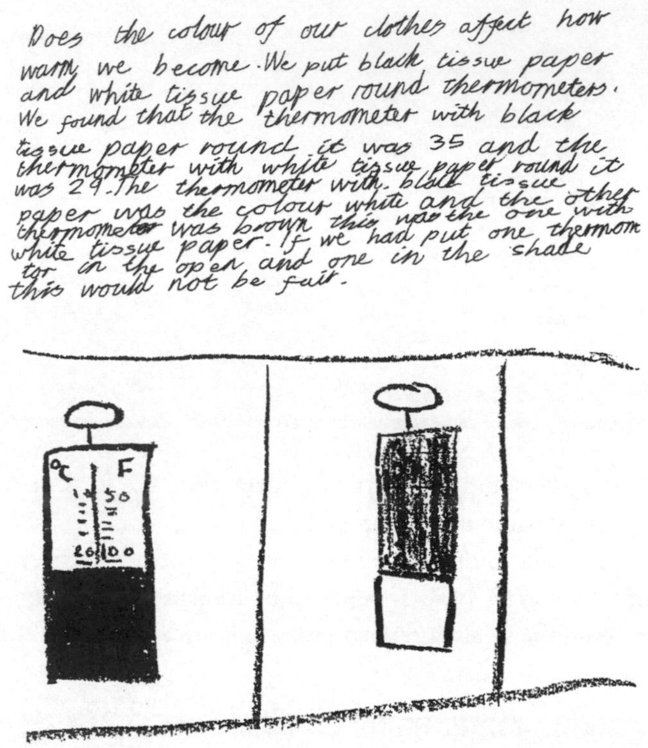

Does the colour of our clothes affect how warm we become. We put black tissue paper and white tissue paper round thermometers. We found that the thermometer with black tissue paper round it was 35 and the thermometer with white tissue paper round it was 29. The thermometer with black tissue paper was the colour white and the other thermometer was brown this was the one with white tissue paper. If we had put one thermometer in the open and one in the shade this would not be fair.

Figure 16.2 A 9-year-old's account of her group's investigation

The account gives a good idea of what the children did and we will assume that the teacher was able to observe the investigation as well as reading the account. How might this information be interpreted in relation to the child's process skills? Box 16.1 suggests some interpretations and identification of next steps resulting from using the developmental indicators in Boxes 15.2 to 15.5.

A similar approach can be used for attitudes, but this requires information to be brought together from a very wide range of activities and it's not helpful to discuss just one event. Suggestions in Chapter 10 for helping the development of inquiry skills may be useful in deciding how to take the next steps.

Interpreting information about children's ideas

A good deal of information about children's ideas will come from their explanations of events, whether written, drawn or spoken. To interpret this information it is first essential to be clear about what the evidence is. We have to be careful to distinguish evidence from interpretation

Box 16.1 Interpretation of information in Figure 16.2 using developmental indicators for inquiry skills

Inquiry skills	*Interpretation of information using indicators*
• Gathering evidence by observing and using information sources (Box 15.2)	Some information in relation to statement 3: identifying differences… Apparently only one measurement (statement 5). No information from this investigation in relation to statement 4. *Next steps:* not enough information here to inform a decision.
• Questioning, predicting and planning (Box 15.3)	Information that a useful approach taken (3) and the variable to be changed was appropriately selected (4) (although not clear how much of the planning was the children's own); some variables controlled. *Next steps:* give further opportunities for child to plan a fair test independently.
• Interpreting evidence and drawing conclusions (Box 15.4)	Results not interpreted in terms of initial question (1) and no explicit connection between the colour of the paper and the temperature (2). *Next steps:* question child about relation between findings and question being investigated. Ensure children understand reason for their investigations.
• Communicating and reflecting (Box 15.5)	(Assume information for statements 1 and 2). Evidence of use of drawing to show what was done, but not findings (3). *Next steps:* discuss with child how to make drawings more informative and how to structure reports of investigations.

and to be as objective as possible about what the child actually says, writes, draws or does. This means taking a scientific approach to interpretation – clarifying the questions we are trying to answer ('What are the children's ideas about …?') and the information that we can use to answer it. Looking at the process in this way reinforces the point that any conclusions that are drawn (about next steps) are tentative and subject to change in the light of further evidence.

For example, if as part of exploring light sources children are asked to draw things that they think give out light, and they include a mirror and the moon in their drawings, the *evidence* is what is in the drawings. The *interpretation* might be that the children do not distinguish between things that give out light and those that reflect it. Before deciding what action to take it would be wise to check this interpretation. Is this really the problem, or did the children mistake 'things that are bright' for 'things that give out light?' Is there supporting evidence from other things the children have done or from what they say about the things they have drawn? Is it reasonable for these children to be expected to know that the light from the moon is reflected light? If the interpretation is confirmed, the next step becomes clear – to provide opportunity for children to test their ideas by exploring what happens to a mirror in the dark, compared with a torch or other source of light, for example.

Similarly, if a child produces the drawing in Figure 16.3 of an electric circuit with two bulbs, it is necessary to make sure that the connection to the left-hand bulb is not just a mistake in drawing. If the child does not see anything wrong, then the next step might be to test the circuit in practice, following the diagram carefully.

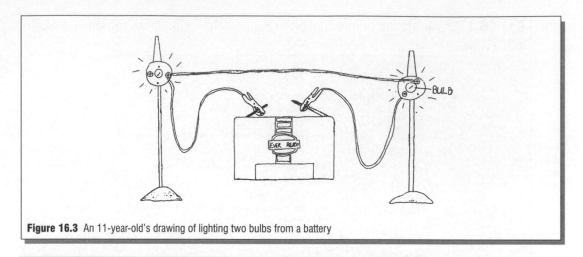

Figure 16.3 An 11-year-old's drawing of lighting two bulbs from a battery

Box 16.2 Generic indicators of development of scientific ideas

1. Little attempt to explain – description only.

2. Attempt to explain but using a preconceived non-scientific idea (about …).

3. Reference to the idea (about …) but without showing how it explains the event.

4. Uses the idea (about …) to explain a familiar event but not related ones newly encountered.

5. Uses the idea (about …) to explain situations different from those encountered before.

6. Refers to a larger idea (about…) and how it explains a number of linked events.

7. Uses the larger idea (about …) to predict events not encountered before.

Identifying development in ideas

In principle it would be possible to use what is known from research about the development of children's scientific ideas to describe development in terms of indicators, as we have done for inquiry skills in Chapter 15. It would require a very large number of lists, of course, and would be unmanageable. A more practical way is to consider the overall development of ideas as they grow from 'small' ones (which explain particular events or phenomena) to 'bigger' ones (relevant to a range of linked phenomena). In helping this development the aim is to help the children to construct more widely applicable ideas that are shared by others in making sense of the world around.

For each idea, then, we can think of a sequence in the different ways it is used in giving explanations, reflecting the 'growth' of the idea. The generic indicators of development in Box 16.2 can be applied to particular ideas by inserting them in 'about …'

To exemplify this approach, we refer back to the children's work in Figures 5.6 and 5.7 (p. 72). There the children were giving their explanations of how the drum makes a sound and how we hear it. The two ideas that the teacher was probing were that 'sound is caused by vibration' and that 'we hear sound when the vibrations reach our ears'. We consider the evidence in relation to the first of these.

In Figure 5.6 the child claims to give an explanation but it is really just a description (the sound is very loud). So the next step is perhaps to give some experience of what is the difference between a drum that is making a sound and one that is not. In Figure 5.7 the word 'vibration' is used directly in relation to the production of a sound. The child has used the idea about sound being caused by vibration in the situation given (indicator 4). We have no evidence that this can be applied in other situations (indicator 5). So the next step might be to give experience that enables the child to see if the idea explains other events where sound is produced. Identifying useful next steps is the purpose of formative assessment; as noted in Chapter 15, there is no need to pin down the children as working at a particular level. Suggestions in Chapter 9 may be helpful in deciding how to take the steps identified.

Feedback

The essential feature that makes assessment formative is that information from the evidence gathered is used to help children take the next steps in learning. This requires information to be fed back into the teaching–learning process. Teachers and pupils can both use this information, so we have to consider feedback to the teacher and feedback to the children.

Swaffield (2008) suggests that there are three models of feedback which are related to different models of learning. When learning is equated with 'being taught', feedback is one-way, from teacher to pupil. Learning viewed as being actively constructed by the learner means that information is needed about how new ideas are being understood in relation to previous ideas. So feedback is two-way, from pupil to teacher and teacher to pupil. In the third model of learning, the socio-cultural model, where learning is regarded as arising from interactions with others, feedback will also come through this interaction 'which is as likely to be initiated by pupils as by the teachers, and to which pupils contribute their expertise so that everyone learns, teacher included' (p. 60). Swaffield notes that this third model is not often found in classrooms. Thus our focus here is on the pupil to teacher and teacher to pupil feedback.

Feedback into teaching

A good deal of children's responses to particular activities reflects the decisions made by the teacher in planning the lesson. These may not always turn out to be the best decisions, and one of the great values of using formative assessment is the opportunity to revise and change teaching decisions. In so doing the teacher can adjust the challenge so that, in the words of the Plowden Report (CACE 1967) quoted in Chapter 4, there is 'the right mixture of the familiar and the novel, the right match to the stage of learning the child has reached'. In Chapter 1 we have an example of the teacher, Chris, using the feedback from observing the difficulty her class had in using the worksheet she had prepared. She decided to introduce a less demanding way for the children to record their findings. This is just one instance of a not uncommon event where the 'next step' is for the teacher rather than the children. The decision based on the children's reactions is to change the teacher's plans rather than leave these unaltered and risk a sense of failure in the children.

Older children can indicate more explicitly where they are having difficulty (see Chapter 17) and come to expect the teacher to respond to the feedback they give. Black *et al.* (2003) cite the case of a class where pupils had become familiar with assessing their own work who, when taught by a teacher not emphasising the formative use of assessment, complained to the teacher when their inability to understand appeared to be ignored (p. 67).

Feedback to children

There are different *ways* of feeding back to children about the next steps to take and different *kinds* of feedback to give. We must consider both.

There has been a good deal of research into feeding back information to children, through marking their work. It indicates that the form of the feedback has an impact on children's motivation as well as on their achievements. The importance of this is underlined by reflecting that motivation and enjoyment are as relevant to future learning as is information about how to correct errors. Thus the *way* in which feedback is given to children is as important as the focus of the feedback. Indeed some research shows that feedback can have a negative impact on performance as well as a positive one (Kluger and DeNisi 1996).

A study that has influenced thinking about feedback, and which was highlighted in the review of Black and Wiliam (1998a), is summarised in Box 16.3. This study leads to the conclusion that children seize upon marks and ignore any comments that accompany them. They look to the

---

Box 16.3 Research into different kinds of feedback

In this study by Ruth Butler (1988) the effect of different types of feedback by marking were compared. In a controlled experimental study she set up groups which were given feedback in different ways. One group of pupils was given marks, or grades only; another group was given only comments on their work and the third group received both marks and comments on their work. These conditions were studied in relation to tasks which required divergent and convergent thinking. The result was that, for divergent thinking tasks, the pupils who received comments only made the greatest gain in their learning, significantly more than for the other two groups. The results were the same for high and low achieving pupils. For convergent tasks, the lower achieving pupils scored most highly after comments only, with the marks only group next above the marks plus comments group. For all tasks and pupils, comments only led to higher achievement.

---

marks for a judgement rather than help in further learning. When marks are absent they engage with what the teacher wants to bring to their attention. The comments then have a chance of improving learning as intended by the teacher. In order to do this, of course, the comments should be positive, non-judgemental and where possible identify next steps.

Turning to the content of the feedback, the main point to emerge both from research studies and from experience of effective practice is a distinction between feedback that gives information and feedback that is judgemental. Feedback that gives information:

- focuses on the task, not the person;

- encourages children to think about the work not about how 'good' they are;

- proposes what to do next and gives ideas about how to do it.

Feedback that is judgemental:

- is expressed in terms of how well the child has done rather than how well the work has been done;

- gives a judgement that encourages children to label themselves;

- provides a grade or mark that children use to compare themselves with each other or with what they want to achieve.

Interestingly, praise comes into the judgemental category; it makes children feel they are doing well but does not necessarily help them to do better. It's fine to acknowledge what is good about a piece of work, if this reinforces the goals, but praise in itself will not improve learning. A remark or mark that indicates a judgement on the work will divert children's attention from any comment that is made about improvement. Children are more motivated by comments that help them think about their work and realise what they can do to improve it and which give them help in doing this. This means oral or written questions and comments such as:

- How did you decide which was the best …?

- Is there another way of explaining this by thinking of what happened when …?

- Next time, imagine that someone else is going to use your drawing to set up the circuit and make sure that you show them clearly what to do.

Do's and don'ts of feedback through marking

Some very practical guidelines for marking, particularly applied to science, were proposed by Evans (2001). The 'do's and 'don'ts' in Box 16.4 are derived from his list.

Feedback to children is more effective in improving learning when children realise the goals of their work and then begin to take part in the decisions about next steps. This takes us to the subject of pupils assessing their own work, which is discussed in the next chapter.

Box 16.4 'Do's and 'don't's of marking

Do:

1. Plan the task with specific learning goals in mind.

2. Identify one or two aspects for comment, and review which are related to the planned learning goals.

3. Comment first (and perhaps only) on aspects specific to *science* since the task was set to help learning in science.

4. Think carefully about whether or not any other comment is needed at all, for instance about neatness or effort, deserving though these may be. By all means acknowledge and encourage effort and progress, but not in a way that diverts attention from how to improve and move ahead.

5. Pinpoint weak aspects, e.g. misuse of a technical term (but don't be pedantic about the use of words), or assertions the children may have made that are not supported by their own evidence.

6. Indicate next steps.

7. Give children time to read, reflect on and, where appropriate, to respond to comments.

Don't:

1. Give judgemental comments and, above all, scores or symbols (such as B+ or 7/10) since these divert children's attention from learning from what they have done.

2. Don't pose rhetorical questions ('Do you think so?', 'I wonder why?').

3. By all means pose questions, so long as the child understands that a response will be expected and will be read.

4. Don't waste precious time on evaluating tasks that are mainly about reinforcement. Concentrate on work that is really worth evaluating *for its science*. Any other work should be acknowledged by signature, not by the ubiquitous and ambiguous tick, which is often interpreted by children (not to mention parents and others) as commendation.

Summary

This chapter has continued the discussion of how to conduct formative assessment by considering the interpretation of information in a way that enables next steps to be identified. The main points have been:

- deciding next steps requires a clear view of the nature of progression;

- next steps in process skills can be identified with the help of developmental indicators such as those given in Chapter 15;

- next steps in ideas can be suggested by using indicators suggesting where children are in the progress from 'small' to 'big' ideas;

- learning is helped by providing feedback to children and to teachers who use it in adapting teaching;

- feedback to children on their progress should be non-judgemental and give information about next steps and how to take them.

Further reading

Swaffield, S. (2008) Feedback: the central process in assessment for learning, in S. Swaffield (ed.) *Unlocking Assessment*, London: David Fulton.

17

Children's role in assessing their work

Introduction

Children always have a role in the assessment of their learning, of course, if only as passive objects of assessment and receivers of others' judgements. This chapter, however, is concerned with the active part they can take in assessment for learning. We begin by setting out reasons – from experience, research and ideas about how people learn – for giving children this active role in the assessment of their work. But they cannot take part in assessment of their learning unless they know what learning they are aiming for and so we discuss ways of communicating goals and standards of quality. We then consider how to help children to reflect on their work with others as well as individually and how to provide them with opportunities to decide their next steps and take greater responsibility for their learning.

The role of children in assessing their learning

Placing children at the centre of the formative assessment cycle (Figure 16.1) draws attention to their pivotal role in the way learning is conceived in this book. Learners are in any case responsible for learning, but whether they *take responsibility* for it depends on their participation in the decisions represented by the two-headed arrows in Figure 16.1. The inward pointing arrows indicate the children are the subject of the teachers' decisions about goals, evidence, interpretation and so on. The outward pointing arrows indicate the children's role in all these decisions.

Although we loosely refer to this involvement as 'self-assessment', the focus should be on the actions and the work rather than the 'self' so it is more accurate to refer to children taking part in the formative assessment of their work. Expressed in this way it includes assessment of each other's work, which has particular value, as we discuss later. So children's participation in assessment means reviewing their work, interpreting their progress in relation to the goals and taking part in deciding their next steps. A good deal of these processes depends, as it does for teachers, on knowing what to aim for; the learning goals of their activities. Helping children to understand what they are intended to learn is important, but not at all easy, particularly in science, as we see later. But first we look briefly at the reasons that make this effort worthwhile.

Box 17.1 Some reasons for involving children in using assessment to help learning

- The children are the ones who ultimately have to take the actions that lead to learning.

- Knowing their goals puts any learners in a better position to achieve them.

- Taking part in assessment of their own and their peers' work means that children see assessment as something in which they have an active part.

- There is less need for feedback from the teacher if the children are involved in assessing their work and deciding next steps.

- Involvement in self-assessment facilitates ownership of their learning and enables children to be responsible for and accountable for their learning.

- It provides for independence and can lead to self-regulated learning.

- It raises children's self-esteem.

- It promotes higher order thinking since it requires children to think about how they learn (metacognitive thinking).

Why involve children in assessing their work?

When asked this question a group of teachers came up with the list in Box 17.1. In addition, research studies reviewed by Black and Wiliam (1998a) highlight the central role of children in their own learning. The involvement of children in assessment of their own and each others' work was among the approaches that were most successful in raising achievement. In the studies reviewed, there were examples of successful strategies for involving children from the age of 5 upward in assessing their work.

Theoretical reasons for involving children in decisions about their learning derive from general ideas about how people learn. The kind of learning we need to aim for, as discussed in Chapter 6, is not a matter of absorbing information and ready-made understandings. Instead, it involves the active participation of learners in using existing ideas to try to make sense of new experiences. Learning goes on inside children's heads and so they must be willing to undertake it and to make the necessary effort. This being so, the way to help learning is to give the learner as much opportunity as possible (appropriate to their age and stage) to know what they are intended to learn and how to go about it. This may seem an obvious point but it is in fact quite uncommon for children to be able to articulate what the teacher intends them to learn from a particular activity, as opposed to what they are supposed to do.

Communicating goals

When any of us try to learn something or improve performance, whether it is a physical activity such as playing a sport, or a mental one such as learning another language, we like to be able to tell how we are doing. We can only assess our progress, though, if we have a clear notion

> **Box 17.2** Missing the point about testing the strength of paper
>
> A group of 11-year-old boys spent three lessons finding out which of three kinds of paper was the strongest. After the lesson an observer interviewed the boys.
>
> *Interviewer* What do you think you have learnt from doing your investigations?
>
> *Robert* That graph paper is strongest, that green one.
> *Interviewer* Right, is that it?
> *Robert* Um…
> *Interviewer* You spent three lessons doing that, seems a long time to spend finding out that graph paper is stronger.
> *James* Yeah, and we also found which … papers is stronger. Not just the graph paper, all of them.
>
> The boys appeared to be unaware of the process of investigation as a learning goal, in contrast with their teacher. It seems reasonable to assume that, had they been aware of this goal, they would have reflected more on the way they were investigating, found more satisfaction in the investigation, and made more progress towards the goal that the teacher had in mind but kept to herself.

of what we are aiming for. It is the same with children: they need to be aware of the goals of their learning. However, as just mentioned, often children do not have a clear notion of the purpose of their activities. Consequently, classroom activities appear to children as collections of disconnected and often meaningless exercises.

One way of giving activities meaning for the children is to set them in a real context – or at least one that simulates reality. The case studies in Chapters 1 and 2 all provided a purpose for the activities involved. For instance in the science week (pp. 28-30) there was real interest in finding out whose fingerprints were on the ginger-beer can. Similarly, finding a suitable ball for the dog motivated the children the think about what properties to test and how to do it. However, the solution to these problems was not the same as what they were learning, or the teachers hoped they would be learning. There was no great value in finding whose fingerprints they were or which ball was most bouncy; the point of the activities was in the process of finding these things out. Similarly in many activities, such as the common one of finding which of certain different kinds of paper is strongest (see Box 17.2), the learning is not about paper but about how to make fair comparisons.

Giving reasons in terms of learning

To improve understanding of the purposes of activities, teachers need to find ways of conveying the goals. In practice this means communicating the intended learning and not just what they are to do. Graham, in the case study about soils in Chapter 2 (pp. 26-28) did this in setting up the soil investigations. Three of his instructions were about what to do, but the fourth gave a reason for doing it – so that they could think about what makes a difference to how well plants will grow in the soils. Without this fourth part, the children would probably have investigated the soils, but if asked what they were learning would have answered 'about soils'. The reason for the investigations given by the teacher focused their observations on relevant differences and thus not only made them aware of why they were investigating the soils but made the intended learning more likely.

It is not helpful to be too mechanistic about how to share learning goals with children by insisting on it at the start of every lesson or on the use of a particular form of words to say what the children will be learning. Graham gives an example of a subtle approach which avoids the pitfalls of telling the children what to think about without giving the answer or using words that they would not understand. In communicating concept-based goals it is important also to avoid telling children what to do or telling them what they will find. In the case of activities where the goals include the development of inquiry skills, this should be made clear; otherwise the children will assume that the answers they get are the main aim rather than the way in which they go about finding the answers. Box 17.3 gives examples of both kinds of goals in the context of an investigation of the heat insulating properties of different materials by using them to prevent ice from melting.

Box 17.3 Communicating goals of science activities

Concept-based goals

Suppose that the teacher's goal is for pupils to understand that *materials differ in their heat insulating properties* through investigations with ice.

The goal cannot be shared with the children in this form. So the teacher might say to the children: *In this activity you are going to find out how well these different materials keep ice from melting.* (This gives the children a reason for the activity in terms of what they will learn but does not tell them 'the answer'.)

Contrast this with: *You are going to try wrapping ice cubes in different materials and see how long they take to melt.* (This tells the children what to do but not why.)

or: *You are going to see that how quickly the ice melts depends on the material you use to wrap it in.* (This tells them what they are intended to find and takes away the opportunity to think about the evidence for themselves.)

Skill-based goals

In the same context of activities with the ice, one of the teacher's goals for the children might be: *To plan an investigation that will be a fair test of which material will keep an ice block from melting for the longest time.*

This might be best shared with the children in this way: *When you test these materials, see if you can do it in a way that the test is fair and you are quite sure any difference is because of the material used.*

Reinforcing the goals

It is not enough, however, to talk about goals only at the beginning of an activity. The purpose of what they are doing needs to be reinforced during and at the end. Ensuring that discussion of results picks up on these intentions will help to set the pattern of taking the purpose seriously and working towards the intended learning.

One teacher regularly asks the children to explain to others what they have learnt, making explicit reference to what they hoped to do or find out. If, as often happens, there was some unplanned feature of the inquiry, she asks them 'what did you learn from that?' Sometimes she asks the children to think of questions to ask each other about what they have learnt; she finds that these are often more probing and difficult than her own questions. All these things combine to reinforce the learning atmosphere, and support learning as a shared endeavour.

Communicating expectations of quality

In order to consider the quality of their work, children not only need to know the purpose of what they are doing but have some notion of the standard they should be aiming for, that is, what is 'good work' in a particular context. This is less easy in science than in an area such as language development, where children might be told that in a piece of writing they are to use whole sentences or make sure that the events in a story are in the correct sequence. The children then know what to look for in assessing their work. In science it is more difficult to make general

---

Box 17.4 Communicating what is 'good work' to young children

The process can begin usefully if children from about the age of eight are encouraged to select their 'best' work and to put this in a folder or bag. Part of the time for 'bagging' should be set aside for the teacher to talk to each child about why certain pieces of work were selected. The criteria which the children are using will become clear and may have messages for the teacher. For example if work seems to be selected only on the basis of being 'tidy' and not in terms of content, then perhaps this aspect is being over-emphasised. At first the discussion should only be to clarify the criteria the children use: 'Tell me what you particularly liked about this piece of work.' Gradually it will be possible to suggest criteria without dictating what the children should be selecting. This can be done through comments on the work: 'That was a very good way of showing your results. I could see at a glance which was best.' 'I'm glad you think that was your best investigation because although you didn't get the result you expected, you did it very carefully and made sure that the result was fair.'

Through such an approach children may begin to share the understanding of the goals of their work and become able to comment usefully on what they have achieved. It then becomes easier to be explicit about further targets and for the children to recognise when they have achieved them.

statements that convey meaning to the children. Thus the required features are better conveyed through examples; over time the children come to share the teacher's criteria. Box 17.4 outlines an approach that can be used with young children.

Teachers of older children can more explicitly share with them the criteria they use both in assessing practical skills and marking written work. One science teacher, for example, did this by writing his own account of a class investigation and distributing copies for the children to mark, looking for particular features. It led to lively discussion and a keener understanding of what was expected in their own accounts (Fairbrother 1995).

Box 17.5 Examples of helping children to identify quality standards

Using examples

One teacher of 10-year-olds spent some time at the beginning of the year discussing with her class what made a 'good' report of a science investigation. She gave each group of children two anonymous examples of children's writing about an investigation from children in the same class in earlier years. One was a clear account, well set out so that the reader could understand what had been done, although the writing was uneven and there were some words not spelt correctly. There were diagrams to help the account, with labels. The results were in a table, and the writer had said what he or she thought they meant, admitting that the results didn't completely answer the initial question. There was a comment about how things could have been improved. The other account was tidy, attractive to look at (the diagrams were coloured in but not labelled) but contained none of the features in the content shown in the other piece.

The teacher asked the children to compare the pieces of work and list the good and poor features of each one. Then they were asked to say what were the most important things that made a 'good' report. She put all the ideas together and added some points of her own, to which the children agreed. She later made copies for all the children to keep in their science folders. But she also went on to explore with the children how to carry out an investigation in order to be able to write a good report. These points too were brought together in the children's words and printed out for them.

Brainstorming

A variation on the above is to brainstorm ideas about, for example, how to conduct a particular investigation so that the children can be sure of the result. The list of what to think about can be turned into questions ('Did we keep everything the same except for …?', 'Did we change …?', 'Did we look for …?', 'Did we check their results?', etc.). Before finishing their investigation they check through their list, which becomes a self-assessment tool for that piece of work.

Another approach is to use examples of other children's work, which could be collected for the purpose and made anonymous. Alternatively, the examples from the collections published or created in the school to help teachers assess work could be shared with the children. The discussion of these examples should lead to the children identifying the criteria for 'good work'. If they have done this for themselves, the teacher does not have to convince them of 'what is good'. Other ways in which teachers have helped children to recognise criteria of quality are outlined in Box 17.5 (based on Harlen 2006b).

Involving children in deciding next steps

When children have a view of what they should be doing and how well they should be doing it, they are in a position to share in deciding the next steps to be taken. 'Sharing' is meant to recognise that the responsibility for helping children's learning is ultimately the teacher's, for we are in no way suggesting that children decide what they do and don't do. However, sharing means that the children understand why they are being asked to do certain things and have a firm grasp of what they should do. Moreover their involvement is likely to lead to greater motivation for the work.

Ways of involving children

In Box 17.6 a teacher of 9–10-year-olds describes how she helps the children to decide what they need to do. Note that the teacher 'makes time' for this which, she reports, is time well spent. It saves time for teaching and learning in the end by obviating the need to repeat explanations of what children are to do, and the children learn more quickly by thinking rather than from making mistakes. This teacher treats the group as a learning unit and encourages them to help each other. Since the purpose of the assessment is formative, and since they learn as a group, the

---

Box 17.6 An example of involving children in deciding next steps

I make time to sit down with each group after an activity and talk about what they found difficult, what they thought they did well and what they could have done better. I ask them if they thought about particular aspects relating to the processes and then about how they explain their results. This is important for me because I won't have followed every step of their investigation and it helps me decide how much they have progressed from earlier work and whether they have taken the steps we agreed previously. I then ask questions that indicate my view of what they need to do, but by expressing this as questions, they actually identify what they are going to do. The questions are: 'What can you do in your next investigation to be more sure of your results?', 'What sorts of notes could you make as you go along to give you all the information for preparing a report at the end?', 'Where could you find out more information to explain what you found?'

(Personal communication)

---

decisions made together are important for their learning. However, she also looks at the work of each child individually and makes sure that they recognise their own next steps in learning.

Other approaches in which children assess their work to identify next steps are encouraging reflection through questioning and peer assessment.

Questions to aid reflection

Building on the approach in Box 17.6, children's reflection on their work and how it can be improved can be stimulated by questions such as:

- What do you think you have done well?
- Did you do what were you trying to do in this section?
- Why did you do this, in this kind of way?
- Do you think now that you could do it a better way?
- Which bits are you unsure about?
- What would you change if you did it again?
- What could you add to strengthen this part?

In the same way as for the quality criteria these can be provided to children in their note books or displayed on the classroom wall, to think about as a regular part of their work.

Peer assessment by children

In the context of formative assessment, children assessing other's work means something quite different from marking each other's books. In essence it means children helping each other with their learning, by suggesting the next steps to take to improve the work.

One of the advantages of peer assessment is that it requires less one-to-one attention from the teacher than some other approaches to involving children in formative assessment. Children can more frequently discuss their work with each other and help each other to improve. But there are other more important reasons, summarised in Box 17.7 overleaf.

Box 17.7 Advantages of peer assessment

Saving on teacher time is not the only reason for encouraging peer assessment. Having children talk to each other in pairs about their work requires them to think through the work again and find words to describe it without the pressure that comes from the unequal relationship between the child (novice) and the teacher (expert). It is also consistent with the understanding of learning as being the development of ideas through social interaction as well as through interaction with materials. It can help children to respect each others' strengths, especially if pairs are changed on different occasions.

The paired discussion needs to be structured, at least when it is new to the children. For example the children can be asked to exchange work and then think about two or three questions about it reflecting the criteria of quality. For instance if the work describes a conclusion from something that has been observed or found from an investigation the questions might be: 'Can you tell what was found?' 'Does the conclusion help to answer the question that was being investigated?' 'What would help to make what happened clearer (a diagram or series of drawings)?' After such a discussion one child said about having her work assessed by another: 'She said it was hard to understand my investigation so I asked her what sort of thing I should have put to make her understand. Next time I will make sure that I describe things more clearly.'

This approach to peer assessment clearly requires a class atmosphere where cooperation and collaboration, rather than competition, are encouraged. When they have confidence in gaining help from a structured exchange with a peer, children begin spontaneously to ask each other for their opinion. The recognition of being able to help themselves and each other enables learning to continue when the teacher is occupied with those who need extra help.

(Based on Harlen *et al.* 2003: 132–3)

Summary

This chapter has discussed the value of helping children to take part in the formative assessment of their work. The main points have been:

- there are important theoretical and practical reasons for involving children in assessing their own work;

- acting on this means sharing learning goals with the children, conveying an operational meaning of quality and helping them to identify their next steps;

- sharing goals means communicating to children a reason for their activities in terms of learning and referring back to this in discussion during and at the end of the activity;

- helping children to judge the quality of the work requires the subtle communication of criteria of quality through discussion of examples;

- involving children in deciding next steps follows from a review of what they have done and how they have done it and agreeing ways of improving it or moving on from it;

- children can take part in deciding their next steps through self- and peer-marking.

Further reading

Earl, L. and Katz, S. (2008) Getting to the core of learning: using assessment for self-monitoring and self-regulation, in S. Swaffield (ed.) *Unlocking Assessment, Understanding for Reflection and Application*, London: David Fulton.

CHAPTER 18

Summarising achievement

Introduction

Following the discussion in the last three chapters of formative assessment, we turn here to the second of the two main purposes of assessment noted in Chapter 14 (p. 171). Summative assessment is probably the first thing that comes to mind for many people, including parents, when assessment is mentioned since receiving reports is the most visible sign of assessment taking place. Although they tend to be seen as contrasting – formative as assessment *for* learning, summative as assessment *of* learning – both should help learning in different ways.

After briefly reviewing the properties that summative assessment needs in order to serve its purposes, the main sections discuss and illustrate three different approaches to assessing pupils' achievements at particular times. Two of these approaches – building a profile over time, and summarising, at a particular time, evidence collected across a range of activities – depend on teachers' judgements, which require some quality assurance procedures. The third involves tests or special tasks. Echoing some concerns expressed in Chapter 14, we acknowledge some disadvantages of frequent testing and suggest some ways of ensuring that these are minimised.

Information for summative assessment

The characteristics of formative and summative assessment (p. 177) indicate that formative is close to the learning, providing quick feedback into decisions about learning activities. Summative assessment is more distant from the learning and less detailed but nevertheless its impact should be to help in decisions that improve children's learning opportunities, albeit through a much longer feedback loop.

To serve its purpose, information for summative assessment needs to be:

■ a summary of what has been achieved at a particular time in relation to the full range of goals including social, emotional and physical as well as cognitive development;

■ succinct, giving an overview of progress, preferably in the form of a profile where main aspects of development are identified;

■ criterion-referenced to standards or levels that have the same meaning for all children;

■ as reliable as possible; ideally involving some procedures for quality assurance.

Ways of summarising achievement

The main ways of providing a record of achievement at a particular time are:

- building a record over time based on teachers' judgements;

- summarising information gathered by teachers over a period of time;

- using tests or special tasks to determine what has been learnt at a particular time.

We now look at each of these in turn.

Building a record over time

This method depends on the existence of some means of describing expected progress in steps or stages so that as each step is reached it can be recorded. A good example of this approach is the Foundation Stage Profile trialled in 2000 and introduced as a statutory requirement in England in the school year 2002/3. It is intended to support both formative assessment and summative assessment and as such is quite detailed, comprising 13 scales within each of the six areas of learning (see Box 18.1). Within each scale there are nine points of progression where:

- points 1 to 3 describe a child who is still progressing towards the achievements set out in the early learning goals, and are based mainly on the stepping stones;

- points 4 to 7 describe a child who is making progress in achieving the early learning goal;

- point 8 indicates completion of the early learning goals;

- point 9 describes a child who is working consistently beyond the level of the early learning goals.

Box 18.1 The Foundation Stage Profile

The Foundation Stage in England refers to the pre-school years when children may be in nursery education or the reception year of a primary school. The Foundation Stage Profile (FSP) was introduced in 2002 to summarize children's achievements at the end of the Foundation stage. The FSP comprises 13 scales relating to six areas of learning: personal, social and emotional development; communication, language and literacy; mathematical development; knowledge and understanding of the world; physical development; and creative development. For each scale a judgement is made in terms of nine points, relating to the child's progress towards achieving the 'early learning' goals. It is intended that the profile is built up over the foundation stage so that the evidence can be used formatively and then summarised against the performance descriptions of the scales for reporting at the end of each term. The process is entirely teacher-based and the evidence for completing the profile is derived from ongoing learning activities. Occasionally, additional observations (of behaviour in different contexts) may be required although these should still be situated within the normal curriculum provision.

A handbook (QCA 2003) provides information and advice on using the scales, case studies and exemplification, guidance on moderation and on use with children having special needs or English as an additional language. It also provides help for practitioners in judging a child's typical attainment at a particular time, through a process of 'best fit' between the child's behaviour and the performance description/exemplification materials. However, unless this is done regularly and the record built up gradually over time, the number of judgements to be made for each child at the end of the Foundation Stage can seem unmanageable. Moreover it is only when the records are updated frequently that the FSP has a formative function. The Foundation Stage optional booklet (QCA 2007b) (and its electronic version, the eProfile) contains the 117 scale points for practitioners to use as a record throughout the year.

Summarising information gathered over time

This approach differs from the one just discussed because, although information is gathered over time, it is brought together and judged at the time when reporting is required. Ideally the information will have been gathered in the context of formative assessment and used to help learning. However it is not appropriate to rely on the interpretations made for formative purposes since these will have an ipsative element; that is, will take into account the individual child's progress and effort. Whilst this does not matter for formative assessment, where identifying the levels at which children are working is not necessary (see p. 188), things are different for summative assessment. In summative assessment, levels are used as ways of communicating to others what children have achieved and so their work has to be judged against the same criteria for all children. Whilst the *evidence* used for the two purposes might be the same, the judgements in summative assessment are made differently.

In England, teachers are required to summarise their 'teacher assessment' judgements at the end of each key stage in the form of a level for each attainment target in the curriculum in science (and in mathematics and English). The way in which this is done at Key Stage 2 is indicated in the Assessment Arrangements, quoted in Box 18.2.

Arrangements for Key Stage 1 at the time of writing are similar but at that stage (Years 1 and 2) there are no tests and tasks in science to be administered in addition, as there are for English and mathematics. Teachers are required to record a level for each attainment target. An overall subject level is calculated (automatically by the school's information management system) by giving a weighting of three to 'Scientific Inquiry' and one each to the content-based attainment targets.

Quality assurance of teachers' assessment

There are clear advantages in using teachers' judgements in terms of the validity of the results since teachers can collect information about a wider range of achievement and learning outcomes than formal testing allows. The whole curriculum can in theory be assessed, thus eliminating the narrowing effect of a special focus on those parts included in a test (to which we referred in Chapter 14 (Box 14.1)). Further, pupils are not subject to the anxiety that accompanies tests and

---

Box 18.2 Teachers' summative assessment in the National Curriculum in England

The level descriptions in the National Curriculum are the basis for judging children's levels of attainment at the end of the key stage. Teachers use their knowledge of a child's work to judge which level description best fits that child's performance across a range of contexts. In reaching a judgement, teachers should use their knowledge of a child's work over time, including written, practical and oral work in the class, homework and results of other school examinations or tests.

The aim is for a rounded judgement which:

■ is based on knowledge of how the child performs over time across a range of contexts;

■ takes into account strengths and weaknesses of a child's performance;

■ is checked against adjacent level descriptions to ensure that the level awarded is the closest match to the child's performance in each attainment target.

(QCA 2007c)

---

which can affect the outcome, reducing validity. Indeed it is feasible for pupils to have some role in the process through self-assessment.

However, there is a commonly held view that teachers' judgements provide unreliable results. This can be the case when no steps are taken to assure quality. The main causes of low reliability in this process are the inclusion of irrelevant information (such as neatness, when this is not a specific goal of the task), variation in interpretation of the criteria, and the problem of relating performance in specific contexts to necessarily general criteria. There are several effective ways in which reliability can be improved to equal and even exceed that of tests. The main ones are using examples, group moderation and using a test or tasks as a check.

Using examples

There are many sources of examples of pupils' work or behaviours, annotated to highlight features which are significant in relation to the judgements to be made. For instance the materials published by the QCA for the FSP contain examples from observing and listening to pupils. Some curriculum materials contain examples of children's actions, words, talk, writing or drawings and discuss aspects which lead to a decision about whether certain key criteria have been met, for example in the Nuffield Primary Science (1995). In the US the *Performance Standards* of the *New Standards* (1997) serve a similar purpose. These examples indicate the importance of not taking some features into account when they are not relevant.

Since teachers should be basing their judgements on a range of each pupil's work and not judging just from one piece; it is most useful to have exemplar material in the form of a portfolio of work from one child than single pieces of work. This helps teachers to apply the criteria in a holistic manner. A glance at the level descriptions for inquiry skills in the National Curriculum, for instance, shows that not every piece of work will fit the descriptions and neither will each and every part of the criteria for a level be represented in the portfolio. This may seem rather a loose procedure, but assessment is not an exact matter and it is better to be aware of the uncertainty than to assume that we can describe children's learning more accurately than is the case.

Group moderation

This involves teachers meeting together to discuss examples of pupils' work. These meetings enable teachers to share their interpretations of the level descriptions as well as to discuss their judgements of specific sets of work. Experience of group moderation where it is developing in the UK, and of other countries where teachers' judgements are used, suggests that it has benefits beyond the quality of assessment results. It has a well-established professional development function. Meeting to discuss the inferences that can be drawn from studying pupils' work provides teachers with insight into the nature of the assessment process which improves not only their summative assessment but also their formative use of assessment.

The rigour of the moderation process that is necessary depends on the use of the results. For internal uses of summative assessment, such as reporting to parents and informing other teachers, within-school moderation meetings are adequate. However, inter-school meetings are advisable when the results are used for external purposes, especially if these involve evaluation of the school. In Wales, secondary schools and their cluster primary schools are, in 2008/9, putting in place group moderation procedures and arrangements for transferring information between primary and secondary schools which increase the reliability of information provided from teachers' assessment. At the secondary level in Wales there are moves to accredit schools to conduct assessment. Similarly in England, teachers will be able to gain professional qualifications in assessment through the Chartered Institute for Educational Assessment (CIEA 2008). However, it is too early to consider the effect of these innovations.

Using tests or special tasks to check teachers' assessment

What is meant here is the use of special tasks or tests as a means of moderating or checking teachers' judgements but not as a separate measure of achievement. Tests are used in this way in the Scottish system for English and mathematics. Teachers decide on the basis of a range of evidence from everyday activities about whether a pupil has met the criteria at a particular level in the subject. Assessment against the level criteria is an ongoing process; a pupil may be judged to have reached a level at any time. When confirmed by moderation, this is recorded and then reported at the appropriate time. The moderation can be through taking part in collaborative moderation within and across schools or the use of tests, which are described as 'another way for teachers to check their judgements against national standards' (SEED 2005). If they choose to do so, although currently only for English and mathematics, teachers can use a test, drawn from an externally devised bank of items, which they mark themselves, and compare with the results of their own classroom assessment. This use is rather different from that of the 'single level tests' to be introduced in England, which we discuss later.

Using tests or special tasks to sum up achievement

A summary assessment can also be arrived at by 'checking up' rather than 'summing up'; that is, giving some special tasks which are devised specifically to assess the point reached in the development of ideas or skills. Tests may be preferred to the use of teachers' assessment for certain purposes because they give each child the same task and conditions in which to attempt it. This contrasts with using teachers' judgements of regular work where the evidence arises from situations which vary from pupil to pupil. However it should be noted that giving the same task does not necessarily provide the same opportunities for children to show what they can do.

National tests

National tests are used to check up at the end of each key stage in England. Until 2005 this was also the case in Wales, but from that date the assessment of levels reached by pupils had to be based only on 'best fit' judgements by teachers in relation to national curriculum levels.

The end of key stage tests are intended to provide 'a snapshot of a child's attainment at the end of the key stage' (QCA 2004 and 2007c). The results are used for more than this, however. They

---

Box 18.3 The impact of high stakes testing on motivation for learning

Findings from a review of research (Harlen and Deakin Crick 2003):

- The introduction of Key Stage 1 tests in 1992 was associated with a reduction in self-esteem of those pupils who underachieved.

- When tests pervade the ethos of the classroom, test performance is more highly valued than what is being learnt.

- When tests become the main criteria by which pupils are judged and by which they judge themselves, those whose strengths lie outside the subjects tested have a low opinion of their capabilities.

- The results of tests that are 'high stakes' *for individual pupils*, such as the 11+ in Northern Ireland, were found to have a particularly strong impact on those who receive low grades. (The 11+ will be terminated in Northern Ireland in 2009.)

- Pupils are aware of repeated practice tests and the narrowing of the curriculum.

- Low achievers become overwhelmed by tests and de-motivated by constant evidence of their low achievement. The effect is to increase the gap between low and high achieving pupils.

- The use of repeated practice tests impresses on pupils the importance of the tests. It encourages them to adopt test-taking strategies designed to avoid effort and responsibility. Repeated practice tests are, therefore, detrimental to higher order thinking.

---

are collected centrally and used for the 'high stakes' purpose of evaluating schools and LEAs. The consequence is that they attract a great deal of public attention as well as having serious effects on teachers and pupils. Some of these effects, such as the tendency to focus on what is tested, to spend time on practice tests and to 'teach to the test', are well known. What is less well known is the impact on children's motivation for learning. A review of research focused on this issue, by Harlen and Deakin Crick (2003), shows 'strong evidence of a negative impact on pupils' motivation' (ARG 2002: 2). The main findings of the review are summarised in Box 18.3.

These effects have to be avoided as far as possible since they are clearly impair enjoyment of and willingness to continue learning, as required for lifelong learning. As long as the tests continue it is important for teachers to do what they can to minimise the negative impact on children. Some general advice, given by the Assessment Reform Group (ARG 2002), based on the Harlen and Deakin Crick review, is reproduced in Box 18.4.

The proposal of new single-level tests in the consultation document entitled *Making Good Progress* (DfES 2007) and built into *The Assessment for Learning Strategy* (DCSF 2008) may well increase the difficulty of avoiding teaching being driven by tests. The new tests, on trial until 2009, for pupils in Key Stages 2 and 3, are designed so that each test assesses achievement at a particular level, which a pupil does or does not achieve, as contrasted with end of key stage tests which assess achievement across a range of levels. The tests are for levels 3–8 in mathematics, reading and writing only, but may be extended to include science. The intention is that pupils sit a test when their teacher judges them to be able to pass, with testing opportunities twice a year, in December

---

Box 18.4 Suggestion for action to avoid the negative effects of testing

Teachers should:

... do more of this ...

Provide choice and help pupils to take responsibility for their learning.

Discuss with pupils the purpose of their learning and provide feedback that will help the learning process.

Encourage pupils to judge their work by how much they have learnt and by the progress they have made.

Help pupils to understand the criteria by which their learning is assessed and to assess their own work.

Develop pupils' understanding of the goals of their work in terms of what they are learning; provide feedback to pupils in relation to these goals.

Help pupils to understand where they are in relation to learning goals and how to make further progress.

Give feedback that enables pupils to know the next steps and how to succeed in taking them.

Encourage pupils to value effort and a wide range of attainments.

Encourage collaboration among pupils and a positive view of each other's attainments.

... and do less of this ...

Define the curriculum in terms of what is in the tests to the detriment of what is not tested.

Give frequent drill and practice for test taking.

Teach how to answer specific test questions.

Pupils judging their work in terms of scores or grades.

Allow test anxiety to impair some pupils' performance (particularly girls and lower performing pupils).

Use tests and assessment to tell pupils where they are in relation to others.

Give feedback relating to pupils' capabilities, implying a fixed view of each pupil's potential.

Compare pupils' grades and allow pupils to compare grades, giving status on the basis of test achievement only.

Emphasise competition among pupils.

(Assessment Reform Group (ARG) 2002: 8)

---

and June. Thus they are intended to confirm teachers' assessment of the level at which a pupil is working. It is proposed that the results of the tests would be the basis of 'progression targets' for teachers and schools, adding to the targets based on end of key stage tests. Schools will be given 'progression targets' measured by 'the percentage of pupils who make two levels of national curriculum progress during Key Stage 2' and a 'progression premium (to reward schools which help pupils who entered a key stage behind national expectations to make good progress)' (DCSF 2008: 4). Thus it is clear that these proposed new tests would be used in the evaluation of teachers and schools, adding considerably to the pressures felt by teachers and pupils.

This additional testing adds weight to the case for using the results of tests, as far as is possible given their limited nature, for feedback into teaching. Teachers can use test results formatively if they analyse returned scripts to pinpoint errors in children's thinking that will inform aspects of the future thinking. Other ideas for the formative use of summative assessment can be found in Black *et al.* (2003).

Special tasks embedded in normal work

The use of special tasks or tests embedded in regular work provides the opportunity to set children a standard task without the anxiety of a formal test situation. This may be desirable even when evidence from regular activities is used as the main source of information if it has not been possible to collect some kinds of information in the course of normal work. Banks of optional tasks are available for teachers to use in Wales to support teachers' assessment and of course there are commercial tests available. These generally take the form of 'stand alone' items with well-defined 'right answers'. Such question formats are not well suited to assessing science, especially inquiry skills. An alternative is to embed questions in a theme which is not only more interesting for the children but cuts down on the amount of reading the children have to do to establish a fresh context for each item.

An example of this approach is given in Schilling *et al.* (1990). Written questions assessing process skills were devised on the theme of the 'Walled Garden', which teachers could introduce as a topic or as a story. Questions were grouped into seven sections about different things found in the garden: water, walls, 'minibeasts', leaves, sun-dial, bark and wood. For each section there was a large poster giving additional information, and activities and a booklet for children to write their answers. Children worked on the tasks over an extended period, with no time limit; they enjoyed the work which they saw as novel and interesting, in no way feeling that they were being tested. The examples in Figure 18.1 on pp. 224–5 are of the questions on 'minibeasts'. They can be used as guides to setting inquiry-based tasks in other contexts to suit the class activities.

Special tasks for checking up on inquiry skills can be written or practical. Practical tasks designed to require all groups of inquiry skills to be used, to the extent that children are able, were employed in the APU surveys (DES/WO 1983) and for research purposes (for example, Russell and Harlen 1990). As they require the full attention of an administrator/observer they are not practicable in the classroom as regular tests. Their value to teachers is in the ideas and hints which they give about the kinds of tasks, ways of presenting them and of questioning children, which can be adapted and applied in planning children's practical work.

Minibeasts

Dan and Tammy kept a note of all the 'minibeasts' they found in the Walled Garden. They drew the minibeasts as well as they could.

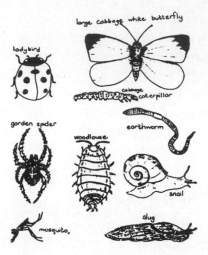

Read about 'minibeasts' in the project folder before you try to answer the questions.

Later, back at school, they used some books to get information about the minibeasts. They made a special chart, called a table, which showed the information, and put it in the Walled Garden project folder. Here is a copy of it.

Minibeast	legs	where eggs laid	eggs hatch into	sheds skin	adult feeds on
woodlouse	yes	under stones, logs	young woodlice	yes	dead animals and plants
snail	no	soil	young snails	no	dead and living plants
ladybird	yes	plants		yes	live greenfly
slug	no	soil	young slugs	no	dead and living plants
earthworm	no	soil	young worms	no	dead things in the soil
cabbage butterfly	yes	leaves	larva caterpillar	yes	plants
spider	yes	in cocoon on leaves	young spiders	yes	flies
mosquito	yes	on water		yes	

Figure 18.1 Examples of test items embedded in a theme (Schilling *et al*.1990)

1. Use the information in the table to answer these questions:
   a) What do ladybirds feed on? ....
   b) In the table all the minibeasts with legs have something else that is the same about them. Can you see what it is?

   ....

2. When they made the table they could not find all the information about the ladybird and the mosquito. Please fill in this information for them on their table:

   a) A ladybird's egg hatches into a LARVA.

   b) Adult mosquitos feed on ANIMALS and PLANTS.

3. Dan and Tammy's table shows that snails eat dead and living plants, but it doesn't say whether they like to eat some plants more than others.

   Suppose you have these foods that snails will eat:

   strawberries   porridge oats   lettuce   carrot

   and as many snails as you want. Think about what you would do to find out which of these foods the snails liked best.
   a) Say what you would do to start with. (Draw a picture if it will help.)
   ....
   b) Say how you will make sure that each food has a fair chance of being chosen.
   ....
   c) What will you look for to decide which food was liked best?
   ....

4. What other things could you find out about snails by doing investigations with them? Write down as many things as you can think of to investigate.

   ....

5. Dan and Tammy went to visit their Aunt and looked for minibeasts in her garden. They found them all except for snails although they looked carefully for a long time.
   a) Write down any reasons you can think of to explain why there were no snails in their Aunt's garden.

   ....

   b) Their Aunt thought it could be because of the kind of soil where she lived; there was no chalk or limestone in it.
   What is the main difference between snails and other minibeasts which Dan and Tammy found?
   ....
   c) Why do you think snails only live where there is chalk or limestone in the soil?
   ....

Summary

This chapter has discussed some procedures and issues in using assessment for summative purposes. We have considered the use of teachers' judgements and of tests or special tasks.

The main points have been:

- summative assessment essentially provides a summary of information about a child's attainment at a certain time; compared with formative assessment it has to be more succinct, strictly criterion-referenced and as reliable as possible;

- summative assessment can be obtained by building a record over time based on teachers' judgements, summing up at certain times evidence gathered across a number of contexts, or by giving special tasks or tests that give a snapshot of what has been attained at a particular time;

- when teachers' judgements are used, criteria have to be applied uniformly so that comparable information is provided about each child – this requires some form of quality assurance;

- procedures for quality assurance of teachers' judgements include the provision of assessed examples, group moderation and the use of reference tests;

- over-use of tests, particularly when they have 'high stakes' attached, has adverse effects on children's motivation for learning;

- teachers can take steps to minimise the negative impact of testing on children's learning and where possible make formative use of the results.

Further reading

Black, P., Harrison, C., Lee, C., Marshall, B. and Wiliam, D. (2003) *Assessment for Learning. Putting it into Practice,* Maidenhead: Open University Press, Chapter 4.

PART

5

Materials and ICT to support inquiry

19

The role and organisation of practical inquiry

Introduction

For many years primary science has been seen as essentially a practical, hands on, endeavour where children learn by doing, feeling, touching and finding out 'what happens if …?' However, in recent years our understanding of the role of practical, first-hand experience has become more sophisticated. The relationship between doing science and learning science is conceived as more complex than simply 'seeing is believing'. Clearly young children do need to experience the world, to see where apples grow, or where milk comes from or how rivers flow to the sea, or to know what size a butterfly is, or to feel for themselves the effect of spinning on a roundabout. But learning science means going further than observing and in this chapter we begin by addressing two of the signature and related features of primary science: practical work and group work. In each case we consider two broad questions: 'Why?' and 'How?' Having considered these key elements of pedagogy we move on to the ways in which practical work is supported, first by looking at resources, their selection, storage and maintenance, and then at matters relating to safety.

The value of practical work

Why practical work?

Science goes beyond simple sensations to attempts to explain the world, and to make predictions about it. This requires more than experiencing; it needs us to be able to explore ideas by manipulating objects, to ask questions of our world. In turn this needs individuals to possess the cognitive skills to engage with ideas and to explore them through the manipulation of objects, and the opportunity to raise their own questions, plan how to obtain evidence, predict what might happen and think about how to capture and share their findings. For young children to develop this complex set of skills for learning they need to go beyond being shown or told. It is not sufficient to illustrate a point through practical work; children need to learn how to explore ideas through practical inquiry.

Despite the squeeze on practical work reported in, for example, the report on primary science in England, Ireland, Scotland and Wales by the Wellcome Trust (2005) and teachers' concerns that it takes up too much time, arguments from a range of authorities in science education are consistent in asserting the value of practical work. The school inspection service in England, Ofsted (2004), states that 'Teaching remains most effective where pupils are actively involved in thinking through and carrying out scientific enquiry' (p. 2). Murphy *et al.* (2000) looked at classroom practitioners and concluded that the most effective in developing children's understanding were those who promoted interaction, where classroom talk was a central feature of classroom inquiry. Bianchi (2003) found that teachers placed a high value on the provision of time for reflection during lessons, where children could think about what they were doing and discuss their ideas. What is emerging is that for practical work to be effective in facilitating learning it must involve discussion, exploration, investigations and time to reflect. This all takes time, so the rewards need to be demonstrable.

A study by Mant *et al.* (2007) goes some way towards demonstrating the rewards achieved through well-constructed practical work. Taking a lead from lessons learnt in teaching gifted and talented young people, they selected for study two matched groups of 16 classes of 10–11-year-olds. Teachers and subject leaders of one group of 16 classes undertook CPD (Continuing Professional Development) aimed at providing them with strategies for creating cognitively challenging, practical science lessons, with plenty of space for thinking and discussion. The CPD promoted science lessons that had:

1. Increased time spent in discussion of scientific ideas.
2. An increased emphasis on the encouragement of higher order thinking.
3. More practical work and investigations.
4. More focused and purposeful recording by pupils, less writing.

(Mant *et al.* 2007: 1712)

Mant and her colleagues found that pupils enjoyed their science lessons more and welcomed the challenge they provided, which in turn increased their engagement with learning. This finding reflects an earlier study that concluded that pupils want to be challenged by new ideas and find things out for themselves (Braund and Driver 2002). However, Mant *et al.* also found that performance by pupils on national tests increased significantly as a result of these challenging, exciting lessons. What most writers, inspectors and many teachers have suspected to be the case seems in fact to be so. The key then is to give sufficient time to practical science to make it worthwhile for the pupils, to give them real, quality learning time.

The link here with research focused on developing thinking skills is interesting. Mant *et al.*'s (2007) findings are that providing cognitively challenging science lessons enhances learning. Carol McGuinness and her colleagues' in the ACTS (Activating Children's Thinking Skills) project (McGuinness *et al.* 2005) found that with careful planning teachers are able to infuse their teaching with activities designed to promote the development of thinking skills. The opportunities for extensive discussion and exploration, and the encouragement of children to make their thinking explicit are all part of this. Alexander (2004) and Mercer *et al.* (2004) emphasise that what is needed is a focus on *dialogic* teaching, which goes beyond simply more interaction and cuts across the distinction between whole class versus group work, as discussed and illustrated in Chapter 8. Once we see practical science activities as a means by which real learning can be facilitated, the cost-benefit analysis falls firmly on the side of practical inquiry.

How?

Sufficient time

The lesson described in Box 19.1 illustrates that the value to learning of direct experience and physical interaction with materials is vastly increased by discussion among the children as well as between teacher and children. The ability of the teacher to extend the children's thinking is clearly demonstrated. Having provided the pupils with time to explore the various string telephones, to talk to each other about them and to use them, she then brought them together to discuss their ideas. In doing so Sue encouraged their creative thinking skills to generate and extend ideas, to suggest hypotheses and to apply imagination.

19.1 Ideas about sound and the string telephone

Sue was working with a class of 6- and 7-year-olds looking at string telephones. The children had been given a variety of 'phones', some with long and some short strings, some made from tin cans, some with paper cups and some with plastic cups. The class enjoyed discovering that they could speak to one another through the phones. After a while Sue asked them to start thinking about what was happening. They then gathered together, with the telephones, to discuss their ideas. An enthusiastic discussion ensued.

Robert   It was pressing through the string gaps.
Teacher   Little gaps in the string?
Hayley   When we said something the sound bounces along the string (*indicates with hand*).
Louis   I thought I saw a bit of electric going along the string ...
Teacher   Louis thought he saw the string moving.
Robert   I thought it was following along the string.
John   There is a crack in the bottom of the cup and the voice gets out.
Teacher   How could you test it?
John   Try a thin gap and a bigger gap and see if it gets through.
Alex   It went along the string and bounced.
Claire   It goes along the gap.
John   We could try a metal cup. If you speak into a metal cup it will be better because if you tap it (*shows vibration with hand*).

Sue recognised that John was beginning to consider the idea of vibration and that the children were ready to begin to test out their ideas. The discussion moved on as the children were asked about ways to test out their ideas. Different tests were considered and pairs of children decided what they would like to try.

(Qualter 1996: 73)

The arguments presented above suggest that practical inquiry takes time if children are to learn. Seeing for oneself is important, especially for young children who, unlike adults, have not got a wealth of other experiences to fall back on when trying to make sense of events. Adults might be able to learn in more abstract ways but children need both physical and intellectual interaction with the world. The most effective teachers do not allow the pressure to move on to prevent them from allowing the children time to explore. Sue, as described in Box 19.1, gave the children plenty of time to explore the string telephones before they began to discuss their ideas.

Clarity of purpose

Goldsworthy *et al.* (2000) as part of the AKSIS project, found that often children's understanding of the purpose of an investigation was not that intended by the teacher. They give the example in Box 19.2 where the teacher's focus was on the pupils developing particular process skills.

It is clear that learning by seeing and doing is much more successful if the pupil knows the purpose of the activity and can therefore focus on what is important (see Chapter 4). Again the AKSIS project (Goldsworthy *et al.* 1998) found that teachers tended not to teach the skills of investigating explicitly and yet this is the key to pupils knowing what to attend to. This contrasts sharply with the example given in Chapter 2 of Anne's class. They were responding to a letter from an industrialist asking for help in finding good sealants for pipes that would need to carry hot water in a power station. The 8- and 9-year-olds were able to choose from a wide selection of potential sealants for their pipes. All chose materials that were likely to be successful because

19.2 What is the investigation about?

Interviewer	Whilst Daryl is running around, tell me, what do you think you are learning in this investigation?
Robert	How fast you can run.
Jody	The length of your legs.
Interviewer	What about the length of legs?
Jody	Well, if there are bigger legs you can run faster and with shorter legs you can run a bit faster.
Interviewer	And anything else you think you are learning?
Jody	How much muscle it needs to go, how fast it can take.
Robert	About forces.
Interviewer	What about anything about doing investigations?
	(interrupted by Daryl returning from running)
	Do you think you are learning anything about how to do an investigation?
Jody	Yes.
Interviewer	What sort of things are you learning?
Jody	Hot and cold and stuff.
Robert	Body.

(Goldsworthy *et al.* 2000: 1)

they had thought about the purpose of the investigation and knew what function the sealant needed to serve. It seems then that teachers having a clear view of what it is they want pupils to learn from practical work and discussing this in detail with the children is the way to ensure that children learn by seeing and doing, and talking.

Feasey (1998) argues that it is crucial that science investigations are set in a social context, thus providing a purpose, and a specific audience where children have responsibility to that audience and so to communicate appropriately. The children in the school described in Chapter 2 (science week for Year 6, p. 28) who undertook the forensic science work were able to engage with very complex scientific ideas, undertake accurate tests and write well constructed articles for the school newsletter because the context they were operating in was realistic. This contextualisation provides a platform for authentic discussion and debate.

It is perhaps the lack of real contexts that results in less time being given to the consideration of evidence than planning and doing. In the example of Daryl and his friends given in Box 19.2, a more lively discussion with more focus on how to investigate more might well have been achieved if the children were responding to, say, a suggestion by the Head Teacher that on school sports day pupils should be in teams of similar heights rather than the usual year or class groups. In this way pupils get to exchange and challenge each other's ideas, to construct appropriate ways to investigate their ideas and to develop theories based on that evidence. This learning about how science works should be implicit in the way science is taught, but made explicit through reflecting on how experiments help to build theory, and how theories then lead to other experiments (Hodson 1993).

In summary, the disaffection with science among young people (European Commission 2006) can only be improved if they are re-engaged with science. The way forward is not to give it less time, not to focus exclusively on learning facts, but to open it up. The value of science is most likely to be obtained when:

- discussion between pupils and between teacher and pupils is seen as key to real learning with teachers modelling ways of asking questions and exploring ideas;

- the problem is set in a social, meaningful context such that there is a reason to puzzle over observations, to raise interesting questions, to take care when collecting the right sort of evidence and to make sense of that evidence in light of the original problem that was posed. Meaningful contexts also give a reason to communicate findings to others;

- the children feel challenged intellectually and in terms of the skills and processes they need to employ; children enjoy thinking hard, employing a range of thinking skills and developing, through hands on experience, their ability to learn independently.

Organising practical work

Why group work?

Almost invariably practical work needs to be undertaken in small groups. First for the efficient use of resources but most importantly for the opportunity it affords for children to share ideas, to challenge each other's ideas and to reflect on their learning. In addition they need to learn how to work in groups and to plan together as a team. Group work done well, that is where children are working as a group not sitting in a group working individually, produces significant benefits to learning. A project funded by the Economic and Social Science Research Council as part of its Teaching Learning Research Programme studied large numbers of children in Scotland as their teachers implemented increased amounts of group work. The findings from this project were quite remarkable (TLRP 2005).

> Despite some views that group work is only beneficial for children's social development, we showed that group work can more positively influence academic progress than other forms of learning.
> (Teaching and Learning Research Programme Briefing No. 11 (November 2005)

One reason for the value of group work, as has already been mentioned, is the opportunity it affords for discussion. Naylor *et al.* (2007) go some way to explaining why. They observed that when working with concept cartoons, argument and discussion amongst pupils does happen, but that the debate is at its richest in the absence of the teacher, a point made by Barnes (1976) as noted in Chapter 8. However, as the Scottish project described above pointed out:

> It is well known that pupils need to have the skills to communicate effectively through listening, explaining and sharing ideas. But pupils also have to learn to trust and respect each other, and they need skills in how to plan, organise and evaluate their group work.
>
> (ibid.)

The value of discussion and debate is clearly important to the successful operation of a group. This might suggest that the most fruitful groups are likely to be made up of children with different starting points. Howe (1990) and Howe *et al.* (1992) undertook a study of group composition that convincingly demonstrated that compared with groups where children had similar initial ideas, those where the ideas were more varied made most progress. Crucially the progress made by these mixed groups was more apparent six weeks after the group work than it was immediately after the lessons. Although other explanations for these differences were sought, none were found.

In a later study, Howe and colleagues (Howe *et al.* 2007) identified some key principles of group organisation in primary science. Their study was designed to draw together all the features that various research projects have identified as important in successful group work to explore their effects on attainment. Their findings revealed that classes where teachers supported group work effectively made greater progress than others. This was equally so in classes of mixed age pupils. The evidence suggests that where teachers monitored groups, briefing children on the task in hand, ensuring good time management, encouraging the development of good group skills and modelling good interaction skills, their pupils engaged in more productive dialogue including the sharing of ideas, discussing disagreements, sharing and explaining ideas.

How can effective group work be achieved?

Develop good team working skills

In order to facilitate good group work teachers need to concentrate on teaching children how to work as part of a team. One way to do this is to allocate roles. Anne, in her project with industry (Chapter 2) provided children with badges, HR manager, Health and Safety Officer, Resources Officer and Communications Officer. This helped her to direct the children and gave them an insight into how industry works in teams with assigned roles. It has also been noted that boys can dominate, in particular when it comes to laying claim to the equipment. It is the teacher's role to ensure that this is not the case. Developing good team working skills is important for science learning and for life. Science lessons are the ideal opportunity for this.

Different starting points within the group

The research by Howe *et al.* (2007) clearly indicates the importance of there being different ideas among the pupils at the start and shows that mixed age groups can be as successful as more homogeneous groups. This suggests that mixed ability grouping is likely to be as effective as more homogeneous groups. The point seems to be to ensure an equality of status within the group by encouraging the valuing and sharing of ideas. Hence group composition can be determined by a range of other factors based on a simple issue of expediency. Where a teacher feels the need to carefully target assistance then more homogeneous groups might be best, but on the whole ensuring a mix of ideas and a willingness to work together should guide decisions.

Opportunity to discuss and share ideas

Teachers can support this process by modelling the kinds of thinking and discussion required. The literature on 'thinking skills' and 'argumentation' discussed in Chapter 8 provides a useful framework and a common language with teachers playing a relatively 'hands off' role while pupils 'propose and justify ideas to other group members' (Howe *et al.* 2007: 561).

Allocation of group activities

It is likely that, if all the pupils in the class are working on the same general problem then the discussion between groups will be richer and the teacher will be able to draw together the ideas from different groups to create a really challenging discussion. However, the nature of the problem that is being looked at, and the availability of the equipment will have a bearing on how the work is organised. What is probably most important is that the pupils and the teacher can see how and why the work is distributed as it is and how it contributes to the whole.

Written instructions

A large and busy classroom, especially where there is group work and practical equipment is being used, requires a good deal of organisation. Thus in Anne's lesson on sealants, buckets of water were placed by each table in order to avoid too much moving about. Children should be aware of what they need to do. However, there are times when they will need instructions of some sort, for instance:

■ Where pupils need to follow a set approach in setting up some equipment, a workcard can be used, or instructions projected onto a screen visible by all. However, given the role and purpose of most group work, such instructions are not likely to be the norm.

■ Often it is possible for the pupils and their teacher to discuss the investigations as a class and to agree on some ways forward. These can then be written onto the computer and projected onto a screen or interactive whiteboard, or printed off for each group.

■ What can be useful is some form of simple writing frame to help the children to structure their thinking and record outcomes. It may also be useful to have a table set up for results. In the case of Sue's lesson on string telephone (Box 19.1) she did not know what ideas the children would come up with and so could not prepare worksheets in advance. What she did was to use a basic 'experiment sheet' with the headings 'I want to find out', 'To make it fair I will ...', 'What I did', and 'I found out' (see Chapter 10, Figure 10.1). Then in discussion with the groups she helped them to add extra instruction, for example John's group needed tin cans, paper cups, and strings of the same length. Using a computer and interactive board would enable the whole class to give advice here. What this approach does is to provide attention focusing and an indication of the materials they needed to collect, whilst at the same time ensuring that they retain ownership of the problem they are addressing. It must be disheartening to spend ten minutes discussing exciting possibilities and then to find that the investigation to be carried out is the one that was in the teacher's head all the time.

Equipment and resources

On the whole the equipment and resources used in primary science are not complex. Often everyday items are more appropriate than specialist science equipment. The important thing is that the resources the children need are readily available, well maintained and efficiently deployed.

Selecting resources

Clearly the resources used in primary science are dictated by the planned activities, which are in turn guided by learning goals. Hence planning and resourcing are closely linked. Good published schemes tend to provide lists of resources needed as does the QCA Scheme of Work for Key Stages 1 and 2 (DfES 1998). Other help is available from organisations including Cleapss (Consortium of Local Authority Provision of Science Services www.Cleapss.org.uk). Teachers' TV provides video reviews of selected resources, especially electronic resources (http://www. teachers.tv/). The Association for Science Education (www.ase.org.uk) provides a good deal of support. In particular *Primary Science*, one of ASE's journals, includes a useful section of reviews of materials for teachers and pupils. ASE conferences are the ideal venue for finding out and trying out resources and finding out how others have used them.

If we have in mind the kinds of practical activities discussed elsewhere in this book, such as floating and sinking, growing plants, dissolving materials, collecting woodlice or using string telephones, it is clear that the resources we need are everyday. Some of these resources can be used over and over again. Others, such as flour or pieces of wire will be used up. Shortage of these things causes the greatest frustration because this is what many of the children's activities are all about, so some money needs to be set aside for their purchase throughout the year.

In addition to the 'everyday' items there are some more specialist items that can enhance learning without being so difficult to use that they act as a barrier to learning. Work on electricity is an obvious example, and measuring instruments such as stop clocks or light metres can provide clear and accurate recordings that would not otherwise be possible. Other equipment such as data loggers and mini-solar panels have become common in schools, with children, if not always adults, seeing them as 'everyday'. In addition there is now a dazzling array of software, Internet resources, posters, models and of course books available to support learning. The following provides brief lists of the resources you might need.

The lists in Box 19.3 are not extensive; the first column in particular could be much longer, including items brought in from the seashore, from visits to grandparents or objects brought in by the teacher. The list could be endless, but the storage space is not. Hence the imperative is to consider what needs to be in the collection of resources.

In all this, the key is to link resource needs to planning and so to the intended learning outcomes. Here the science coordinator or subject leader has a key role. It may, for example, not be value for money to buy something like a model of a human eye if it is only to be used by the oldest pupils once in a year. It may be better to arrange to borrow one from the local secondary school, local teachers' centre, science learning centre. ICT resources are discussed in more detail in Chapters 21 and 22.

19.3 Resources of science

Everyday objects and materials	Consumables	Specialist equipment	Support resources
Boxes, plastic bottles, other containers, string, scissors, rulers, paper clips, sticky tape, drawing pins, elastic bands, glue, card, plasticine, plant pots, spoons, straws, marbles, toy cars, rocks, pieces of fabric,	Flour, bicarbonate of soda, soap powder, plaster of Paris, mirror card, wood for hammering, batteries, wire for shaping, aluminium foil, fruits or flowers for cutting, seeds for planting.	Posters for collecting insects, torches, mirrors, glass blocks, triangular prisms, hand lenses, measuring cylinders, spirit thermometers, data loggers, tuning forks, stop clocks and watches, springs, bathroom scales, pulleys, filter paper, gardening and other tools, magnets, bulbs, wire etc.	CD ROMs or a list of appropriate websites containing resources that show events (e.g. volcanos or plant growth), or that model phenomena (e.g. the solar system or trajectories). Models (such as of the digestive system, or a 3D eye). Appropriate resources for use with the interactive whiteboard. Hardware such as posters, books and other paper resources.

Storing equipment and materials

Access is the key word in deciding a system of storage for equipment and materials. There are various possibilities and the advantages and disadvantages of each in a particular case will depend on the size, physical layout and curriculum planning of the school. We can do no more here than point out options.

A central store?

A decision has to be made about central storage versus distribution of the equipment among classes. Apart from physical availability of a central store a major consideration is having someone to look after it. There are obvious advantages in sharing expensive items which are only infrequently used but some of these advantages are lost if the equipment is not kept in good order. Clearly the science subject leader, or coordinator, has to be willing and able, in the sense of having the time, to organise a central store and to check that items are not 'lost' by being put back in the wrong place or in an unsatisfactory condition. In schools where teaching assistants and other support staff are available it is helpful to put time aside for them to take on the role of maintaining resources. This is more easily achieved in a central store.

Giving children access

Another decision is whether children should have access to the equipment as well as teachers. The problems of maintaining an orderly central store can be exacerbated by too many having access, yet the teacher will want children to help in the collection and return of equipment. The suggestion of appointing a few children to be 'monitors' or 'storekeepers' may be a solution. If the store is within each class, the same considerations apply. If children are to have access then the labels used to classify the equipment should be ones that they will relate to and understand. There are considerable dividends for the initial investment of time when children are, perhaps, involved in drawing up lists of what equipment there is and creating rules for using the store.

Whether or not there is a central store, within a class the equipment for certain sessions needs to be accessible to the children. The demands of providing group activities for all the children at once are of course considerable and require preplanning and preparation. The materials and equipment needed for a set of activities can be anticipated and a suitable selection made available without limiting what the children will be able to do using their own ideas. It is handy to have these materials on a trolley if possible so that they can easily be put safely out of the way when not being studied. When the equipment is being used, the teacher should be able to depend on the help of the children to take responsibility for choosing, collecting and later returning it to its proper place. Building up a system for this is important in developing children's ability to take a part in facilitating their own learning as well as for the teacher's sanity. It involves making sure that children know what is available, where, and how to look after it and keep it tidy.

Topic boxes

A third major decision point, which applies where a school or class organises science within topics, is whether equipment should be boxed by topic or stored as separate kinds of items. The topic box is a great convenience, but can tie up equipment which could be used for work outside the topic. This can lead to 'plundering' from the box with the chance of the item not being there when that topic is being used. The effort put into developing topic boxes is also a disincentive to changing topics, when perhaps they have outlived their freshness. The device of temporary topic boxes is a useful compromise. The box exists for as long as the topic is being used and is dismantled when moving on to another topic.

Safety in and out of school

Despite the fact that science is now taught by most primary teachers and in all primary schools, it remains very safe. Teachers and others take sensible precautions and hence very few accidents are related to science activities. However this situation should not lead to complacency. Part of the reason science is so safe is that there is a good deal of high quality advice available to support science coordinators and teacher. The ASE produces and updates an essential guide called *Be Safe* (ASE 2001); there is also an INSET pack (ASE 2002). A school may have a health and safety policy or statement. Teachers and other educators in the school must be aware of the issues, and indeed Peter Burrows (2003) argues that every school should have at least one copy of *Be Safe* which is a short booklet setting out the main points (see Box 19.4). More detailed information can be obtained from regular publications which are distributed to member schools by CLEAPPS (of which all local authorities in England and Wales are members), or SSERC which has a similar role in Scotland. These materials include regular updates and the opportunities for teachers to phone or email specific queries.

Ensuring safety in science is not achieved by simply reading booklets, no matter how good. It requires the application of common sense. Burrows (2003) comments that an activity that is safe for a group of children with high levels of literacy may be less so where many of the children are bilingual or refugees with limited experience of formal schooling. Notes to this effect can be added to the school scheme of work, and to the policy for science, but staff training is essential to ensure that all know about and can apply safety procedures. This applies as much to support staff and parent helpers as it does to teachers.

Safety is not only a matter for the staff to consider. These considerations need to be shared with the pupils. Health and safety rules should not simply be presented to the children. Most curriculum guidelines require the explicit development by children of ideas relating (for

---

19.4 Topics covered in *Be Safe* (ASE 2001)

Be Safe contains essential safety codes for using tools, glues, sources of heat, chemicals and electricity. It also covers the preparation of food in the classroom and related matters of hygiene. Precautions to take in studying 'Ourselves' are set out. There is an important section on the selection and care of animals kept in the classroom and a list of those that should not be kept. Advice is also given about growing micro-organisms. Finally there is information about poisonous plants and safety codes for working out of class and for visits and field trips.

19.5 Safety matters within a school science policy document

Learning and teaching

Children will be taught to make their own 'risk assessment' before undertaking work.

Health and safety

Teachers should make themselves aware of any safety issues before undertaking work with children.

In order to ensure the safe teaching of science it is required that all staff read the ASE *Be Safe* booklet and read any safety bulletins which are circulated by the post-holder.

There are also a number of CLEAPS publications which deal with a wide range of safety issues – these and the *Be Safe* booklet will always be available in the staff-room.

If any safety issues are unclear the science coordinator will seek clarification from CLEAPS.

(Excerpts from the science policy of Hillside Primary School, Orpington)

example) to road use, mains electricity, and the health hazards of smoking or drug abuse. All these ideas need to be discussed with children in such a way as to encourage understanding and therefore self-discipline in terms of obedience to the rules. Rules and obedience to them is necessary where safety matters are concerned but the sooner compliance becomes voluntary the sooner the temptation to break them is eliminated – hence the item in the school science policy presented in Box 19.5 where explicit mention is made of pupils undertaking their own risk analysis. The prime importance of safety should not be to curtail children's investigations but to ensure that the necessary precautions are taken and that children gradually come to understand the reasons for them. The same arguments apply to health and safety issues when taking children out of doors and on school trips. This is discussed in more detail in the next chapter.

Summary

This chapter has concerned questions of why and how relating to practical work in primary science including its rationale, organisation, equipment and safety precautions. The main points have been:

- the value of practical work in primary science is not simply 'learning by doing', but rather providing children with real experiences and the opportunity to explore, discuss and test their ideas to construct their own knowledge and understanding about the physical world and the nature of science;

- for practical work to be successful and sufficient time needs to be set aside;

- children need to see the purpose of their investigations and for that purpose to be meaningful; in this way they will develop their skills as scientists;

- working in groups of four or five, with the teacher monitoring the work of the group, modelling the skills of debate and discussion but giving control to the group provides the ideal basis for real learning to be achieved;

- when selecting materials for use in primary science it is important to keep in mind the centrality of first-hand experience – children learn best when they explore things around them; therefore simple, familiar utensils are to be preferred over more complex laboratory apparatus;

- when building up a stock of resources it is essential to consider the curriculum and the activities planned and to ensure that consumables are available as appropriate; the responsibility for maintaining resources must be clear and care taken to maintain and store equipment and materials in good condition, this is particularly so if a central store is to be used – children should be involved in keeping all the things in good order;

- a wide view of safety has been taken, so that risks involved in certain activities can be minimised without inhibiting children's experience – helping children to understand reasons for safety codes has to be seen as an important part of learning in science.

Further reading

Burrows, P. (2003) Managing health and safety in primary science, *Primary Science Review* 79: 18–20.

Mant, J., Wilson, H, and Coates, D. (2007) The effect of increasing conceptual challenge in primary science lessons on pupils' achievement and engagement, *International Journal of Science Education* 29 (14): 1707–19.

Naylor, S., Keogh, B. and Downing, B. (2007) Argumentation in primary science, *Research in Science Education* 2007 37: 177–239.

Teaching and Learning Research Programme (November 2005) Briefing No. 11: Improving pupil group work in classrooms, a new approach to increasing engagement in everyday classroom settings at Key Stages 1, 2 and 3.

http://www.groupworkscotland.org/ (accessed July 2008).

Learning outside the classroom

Introduction

A growing support for learning outside the classroom can be seen as a rebalancing after a period where the tightly prescribed curricula in various countries has led some teachers to feel constrained, needing to 'fit everything in'. The renewed focus is reflected in the conclusion of the House of Commons Select Committee on Skills that 'education outside the classroom is of significant benefit to students' (Select Committee 2007: 7). In this chapter we consider the benefits of learning outside the classroom and its particular value for primary science. We provide examples of different types of experiences and locations and make some suggestions about how to plan for and make the most use of these precious events.

Why learning outside the classroom?

The need to extend learning experiences

After the introduction of the National Curriculum in England the amount of 'field work' being experienced by secondary school pupils plummeted because teachers did not see how it related to the curriculum, could not link it directly to assessment and worried about finding the time in a crowded curriculum (Fisher 2001). Similarly in primary schools the time taken to visit a museum or local supermarket became more difficult to justify when so much needed to be 'covered' in the prescribed curriculum. In addition to these curriculum constraints the issue of health and safety became such that, in some cases, teachers shied away from taking the risks associated with journeys out of school. The increase in the costs of school visits, especially transport costs has added to the problem. Few would disagree that this is a loss to the general education of young people.

Fortunately a certain relaxation of the curriculum, and in particular a reduction in the specificity of prescription (see Chapter 3) has left teachers feeling a little more free to include more variety and excitement in their planning. However, this is not the whole story. A number of factors have come together to bring learning outside the classroom to the fore. These include concerns about a lack of exercise by young people, and poor diet leading to health problems. Understanding more about food production as well as developing an appreciation of the outdoors is seen as a way to counteract this. Further, there are worries that a lack of understanding of the natural world could lead to citizens who are unable to take informed decisions about their impact on the environment. There is also a growing unease at the lack of freedom for children to learn through play and exploration which in turn means that they are not learning how to take risks and make decisions for themselves. In terms of primary science, the opportunities offered for relevant, exciting and memorable experiences with resources, environments and experts not normally found in the classroom means that learning outside of the classroom is essential.

In our increasingly controlled and technologically rich world young people are more protected and less active than they were in the past. Peacock (2006a) describes an idyllic childhood in the Lake District where he roamed far and wide, fishing in streams and climbing trees. We may not all have had such freedom or such opportunities to discover the natural world by ourselves, and simple nostalgia for our own childhoods may not be sufficient reason to go to the trouble of trying to recreate these experiences. However, it is clear that children do need to play and learn in this way, even if we now feel there needs to be more control and protection. The *Learning Outside the Classroom Manifesto* linked this to other English education policy statements by arguing that outdoor education is a 'powerful route' to the 'every child matters' agenda. This includes, in particular, 'enjoying and achieving, staying safe and being healthy' (DfES 2006: 3).

Arguments for teachers spending the, not inconsiderable, time and effort involved to provide opportunities for learning outside the classroom include the mounting evidence that such experiences have a significant impact on children's learning, their motivation to learn, their social skills and general attitude to school. In relation to science, in addition to the development of positive attitudes to science learning, children get the opportunity to develop and apply scientific skills and understanding in the real world. Interactive and informal learning environments have an important role in demystifying science, for parents and the general public as well as for children.

Finally there is access to resources that would otherwise be unavailable, including the physical environment, and specialist or expensive equipment from which to learn, and also the intellectual resources of the specialists who offer support for learning in certain sites, such as countryside rangers, museum curators, farmers, employees in factories and other industrial settings.

The contribution to learning in general

There is a broad consensus that taking children out to experience the environment and to work in exciting and different settings has a significant impact on the quality of their learning and on the relationship between teacher and pupils. Pupils learn about society and how to work together. They develop an understanding of the relationship between nature and society. Dillon and his colleagues (2005: 22) describe the cognitive, affective, interpersonal/social and physical/behavioural impact of learning outdoors. Similarly in its *Learning Outside the Classroom Manifesto*, the DfES listed the advantages as in Box 20.1.

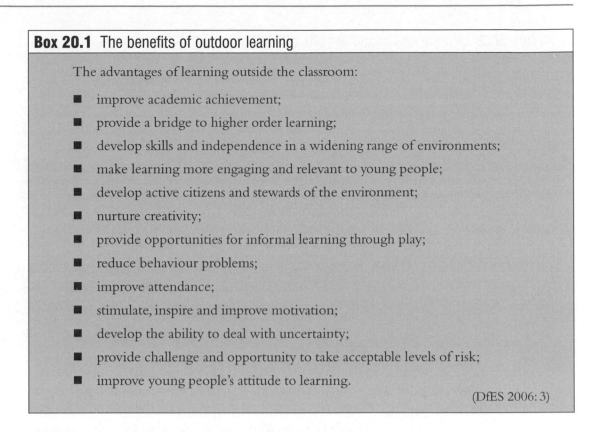

Box 20.1 The benefits of outdoor learning

The advantages of learning outside the classroom:

■ improve academic achievement;

■ provide a bridge to higher order learning;

■ develop skills and independence in a widening range of environments;

■ make learning more engaging and relevant to young people;

■ develop active citizens and stewards of the environment;

■ nurture creativity;

■ provide opportunities for informal learning through play;

■ reduce behaviour problems;

■ improve attendance;

■ stimulate, inspire and improve motivation;

■ develop the ability to deal with uncertainty;

■ provide challenge and opportunity to take acceptable levels of risk;

■ improve young people's attitude to learning.

(DfES 2006: 3)

The contribution to science learning in particular

The specific benefits to be gained for science from working out of the classroom include, for example, the development of an understanding of the relationship between the food we eat and farming. Dillon *et al.* (2005) point out that, although farming takes up a significant proportion of the countryside and is a huge industry in the UK, as in much of the developed world, farming and food have become disconnected for many people. If young people are to contribute to debates about sustainability a reconnection needs to be made. Similarly in terms of the environment, the issues are complex, but without an understanding of the interrelationships between people and the environment young people will be unable to make informed decisions about such matters as the need to recycle materials. A national poll in 2008 found that a third of the adult population of England did not believe that changes in weather patterns were related to global warming, or that they were anything other than 'natural' (*Independent* 02/05/08). Having the chance to explore the natural world and to see the interrelationship between people and their environment gives young people a foundation on which to build their views of the world and their own relationship to it.

The quotations in Box 20.2 bring together some of the important aspects of learning outdoors. In the first case the girl experienced something brand new and learnt not to be afraid of the animals she found. Her interest was aroused and she really enjoyed the experience. In other cases, where children might have been expected to know a lot about the environment (Ambleside being in the heart of the Lake District National Park), having a project to work on focused their

---

Box 20.2 Some views on the benefits of getting out of the classroom

An 8-year-old from inner London on her first experience of pond dipping:

There were lots of different animals, lots of legs and all slimy. It took away my fear.
Getting out of the classroom – a day with the RSPB (Teachers' TV)

A 14-year-old girl living in a rural area after working in her local environment:

We used to take it all for granted – you know, the hills and the trees … now, we take it for granted that we don't pick wild flowers, things that are illegal and anti-social, like litter and campfires.

(14-year-old girl, Ambleside, Peacock 2006b: 15)

A ranger discussing the value of school visits:

Children's memories and learning from the visit were closely related. Strong themes are positive personal and social gains of direct and novel outdoor experiences in big landscapes, appreciation of methods of enquiry into the natural world (scientific and artistic) and interest in revisiting the National Park.

(Dillon et al. 2005: 23)

---

energies and helped them to value their own beautiful surroundings. Without this they might not have appreciated the need or the means to preserve it. In the final quote the ranger makes a link between memory and long-term learning similar to that described in Chapter 4 where we discussed neuroscience and Susan Greenfield's description of memory as the 'cornerstone of the mind' and the basis of our ability to adapt to our environment, that is, to learn. In this case, as in the other two, children were also motivated to revisit these sites and to continue to use and learn from them.

Access to resources

Physical resources

Throughout this book we have emphasised the need for pupils to learn science through first-hand experience in which they are able to explore objects, materials and events. Mostly the resources for learning can be simple, familiar everyday objects, and may be easily accessible. However, there are times when so much more could be learnt with access to appropriate equipment or environments. In Chapter 1 we described the visit of a class to the beach with David. Clearly the beach in itself is a valuable resource, but also the classroom provided by the oil company and the photographs developed with the support of the local oil company meant that key images could be presented and discussed in relation to the topic under study. The opportunities provided by museums and hands-on science centres are considerable, such as the example given later in Box 20.7 of a model of NASA mission control and the chance to 'fly' in a space ship. No less significant are the opportunities offered by the local supermarket to help children understand how groceries are organised, how bread is made, how food is stored and kept fresh are all valuable additions to the curriculum.

Intellectual resources

No teacher can hope to be an expert in all areas. Learning from experts is a valuable extension of the resources that can be harnessed to support the curriculum. This might mean making use of an amateur photography club to produce photographs of a local site for a visit, or the expertise of parents, carers and others in the community. Shirley Davids describes how Howarth School gardening club developed under the guidance of the school caretaker and a parent who is also a professional gardener. The garden is used by all children throughout the school as part of their curriculum. 'The day I learnt most was when I went outside to look at the flowers. I sucked in quite a lot of learning that day' (Davids 2008: 6).

Museums, galleries, gardens, farms, and other places of work also provide access to a great deal of expertise. Museums and galleries, and especially hands-on centres have worked extremely hard over recent years to develop materials to support pupil learning and to explore ways of presenting exhibits that support learning. These locations are now much more child and teacher friendly, providing hands-on experiences, specially designed exhibits and specially trained educators. Most centres have developed materials that can be sent out to schools to help prepare for a visit and that suggest follow up work (for example, Baraclough and Bracey 2005). Linked to this is a whole wealth of material online that can be used to support visits, or independently. These can be found through websites such as the 24 Hour Museum (www.24hourmuseum.org.uk/). A number of businesses have also opened their doors to educational visits, often providing educators based in specially designed centres to support learning. It remains the role of the teacher to make the best use of these resources as we discuss later in this chapter.

Locations for learning outside the classroom

There are many ways to categorise locations for learning. We divide them here into natural locations, museums and wildlife centres, places of work and a few 'others'.

Natural locations

This includes parks, seashores, woods, meadows and school grounds. In some there may not be a formal structure for visitors and so the teacher's knowledge of the area is important. The school grounds and immediate surrounding area is probably the most inexpensive outdoor opportunity which still remains under-used. One great advantage of making more use of the local environment is that repeat visits can be made. Fradley (2006: 15) wanted to include the outside environment more and in particular to take the children out for a weekly walk. Making sure that her pupils were adequately clothed and shod was a challenge. She sent a letter home to parents as in Figure 20.1.

The option of walking around the local area is necessarily dependent on parental permission, and the environment. A busy city location might be inappropriate, but getting out into the grounds to experience rainfall or to measure wind speed with paper windmills is possible for many schools. Many teachers recognise that the pedagogic skills needed for a successful trip are not quite the same as those needed in the classroom (Kiseil 2007). This can lead to a lack of

Dear Parents

Welly Walks from Elm Class

This year I would like to use the outside environment more within my teaching; the children are really interested in the world around us. This week we went for a short walk and had a great time talking about bees and collecting nectar, the lifecycle of a caterpillar and seed dispersal linked to sunflowers. When we returned to the classroom the children wrote beautifully about aspects of the walk they enjoyed and did colour mixing to paint sunflowers in the style of Van Gogh as well as pastel pictures. Real experiences such as these are very valuable.

I would like the children to bring in wellies and a very waterproof coat every Friday in order for us to go out for short walks. Sometimes we will go around the village to link in with our geography topic; at other times we will be collecting thoughts, ideas and possibly creatures to fit in with our other subjects. It will be great to find out more about the rain. All the children will obviously need to be adequately protected from the weather so if you have any spare wellies or waterproofs I would like to have some for the classroom

Figure 20.1 Preparing for working out of doors

confidence, especially on the part of inexperienced teachers. Accompanying more experienced staff on visits is a good way to learn, as is making use of organisations that provide expert trained staff. There is a wide range of groups who work with schools. Forest School, for example, provides trained specialist staff take the lead (NEF 2003).

Welly Walks, Forest Schools and others focus on general learning although they include many opportunities for science learning, as Jane Adams describes when writing about her school's involvement with the National Trust Guardianship Scheme which enables links with National Trust wardens (Adams 2006: 7). Other activities can have science as the main focus of work. The children in Neston School are lucky enough to have plenty of greenery around their village school, and making use of this for science is an important part of the planned curriculum as indicated in Box 20.3.

Working outside the classroom as described in Box 20.3 provides children with the opportunity to use and develop their skills of observation and prediction, in this case when seeking out the woodlice. Continuing outside seemed like the most natural thing to do. Many other natural locations present themselves as places to learn. In Chapter 1 we described a trip by a class of children in North Wales. Carefully organised beach scavenger hunts offer so much that is exciting and interesting, providing schools with a sound basis for further class work on identification of items found, to online research to find out more about the shells and seaweed discovered. Other opportunities can come from links with university departments who are keen to develop links with schools. Owen *et al.* (2008) describe how a school gained through children working with professional scientists to do environmental research on their local river, something that might otherwise have been beyond the ability of the school staff to offer.

Box 20.3 The outdoor classroom

Year 2/3 class in Neston School – the classroom outside

A class of 5–7-year-olds were continuing their topic on 'minibeasts' in a lesson in the school grounds looking for and studying woodlice.

The teacher introduced the lesson briefly because the class was excited to be going outside. Each group had a small plastic tray to collect woodlice and a handheld magnifying glass, a clip board and Post-it notes and a little pack of laminated words. Having reminded the children about safety issues and revisited the questions they had raised about woodlice, the class of 22, in groups of three and four plus two helpers, went to different places in the grounds to see what they could find.

The children looked under stones and in long grass, and in the woodpile as well as less likely places. They were clearly making predictions about where woodlice could be found and learning a good deal about their habitat. Each group gathered between five and ten woodlice before the teacher called the class together.

The children gathered at the picnic tables picked up their clip boards and were asked to spend a little time just taking turns observing the woodlice and wondering about them. They were encouraged to take turns and to 'tell each other what you notice'.

Teacher	Are they all the same?
Pupil	The smaller ones are usually like grey.
Teacher	Are they all grey?
Pupil	Maybe the younger ones are more grey.
Pupil	Some have spots.
Teacher	Do you think they are all the same species?

Once the class had taken time to observe the woodlice their teacher called them all together.

Teacher Well everybody, that was really really good observations. You have all been noticing lots of things about your woodlice.

The children were then asked to take their Post-it notes and pack of words. The words included 'do', 'who', 'what if…', 'would', 'where' and 'can'.

The teacher asked the children to take out one word at a time and to write a question about the woodlice to include that word. One group began working immediately, asking questions such as:

Do you like the feeling of them?
Would you touch them?
Where do they come from?
What if it got sick?/had an orange head/had an orange bottom?

The teacher joined the group and selected 'can' from the pack of words.

Pupil: Can it fly?
Pupil: Can it run? Yes, because it's got legs.

Box 20.4 On the farm

Docking school in Norfolk teamed up with Courtyard Farm that supplies the school with organic meat under the auspices of the 'Food for Life' partnership scheme. The farmer was worried that children, even from relatively local schools, did not understand the industry. At the start of the project the Docking School council was consulted about how they would like a project to develop. This proved to be a really useful process which demonstrated pupils' interest in the farm and their desire to learn new skills and get to know how the farm worked. They also wanted to 'feel that they could help the farmer'. Older children visited first and, later in the day, partly as a way to reduce transport costs, younger children arrived. The older children then acted as guides for the younger children, parents and teachers. The farmer, well used to visits from schools, reported that these were the best he had had. He found the older children had become identified with the farm and acted as hosts. Small groups worked well. Further trips were planned to extend the partnership and build on the considerable amount of interest and goodwill the project had created.

More information about this visit can found at http://www.foodforlife.org.uk/resources/case_studies/CaseStudy221

Places of work

Children's learning is enhanced where they see its relevance to their lives and to the world beyond school. The Every Child Matters agenda (DfES 2004) refers to economic well-being, within which an understanding of the world of work is considered important. Visits to places of work can promote an understanding of how science contributes to our lives, and how useful an understanding of science is to future employment. Local supermarkets, fire stations, greengrocers and garden centres can provide valuable locations for visits. Farms, as mentioned earlier, provide opportunities for many links between science and everyday life; they are also places of work. School visits to farms can provide a wide range of benefits as the children from Docking school discovered in Box 20.4.

Building up a long-standing relationship with a local company can provide continuity for pupils and additional advantages as pupils become familiar with the site and make links with the work that some of their parents do. In the case of a local power company as described in Box 20.5, the school gains considerably from the continued connection.

Science museums or centres, zoos and wildlife centres

Unlike classroom learning where there tends to be a linear sequence of activities and ideas, one building on the other, each relying on what has previously been learnt, museums, galleries and hands–on centres tend to provide non–linear units of activity. These may be around a theme, such as 'Light and colour' or 'Lavatories through the ages', but visitors can experience exhibits in more or less any order they want to, remaining at each for as long as they wish. Thus the museum relies

Box 20.5 Getting to know local industry

A class of 7-year-olds visited a local gas-powered electricity-generating power station. The company has a staff-training centre that is also used to host school visits. The company funds a significant number of class visits for local schools each year as part of its community responsibility. The children from this local school will visit the station at least twice during their primary school career. On each visit, where possible a member of staff who is also a parent of a child in the school is released to join the group. This helps to make the link with employment and also adds to the expertise available to the children on their visit. Older children have a chance to look around the power station while, for health and safety reasons younger ones remain in the classroom at the site.

After safety talks, including dressing up in reflective clothing and hard hats, the children worked in small groups with helpers provided by the company to study electricity. They made circuits, tried out switches, looked at a prototype electric car and then worked with a small model electric car studying conductors and insulators. Each group tried each activity. One involved generators.

Generators

A group of five children were shown pictures in the power station exhibition of the large gas-powered electricity generators in the main power station. They also looked at scale models of wind turbines and water driven turbines. The parent who worked in the station was able to explain that some energy is needed to turn a generator in order to produce electricity. In this station the energy comes from gas.

Each pupil was then handed a small, hand held generator, wires and a bulb in a holder. They were asked to connect up the generator and turn the handle. This caused much excitement. One pupil commented 'The faster you go the brighter the bulb'. The teacher used this to ask pupils to try for themselves. 'Go slower. What happens to the bulb? Go faster. What happens to the bulb?'

The teacher then gave each child a cell to connect up instead of the bulb. This caused the generator handle to turn, much to the delight of the pupils. Although the teacher did not elaborate he simply said that the electricity was causing the handle to turn, so energy was coming from the 'battery' to the generator, instead of the other way round.

on curiosity and intrinsic motivation on the part of the general visitor. For school visits this can mean that the amount learnt is fairly limited. In a study of pupils visiting fairly formal museums, Bamberger and Tal (2007) concluded that learning in museums is optimised when pupils have a limited or rather guided choice as to the areas that they are encouraged to explore. This gives the opportunity to make links with their classroom learning and enables the best use to be made of the expertise and knowledge of the museum staff.

Tunnicliffe (2001) found that groups visiting museums with adults asked significantly more questions and made more statements of knowledge than groups without adults. The importance of adults, of prior preparatory learning and of information available to pupils at their level was suggested by Bowker (2004). When researching visitors to the Eden Project, he found that children change their views of plants even in a single day visit (from 'boring' to 'interesting'), but that, unless interesting plants and information are pointed out to them they do not always notice things for themselves. In a further study of the learning achieved in an Eden workshop focused on teaching children about the use of tropical plants for survival, Bowker and Jasper (2007) found that although pupils' understanding did increase significantly, they did not make the link between what they had learnt and the way indigenous peoples might use these plants. Such connections need to be made explicit by those leading the workshops. All this suggests that, for maximum benefit to be obtained by pupils, careful planning is crucial, with teachers, helpers and museum educators sharing an understanding of how best to support the visit.

Jarvis and Pell (2005) investigated any influence on children's attitudes to science of a visit to the UK National Space Centre (Box 20.6). They found that in the main exhibits, where helpers had a knowledge or interest in science or were experienced teachers or helpers, the children were more focused and engaged more with the exhibits. However, a number of the groups were fairly directionless. Questionnaires before and some time after the visits showed that these experiences had not contributed to increased interest in science in general or space in particular. However the feedback from the Space Challenger experience was more positive.

> The spacecraft was amazing. I've never had an experience like this before. It felt real. It's really exciting science. You felt important because you had your own little job.

Box 20.6 Out of this world

In visits to the National Space Centre (http://www.spacecentre.co.uk/home/) teachers were keen to ensure that pupils learnt about the relationship between the Earth, moon and sun in order to meet the requirements in the English national curriculum at the time (2002). Children visited the main exhibitions looking at models of the solar system and many other exhibits touring in groups accompanied by a parent or school helper.

The Space Centre included a section called the Challenger Centre which consisted of a NASA-like 'Mission Control' with a bank of computers sending electronic messages to the 'space craft' (entered through an air locked door). Flight directors, from the museum, ran a role play in which pupils were allocated roles, with half in mission control and half in the spacecraft. The challenge was to find and send a probe to a comet. The flight directors asked questions to bring out children's knowledge and understanding before starting. Half way through the visit the pupils had the opportunity to change over so that all had a chance to experience mission control and space flight and to take on roles such as the life support team who conducted water supply tests.

(From Jarvis and Pell 2005)

Other locations

Almost any location can provide learning opportunities. Visits to castles with a focus on history can also contribute to the science curriculum. Pushes and pulls and levers and pulleys are fascinating when linked to the mechanisms for a portcullis, or how a magellan operates. Visits to a concert hall can provide just the background for work on sound and music, and regular trips to the swimming pool offer obvious opportunities to study floating and sinking. All visits, whether they are in the school grounds, or week-long school trips abroad require careful planning. We now consider some key points that have emerged from research in terms of planning to ensure learning.

Preparing for a visit

The AZSTT website has an excellent section on planning for visits to hands-on science centres. The advice applies to many other visits. See http://www.azteachscience.co.uk/code/development/enrich_science_learning/index.html.

Research suggests that the most effective visits, wherever they might be, are those where the aims and objectives are clear and planning is carefully designed to achieve these objectives. Where possible all those involved in the visit should contribute to and be aware of the aims of the wider project that includes work prior to the visit and follow up work. DeWitt and Osborne (2007) developed guidelines as a result of extensive research where they focused particularly on developing interaction and dialogue as the means to engender learning (see Box 20.7).

Making the most of a visit

One of the major factors limiting the number of experiences schools can offer outside the classroom is the cost. This was cited as the third most important factor in limiting teachers' choice in the Wellcome Trust science survey of primary teachers (Wellcome Trust 2005). Other issues include concerns about health and safety, worries about the time taken by visits and the effect this might have on coverage of the curriculum and, finally, concerns that inexperienced teachers and others have about coping in very different teaching situations. Although there are no perfect solutions, we can see some solutions in the various examples given in this chapter. The following therefore is not an exhaustive list, rather it constitutes a few suggestions that might help in appropriate contexts.

The costs involved

- It is worth thinking about the immense value that school visits can bring to pupil learning. Once this is factored in, finding the funds becomes less difficult.

- Docking School, mentioned earlier, used the same bus throughout the day to bring all the children to the farm. This cut down on transport costs.

Box 20.7 Guidelines for planning visits

Select a good venue	The best organised locations produce resources that are attuned to the needs of the teacher and pupils, that fit with the curriculum as planned by the teacher. This means that museums, hands-on centres, etc., that are willing to meet teachers beforehand and adapt their materials to suit are likely to be more effective. In turn, visits where teachers have taken up the offer of a pre-visit and shared planning are likely to be the most successful both in terms of pupil and adult enjoyment and in terms of learning achieved.
Provide a clear structure	A clear structure and purpose for the planned activities for the visits, linked to pre-visit activities (including the opportunity to practise any skills they might need on the visit) and post-visit follow up lessons enhance pupil learning. Pupils should know what to expect before they arrive and have a clear idea about what they need to focus on during their visit. Ideally they will have planned strategies for recording experiences, observations and information to take way with them.
Encouraging joint productive activity	During a visit it is helpful to have pupils working in pairs or small groups with an objective, such as a display, or some other need to report back on what has been learnt. This gives a focus for and encourages dialogue with each other and with the group helper. A degree of choice in selecting displays or activities enables them to select things of greatest interest to the group and which have personal relevance to them.
Support dialogue, literacy and/ or research skills	Visits where pupils are encouraged to discuss ideas and to think of follow-up research and ways to report back on their finding encourages productive dialogue during the visit and sustains interest and learning beyond it. Use can be made here of online materials provided by the centre visited or other similar places. Jarvis and Pell (2005) also suggest sending letters home to parents telling them what is planned or what was learnt can encourage discussion at home, so extending the learning further. They also recommend that teachers should review and recall learning and experiences from visits later in the year and when working on related science topics.

(Adapted from DeWitt and Osborne (2007))

- In a number of areas schools have clustered together as networks. This means that three classes from three different schools can make use of the same bus, thus reducing the overall cost to any one school.

- Carol Fradley's idea of Welly Walks is inexpensive and the children gain a great deal from this approach. Making use of free sites close to school, such as supermarkets, greengrocers and other businesses can keep the costs to a minimum.

- There are many businesses willing to fund and otherwise support schools. Making links in this way can bring a range of benefits, particularly where longer term relationships are established.

Health and safety

- The key to safe learning outside the classroom is careful planning and taking good advice. Teachers who are inexperienced at managing trips should always get advice and guidance from more experienced staff, and wherever possible, should have the opportunity to accompany others as a helper in order to develop some of the skills necessary. This is where putting two or more classes together can help.

■ It has been emphasised above that pre-visits are important in planning the learning. These same visits help to ensure that a risk analysis is thorough. There is a wealth of guidance including 'Health and Safety of Pupils on Educational Visits' published by Teachernet and available free or to download from the website. Local authorities often have an outdoor education officer, and advice on their websites, and schools should have their own policies in place. Most museums, hands-on science centres, national parks and other places that host school visits regularly will publish their own risk assessment which can help guide teachers in their planning.

■ All those involved in a trip, or undertaking any activities outside the classroom should be aware of the risks and the procedures to deal with any problems. This includes all helpers. For example, in the visit to the power station, the staff at the station briefed all the helpers separately from the children. This was followed up with a briefing for the children.

Summary

This chapter has considered the value to learning in general and science in particular that comes from working out of the classroom. The main points have been:

■ the value of learning outside the classroom is significant, and hence worth taking the time to do;

■ the prescribed curriculum in a number of countries is now being relaxed, in part in order to give teachers the freedom to provide a richer and more varied curriculum;

■ well planned visits, especially those that fit into the year planning and are not simply a one off with no prior work or follow up, will cover a swathe of the curriculum and provide the motivation for pupils to continue their learning back in school;

■ learning outside the classroom has significant benefits for pupil learning in terms of social, personal and academic development as individuals and as citizens; it is also recognised to increase motivation and enhance learning and attitudes towards learning – this has been increasingly recognised by policy makers who are making efforts to encourage more learning outside the classroom;

■ making use of many locations outside the classroom provides access to a wealth of resources for science learning that could not otherwise be available;

■ there are many locations to choose, and these offer different opportunities; knowing how best to use these resources is an important part of the success of any visit;

■ careful planning with pre-visits to plan good curriculum coverage and a rigorous risk assessment ensures a productive and enjoyable visit; the learning can be built upon back in school, thus increasing the value for money.

Further reading

Adams, J. (2006) Starting out in your own backyard, *Primary Science Review* 91: 7–10.

Davids, S. (2008) Growing faster than their sunflowers, *Primary Science* 101: 5–8.

Fradley, C. (2006) Welly Walks for science learning, *Primary Science Review* 91: 14–16.

Useful websites

The AZSTT website has an excellent section on planning for visits to hands-on science centres: http://www.azteachscience.co.uk/code/development/enrich_science_learning/index.html

Teachernet health and safety website:

http://www.teachernet.gov.uk/wholeschool/healthandsafety/visits

21

Children using ICT

Introduction

In this chapter we look at the role of information and communication technology (ICT) in the learning of science. We focus here in particular on the ways children can use ICT in their learning in and beyond the classroom. What we say about using ICT is firmly linked to discussions in previous chapters about the importance of learning and understanding constructed through children discussing ideas, thinking, exploring and developing the skills and attitudes of science.

We begin this chapter with a discussion about how children interact with technology and then how ICT is being included in the curriculum. Different resources, hardware and software can be used in many combinations, hence we then provide three examples of children using ICT in school, before moving on to consider the various functions of ICT more generally and the role of the learner in using the various tools.

Digital citizens

Baby Miles, aged 3 weeks, was lying on his new mat kicking his legs. His foot hit the centre of a large toy flower and set off a little tune. This attracted Oscar, Miles's 15-month-old brother's attention. Very soon Oscar had worked out that all three large flowers play a tune, each one different. Soon Oscar had decided he liked the blue flower tune best. Oscar is also able to play his own CDs and select different operations in his toy car.

Many children in the developed world at least are virtually born using information and communication technologies. They expect to use ICT for play and for learning. Indeed Frand (2000) has argued that for young people computers, digital cameras, mobile phones, and the like are not seen as 'technology'. He suggests that, 'if you can remember using your first one ever, it's technology' (p. 16). For people over 60 the landline telephone is not considered to be technology, for people over 50 the television is hardly 'technology'. In the same way as older people take the telephone for granted, primary-school-aged children now take mobile phones and other hand held mobile devices in their stride. They see computers and the Internet as simply a part of the normal world, and the ability to use devices to control their world is normal.

People who remember first using digital technology may well have become competent users, but they will generally remain 'digital immigrants' as compared with their younger counterparts the 'digital natives'. Natives expect to use these objects to learn with. Why wouldn't they? Yet confidence and familiarity with ICT does not necessarily mean competence, and, like any other tool, the support it provides for learning is very much dependent on how the teacher incorporates its use into the curriculum.

ICT in the curriculum

ICT is seen by governments as a key element in ensuring that education contributes to economic competitiveness. There have been huge investments made over recent years. Hall and Higgins (2007) report that, between 2001 and 2004, the UK spent £1 billion on ICT in schools while between 1999 and 2000 Australia spent $4.3 billion. At the same time, and partly as a result of this massive investment, new products have become available that are designed especially for use in primary classrooms, for instance:

- Lighter, easy to use digital cameras with associated software are now relatively cheap. At least one digital microscope is, or should now be, in every school in England.

- A whole range of hand-held devices are available to schools, including lunch box sized computers, and PC tablets.

- With the wider adoption of wireless technology another phase in classroom information technology is beginning to open up. This is the ability to go mobile. This opens up a whole vista of opportunities as it becomes possible to move away from the computer suite, and even out of the classroom all together whilst remaining connected.

Children using ICT in learning science

The learning opportunities provided by putting various forms of ICT into pupils' hands are best conveyed through real examples. In all cases these make use of information from the Internet and more information can be found about them and other examples through the sources listed.

Example 1: getting out of the classroom with a tablet PC

Tablet PCs look rather like 'etch-a-sketch' as they are computer screens that lie flat like a slate and are robust enough to survive normal classroom handling by all ages. Pupils interact with them using a stylus (pen) on the screens. When first widely introduced, teachers tended to use tablets in literacy work, as they have real value in helping children to develop their handwriting and, for example, sharing in the writing of stories (West Sussex Grid for Learning 2004). For children, and those who are less confident in coming up to the front, tablet PCs allow them to contribute from where they are sitting. However, their real value emerges as teachers and pupils see how they support group work. This was pointed out by one of the early users in the blog in Figure 21.1. As teachers and pupils become more familiar with tablets, and more schools are

> *posted by port ellen at 5:36 PM* 2 COMMENTS
> TUESDAY, NOVEMBER 22, 2005
>
> ....
>
> ## Collaborative Learning and Peer Support - KJ
> Today I want to talk about the effect the tablets have had on collaborative learning and peer support. Our school does make good use of both these strategies. Our children enjoy working together to support each other and to share the learning experience. However, I have noticed that this is particularly evident in the original tablet children. Their teamwork skills are excellent. They make use of individual skills within each group in order to succeed in the task set. I have noticed that even if they don't get on particularly well with their tablet partner socially, they make a good effort to work well with them during the set task. This is not just evident in ICT but is becoming increasingly more noticeable in other curricular areas.
>
> ....

Figure 21.1 A teacher's blog

using them through wireless connections, the flexibility of this tool is recognised and is being used more in science worldwide. In Asahi East Primary School in Japan where drawing skills are highly valued, children use pen tablets for sketching. For example, they planted seeds and watched seedlings growing taking photographs and making drawings of their plants at regular intervals. Drawing, their teacher argues, encourages children to focus on detail that they would not notice if they simply took photographs. The children then created animations of their plant growing using their own drawings and also their digital photographs (http://www.wacom-asia.com/casestudy/asahi_east.html).

Fairfield Junior School in Hertfordshire took to new heights with their class set of tablets used as part of a project funded by the computer company (Ergo computing 2007). The tablets had a wireless connection that allowed children to use them out of doors in the school wild area. Some pupils visited the grounds making notes, keeping in contact with fellow pupils in class who undertook Internet research, for example to identify plants, at the request of their outdoor collaborators. Pupils were able to connect the tablet up to a digital microscope, and send the image back to the classroom. The microscope was then used to identify creatures dipped from a pond, and the image of a water flea was projected on to an interactive whiteboard in the classroom allowing identification and another addition to the information gained during field work

Example 2: creating and using a database

Byrne and Sharp (2002) suggested a series of lessons that could make use of databases. A teacher of 9-year-olds in an urban school used some of these ideas in a topic that involved the use of databases. The RSPB (Royal Society for the Protection of Birds) annual National Bird Survey provided the staring point. A member of the local RSPB came into school to talk to a class about the Garden Watch project and about birds in their locality (see websites at the end of this chapter)

The children decided to set up a bird watch project of their own to run throughout the spring term. Groups of children took on different tasks. One group found images of birds on the Internet and explored the different identification keys available to find one they could easily work with. They then created a display to place on the wall next to the window by the bird table. One group experimented making bird seed cakes and deciding where best to place bird feeders. Another group explored the best bird tables to use and sourced an inexpensive one. The children's teacher found out about a project in another authority that involved movement activated web cams being placed in each of a number of school bird boxes over the spring and summer. (http://www.lea.derbyshire.sch.uk/birdcam/, and http://www.wynyardwoodlandpark.org.uk/BirdBoxWebcam.htm). The children then monitored the website looking into the nests.

Once the bird table and feeders had been set up the children organised a rota to observe the birds on the table at different times in the day (including during breakfast club and after school club) over a two-week period. Groups used the digital camera to film birds on the table and took photographs. A database of birds and times of visiting was built up and explored to find out which birds visited at different times of the day. The children were able to compare their data with the national data produced as a result of the RSPB project. They designed a web page for their school site, which included profiles of the most regular visitors and of the rarest. They were able to insert a video clip into their web page and an animation based on photographs taken at different times of the day. A group of children wrote a report on the nest box experiment in the local authority bulletin and another negotiated with the head teacher for the school to get involved in the following year's garden and school birdwatch survey with the RSPB.

Example 3: data loggers

At Willesborough Junior School in Kent the Year 5 children were introduced to data loggers through a revision lesson on shadows. Children revisited the concept of shadows and how they are formed before exploring them again using data loggers. They found out how the equipment worked, and produced and labelled graphs to show the changes in light intensity measured (see Figure 21.2). Once the class was familiar with the equipment they were then able to tackle a real problem to find the best materials for keeping drinks hot using a temperature sensor (http://www.kented.org.uk/ngfl/subjects/science/Ecolog/index.html).

The functions of ICT and the role of the learner

The three examples illustrate how different ICT resources can be used in an authentic way to enhance learning. In looking further at the different functions of ICT, it is important to recognise that these can be integrated in a topic in different ways. As the range and variety of ICT and associated software increases it becomes more and more difficult to categorise the different tools since one tool may have different functions. Here we consider the functions under the headings of enabling children to find information, explore ideas, practise or revise, record and collate and present and report.

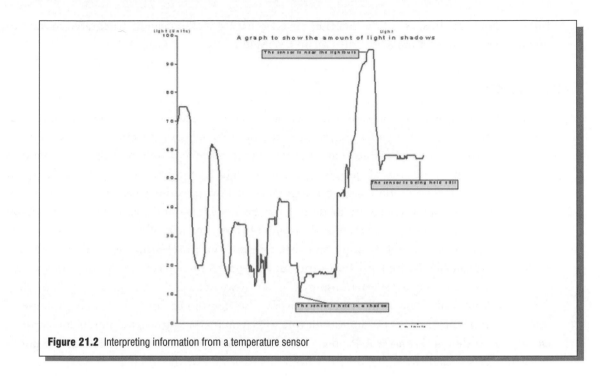

Figure 21.2 Interpreting information from a temperature sensor

As a reference source

In the early days of CD-ROMs and the Internet much of the material available could be described as 'books on screen'. This offered the opportunity of a greater number of reference sources and ease of browsing. Now the sources available are often more interactive, including animations and video, and can be tailored to suit the age range and interests of pupils. Using the ICT as a reference source remains the most widely recognised use in the population at large; especially in the case of the Internet. In a study of primary teachers' use of ICT in Belgium this was by far the most common use for children in the classroom (Tondeur *et al.* 2007). In Example 2 above we saw how pupils were able to use websites to gain information about birds and bird feeders and used search engines such as Ask Jeeves for Kids. Similarly, knowing clearly what is wanted is important in using sites such as Wikipedia and encyclopaedias in general.

Children enjoy finding out for themselves. Here it is crucial that there is a clear purpose for finding information, otherwise the tendency is to copy large tracts of information, which is little understood and hardly read. On the other hand, a common characteristic of 'digital natives' is to flick around screens and pieces of information from one to another (as they do in computer games) and to make little sense of anything they are looking at. This is why information that is well structured and age appropriate is often more useful for teaching. Thus the RSPB website with its sections entitled 'In the classroom' can provide a useful starting point. Similarly in Example 1 the children were able to make use of websites such as Nature Explorer which provides simple keys, and diagrams of pond animals (see websites). With greater access to the

Internet in classrooms, use of the Internet for information seeking can be integrated more into normal classroom learning as was the case in Example 1.

Exploring ideas

Simulation and modelling software, and spreadsheets and databases that let pupils test out ideas – for example, the trajectory of a cannon fired at different angles, or the effects on fox numbers of reducing the number of rabbits – are extremely useful, fun and well developed. Simulations such as seed growth are also valuable. With the introduction of digital cameras that are easy for children to use in schools, time lapse photography has now become accessible to them. Once children see how such artefacts are made they are better able to understand those they see on screen. Clearly in other situations simulations provide the only way of exploring ideas as in the case of the Earth in space. It is important that care is taken in selecting from the wide range of materials available. Many local authorities and science centres have information and advice that is helpful here (see websites). In using ICT in this way pupils can test ideas in groups, then discuss and build on these ideas. Group discussion also helps in the process of making sense of information. The teacher has an important role to play in mediating what children are learning, because, as Sutherland *et al.* (2004) observed, with simulations, often the knowledge the pupils constructed as a result was quite different from that expected by the teacher.

Practice and revision

There are some high quality CD-ROMs and websites available for revision. These include sites that are structured in such a way as to closely match the curriculum, such as BBC Bite Size. Published schemes now often include CD-ROMs (or websites) that can help provide additional exercises. Some simulation software and quizzes can be used to help pupils to revise in a fun way. However, it is important to ensure that, if revision is essential, it is motivating for the pupils rather than a drudge. This can be done in many ways. For example, if over the course of a project pupils have kept a record of their work – reporting findings from investigations as a Big Book (as described in Kathy's class in Chapter 1) or a website as described in Example 2 in this chapter. Groups of pupils can go back and review that information and perhaps re-present it, as the children in Example 2 above will be asked to do in preparation for the next annual RSPB bird survey. Different groups could take a different topic and present it to the rest of the class, thus giving purpose and meaning to revision (and sharing the load).

Recording and collating

We have already mentioned different types of equipment that are available to schools to support data collection and recording. The principal tools include the digital microscope, digital camera and data loggers.

The digital microscope

This is described in detail on the planet science website http://www.planet-science.com/. The microscope is designed to be robust enough for school use and simple enough for even the youngest of pupils (Evans and Dunne 2006). The microscope can be linked up to a computer through a USB port. It can also take photographs that can be uploaded and stored.

The digital camera

Specially designed cameras for use by children are being used in many schools. This allows the children to use them for recording information, time-lapse photography and video recording. In addition, with appropriate software they can be used as a starter for use in making animations as part of a multimedia presentation. Their use then is in the collection and recording of data and in presenting and reporting information.

Data loggers

Although data loggers have been available for use in schools for longer than digital microscopes and cameras, they have become more sophisticated. They use sensors (temperature, sound, light) to create a database from which information can be represented in the form of graphs, bar charts, tables or pie charts. Once data have been collected the results can be presented to the whole class, possibly in the form of graphs or pie charts so that patterns in the data can be discerned. For example, as part of a sustainability project, Moorefield Primary School installed an electronic utilities monitor for collecting data about energy use at the school over a period of time. This system uses sensors and a data logger to record external and internal temperatures and electricity, gas and water consumption. Pupils collected this information and investigated relationships between the different factors. The project is described on the Teachernet website (see websites).

Presenting and reporting

Over recent years the possibilities for producing high quality reports by primary children has increased exponentially. Desktop publishing and word-processing have become much more accessible, even to young children where, for example, 'read back' options can be used to help them with their writing. Software is now available to enable pupils to build web pages, that could, for example, be uploaded onto the school website (as was the case in Example 2 above) and used to report work to parents and carers. Using child-friendly video cameras and associated editing software, films and animations can be made, or short clips inserted into web reports. In addition many schools are experimenting with podcasting where children can produce audio files to upload onto a website, CD or iPod. These can be listened to by parents, younger pupils, and by the children themselves at home or later for revision. Here pupils are acting as creators of knowledge, synthesising and re-presenting it for discussion and development. The possibilities are considerable; the challenge is to ensure that science learning remains central to the activity.

Summary

This chapter has discussed the use by children of information and communication technologies in their science activities. The main points have been:

- young people have grown up with new technologies and many readily make use of ICT as part of their normal experiences but this does not mean that they always learn what teachers might want them to learn – what is needed is a clear purpose for their activities;

- ICT is moving ahead at a great pace and developments mean that more and more possibilities are opening up to support learning in the primary classroom; in particular the development of cheaper, lighter, child friendly equipment, a wider variety of software and the increasing use of wireless technology, offer the possibility of untying children from the computer desk and allowing them to take their ICT learning tools with them wherever they are learning;

- there is a vast array of material on the Internet for children to exploit to gather information and to explore ideas; however, they need a clear purpose for what they are doing if they are to engage with the material and learn from it;

- ICT is a tool that can be harnessed and used by children to find information, explore and revise ideas, collect data and record and collate it as well as to represent their learning in ways that are attractive and creative. It is a marvellous tool when used well.

Useful websites

Although science year has been and gone the ASE SY CD-ROM now exists as web pages which are still full of useful information and links:

http://www.sycd.co.uk/primary/managing-science/web-search.htm

MAPE link to a wide range of primary ICT support sites:

http://www.supporting-ict.co.uk/weblinks/science.htm

Nature explorer:

http://www.naturegrid.org.uk/children.html

RSPB birdwatch and schoolwatch:

http://www.rspb.org.uk/birdwatch/ and
http://www.rspb.org.uk/schoolswatch/

Sheffield Local Authority, primary science links:

http://www.sheffield.gov.uk/education/information-for-learners/pupils/primary/science

Teachernet:

http://www.teachernet.gov.uk/CaseStudies/casestudy.cfm?id=509

Further reading

Byrne, J. and Sharp, J. (2002) *Using ICT in Primary Science Teaching*, Exeter: Learning Matters.

Warwick, P., Wilson, E. and Winterbottom, M. (eds) (2006) *Teaching and Learning Primary Science with ICT*, Maidenhead: Open University Press.

Teachers using ICT

Introduction

In this chapter we focus not so much on the information and communications technology (ICT) resources used by pupils to enhance their learning, but on the teacher as orchestrator of the learning environment for pupils. We begin by considering one particular revolution in classroom teaching, the interactive whiteboard (IWB), looking at why this is the most visible technology-related change in schools over the past ten years. One way in which the IWB has enhanced teaching is by offering wider horizons, providing a shared window onto the world. Taking up this image we then look in turn at a number of possibilities for 'wider horizons' being offered by ICT. In some cases we are just on the verge (in 2008) of finding ways to use these new resources, so we consider what they may mean for the way teachers plan and manage teaching of primary science. Finally we consider the ways in which electronic resources are available to teachers, and strategies for keeping up with changes without being swamped.

ICT transforming the curriculum

The rapid growth in the availability and variety of ICT both in schools and in our wider social and business world mean that there is a great deal for teachers to take on. The 'digital immigrants' (see Chapter 21, p. 258) amongst us are often painfully aware of the challenge of keeping up with the times, but even for teachers who are newer to the profession, who are more comfortable with ICT and for whom ICT was a substantial part of their initial teacher training, incorporating ICT into effective pedagogy and continuing to keep up with changes is a challenge. 'There is a tendency to think that ICT is so "new" that its use will be accompanied by new pedagogies that will somehow transform teaching and learning' (Sutherland *et al.* 2004: 413). Teachers not only need to learn how to use new technologies but also how to use them to support learning. In previous chapters we have discussed the importance and value of practical work that encourages pupils to engage with ideas, with each other and with the teacher in a way that enables the collaborative construction of knowledge. ICT holds out the prospect of helping in that process, and taking this further by breaking through the walls of the classroom, widening children's horizons and bringing new opportunities for learning into their world.

ICT is likely to contribute most effectively to learning where the teacher employs sound pedagogic principles to its incorporation. Rudd (2007: 7) suggests that there are three levels in the adoption of new technologies.

1. Infusion – the spread of use into more and more classrooms; the new technology simply serves to reinforce existing practice.

2. Integration – the technology becomes embedded in the curriculum, adding new ways in which it can be used.

3. Transformation – where technology is used to 'add value' to the whole learning process, where learners become centrally involved in its use and where they actively construct knowledge through interaction.

It is clearly not automatic that adoption will move inexorably from points 1 to 2 to 3. Indeed, development may not be the same across the curriculum. The use of ICT in primary science seems to be less well established than in English and mathematics (Harrison *et al.* 2002). The type of use made of ICT in science tended to be highly focused on developing subject knowledge for national tests, yet, unlike in English and maths, high use in science was not correlated with higher test performance. Sutherland *et al.* (2004) researching the impact of ICT in schools noted that in secondary science, too, ICT was used less than in other subjects. They suggested that this might be due to the traditional focus on practical work in science in the UK and that the difficulties of taking science into the computer suite or getting computers and other electrical equipment into the lab or out on a field trip might go some way to explaining this. The changes and extensions to the equipment now available to schools (as discussed in Chapter 21) may well be enabling more infusion of resources into classrooms. One such change has been with the use of interactive whiteboards (IWBs) or smartboards. The change has been dramatic in some cases such that one teacher in a Canadian elementary school described the transformation that she felt had occurred when IWBs were introduced as part of a whole-school project as 'My teaching took off sideways' (Naylor *et al.* 2008).

Interactive whiteboards

An interactive whiteboard, according to Becta (2003) is a large, touch-sensitive board which is connected to a digital projector and a computer. The projector displays the image from the computer screen onto the board. The computer can then be controlled by touching the board, either directly or with a special pen. Among the potential applications are the shared use of web-based materials, the showing of video clips, sharing pupils' work, creating digital flip charts, and many more.

> The Smartboard permits a multimodal approach that allows participants to move beyond language barriers or abstract content by presenting a variety of means, including colour, image, sound, spatial and kinaesthetic modalities for students to make meaning.
>
> (Jewitt *et al.* 2007 (quoted in Naylor *et al.* 2008: 8))

Box 22.1 Pros and cons for teachers and pupils of the use of interactive whiteboards

For teachers

Positive
Allows use of web and other resources
High quality of presentation
In touch with ICT
Ownership – teachers can tailor materials to suit
    the topic and the children
Allows better planning and sharing of resources
Enables easy recall of previous work
Responds to children's needs
Increases children's motivation
Enables collaborative learning

Negative
The equipment can be expensive
The need for training and continued practice
The need for technical support
A tendency to over-reliance on visuals
A tendency to more exposition (teacher
    dominated)
The challenge of finding materials on the Internet
    and elsewhere
The time it takes to download materials
The difficulties of downloading large files
LCD vs whiteboard (the TV-like flat LCD screen
    has a higher resolution and additional functions
    to the IWB). Should we wait and invest in the
    next development?

For pupils

Positive
Versatility (accurate, clear diagrams, unlike those a
    teacher might draw on a normal board)
Multimedia (colour, movement, audio, video)
More fun and so maintains attention
Can be interactive

Negative
Teacher exposition
Technical problems (such as slow or disrupted
    Internet connections, pens that don't work)
Seeing the IWB (often too small, children not sitting
    in the right place, or sunlight on the board)
Sense of unfair distribution of opportunities to
    interact themselves with the medium
Height of the board

Between 2001 and 2004 the UK spent £1 million on installing interactive whiteboards into schools, many of them in primary schools. As IWBs become widespread in schools, resources to support them are growing. The expansion of broadband Internet connections in many schools makes downloading materials easier and so encourages the production of more. With the growth of use of IWBs there has been a growth in the amount of research considering their use in classrooms. Box 22.1 brings together some of the positive and negative findings from a number of projects considering views of both pupils and teachers.

Most of what can be done with an IWB could be done in other ways. Regular whiteboards, or flip charts, are very flexible and allow diagrams to be drawn in discussion with the pupils, and they allow ideas to be collected and stored (flip chart). What IWBs offer is a way in which whole classes of children and their teacher can interact to share ideas, build new ideas together in an enjoyable way that can be stored easily and reviewed and revised later. Teachers and pupils tend to believe that the IWB does improve learning, although the research on this is not conclusive.

What the research says

Research into the ways in which IWBs are being used has tended to focus on the interactivity that they offer. In the national literacy, national numeracy, and national primary strategies in England, for example, the emphasis has been on lesson pace, interaction and questioning. Kennwell *et al.* (2007) found that lessons using IWBs did in fact have more pace and questions, but that the questions were of a more superficial type and that thinking time for pupils was being sacrificed to pace. In a thorough, large-scale study Smith and his colleagues (2006) found that the pace of the lessons was, as suggested by both teachers and pupils, faster and included more open questions and more responses by pupils. However, the length of the pupils' responses was shorter as was the wait time between question and answer. The amount of time given to explaining by the teacher remained about the same at 28 per cent and presenting at 17 per cent of the time. In the first flush of IWB use, pupils had more involvement in presenting material, but this had dropped back in the second year of use. The findings suggest that traditional patterns of whole class teaching persist despite the emphasis on interactive whole class teaching in the national strategies.

In a study of IWB use in six local authorities Higgins *et al.* (2007) found no discernible improvements in pupil attainment as a result of IWB use, despite the fact that teachers and pupils all believed this to be the case. In a very large-scale study by Moss *et al.* (2007) for the Department for Children, Schools and Families (DCSF), differences were identified by pupils in classes that had been using IWBs for between 1 and 2 years. In Key Stage 2 (7–11 years) all pupils, except high attaining girls, obtained higher than expected performance in science, with low attaining boys showing most improvement. In Key Stage 1 (5–7 years) all girls, and average and above average boys, showed better than expected attainment. In addition, the study found that, in some subjects, the amount of experience the teacher had of using the IWB was a significant factor in enhancing pupil performance.

A number of examples of ways in which teachers are using IWBs can be found on the Internet (http://samples.embc.org.uk/primary/), although, of course, these change over time. Box 22.2 described Greg's use in enabling his 4-year-olds to group materials in different ways. Greg's approach ensures that his children have first-hand experience of materials and are able to explore them directly. Use of the digital camera helps the children to make the link between the two-dimensional image and the actual object, and the children were able to discuss the properties of the materials and how they would group and describe them by manipulating images on the interactive whiteboard. This enabled language development, discussion and reflection.

As with every new tool in teachers' kit for teaching, IWBs are only as good as the teaching and learning that they support. On the whole it would seem that, in England, where whiteboard use has been heavily promoted, 'infusion' has been successful, and the technology has become 'integrated' into the curriculum. This then has helped teachers to run whole class teaching as they would normally do, but with a better, more enjoyable and engaging medium. However, it would seem that it is not always the case that IWBs 'add value' (see Rudd 2007, mentioned earlier).

It is likely that, for real transformation, there needs to be a reconsideration of when it is appropriate to use this technology, and how and when it is not. In previous chapters we have pointed out the importance and value to learning of children having the opportunity to exchange,

Box 22.2 Using an interactive whiteboard to group materials

Greg's reception class (4-year-olds) were looking at materials. They had a variety of everyday objects such as coins, postcards, plastic cups, pencil sharpeners and erasers and were discussing the materials and what they were made of. In groups the children observed their objects closely, discussing the properties of the materials and developing appropriate language to describe them. They then used a digital camera to take images of their objects to put on the computer. Greg made some files containing descriptions based on what the children had said. The images were then shown on the interactive whiteboard. The children recognised their objects and together the class discussed their observations and findings. Children were asked to use their 'magic fingers' to move the images of the objects around the board, to group them in different ways and to link their objects to the labels and descriptions that Greg had made using the children's words, which were then projected onto the whiteboard. In this way the sharing of ideas was encouraged and decisions about materials and their descriptions could be discussed. Additional words could be added as decisions were made. The children loved using their magic fingers, finding it much easier than manipulating a mouse and more visually attractive because of the large screen. They could save their work and print it off for display.

discuss and question each other's ideas and to be challenged to present their own reasoning for others to consider. Research suggests that this is best done in groups with the teacher acting as monitor and guide rather than leader. The temptation with IWBs is for teachers to take on the role of leader and so reduce the opportunities for children to develop their thinking skills.

Widening horizons

As information and communications technology develops we seem to be moving away from a focus on *information* and towards an increasing emphasis on *communication*. It has been argued, by the original inventor of the Internet, Tim Berners-Lee, that communication was the original purpose of the Internet and that it is only now that we are beginning to capitalise on its potential, moving not just into communication but towards greater collaboration. Opportunities for greater and more personalised communication come with blogs, Wikis, instant messenger software, Internet telephone systems and video conferencing. These various technologies are described in greater detail elsewhere; here we can only give brief examples of their use in general and in supporting the teaching of primary science in particular.

Blogs

The word blog derives from 'web log' and is essentially a diary or log of ideas and information put up on the Internet for others to read. They can be open or restricted to an identified group of people. Blogs are used in general by, for example, gap year pupils to record their travels for family and friends to keep track of them while they are away. Teachers too can use blogs to share information and comments. In the previous chapter we quoted a teacher's blog as she embedded tablet PCs into her teaching (Box 21.1). Free resources for setting up classroom blogs are available to schools. One way to use them is to set up blogs between a number of schools, for example in keeping a record of the weather, or of the activity of birds in bird boxes across a number of school sites, or phases of the moon at the same time in different parts of the world. As part of the Learning2Go project a blog of podcasts was set up (http://www.learning2goblog. org) including a report in the form of a rap from Trinity Foundation School about their Forest School (see Chapter 20).

Wikis

These are editable websites, the best known of which is Wikipedia. A number of primary school sites are now open to specific members of the school for editing. This allows school staff to post information and Parent Teachers Associations to contribute, as well as children, to share information and ideas with the school community. Again, these can be open or password protected. A class undertaking different aspects of a science topic can upload text, images, video and sound files to produce a multi-media, collaborative report that can be shared with other classes and the wider school community.

Internet telephone and instant messaging

Many people now use messaging and Internet telephones in their day-to-day life. Their application in school is beginning to be developed, as in Neston School (Box 22.3).

The approach at Neston gives the children the opportunity to work independently whilst keeping in touch so that the teacher can act as a guide and support. Of course instant messaging and Internet telephones are not restricted by geography and so it is possible for communication of this sort to be national and international. The BBC has a project running to support links between schools in different countries. These might have a theme, such as schools following the migration of starlings from Poland; or something more broadly based so that children ask one another questions about family, or playground games or, as was the case with a school from Ghana, 'What is snow?' (www.bbc.co.uk/worldclass/).

Box 22.3 Keeping in touch with the Moonbase

Each term, different classes in Neston Primary School in Wiltshire work on a Moonbase project. The Moonbase is a geodesic dome constructed in the school grounds. Groups of children work in the Moonbase, supported by a teaching assistant where appropriate. They undertake aspects of their project and send information (such as tables of data) back to the classroom via email. They are able to send questions instantly to their teacher or classmates using instant messenger and Skype telephone.

Video conferencing

Video conferencing has moved out of the business world and is increasingly used for education. The technology does not now require special rooms, and the equipment is not prohibitively expensive. Once the equipment is set up groups of staff can work together across schools on specific projects. Given the difficulties that travelling often poses for teachers wanting to work together, the value of video conferencing, once the equipment is installed, can be significant.

Video conferencing also enables groups of children to work together. For example, it would be possible for small schools to share lessons. The example in Box 22.4 is of a very early experiment in video conferencing for science lessons. There is clearly a lot to learn to make this effective, and decisions about whether it is the best use of the resource will need to be considered. In another example, a high school working through the Global Gateway (http://www.globalgateway.org/) linked up with a school in South Africa with two classes of pupils being challenged to design and build a motorised vehicle. The video conferencing system was left on for four hours while pupils worked and exchanged ideas and finally produced a range of working cars.

A more common use of video conferencing is to put school children in touch with experts such as scientists and museum educators. In the March science week in 2006 in London, children had all these opportunities. They were also able to communicate with other children in distant schools and to share ideas and see each other's work. They were highly motivated, prepared well and studied hard to have good questions and be knowledgeable when speaking to experts. The class teachers and head teacher alike were keen to continue to use the resource as a means of motivating the children and broadening the curriculum.

Box 22.4 Building experience of video conferencing in primary schools

Branscombe and Farway are two small, rural primary schools in Devon who first tested out the use of video conferencing by linking up with the Ocean Institute in California. The children planned some questions and then linked up for an hour. The project was not directly linked to the curriculum but the children benefited from it, and also found out about Christmas in California. The schools decided to take the idea of video conferencing further by linking the two schools up to allow children to discuss and share their science work. Classes were timetabled such that those children of similar ages working on the same topic could show each other their work and discuss their findings and ideas. There were some technical problems and the younger children in the schools were intimidated by the idea of 'being on the television', while older children tended to prepare for the link up and then stick to their script, thus limiting the amount of real discussion. There were some instances where children were able to share and learn from each other. The evaluation of the project was that staff needed better insights into how to organise video conferencing and that children needed to become more experienced in using it before it could be said to contribute to learning.

(Becta Video Conferencing Case Studies)

Virtual learning environments (VLE)

Most recent university graduates will have had some experience of using virtual learning environments. Virtual learning environments generally have a combination of some or all of the following features:

- communication tools such as email, bulletin boards and chat rooms;
- collaboration tools such as online forums, intranets, electronic diaries and calendars;
- tools to create online content and courses;
- online assessment and marking;
- integration with school management information systems;
- controlled access to curriculum resources;
- student access to content and communications beyond the school.

(Becta Virtual Learning Environments 2007
http://partners.becta.org.uk/index.php?section=rh&rid=13640)

Today many university courses involve some element of VLE. This can be fully online, or 'blended' where pupils undertake some work in a virtual environment but also work together in more traditional settings. A number of universities are providing online postgraduate programmes for teachers, and their use is likely to grow as systems become more sophisticated and adults become increasingly comfortable with this form of learning.

The use of VLEs in primary education is in its infancy. The VLE could not replace face-to-face learning, but it has the potential to supplement it, supporting and extending the day-to-day curriculum. The value of VLEs is that they are bounded learning environments in which teachers can place appropriate learning materials that children can use independently as individuals or as groups. The materials, once designed can be used again, added to or modified. They can include interactivity through blogs, Wikis, video conferencing, and message boards. Teachers can also feed back marking and keep records of formative comments as well as summative marks.

Implications of 'widening horizon' ICT for the teacher

The discussions on blogs, virtual learning environments, interactive whiteboards and the rest all suggest that, if they are to be used at all, certain conditions are required. Some important considerations are:

- they are often expensive, so funding needs to be available;
- technical support needs to be available;
- good Internet connections are essential;
- teachers need to be trained in their use, and to keep in practice;
- children need to be trained in their use, and to keep in practice;
- teachers need to have access to a wide range of software;
- teachers need to have access to good advice and support re pedagogy;

- implementation needs a system–wide shift to greater networking amongst schools and teachers;
- the activity must be purposeful.

This last point is crucial. Using the resources in a meaningful way is as important for children learning to use ICT as it is for their learning in science. A blog makes no sense if the only people reading it are one's classmates; it would be easier just to have a 'news' slot in the school day. The same argument applies to Wikis. Video conferencing requires participants to be at a distance from one another. It also requires teachers to be linked up with others, in other schools or other institutions (such as museums, space stations and bird sanctuaries). This necessitates a good deal of coordination and planning. Similarly, although a class teacher could set up a VLE and populate it with resources for learners, the amount of time and effort needed would be prohibitive. It might be worth setting up something across one primary school (as some schools have done) but even in this case the availability of high quality learning materials externally is likely to provide an essential contribution to success. We return to the value of wider networks of schools and teachers in Chapter 26 in the context of continuing professional development. Clearly such networks, whether virtual, or face to face to face, are crucial if some of the developments discussed in this chapter are to be taken further.

One way in which teachers are supported is through specially targeted learning platforms. In the UK the National Grid for learning, Becta, offers a wealth of information while the more local grids offer opportunities for the exchange of ideas and information.

Learning platforms

Government policy in many developed countries, including England, is that the use of ICT for teaching and learning is not an option, but must be integrated into the infrastructure of the school. Now that most schools in the UK have good, networked, broadband connections, teachers and pupils should be able to access information and resources in school, and can go beyond this to access materials and resources outside school. A learning platform is generally a custom designed collection of hardware and software that allows schools to run management information systems (MIS), a VLE, assessment management and a website. The DCSF e-strategy sets the expectation that by 2008 every school pupil should have access to a personalised online learning space and that by 2010 every school should be working towards an integrated learning management system (Becta 2008). Becta provides a wide range of resources at a national level (http://schools.becta. org.uk/) for learning and for school management. There is a Welsh National Grid for Learning, and in Scotland there is a national intranet for education, 'Glow', managed by Learning and Teaching Scotland (http://www.ltscotland.org.uk/glowscotland/index.asp), which provides support for Curriculum for Excellence, and all the facilities of a learning platform listed in Box 22.5. In England there are also local grids for learning which include resources, advertise courses and workshops for teachers, provide a platform for teachers to network and often a means of swapping good ideas and sources of expert help and advice.

Box 22.5 Advantages of a learning platform in schools

To teachers	To pupils	To parents	To administrators and management
Create and share teaching materials to use online, print or use with IWB	Access learning materials online from home, or elsewhere	Play a greater part in children's learning (online from home)	Provide up-to-date management information on attendance and attainment
Place resources online for teachers to access at home, etc.	Store notes and work online	Access to child's personal home page to keep track of their work	Track the progress of individuals
Access wide variety of materials to customise	Work at own pace and in own way	Review assessment and other data on pupils	Collate summative and formative assessments
Access lesson plans from colleagues to support supply staff	Create online portfolios, store digital artefacts	Communicate effectively with teachers and administrators	Reduce administrative burden of teachers
Monitor and track pupil progress	Improve ICT skills	Engage with the wider school community	Enable communication within school and between schools
Receive student work for assessment	Submit homework on line	Become an active partner with the school	Increase communication between parents
Manage timetables and diaries	Communicate by email and online discussions with other pupils and teachers		

(Adapted from schools.becta.org.uk/index.php?section =lv&catcode=ss_lv_lp_03&rid=12889)

Learning platforms can be accessed from outside the school (Luckin *et al.* 2005). One exciting example of the possibilities opening up for learning is described in the Learning2Go project. The project was set up in Wolverhampton to explore the use of mobile technology using hand-held devices. Children from the project schools, which included both primary and secondary, were given these devices to carry with them. Applications included pupils using them at home to study in their own time, and sharing learning with parents and friends. In addition the devices were used on field trips, visits to museums and other out-of-classroom events (see Box 22.6). Project staff suggest that the applications used must be 'cool', that is of a high quality and attractive to pupils such that learning and play overlap.

Social networking

It is difficult to keep up with the pace of change; for example, since the publication of the previous edition of this book the development of social network services has become ubiquitous. A recent report on children's use of social networking defines these services as 'Internet- or mobile-device-based social spaces designed to facilitate communication, collaboration and content sharing across networks of contacts' (Digizen 2008: 5).

Box 22.6 Mobile learning – anywhere, any time

Extended Learning2Go falls into ten categories:

- continuation of school-based tasks that have interested learners who want to take them further and develop them using their own time;

- reading ebooks anywhere, any time;

- use of specific software purchased for home/school use, e.g. grid club. This is important as it encourages a cross between playing and learning – plearning;

- independent exploration and gathering of new software and applications by learners;

- personalisation of the device with appropriate today screens, games and music, and picture and video files;

- assistance in completing set tasks or homework;

- sharing ICT expertise with other members of the family;

- use of the device in other locations around school such as playtime or lunchtime use;

- use of the device on trips to museums or art galleries.

Some of these sites are simply ways by which large companies can market goods to children. Many are for adults, including teachers, who use them for keeping in contact with friends and family. Others such as the new MyBBC (which is designed to be a very safe environment for young children) are aimed at 6–13-year-olds allowing them to store favourite television programmes and, among other things, to link with friends, who they may meet in their Avatar forms (virtual online selves). There have been some experiments where children from different countries have worked together to share information and produce new knowledge (Ligorio and Van der Meijden 2007) but this use requires levels of organisation and planning beyond the scope of most schools at the present time (2009). Questions about how teachers can use this resource or whether they should, are beyond the scope of this chapter. Digizen (2008) provides some very useful discussion of these matters. What is clear is that the explosion of social networking serves to underline the extent to which the 'digital natives' in our classrooms are interacting with ICT in many aspects of their lives.

Summary

This chapter has focused on ICT that is on the cutting edge of moving pedagogy and the curriculum forward. As the case of the interactive whiteboard has demonstrated, the introduction of such innovations takes a concerted and centralised effort to inject the hardware, software and training into schools. This is not something that can be done by a lone 'early adopter'. Despite the financial investment it is still not clear that real strides have been made in changing pedagogy; which is always a slow process. If the promises of ICT are to be realised then the way teachers work together, plan and interact will need to change. Only then can ICT help to transform primary science teaching such that:

- children are able to work within and outside school to build and develop their understanding of science and how it works;
- teachers can access and use the vast array of resources available to enhance pupil learning; this requires a more collaborative and democratic approach to teaching and learning;
- teachers can access efficient information management systems to reduce the administrative burden on planning, assessment and record keeping;
- teachers can work towards seeing alternative ways of teaching that can be supported, but not led, by ICT.

Further reading

Kennwell, S., Tanner, H., Jones, S. and Beauchamp, G. (2007) Analysing the use of interactive technology to implement interactive teaching, *Journal of Computer Assisted Learning* 24: 51–73.

Smith, F., Hardman, F., and Higgins, S. (2006) The impact of interactive whiteboards on teacher–pupil interaction in the national literacy and numeracy strategies, *British Journal of Educational Research* 32(3): 443–57.

Sutherland, R., Armstrong, V., Barnes, S., Brawn, R., Breeze, N., Gall, M., Matthewson, S., Olivero, F., Taylor, A., Triggs, P., Wishart, J. and John, P. (2004) Transforming teaching and learning: embedding ICT into everyday classroom practices, *Journal of Computer Assisted Learning* 20: 413–25.

Useful websites

The Hertfordshire Grid for Learning provides links to a lot of material on IWBs including:

http://samples.embc.org.uk/primary/

http://www.thegrid.org.uk/learning/ict/technologies/whiteboards/index.shtml#research

Lewisham ICT Training website offers a plan of where there might be opportunities for using ICT in the primary science curriculum linked to the QCA scheme of work:

http://ecs.lewisham.gov.uk/talent/pricor/science.html#How

Becta report on the use of video conferencing in schools:

http://schools.becta.org.uk/upload-dir/downloads/vc/vc_classroom/case6.pdf

Managing science at the school level

23

Aspects of whole-school planning

Introduction

The move towards greater flexibility in lesson planning and the increasing recognition of the value of allowing children to participate in decisions about their learning are just some of the influences which have shaped curriculum planning over recent years. At the same time it is recognised that planning cannot simply be a matter of listing the topics taught or learning outcomes to be attained. In this chapter we take a closer look at the wide range of factors to be taken into account when planning a whole-school programme. We argue that in order to provide a flexible and open delivery of the curriculum in the classroom more careful and rigorous planning is needed at the school or year level. We begin by looking at what a school might identify as important when planning a programme, then move on to a consideration of a few of these issues as they apply to science including a discussion of the links between science and other subjects.

Overview of planning

In Chapter 3 we looked at the changing nature of the various national curriculum requirements or guidelines from England, Scotland, Northern Ireland and Wales. The picture remains fluid, but the changes broadly suggest that the science curriculum should:

- provide for greater relevance to real life and other learning;

- make a place for current issues of concern, such as sustainability;

- reduce content to allow greater attention to skills and processes;

- give teachers more freedom by less prescription;

- identify progress in skills and ideas;

- improve continuity from pre-school to school and from primary to secondary.

In Chapter 13 we addressed the issue of planning at the level of the lesson or group of lessons. In thinking about lesson planning we were concerned to advocate a move away from planning for specific learning outcomes and instead to plan with broader goals in mind. This approach has the advantage of allowing the teacher the flexibility to respond to pupils and to adapt and adjust teaching according to their needs. However, this is not to say that planning can be laissez-faire because the goals a teacher has for pupil learning need to originate in the shared values and goals of the school and the wider community.

We can think of planning as having three main levels:

- school level (long-term): planning at this level is across the whole school and the wider curriculum. This will often be brought together as a curriculum map, showing how different elements are linked;

- programme level planning (medium-term). This involves two elements:

  - ensuring continuity and progression in subject areas such that a sequential learning journey is offered to all children;

  - ensuring that what is valued by the school and community is woven into the curriculum opportunities. This means, not only what is taught but how it is taught and learnt;

- class level planning (short-term): this is where the teacher or groups of educators together translate the long- and medium-term plans into actual learning experiences for the children over a lesson or short series of lessons such that the learning goals reflect both the school values and appropriate progression in the subject matter.

In England the non-statutory QCA scheme of work for science (DFEE 1998) provides a highly structured programme of study covering science for pupils from the age of 5 to 11 years. With its 33 units and four short revision units it provides a balance of biological and physical science topics each fitting into about half a term. The QCA scheme can be seen as falling somewhere between medium- and short-term levels of planning. It received some support from a small-scale qualitative study by Gillard and Whitby (2007), but there were also concerns that it may 'stop teachers being creative and really thinking through what they are doing and why' (ibid: 221).

It is at the level of the overall and longer term planning that such issues are addressed. In the next section we consider just a few of the questions that need to be considered as part of the whole-school approach to planning.

The planning agenda

In recent years there has been a welter of new ideas, initiatives and imperatives in education, all of which seem to result in some additional agenda being set for primary education. They include, in England, with similar agendas across the UK: Every Child Matters; Personalised learning; Thinking skills; the Social and emotional aspects of learning (DfES 2005); planning for transfer and transition; involvement of parents.

In ensuring attention to these overarching matters it is important to keep a balance and not allow science, or other subjects, to be lost (Conroy *et al.* 2008). We can only consider a few topics of particular relevance to science.

Involving parents

Parents are the first and most important educators of their children and yet often they can have little knowledge about, and even less opportunity to contribute to their children's schooling. In recent years the notion of schools as part of, and in some senses accountable to, the community they serve has grown. One of the five key principles underpinning the Every Child Matters agenda in England is partnership with parents, employers, volunteers and volunteering organisations as part of the goal of maximising the life chances of children. Many schools are working actively to engage parents in their children's education. Schools need to decide on the nature of the relationship they want with parents. We can see parental involvement as falling on a continuum. At one end involvement can be simply keeping parents informed about their child's education, for example by sending out newsletters, or providing information about what their child will be covering in different subjects on the school website. Most schools have mechanisms to do this. Further along the continuum is the involvement of parents in school trips, helping with activities in class, and helping with homework. In the example of a visit to the beach given in Chapter 1, one of the helpers was a parent who had worked as a ranger on the beach, and in Chapter 20 a visit to a local power station was enhanced by a parent who was also a member of staff joining the children. In other cases parents can bring particular skills and knowledge into school, such as photography, gardening or sculpture. Building such activities into the school programme can enhance the children's experiences and bring staff and parents closer together.

Still further along the continuum of parental involvement, parents can be encouraged to contribute to the planning and development of the school. One example of this is in the use of learning platforms as discussed in Chapter 22. Here parents are kept informed about their child's progress, can make comment or contribute to discussions, initiate debates and suggest additions or changes to the school programme. We are, perhaps, still a little way from a point where school professionals are able to work together with pupils and parents as co-designers of the curriculum (Leadbeater 2004), but parental involvement is high on the government agenda.

Involving parents does not happen simply by sending a letter to invite suggestions. It requires a lot of hard work on the part of the school to develop trust and shared understanding and it often takes additional resources to implement. The example in Chapter 22 of the 'Learning2Go' project (see Box 22.6) involved all these things. In this case ICT was being used to allow pupils to continue their learning outside school, and in so doing to involve other family members in that learning. Other, more low-tech solutions to engaging with parents include the use of topic boxes. In one school, where teachers were keen to encourage parents to see learning as fun and to play and learn with their children, a set of role play boxes were developed with titles such as 'owls', 'growing things', and other less science focused themes. The boxes contained lots of equipment, books and activities for the children to share with parents and siblings. They were a great success and the science activities in the boxes were very much enjoyed (Qualter 2005). A further development on this approach to home school links was used at Brucehill Education and Childcare Centre where parental involvement was brought far more to the fore. See Box 23.1.

Many schools have science weeks with parents and carers invited into school to share in the fun, or to observe and take part in lessons. These experiences can bring staff and parents together

---

Box 23.1 Taking science home in a box

At Brucehill Education and Childcare Centre parent–school link projects had mainly involved literacy and numeracy, with children taking work home to share with parents. For science, project staff wanted to develop a more collaborative approach by working with parents. Three groups were created, each with a mix of parents and staff, to develop science topic boxes. Science was chosen as it can be seen as quite 'scary and mysterious' for parents, and staff too felt that this subject needed to be reviewed. 'Our aim is to encourage our parents to spend quality time "educating" their child in a relaxed, informal and fun way. We (staff and parents) provide all the ideas, materials and information necessary and they have all the fun'. Thirteen boxes were developed with themes such as 'mini-mania' (minibeasts), 'sing a rainbow' (colour), 'ready-steady cook'. The boxes have been a big success with very little damage and great enthusiasm on the part of children and families. The main problem is not having enough boxes to satisfy the demand.

(http://www.ltscotland.org.uk/earlyyearsmatters/previousissues/issue5/parents/scienceboxes/index.asp)

---

in shared activities. Parents, carers and others may then feel more able to offer to contribute to school life and teaching.

Transfer and transition

Concern about the dip in attainment that tends to accompany the transfer of pupils from primary to secondary schools was highlighted and explored by Galton *et al.* (1999a) who also commented on similar, if less extreme 'dips' between years 3 and 4. In science, 'dips' in attainment and motivation have been identified; for example, the AAP surveys in Scotland showed a decline in the motivation of pupils towards science learning between Year 5 in primary schools and the second year of high school (SEED 2003). In England the emphasis on testing in Year 6 is seen as reducing motivation and so attainment.

As a result of concerns about the impact of transfer between schools a significant amount of work, including a number of funded projects, has provided a wealth of materials that schools working in partnership with others, including secondary schools, can use. These approaches often involve visits by Year 6 children to their secondary schools; Year 7, 8 and 9 pupils acting as mentors for new pupils; and link teachers in secondary schools visiting primaries. Where a school sees tackling issues of transition to secondary school as important they will wish to encourage children to feel comfortable about the move. Transition activities in science provide an ideal opportunity, as science is one of the subjects where primary children are both excited about working in laboratories, but can also be anxious. Braund and his colleagues undertook a number of projects on transition, leading to the general advice in Box 23.2.

Box 23.2 Tips for productive transition projects

Bridging or transition projects should:

1. Contain work based in contexts related to industry/commerce that should interest pupils of this age. Lessons start with a letter inviting the class to investigate a 'real-life' problem such as the effect of temperature on fizziness of drinks.

2. Have a key focus on what we call the 'process skills' of scientific inquiry. We were aware that developing pupils' abilities in considering and evaluating evidence is a major concern amongst teachers and so lessons show clear progression and guidance on teaching in this area.

3. Include a manageable and useable assessment scheme involving pupils in self-review and providing information that Year 7 teachers can build on. We were guided here by the work emerging from Kings College (Black *et. al.* 2002).

4. Allow findings from Year 6 inquiries to form a basis, but not an essential requirement, for further work in Year 7. We had to allow for work to progress from the primary phase but be capable of being carried out by Year 7 pupils that may not have experienced Year 6 lessons.

5. Provide enough 'planned discontinuity' to satisfy pupils' desires to work in new ways and with new equipment following transfer to secondary school whilst at the same time recognising that teaching should have similar and consistent approaches.

(Braund 2003: 12)

McMahon working with colleagues and schools from two local authorities and with the support of BAE Systems developed a project that seems to use Braund's advice (DfES Standards website). They focused on inquiry skills through a topic on 'travelling through air and liquids'. This included the involvement of engineers from BAE systems and hence a connection with industry. Primary teachers undertook assessments focusing on planning and obtaining evidence which was passed on to the secondary school where teachers undertaking the follow up part of the project focused their assessments on interpretation of data and evaluation. Children were also encouraged to self assess in both the primary and secondary context. In the secondary school the pupils presented their primary work to their new classmates, had additional lessons in data interpretation and lab skills before continuing with the topic, and moving on, to additional follow up activities determined as a result of teacher assessment and pupil self assessment. It was highly motivating for pupils to know that their primary project would be followed through in secondary school. For secondary teachers the benefit of a better understanding of approaches to teaching science and to assessment in primary school helped them in their planning and teaching.

The importance of communication between primary and secondary school teachers such that secondary school teachers are able to make use of the records passed on to them was highlighted by Burr and Simpson (2006) who went on to use a passport system as developed in science year (which can be found on the Planet Science website). Using the passport, pupils collect 'visa' stamps to record skills gained and experiments undertaken as well as recording websites visited and other activities. These passports are then taken into the secondary school for use by pupils and to inform teachers.

Other initiatives include, for example, Buckinghamshire Grid for Learning's resources for a project on 'How do Penguins keep warm?' for Year 6, and 'Why do Penguins huddle?' for Year 7. The Astra-Zeneca project at York University (see website) developed different ways to address similar problems. One approach has been to devise science inquiry mini-tasks that can be used across primary and secondary schools, in which similar pedagogic approaches are used across Years 5, 6, 7, and 8, thus moving away from the 'special' transition projects to encourage more seamless continuity and progression.

A key feature of all the projects is that they involve collaboration and communication among groups of primary schools and secondary schools. Often secondary schools have a teacher responsible for primary liaison, but it is also clear that, for these projects to become part of a school's practice, collaboration needs to be ongoing and the activities need to be part of the school's overall curriculum and written into the science programme or scheme of work. 'It is unlikely to be enough for other schools to take up this project, or any other bridging project, as a package, without taking some ownership of it through some process to establish a trusting relationship between teachers at each end of the transfer' (McMahon and Davies 2003: 9).

Similar collaborations are important wherever there is a transition for pupils. Within the same school this can often be addressed through careful collaborative planning where teachers develop a shared understanding about what it is they are trying to achieve in teaching science. The school science programme is not therefore a static entity but both a result of collaboration and discussion and the focal point for ongoing discussion, debate and development.

Cross-curricular links and themes

One of the major dilemmas facing teachers is the difficulty of ensuring coverage of the whole curriculum. The relaxation of some curriculum guidelines can reduce this problem, but it remains a fine balance between meaningful learning opportunities and ensuring coverage within a subject. One of the ways in which this tension can be overcome is to take advantage of any overlap among subjects and any reinforcement that learning in one area can offer to another by planning through topics rather than separate subjects. The advantages of such planning are not limited simply to efficiency, but where real overlaps or synergies arise, the recognition of links between subject by children helps them to make sense of their world and to make connections more easily. Making 'connections' rather than collecting information is how we believe children learn and develop as learners (see Chapter 4).

In Northern Ireland the idea of making connections has been developed in the form of Ideas for Connected Learning (ICLs) which are described as a 'range of active learning experiences' in guidelines that emphasise flexibility in planning the delivery of the revised National Curriculum. Guidelines are provided within a number of themes such as 'Wonderful World'. ICLs have also been developed for Year 6 (primary age) and Year 7 (secondary) and so could support transition (CCEA nd). However, it is important to see, within such cross cutting themes the characteristics of the various subjects within them.

Literacy and numeracy

Concern for the development of numeracy and literacy skills in primary schools over recent years has led to an increase in the proportion of time teachers spend planning for these subjects and has tended to move science to the afternoon when children are less alert (Sutton 2001). Children are taught to use non-fiction texts in literacy lessons. In this way, it is argued, they will increase their knowledge of other subjects. However, care needs to be taken if the intention is to teach science through literacy in this way. The AAAS (1989) found that texts rarely contributed to effective learning. This could be explained in a number of ways. Newton *et al.* (2002) found, for example, that school science texts, like many schemes of work for primary science, do not show a concern for explanatory understanding. That is, they provide information on 'how' and 'what' but not 'why'. In addition Peacock and Weedon (2002) found that 9–10-year-old pupils who had been taught the use of non-fiction texts did not use science texts well to gain information. This, they concluded, was because what is needed is the development of visual literacy, or what Aldrich and Sheppard (2001) call graphicacy. Most science books include more pictures, diagrams and symbols than they do words, yet little emphasis is placed on visual literacy in the National Literacy Strategy. It is therefore important that teachers actively teach children to use science information books, making links between labelled diagrams and text, and seeking to discuss the possible explanations for the phenomena being presented within the pages. The need for these skills is becoming more and more important with the ever-increasing use of the Internet and CD-ROMs, which are even more likely to rely on visual images, and demand the ability to read information in a range of presentational forms.

Increasingly teachers are finding ways to integrate literacy and numeracy teaching with their science teaching. The challenge is to ensure that, by focusing on literacy skills, the science covered will not be trivial. What is important is to look for ways in which science learning can be enhanced or can contribute to literacy and numeracy learning. For example, data from science experiments can be used in numeracy lessons to construct graphs, diagrams and charts. The example given in Box 23.3 shows how science work can inspire literacy work, which in turn can help learning in science. The ASE has two publications which provide useful support in ensuring that the science learning remains central, and the goals of developing science skills and ideas are taken seriously by taking science activities as their starting point (Feasey 1999, and Feasey and Gallear 2000).

Science mathematics and technology

Science has its own distinctive characteristics but this does not mean that it is independent of other ways of knowing about and reacting to the world around. Its closest relationship would seem to be with mathematics and technology. But while there are many occasions when science,

---

Box 23.3 Science learning supported in literacy work

Chris Wardle's class of 6–7-year-olds had been working on the topic of 'light and dark'. The previous term, they had looked at various light sources and explored shiny objects and noted how these cannot be seen in the dark. The class then used their science work to develop some alliterative list poems. In this way the children were able to recap on science work, consider the meanings of science words, use dictionaries, thesauruses and science information books to find more useful words.

Light is …
Shining sun
Twinkling torches
Laser light
Magical match
Golden glows

(Wardle 2000: 27)

---

mathematics and technology are brought together in one activity, they still remain distinct human enterprises, distinguishable from one another by several characteristics. For example, whereas for science, the physical world around is the ultimate authority by which its theories and principles are to be judged, for mathematics the ultimate test is the logic of relationships and numbers; there is no need for the descriptions of mathematics to relate to the real world.

Because science and technology have been intimately linked in the activities of primary school children, there often appears to be difficulty in distinguishing between them. There would certainly be difficulty in disentangling them, especially in relation to their role in practical activities where children are not only devising ways of problem solving and investigating but constructing actual devices to implement their ideas. But there should be no difficulty in distinguishing between science and technology, for they are quite different in aims and the kinds of activity through which their aims are pursued.

Scientific activity, as we have seen, aims at understanding. Technological activity uses 'knowledge and skills effectively, creatively and confidently in the solving of practical problems and the undertaking of tasks' (Layton 1990: 11).

An important difference between science and technology lies in the way in which a solution to a problem is evaluated. As Layton (1993) points out, the over-riding concern in science is that a theory or explanation should 'fit the facts'. But the products of technology must not only function as intended but also meet other criteria such as 'environmental benignity, cost, aesthetic preferences, ergonomic requirements and market size. "Doing science" is different, therefore, from "doing technology"' (Layton 1993: 48). He goes on to state that scientific expertise 'is no guarantee of technological capability' (ibid.).

Coming back to the classroom, we see some of these characteristics of technology in progress when children are building models, especially working ones, but in fact at all times when materials are used. There is some application of knowledge of materials and skill in fashioning them, which compromise with the necessity of using the materials available, and creativity in doing this to achieve the end result intended within the constraints of time and cost.

Distinguishing technological from scientific activities is important in teachers' minds because they are, as this chapter tries to show, different aspects of children's education. It makes sense, however, to continue to pursue both within the same topics and activities, just as these will also serve certain aims in mathematics, English and other subjects.

Science and other subjects

Looking at the relationship with other subjects from the point of view of helping scientific activity and understanding science, the matter does not end with mathematics and technology. History provides insights into how the accumulation of knowledge over the years has led to greater understanding of how things around us are explained. There are two aspects of this: how new ideas have emerged and what these ideas are. These two are the reasons given by the American Association for the Advancement of Science for including historical perspectives in Benchmarks (AAAS 1993).

There is also a strong relationship between science and art in its various forms in that both help to reveal patterns in things around us which help in making links between one object or event and another. These patterns enable us to make predictions, not so much about what will happen in the future as about what we may find happening now if we try to find it. Science and art are also connected in the use and nature of the human senses, and in a particularly enthralling way in such phenomena as optical illusions, colour perception and resonance.

Some examples of science and art are given in the report of an external evaluation of the Leonardo Project (TERU 2007) (see Box 23.4). The success of the project seemed to result from integrating the two subjects rather than simply running them alongside each other. Such projects can be expensive and it may not be possible, or appropriate, to teach in this way all the time. However for practical as well as pedagogical reasons linking subjects where appropriate can enliven lessons, add value to learning, help make links with learning and the wider world, and provide opportunities for creative leaps, especially where children are given the freedom to develop the project in their own way.

Sustainability

Attention to sustainability has recently risen to the top of the schools' agenda. Work in the area will tend to be cross-curricular, involve parents and other members of the community and will require a good deal of planning to ensure a quality learning experience. Most head teachers are now attempting to run their schools in an environmentally friendly manner with recycling by children, staff and parents encouraged. Many local authorities, such as Staffordshire with its motto 'our county, our climate, our choice', run sustainability projects. Projects within the wider community are being taken up by schools, in some cases with additional funding.

However, although the stated intention is that all schools should become sustainable by 2020, in England Ofsted has recently reported that 'most of the schools visited had limited

---

Box 23.4 The Leonardo Project

The Leonardo Project began as a well-funded project in Northern Ireland and later extended into England and Scotland. It is based on the idea that artists and scientists are both searching for understanding and, following its namesake, the aim was the synchronised integration of learning outcomes for art and science.

The essence of the learning experience was based initially in an eight-week integrated programme of activities where children were encouraged to collaborate to explore an aspect of the topic of flight following a planned series of activities:

■ information gathering – finding out about flight from websites, books, and first-hand experiences through visits to bird sanctuaries, flight centres, or museums and similar facilities;

■ development of ideas – pooling of ideas to develop more focused work, in some schools focused investigations of wing structure (including looking at Leonardo da Vinci's drawings), in others exploration of camouflage and the creation of camouflaged habitats, in others the movement and flight patterns of insects;

■ creation – e.g. designing and planning a unique flying creature;

■ extension – the consolidation of ideas through the creation of storyboards, posters, DVDs, poems to name a few.

Teachers, trained in delivering the project, found the experience rewarding: 'I really used the ideas that the children had given me to help me teach more creatively', 'The children too very much enjoyed the experience', 'Doing art and science at the same time was great fun.'

(Hickey *et al.* 2008: 13).

knowledge of sustainability and work in this area tended to be uncoordinated, often confined to special events rather than being an integral part of the curriculum' (Ofsted 2008 cover page). Nevertheless, many schools have embraced the idea of sustainability. For example Bowridge Primary School is reported by the National College for School Leadership to have a 'vision and concept of sustainability (that) is broad and includes aspects that have traditionally been included to promote environmental protection and understanding'. The head considers that education for sustainability is 'a holistic approach to school improvement' and 'provides an appropriate route for addressing the Every Child Matters agenda' (NCSL website).

Summary

This chapter complements other chapters where aspects of whole-school planning are considered. Here we have focused on planning for the involvement of parents, continuity at transfer and transition points, cross-curricular links, and themes and sustainability. The main points to be emphasised are the need for:

- an agreed system of planning that is consistent and well structured to ensure progression and continuity;

- discussion and sharing of ideas, expertise and workload between teachers;

- whole-school agreement about subject coverage and balance;

- a realistic approach to addressing the plethora of agendas that present themselves, keeping in mind the needs of the children, and the resources of the staff and school as a whole;

- clear links with the national or district curriculum requirements;

- avoidance of slavish adherence to topic or separate subject work such that useful links are made and spurious links avoided;

- consistency of aims and values established in the longer term plans, with medium- and short-term plans so that they are translated into clear goals and appropriate assessments and record keeping.

Further reading

Braund, M. (2004) Bridging work in science. What's in it for primary schools? *Primary Science Review* 82: 24–7.

Cassop Primary School, Co Durham (1007) Harnessing wind and sun: using energy wisely, *Primary Science Review* 100: 35–7.

Conroy, J., Hulme, M. and Menter, I. (2008) *Primary Curriculum and Assessment: Primary Curriculum Futures* Primary Review Research Survey 3/3, Cambridge: University of Cambridge Faculty of Education. Available from http://www.primaryreview.org.uk/

Hickey, I., Robson, D., Flanagan, M. and Campbell, P. (2008) Leonardo flies again: integrating science and art, *Primary Science* 103: 9–13.

Qualter, A. (2005) Role play boxes: taking science home, *Primary Science Review* 90: 21–3.

Useful websites

Astrazeneca SEMs project:

   http://www.azteachscience.co.uk/code/trust/york.asp

Buckinghamshire Grid for learning:

   www.bucksgfl.org.uk/science

National College for School Leadership, sustainable schools:

   http://www.ncsl.org.uk/sustainableschools-index/sustainableschools-casestudies/
   sustainableschools-bowbridge.htm

Planet Science website, passport:

   http://www.planet-science.com/sciteach/index.html?page=/sciteach/passport/index.html

24

Recording and evaluating provision for science

Introduction

This chapter deals with making and using records that help teaching and learning in science. The science subject leader, working with other subject leaders, will wish to establish an appropriate general approach to recording that works for all subject areas and with which teachers feel comfortable. It is also important that individual teachers feel able to adapt the system to suit their needs in their day-to-day recording, so that they and other staff, including teaching assistants, can use it easily in supporting their planning and evaluation. In the first part of the chapter we consider records made by teachers of children's activities and achievements. We then consider ways in which children's involvement in their own learning can be supported by encouraging them to keep records of their own development. In the final section we look at the use of records in self-evaluation, proposing some standards for evaluating provision at class and school levels.

Purposes of records

Records are important means of communication among all those involved in pupils' education, from the government department and local authorities through schools' senior management teams and class teachers to parents or carers and pupils themselves. All records are ultimately about pupils' learning experience and attainments and their purpose is to ensure high quality education. However, concern here is not with the form and content of reports on children's work, but with the use of records to monitor and review provision for science at the class and school level. We briefly consider records in general and then focus on those relevant to science.

Records are created by teachers, school management and sometimes by pupils; the records are used by teachers, school management, governing bodies, local authorities and government agencies. Box 24.1 summarises the content and purposes of records created in the school.

The only statutory requirement on schools in England in relation to records is that records must be kept and updated at least once a year, on every pupil, including information on their academic achievements, other skills and abilities, and progress. It is up to schools to decide how to collect the information and how to record it. Examples of how schools do this can be found on the QCA website. For instance, this is an extract from the account of how the Highlands

Box 24.1 The 'who?', 'what?' and 'why?' of school records

Who creates the record?	What information does it contain?	Why is it needed?
Senior management	Pupil data and statistics Pupil progress and attainment in all subjects Staff and school data as required by the LEA or government	To review and develop school policies For forward planning To meet mandatory requirements To inform the governing body and parents
Class teachers	Pupils' activities Pupils' achievements	To inform medium- and long-term planning To contribute to school level evaluation and planning To report to parents or carers To report to other teachers at transition points
Pupils	Activities undertaken Self-assessment of achievements	To supplement teachers' records To encourage reflection on and development of responsibility for learning

Primary School developed and uses a system for using ongoing records to keep track of pupils' progress.

> During the year, teachers keep ongoing records for reading, writing and mathematics. A 'Tracker' sheet relates to assessment focuses or key learning objectives. There is one sheet for each class, and this indicates when the objective was covered and what level the children are working at. One sheet is completed for boys and one sheet is completed for girls. Tracker sheets are also used when setting targets for the following term and feeds into the teacher's medium- and short-term lesson planning.

An 'Analysis of Progress Made' sheet indicates whether children have moved up or down sub-levels or remained the same. These are also completed for different groups. This tool is used to track children and consider where and when intervention might be beneficial (http://www. qca.org.uk/qca_8855.aspx).

Schools in England can use the PANDA (performance and assessment) reports provided by Ofsted (http://www.teachernet.gov.uk/management/tools/panda/). The reports give an overview of each school's performance in relation to other schools and national averages using data from Ofsted, the DCSF and the QCA. The reports are designed to support schools in their self-evaluation and feed into the inspection process. Schools can access their PANDA reports online through the ePANDA website, using their password.

Teachers' records in science

Two kinds of records are needed to inform short-term and medium-term planning. First are records of individual pupils' experiences as these will vary from group to group, and from intentions, where children are able to follow up questions that arise during their planned activities. Second are records of children's achievement so that the teacher can plan for continuity in children's development. These are ongoing records which teachers use for their own planning and on which they can draw when making a more formal report on children's attainments.

Records of activities of individual children

Unless all the children in a class always work on the same activities as each other, there is a need for a system which records what individuals have actually done. Even if the activities were the same for all it would be no guarantee that their *experiences* would be identical, since children attend selectively to different parts of the work, extend some and give scant attention to others. They also become diverted into unplanned avenues to follow their own questions.

It is not always possible, or appropriate, for every child to undertake every activity. For example in the case studies in Chapter 2, in both Graham's and Anne's classes the groups of children each conducted a different investigation. However the different activities were intended to address the same ideas and develop similar skills and the children presented their findings to the rest of the class. There was no need for them all to do each investigation.

The need for a record of science-based experiences is particularly needed when work is undertaken through cross-curricular topics. Box 24.2 describes one such example.

Experiences directed to the same objectives as in Box 24.2 were planned for the next week in another topic on the 'gingerbread man'. This gave them opportunity to investigate ways to keep

---

Box 24.2 Science in a topic at the foundation stage

A reception class was undertaking a week-long topic 'Our New School' in which they considered a wide variety of aspects of the foundation stage curriculum, including knowledge and understanding of the world. A new school building was being erected in the grounds of their very old school. The children talked to parents who had attended the school as children, discussed old photographs, and considered how people felt about their old school being knocked down. Within the Foundation Stage 'Knowledge and understanding of the world' the focus in science was to 'Investigate objects and materials by using all of their senses as appropriate' (DfEE/QCA 2000). The children explored building materials and thought about how to build a stable wall. Within the topic there were many opportunities to develop understanding. For example, an activity table of various play bricks was used to encourage building and testing the strength of a wall. The children were also able to test the properties of different materials (squashy, breaks easily, goes runny when wet) to see which might be good to build with. By the end of the week teachers wanted to be sure that all children had experienced each of these activities. They kept a chart for each activity table, so that children could record their visit to the table (using laminated name labels to stick on a wall chart). At the end of the week gaps could be easily spotted and recorded.

Class .... Term ....

Topic	Our New School (Week 4)		The Gingerbread Man (Week 6)		
Activity	Build a wall	Explore building materials	Baking	Rain cape for Gingerbread	Judge the best Gingerbread man
Goals	Prediction Describes what they did	Investigates using senses Appropriate language	Uses senses to explore Appropriate language	Investigates materials Prediction Describes what they did	Describes simple features Compares features
Ali					
Sam					
Charlene					
etc					

Figure 24.1 Record of science activities undertaken within topics

a gingerbread man dry and, in baking, would look at a variety of materials using their senses. Figure 24.1 indicates the kind of record kept of the activities undertaken by each pupil.

Certain activities will probably be regarded as equivalent to each other, while in other cases it may be that the context is so different that repetition is desirable. Taking these things into account, the teacher will use the record to keep an eye on the gaps in the activities of individual children and act on this, either in planning the next term's work or having one or two sessions in which children are directed to activities which they have missed. The main thing to be avoided is the same children missing out on all experiences relating to materials for any reason such as absence or lack of engagement with an activity.

Ongoing records of children's achievement

The records concerning the ongoing achievements of individual pupils in a class are necessarily detailed. On-going formative assessment involves making judgements about achievement which in turn inform the next steps in learning (see Chapter 16). During a single lesson the teacher may use on the spot assessments to move children on immediately. However lessons are time-limited, while learning should continue from one lesson to another, term-to-term and year-to-year. Moreover teachers will rarely have the opportunity to observe and assess all the children in a class during a single activity. Records need to be kept in order to identify and fill the gaps. Keeping track of assessments made, particularly in respect of inquiry skills and attitudes, which develop throughout the year, is important in building up a full picture of the child's progress. It is best to keep in mind that:

- the over-riding purpose is to help the teacher remember where each child has reached in his or her development so that suitable activities and encouragement can be given;

- these records are for the teacher's own use and so the level of detail can be adjusted to suit the individual's ways of working;

- they will be summarised for other purposes, for school records passed from class to class and for reporting to parents or carers.

Teachers vary as to how much information they can carry in their head and how much they like to write down, and this may be one of the factors which leads to a preference for a check-list, or for a more detailed pro forma which gives opportunity for comments, caveats and explanations. However systems for recording achievement need to be simple and, in most cases, understandable by others. This is particularly important in cases where a classroom assistant or other adult takes part in assessing what has been learned. The class teacher and her assistants in the reception class described in Box 24.2 used a simple record for each topic as shown in Fig 24.2. These records formed the basis of discussions between the class teacher and her assistant and in turn contributed to the individual records for each child (looking down the columns) and helped to identify aspects to focus on in forthcoming topics (looking across the rows).

Nursery – Mrs Cole and Mrs Kahn - Week 4

Building a new school –

Knowledge and Understanding of the world

Objective	Ali	Sam	Charlene	Kylie1	David	Liam	Leanne	Kylie 2	India
Tests Strength of materials	✓	✓	✓	✓	✓	✓	✓	O	✓
Able to make prediction	✓	✗	✓	✓	✓	✗	✗	O	✓
Describes what he/she did	✗	✓	✓	✓	✓	✓	✓	O	✓
Investigates objects/materials using all senses	✓	✓	✓	✓	✓	✗	✓	✓	✓
Uses appropriate language to describe objects/materials *(Smelly, Squashy, hard, cold etc.)*	✗	✓	✓	✓	✓	✓	✓	✓	✓
Comment	Facial expression etc. but not speaking					Needs to slow down too rushed		Did not do wall.	

Figure 24.2 Simple topic record sheet

Science profile. Child's Name:		Date:						
Inquiry skills and attitudes	Circle number of indicator applying							
Gathering evidence by observing, etc.	1	2	3	4	5	6	7	
Questioning, predicting and planning	1	2	3	4	5	6	7	
Interpreting evidence, drawing conclusions	1	2	3	4	5	6	7	
Communicating and reflecting	1	2	3	4	5	6	7	
Willingness to consider evidence and change ideas	1	2	3	4	5	6	7	
Sensitivity to living things and the environment	1	2	3	4	5	6	7	
Ideas about								
Living things and life processes	1	2	3	4	5	6	7	
Interaction of living things	1	2	3	4	5	6	7	
Materials	1	2	3	4	5	6	7	
etc.								

Figure 24.3 Individual science profile: cumulative record

Keeping records is made easier if the record is cumulative and enables children's progress to be identified. The Foundation Stage Profile (see Box 18.1) allows for regular updating on the same form indicating where children have reached using the nine points for each of the 13 scales. A specifically science-based cumulative record can be created based on the indicators of development in Boxes 15.2 to 15.7 (pp. 189–191), for example as in Figure 24.3. As many teachers today keep their records on computer it is a simple matter to update records at regular intervals. The areas of knowledge covered will not be the same from half term to half term, but the 'ideas' can be written in as appropriate. However, the skills and attitudes are likely to be widely relevant and so should be covered whatever the subject matter of the activities.

Many teachers will feel that the problem of records of this kind is not that they contain too much information but that they contain too little. The richness and complexity of children's performance can rarely be captured in a brief note (and even less by a tick). In many systems, therefore, these records are only a part of the material that is available to a teacher about individual children. Samples of work, chosen by the child and/or the teacher, and more extensive notes may be kept in a file for each child.

Records that children can keep

We mentioned earlier in this chapter (Box 24.2) how children in a reception class recorded the completion of particular activities by posting their name on a chart. The next logical step is for children to keep their own records of their achievements, although perhaps when the children are a little older. A number of approaches have been adopted to facilitate this. In some schools the learning objectives are always written on the bottom of worksheets, or put on the board. These objectives are often presented in child friendly language. Children are asked to indicate with smiley (or otherwise) faces, ticks or comments, or 'traffic lights' (Black *et al.* 2003) as to how far they feel they have achieved the goals. Teachers can then moderate this judgement as they make their own records. Children may then mark off the objectives met on an appropriate

	Names of children						
I have experimented to find out about some of the difference between ice, water and steam							
I know what happens when water 'disappears'!!							
I have found out about the evaporation of other liquids							
I have investigated different conditions that can affect the rate of evaporation							
I have found out how to evaporate water and change it back to water again							
I have found out about the water cycle!!							
I know the boiling temperature and freezing temperature of water							
I know how to change water into ice and make it melt again							
I can use a temperature sensor and create a graph on the computer							
I can suggest what might happen and explain why							
I can write clear accounts and explain my results using my scientific knowledge							

Figure 24.4 An end of unit record sheet completed by children

recording device. Figure 24.4 is an example of a class record adapted from Nimmons (2003) of records for a Year 5 class having studied the unit on changing states in the QCA scheme of work (DfEE 1998). The children can write a brief comment or simply check off what they have done. Individual records of the same kinds could be created for children to keep in their folders with the unit work.

Evaluating provision for science

Teachers and schools can use evaluation formatively to improve provision for science by comparing their practice with standards of quality. We use the word 'standards' here to mean something to aim for as opposed to what has been achieved. Teachers and schools themselves could establish what 'quality' means in operational terms, taking into account indicators of widely agreed criteria that exist in the documents provided for school self-evaluation, such as *How Good is Our School* (SEED 2002b) in Scotland, in England *A New Relationship with Schools* (DfES and Ofsted 2004), and in Wales *Guidance on the Inspection of Primary and Nursery Schools* (Estyn 2004).

Standards at the class level

Box 24.3 provides a starter list of indicators relating to provision at the class level. Derived from examples of good practice, these standards are not all easily attainable but may be regarded as goals to aim for. They may be used in occasional (once or twice a year) evaluation discussions but hopefully also kept in mind at other times. Ideally teachers collaborate in collecting information to conduct this self-evaluation. Observing each others' lessons with the standards in mind is a valuable experience for both the observer and the observed. However, where this is not possible, the standards may help personal reflection.

Box 24.3 Standards for classroom practice

Teachers should:

- use a range of methods suited to the achievement of the various goals of learning science;

- provide simple materials and equipment for children to use in first-hand exploration and inquiry of scientific phenomena in their environment;

- regularly ask questions which invite children to express their ideas;

- know where children are in the development of ideas and inquiry skills and use this information to provide opportunities and support (scaffolding) for progress;

- include in lesson plans what children are intended to learn as well as what they will do;

- provide comments that help progress in oral or written feedback on children's work;

- ensure that children regularly have a chance to raise questions and that these are addressed;

- ensure that children always know the purpose of their investigations and other science activities;

- provide opportunities for children to discuss observations, plans, findings and conclusions in small groups and as a whole class;

- provide opportunity for children to obtain information from books, the Internet, out of school visits and visiting experts;

- discuss with children the qualities of good work so that they can assess and improve their own and each other's work;

- provide time and encouragement for children to reflect on how and what they have learned;

- keep records of children's progress based on questioning, observation, discussion and study of products relevant to the learning goals.

Standards at the school level

Box 24.4 suggests some indicators for use by the school's science subject leader or senior management in evaluating provision for science at the school level. It is important for all the school staff to agree to the standards to aim for and to participate in evaluating progress towards them. The indicators in each set of standards can be used in much the same way as indicators of pupils' achievement at a particular time. Evidence relevant to each indicator will come from a range of documents, records, observation, lists of resources, review of pupils' work, discussion with advisers, parents and more besides. The intention is not to judge the provision as 'good' or 'poor' but to draw attention to areas where practice falls short of aspirations and so focus action to develop and maintain agreed standards of practice.

Box 24.4 Standards for school provision for science

The school should:

- have a school policy for science which reflects the above standards for classroom work consistently across the school;

- regularly enable teachers to discuss the policy and update it as necessary;

- expect teachers to use the agreed standards in their lesson planning, teaching and self-evaluation;

- provide regular opportunity for teachers to plan and, where possible, to teach science lessons collaboratively;

- have effective procedures for the provision and maintenance of equipment and materials to support inquiry-based activities and sources of information for children and teachers;

- keep records of individual children's progress in science based on annual or bi-annual summaries of teachers' records;

- ensure that parents and carers are aware of the school science policy and of how they may be able to support their children's learning in science;

- enable teachers to upgrade their science teaching skills and knowledge through regular professional development.

Summary

This chapter has considered how the provision for children's learning in science can be helped by keeping records and by evaluation at class and school levels. The main points have been:

- teachers need to keep separate records of activities undertaken by children and the learning achieved;

- teachers' own records of assessments made as part of teaching should be sufficiently detailed to be useful in aiding planning;

- cumulative records of learning can be made on a single record proforma by adding information at different times;

- as part of their involvement with their own learning, children should be aware of and play a part in the assessment process; they can usefully keep ongoing information which enables them to record their activities and monitor their achievements;

- it is helpful for self-evaluation at class and school levels for schools to identify the standards to which they aspire in provision for science and to evaluate their actual provision in relation to them.

Further reading

Harlen, W. (2007c) Holding up a mirror to classroom practice, *Primary Science Review* 100: 29–1.

Richardson, I. (2006) What is good science education? in W. Harlen (ed.) *ASE Guide to Primary Science Education*, Hatfield: ASE: 16–23.

Wright, L. (2006) School self-evaluation of teaching and learning science, in W. Harlen (ed.) *ASE Guide to Primary Science Education*, Hatfield: ASE: 73-9.

The science subject leader

Introduction

In this chapter we discuss planning and support for science in the primary school from the point of view of the subject coordinator or subject leader. The main concern is with translating the developing philosophy of the school, and in particular the approach taken to science, into practice. There are also more technical aspects of management that need to be addressed if science is to be properly planned and implemented in the school. We begin with a discussion of the role of the subject leader in terms of contributing to the strategic direction of the school, and in particular the school science policy. We then consider the subject leader as the support for learning and teaching, leadership and management of staff and the oversight of the effective use of people and resources to ensure high-quality science learning in the school.

The role of the subject leader

The first of the two main roles of the science subject leader is to lead a team that plans and carries out a teaching programme that engages pupils, achieves high standards and aligns with the National Curriculum for science. The second is to evaluate the curriculum and its impact on pupils (DCSF Standards website). But this has not always been the case, for the role has evolved. The science coordinator began life as the member of staff who dealt with the literature coming into the school relating to science, writing the school policy on science (Ritchie 1998), possibly identifying the materials needed, possibly attending courses in science teaching that could then be 'cascaded' to the rest of the school staff. The role changed and grew and then became science subject leader. As the title implies, this is not simply a 'pulling together' of information but taking a view about what science should be in the school, identifying ways in which it might need to change and then finding ways to make changes, taking staff on the journey. In recent years the role has changed further in some schools. As we mentioned in Chapter 23, planning requires consideration of a wide range of whole-school issues as well as those that fall more easily within a subject. One way to address this across a school is to have teams of staff responsible for a subject, a number of subjects or for specific themes (Burrows 2004), or, for example teachers with responsibility for a year group, or stage. One example of this approach is reported by Barr (2003) as described in Box 25.1.

Box 25.1 The role of a subject leader as part of a team

At Brindishe School a system of teams with team leaders is used to manage all subject work throughout the school. The science and technology team consists of three teachers, a classroom assistant, the school 'housekeeper' plus the subject leader.

The planning cycle in the school begins in June with a whole-school INSET/ development day. During that meeting the development plan is reviewed enabling all team leaders to reflect on their own area of responsibility and on achievements throughout the year. The staff (including teaching assistants and senior teachers) then start to put forward ideas for the following year. These are collated and drawn together by the head teacher in revising the school plan for the year. The team leaders then arrange meetings with their team to develop the plans for the coming year. Because everyone is part of more than one team, plans within any subject area are not independent of what is being developed by other teams.

Although the subject leader has a number of responsibilities in this school (analysis of assessment data, liaising with the senior managers, staff development, lesson audits, etc.), the team approach ensures a shared understanding and a shared sense of achievement.

More commonly an individual teacher will have responsibility for more than one area (science and transition, or science and out of school education). Hence, the role of the subject leader still exists, but has changed as a consequence of the context in which schools operate. Box 25.2 describes the responsibilities of a single subject leader which could equally well apply to a team.

In the next sections we expand on each of these points in turn.

Strategic leadership and direction

We have argued in the previous chapters that schools need to develop a vision based on the values of staff, pupils, parents and carers and the wider community. School policies are, or should be, an expression of these values and priorities. The science subject leader, working with all others in the school who have responsibility for an aspect of the curriculum, needs to spend time discussing school policies, not once, but regularly. This is now an established part of practice in most schools, with a regular timetable of review of specific policies. To do this well a subject leader needs to understand the broader policies of the school, to know the capacity of the staff and school to achieve aspirations, to have a sound understanding of science and science teaching and to be up to date with current developments in the field. In addition, and most importantly, good communication with senior managers as well as colleagues is essential if a policy for science is to be developed collaboratively.

Box 25.2 Key areas of subject leadership

■ Strategic direction and development

Within the context of the school's aims and policies, subject leaders develop and implement subject policies, plans, targets and practices.

■ Learning and teaching

Subject leaders secure and sustain effective teaching of the subject, evaluate the quality of teaching, learning standards and the pupils' achievements, and set targets for improvements.

■ Leading and managing staff

Subject leaders provide for all those with involvement in the teaching or support of the subject, and the guidance, challenge, information and development necessary to sustain motivation and secure improvement in teaching.

■ Efficient and effective deployment of staff and resources

Subject leaders identify appropriate resources for the subject and ensure that they are used efficiently, effectively and safely.

(Adapted from East Sussex School Improvement Service 2005)

A science policy

The science policy should be a clear expression of values and aims and should inform teachers, governors, parents, children and the wider community about what the school sees as important in science teaching. The main topics to be covered in a policy proposed by CLEAPSS (2006) are listed in Box 25.3.

The CLEAPSS document gives examples for each of these topics, taken from a number of school science policies. For instance, for 'the philosophy of science teaching':

> ...we believe that children have a natural curiosity about their world and the enthusiasm to want to make sense of it. We aim to capitalise on this, using first-hand experiences so that our children come face to face with phenomena and learn directly about the ways things are, and why they behave as they do.

In England there is a great deal of emphasis on subject leaders making use of the substantial amount of assessment data that is available about a school and about the individual children within it (see the standards site for example (http://www.standards.dfes.gov.uk/). This can indeed be a useful tool in evaluating the implementation of the curriculum, but should only be done in the clear understanding of the context and a recognition that not all that is valuable is captured in such data.

Box 25.3 Topics in a school policy

The science policy should include statements of:

- the aims of teaching science, reflecting the school aims;
- the philosophy of science teaching;
- the approach to science teaching;
- the approach to assessment;
- how equal opportunities are provided;
- how health and safety are assured;
- procedures for record keeping;
- cross-curricular links;
- outdoor education;
- the approach to planning;
- the use of resources.

Learning and teaching

Monitoring learning and teaching

The subject leader helps to support teachers and other educators within the school to provide the best possible science education for children. This means ensuring that staff both understand the science policy and science curriculum and feel free to plan and teach creatively in a way that suits their own pupils. This is no small challenge. If we are aiming for continuous improvement then the subject must be monitored and evaluated. In a sense the aim here is to ensure that there is a continuing conversation between staff about science teaching.

In Chapter 24 we proposed some standards for the evaluation of science at the class and school levels. Here we focus on some of the strategies subject leaders can use to gather information for monitoring and evaluating science across the school. Monitoring is not policing. It should be simply the process by which the 'conversation' described above can be most effectively conducted.

Scrutiny of teachers' planning
At the level of medium-term planning this should involve whether the plans reflect the overall school curriculum in terms of topics, coverage and approach. Is there a good balance of coverage of different areas of the curriculum? Is there a good range of different approaches being planned (working outside, use of ICT, group and individual work)? Is there good integration of investigative work across the term?

At the level of the lesson or group of lessons the questions can be drawn from those given in Chapter 4 and used again in Chapter 13 on lesson planning. For example:

- Are the activities likely to be interesting and relevant to the children?

- Do the activities build on previous experience and promote progression?

- Will the children be able to use a range of senses and learn actively?

- Will the children talk and represent their ideas in different ways?

- Will the children be able to develop scientific ideas, use inquiry skills and demonstrate scientific attitudes?

Scrutiny of pupils' work

Pupils' notebooks should provide a record of some of the work the children have done in science and should reflect the medium and short-term plans of the teacher and be set at an appropriate level for the children. Thus, it is useful to refer back to teachers' plans when looking at children's work. Crucial questions in respect to inquiry were suggested by the AKSIS project, and quoted by CLEAPSS (2006). These include:

- Whose inquiry is it? The answer should be clearly the child, or group of children, rather than the teacher.

- What is its context?

- What questions are the children trying to answer?

- Have children drawn conclusions? How good is their evidence?

- Has the teacher's marking helped, for instance by indicating what is good about the work, what could be improved or by raising questions for the child to consider?

Of course not all the work produced is presented in books. It is also useful to look at the product of collaborative work, for example a big book from a class topic, or displays on classroom and corridor walls. Wall displays can give an impression of the profile of science in school, the emphasis that is being placed on inquiry, and the extent to which children themselves are involved in the whole process. The work displayed should be something that children themselves feel is worth showing to others. Often wall displays can be used to inform, excite and motivate children and visitors to the classroom. This last point ensures that parents and carers are informed about ongoing science work in school.

Observation of teaching

A really useful way to encourage conversation between staff is for them to be able to observe each other teach. Science subject leaders are often in this fortunate position. However, it is also helpful for others to either observe each other teach, or to team teach. This suggests that 'observation' should be seen as positive, yet some people find it difficult, both to be observed and to act as observer. Observation then needs to be conducted sensitively and to emphasise the positive. A discussion before the lesson between the teacher and observer should identify what is planned for the lesson. More detailed information about individual pupils, for instance, will help the observer to understand what is happening and why. It is helpful to agree beforehand on the focus of the observation. This may be on particular parts of a lesson that a teacher wants to improve, for example, the plenary, or particular ways to organise practical work, such as group work. Teachers might want to consider particularly successful strategies that might be shared with others.

When observing lessons it is helpful to plan how notes will be taken to address particular points, so that feedback can then be in the form of a conversation, focusing on the particular aspects under consideration. As in feedback to children, it is important to highlight features of effective practice and discuss ways in which the individual can develop. In this way agreement can be reached about targets for further development that can feed into whole-school targets, and, along with other monitoring, can inform subject and school development.

Leading and managing staff

Science subject leaders need to provide information, advice and guidance for colleagues in such a way as to support the whole school in moving forward. This can involve providing support in relation to approaches to teaching and subject knowledge.

The science subject leader as an advisor

A major element of the subject leader's role is to advise other colleagues. This requires sensitivity, as some teachers may feel less than confident, for example, about their subject knowledge both of science concepts and about inquiry skills. On the other hand newly qualified teachers may, because of an increased emphasis on subject knowledge in the initial training curriculum, arrive with a sound knowledge of the subject but need mentoring and guidance in understanding how children learn and in effective pedagogy. How the subject leader addresses this issue partly depends on the view of what is needed to be an effective primary science teacher.

The question of the extent to which a primary teacher who is a generalist has the knowledge to provide learning activities of the necessary challenge for children throughout the primary school is a contentious issue. The arguments are clouded by reducing the concept of 'teachers' knowledge' to knowledge of the subject matter, with little regard for other kinds of knowledge which are involved in teaching.

It is through the work and writing of Shulman and some other science educators in the US that the kinds of knowledge needed in teaching have been set out. Writing in relation to teaching science, Shulman (1987) lists the following kinds of knowledge as being required by the teacher:

- content knowledge– about science and of science;
- general pedagogical knowledge – about classroom management and organisation, non subject specific;
- curriculum knowledge – guidelines, national requirements, materials available;
- pedagogical content knowledge – about how to teach the subject matter, including useful illustrations, powerful analogies and examples;
- knowledge of learners and their characteristics;
- knowledge of educational contexts;

- knowledge of educational goals, values and purposes, including the history and philosophy of education.

It is significant that Shulman puts content knowledge first in this list, since several of the subsequent items depend on it. But what he emphasises is not so much the mastery of each and every aspect of a subject, as an understanding of what it is that identifies science; how the discipline of science differs from other disciplines; what its boundaries are, its limitations and the different ways in which it can be conceived. With this understanding, teachers can develop pedagogical content knowledge, which Shulman characterises as building 'bridges between their own understanding of the subject matter and the understanding that grows and is constructed in the minds of students' (Shulman 1991).

Teacher subject knowledge

In the 1990s, disquiet about the effect of poor teacher subject knowledge led to a demand on initial teacher training courses to increase the focus on science and in particular science subject knowledge. This, coupled with the compulsory study of science up to the age of 16 in UK schools for many years, means that recently qualified teachers are likely to have grounding in the subject. The introduction of the non-statutory guidance the QCA scheme of work (DfEE 1998) has also provided increased support for science teaching, including many sources of support for subject knowledge.

One effect of concerns about science subject knowledge was an increased pressure on schools to use specialist subject teachers in the upper years in particular. The disadvantages of separate subject teaching are that science can come to be seen as something different and separate from other subjects and possibly less relevant to the children. The opportunities of maximising learning, increasing motivation, and of making cross-curricular links are much reduced, and the need to move teachers around creates a much more rigid timetable with much less opportunity for children to pursue an interesting idea or complete an investigation. Yet at the same time it is clear that a teacher who is interested in and knowledgeable about a subject can inspire interest and enthusiasm in their pupils.

The importance of considering the interests of the children was underlined by research which suggests what happens to children's learning experiences when teachers with little confidence in this area have to cope with science. Harlen and Holroyd (1995) found that teachers adopt teaching strategies that included:

- compensating for doing less of a low-confidence aspect of science by doing more of a higher confidence aspect: this might mean stressing the inquiry skill aims in science rather than the concept development aims and doing more biology/nature study and less physical science;

- heavy reliance on kits, prescriptive texts and pupil workcards;

- emphasis on expository teaching and underplaying discussion;

- over-dependence on standard responses to content-related questions.

However, the situation is not as simple as 'more science knowledge better science teaching'. Newton and Newton (2001) suggest that teachers who have some science knowledge are

---

Box 25.4 The subject leader as subject knowledge support

Caroline has a BEd science degree. She teaches 7–8-year-olds and has been science coordinator for three years. There is no specialist science teaching in this two-form-entry school which is housed in a new building. The classrooms for each year group are semi open-plan and linked by a shared work area. The year teachers develop their medium- and short-term plans together, with the more confident teacher in each year group taking the lead.

The school's long-term plan is based on, but is not the same as, the QCA scheme of work. Each section of the plan is supplemented by a series of notes developed over the years by Caroline. The notes focus on subject knowledge, with advice on additional sources, websites and books. Each year she makes a note of questions teachers ask her and the research she has done in order to answer the questions. In developing the long-term plan for the following year, she reviews her file of notes and ideas and uses this to inform the development of the next plan. In this way she has built up a file of useful supplementary information and ideas for teachers that is organised in units according to the school plan. Teachers can then use this in their medium- and short-term planning.

---

more likely to develop the pedagogical skills to support pupils' learning. The emphasis is not on facts but on the broad principles which teachers, as adults with much existing relevant experience, very quickly grasp, most importantly, on the understanding of what it is to be scientific.

The support now available online, through guidance books on subject knowledge and initial teacher training courses, as well as published schemes of work, may have added to increasing confidence to teach science. A Wellcome Trust survey of primary teachers found that 80 per cent indicated high levels of confidence in teaching science (Wellcome 2005). The added confidence and support should enable primary teachers to continue to teach science to their own classes rather than separate it from other work by using specialist teachers. As the debate continues, schools need to make decisions about how to support staff in developing their science knowledge and understanding and in how to deploy staff. The subject leader is crucial here in helping to identify the strengths and weaknesses of teachers and to help to develop staff whilst making maximum use of their expertise. One practical way of doing this and then providing the support that is needed is described in Box 25.4.

The subject leader as staff developer

Sharp and Hopkin (2008) in a survey of English primary teachers in 2007 found that 60 per cent of respondents had received no science-focused training either within school or outside over the previous three years. Considering that the subject specialism of the respondents was skewed in favour of science subject leaders, and that science subject leaders had undertaken significantly more training than other colleagues, the situation is not encouraging. In particular the lack of professional development in school suggests that science subject leaders have not had the opportunity to provide this essential support for staff. This is a particularly important gap, especially with the increase in support staff and in the level of responsibility for teaching and assessment that they can have in some schools.

All teachers and other educators should feel comfortable enough to ask for help when they feel they need it; we all need to keep up-to-date and to have the stimulus of learning new things. The science subject leader must not only monitor the curriculum and teaching but must also address weaknesses. The help staff need can be established through professional conversations. We discuss in Chapter 26 ways of providing professional development.

Effective deployment of resources

The subject leader needs to be a champion ensuring that science is afforded appropriate resources, including time within the timetable and sufficient funding for resources and travel to sites outside the school.

Resource management and timetabling

One of the roles that subject leaders have always recognised as important is that of resource manager. Primary science is demanding of resources. In Chapter 19 we discuss the issue of resources in some detail. However it is important to note that the term resources can cover a multitude of things: practical equipment, storage space, the time to carry out science activities and the knowledgeable teachers to support it, the information technology, books and posters that can enhance subject teaching, as well as visitors to the school and places for the school to visit.

One of the findings of the Wellcome Trust study of primary science across the UK was the variability among different schools in terms of funding for science. Given the increased emphasis on sustainability, learning out of doors and ICT, funding for science needs to be realistic. This may mean subject leaders getting involved in bidding for additional external resources, seeking links with local industry or simply persuading senior managers to recognise their concerns.

Time is a major resource for science. Science is often squeezed out in implementing the planned activities for several reasons, including the teachers' lack of confidence in teaching science or the special emphasis given to literacy and numeracy, noted in Murphy et al. (2000), and illustrated in the words of a teacher of 7–8-year-olds:

> If I had science in the morning, pre literacy and numeracy strategies, I could start and let it run. I would have other topic work to feed in for children who had completed a task and I could keep working right down to the slowest. But now I've got to cut off. I find that very frustrating. The children find it frustrating.

(Murphy et al. 2000: 15)

As well as the overall time for science, the timetabling of science activities is important. Where it is felt that science requires extended periods of time, this needs to be set against the demands of other curriculum areas. Getting the balance right when a cross-curricular approach is being taken is also something of a fine art. Where broadly based topic work is the predominant way of working, the timetable needs to allow this to take place for extended periods of time, interrupted only by the essential scheduling of activities where space, staff or equipment have to be shared, providing time for children to carry out investigations which would not fit into small time-slots. In theory this could still be the case where the school organises the curriculum on a subject basis, with the time for each area designated. However, in this case, there is a greater likelihood of time being chopped up into portions which restrict opportunities for children to try things out, discuss them, try other ideas while things are fresh in their minds and so derive maximum learning from their activities. Decisions about having a dedicated science week or the use or otherwise of subject specialist teachers can also restrict choice in terms of how science fits into the timetable.

Summary

The science subject leader contributes to the strategic development of the subject in school, securing and sustaining effective teaching, leading and managing staff and ensuring the most effective deployment of human and physical resources. This is achieved through:

- the development of a science policy that reflects the values of the school and is owned and understood by all those involved in supporting science learning;

- the monitoring of learning and teaching that enables ongoing 'conversations' about ways to improve and enhance learning for pupils;

- the effective leadership of staff so that the subject leader can act as advisor, supporter, collaborator and, where necessary, champion of the subject;

- the effective management of resources including time, equipment, and staff.

The latter includes contributing to considerations of appropriate professional development for staff, a subject to which we turn our attention in the next and final chapter.

Further reading

Lawrence, L. (2006) The science subject leader's role, in W. Harlen (ed.) *ASE Guide to Primary Science Education*, Hatfield: ASE: 83–9.

Teachers' continuing professional learning

Introduction

The teaching profession is, by its very nature, a learning profession. We value learning and are regularly developing our skills as teachers. The pace of change over the last 20 years has meant that keeping up with developments and continuing to learn has become more of a challenge. It is not simply new technology that has changed or that science itself has moved on apace, but also the frequency of appearance of new ideas about learning and teaching. 'Personalised learning', 'assessment for learning', 'learning styles', 'multiple intelligences', 'awe and wonder', 'every child matters' and a whole lot of other terms have emerged since the first edition of this book. How are teachers to engage with all these new ideas and make reasoned judgements about how, or if, they can be useful in enhancing learning and teaching? The answer clearly lies in Continuing Professional Development (CPD), the subject of this chapter. We begin by describing what is meant by CPD for teachers, and then identify various approaches and the range of resources and opportunities that might be accessed in order to support continued learning. With such a wide range of possibilities it is important to consider how to identify needs. Finally we look briefly at the ways the different countries of the UK have chosen to support CPD and the ways in which professional development is recognised and rewarded.

What is CPD and what forms can it take?

Continuing Professional Development (CPD) is the means by which members of a profession maintain, improve and broaden their knowledge and skills throughout their career. It is increasingly recognised that all educators should have access to good quality opportunities for professional development. In the past this might have meant simply 'going on a course' or attending a workshop. However, our understanding of the range of opportunities for CPD has broadened considerably. In part, this is because research has shown that attendance at a short course, off site, with little or no follow up has little impact in improving teaching.

Effective teachers are 'continually learning on the job, because their work entails engagement with a succession of cases, problems or projects which they have to learn about' (Eraut 1994: 16). Eraut emphasises the point that, in order to make the most of these learning opportunities, professionals must have time to reflect on them either individually or with others. Thus, what

Hoyle and Megarry (1980) describe as 'the extended professional', is characterised by continual learning supported by opportunities to reflect on experiences and deliberate on the implications for practice. These opportunities to reflect then constitute the kind of continuing professional learning needed if practitioners are to move from the 'restricted professional' role concerned simply with delivery of the curriculum to the more creative practitioners that most teachers aspire to be.

The Eisenhower programme was one of the largest ever in the USA in funding for teacher professional development. Different states, school districts and schools made use of the funds in a variety of ways. In an extensive survey of take up, Garet and colleagues (2001) found that the most widely used form of CPD was the workshop. However, they also found an increasing interest (at the end of the 1990s) in what they termed the 'reform type' of CPD, which included study groups, mentoring and coaching. They concluded that sustained, mainly school-based CPD involving groups rather than individual teachers was the most effective.

> Timespan and contact hours have a substantial positive influence on opportunities for active learning and coherence. Longer activities tend to include substantially more opportunities for active learning, such as the opportunity to plan for classroom implementation, observe and be observed teaching; review students' work and give presentations and demonstrations. Longer activities also tend to promote coherence including connections to a teacher's goals and experiences, alignment with standards and professional communication with other teachers.
>
> (Garet *et al.* 2001: 935)

Forms of CPD

Short courses

A single day course may not always be the most effective, but if well selected it can be an efficient way of providing what is needed. For example the teacher in Box 26.1 had the opportunity to take a course that she could then make use of in her role as science coordinator. What she learnt from the course fitted her own and the school's needs and so the head and other teachers in the school were supportive in the follow up work. Essentially then, a short course led to an extended project.

Extended courses

The traditional approach to CPD has been to undertake a master's course at a local university, or as a distance learning programme. In England, support for courses deemed appropriate for qualified teachers comes from the Training and Development Agency for Schools (TDA). There are very few master's programmes that focus specifically on science education, and even fewer where the focus is primary science. However, it is possible to select individual modules and also to focus assignments from more general modules on science. What such courses can provide is an opportunity to take a step back and to reflect on practice, seen as important in developing the extended professional.

> **Box 26.1** Impact of a well-selected one-day course
>
> The course was really valuable, and since returning to school, I have implemented everything listed on my action plan. The resources have been loaded on all the interactive whiteboards (the school has one in every classroom) and I have provided a half-day Inset course to all staff on their use. And because of my peripatetic role within the school, I've been able to ensure that the approaches have been used with all pupils. It is impossible to be certain whether the teachers would have used them without my intervention, but I feel now that teachers understand the value and that they would continue to use them whether I was present or not.
>
> (Redmore, Teacher Expertise website)

A full master's programme is a major undertaking which may not always be the appropriate route. Indeed, if we are to see CPD as lifelong learning, one would expect to continue learning beyond the award of the degree. The proposal by the TDA Board (TDA, 2007) to give those enrolled in graduate teacher programmes the opportunity to acquire master's-level credits during their programme, would spread the work over a longer period and encourage continued study at M level.

Increasingly universities are offering programmes that are more integrated with the teachers' own professional setting, making links not just by encouraging school-based research to provide the material for assignments, but rather to extend this into schools. This is in response to the mounting research evidence about what constitutes effective CPD.

> Effective CPD processes included: use of peer support and specialist expertise; use of observation and feedback; teachers experimenting in applying the new skills in classroom teaching; consultation with teachers during the CPD process; and a significant in-school component to CPD.
>
> (Cordingly *et al.* 2005)

Johnson (2007) reported on a CPD project in the US designed to help promote the National Science Education Standards. Science teachers and managers from a number of schools attended a two-week summer school at a local university, extending their subject knowledge and undertaking workshops. Part of the programme involved the one or two teachers from each school designing a sustained course of CPD to deliver back in school over the following year. In the two research schools, university staff continued to act as coaches. In one school, staff then got whole days in-school of training from their colleagues. The approach was found to be effective in changing teachers' practice. However, in other contexts where the school systems were less supportive (in terms of time provided for professional development) there was less impact. Even in this well supported environment the impact was variable. Some teachers who changed their practice very little might benefit from more focused coaching.

Coaching and mentoring

Many teachers are familiar with the role of the mentor as it is common practice in initial teacher training to have a school-based mentor who, ideally, acts as a knowledgeable and trusted counsellor offering support and guidance and sharing his or her expertise. This can also provide a very useful structure for supporting new staff in a school and, in particular teaching assistants and other classroom support staff. In many organisations mentors are identified for new staff as a matter of course. However, in terms of supporting development in primary science there is value in considering coaching. A coach works with an individual to help them to become more effective, working with the teacher's own identified goals. An example of coaching is provided on Teachers' TV. The coach works with two teachers keen to improve their science teaching. They each focus on one lesson and develop approaches to making that lesson more engaging for their pupils. The teachers also support one another and so ensure continuing mutual support when the coach is no longer there.

Although it may not be seen as typical coaching, many teachers find that they learn a great deal when they see others teach their class, especially when away from school. In Chapter 20 we discussed the use of experts in providing valuable opportunities for learning outside the classroom. Class teachers attending with their class have the opportunity to observe a different style of teaching, to acquire useful information, and ideas. They also have the special experience of observing their own class learning and talking to the children in a way that, when managing a busy class, it is not always easy to do. Such trips are not only rich learning experiences for pupils, but have the potential to provide also a rich learning opportunity for the teacher. Many experienced outdoor and museum educators are aware of this as part of their role.

Collaborative groups and networks

Working with a knowledgeable expert coach has many advantages. However, where the coach is from outside the school, this can be expensive and is unlikely to be sustained over a lengthy period of time. It is clear that, where teachers work together to identify shared goals, then these collaborations have a high chance of success. In many primary schools the development plan has tended to focus on more general issues. In England the Every Child Matters agenda (DfES 2004) has resulted in work focusing more on PSHE or cross-school issues. A focus on Assessment for Learning has also been the whole school and not subject specific, as has the personalised learning agenda. Yet teachers can work together in smaller subject focused groups, often under the auspices of the more general issue to develop and support one another in trying out new ideas, observing one another teaching, or planning new topics together. Thus, although it might not have been seen in that light, the case study of the science week described in Chapter 2, where a group of teachers planned the week together, is a very good example of in-school professional development. Another such approach is for science subject leaders to work together in ways that support curriculum development, their own CPD, and help in planning the CPD they will provide in their own schools (see Box 26.2).

Box 26.2 Science subject leaders working together

A group of science subject leaders collaborated to look at developing a more creative primary science curriculum that teachers in their schools could use with confidence. The group worked together, supported by a local authority science adviser to develop, implement and evaluate their ideas. The feedback from schools was excellent, but in working together in this way it is also clear that the science coordinators themselves learnt a great deal from each other and from the process. They were, as a result better able to support their school colleagues' learning through the delivery of effective CPD and implement the new curriculum.

(Liyambo 2005)

Box 26.3 Small scale action research

Within science lessons my aim was to investigate how open questioning affected children's learning and enthusiasm about the unit of study. At the beginning of each unit I aimed to have an open question forum with the children. We would discuss what they already knew about the topic and identify areas that they would like to find out more about. This would then guide my planning and hopefully fire their enthusiasm for the unit.

At the time I was teaching Year 4 and focused on the unit of solids and liquids to try out this approach. We began with a circle time session to promote discussion and I presented the children with a selection of objects as an initial stimulus. We discussed the properties of what makes a solid or liquid and had a debate about the properties of tomato ketchup. We could not decide whether it was a solid or liquid! I then gave each child some coloured slips of paper. They wrote down what they already knew and what they would like to know. These slips of paper then formed part of the science display. A lot of their questions were about mixing different solids and liquids or heating and freezing them e.g. 'What happens when we mix flour, ketchup and water?', 'What happens when we freeze cotton wool?' I referred to these questions during the following science lessons and used them to guide my planning.

The most exciting result of this approach was the children's active involvement and interest in their own learning. A few children carried out investigations at home involving mixing different substances and heating or freezing them. Some of these 'experiments' were also brought into school, and the children explained their observations and understanding to the class. These children were interviewed two months later by a visitor from the university. They were able to recall the exact details of what they did and explain their understanding of what happened. Above all their enthusiasm was still apparent.

(http://www.uea.ac.uk/edu/creativepartnerships/primary/intro.html)

In some areas, groups of schools have formed networks to support professional development. These provide supportive structures which enable groups to get together in the way described by Liyambo. This type of CPD can be seen as a form of action research. Action research is an approach to exploring practice that begins with an issue or problem that a teacher or group of teachers wants to address. The research proceeds in a rigorous manner in which the problem is clarified, possible solutions suggested and tested, and the outcomes interrogated and reflected upon before conclusions are drawn and/or further exploration embarked upon.

Box 26.3 describes some action research undertaken by a teacher in her third year of teaching, as part of her involvement with a group of teachers, 'Creative Partnerships', at the University of East Anglia. She explored the use of open questioning with her class.

Networking with teachers and other educators who have similar interests and needs can be extremely rewarding and motivating. One strategy to support discussion in groups is to share stories of classroom experience. It is not always possible to spend time in one another's classroom, but, as Lemon (2007) explains, using photographs of lessons can provide a useful starting point for teachers to reflect on their own practice and to share insights as a supportive group.

Networked learning communities can provide opportunities to support informal groups. For example, in Liverpool, schools were formed into networks which then supported formal and informal groupings of teachers. Much of the time these groups, meeting in a network centre or in each other's schools, simply provided a forum for exchanging ideas. It sometimes led to more formal action-research type collaborations, or the identification of an expert in a particular field (from one of the schools or an external consultant) who could provide training to the school network. This cuts down the cost, makes use of the expertise that staff in the schools have, and serves as excellent CPD for those who are called upon to deliver INSET (Varga-Atkins *et al.* 2008).

The Internet provides another means of networking and collaboration that has only recently become widespread. There are many websites that provide information, but also offer opportunities for teachers to communicate with each other offering help and support. For example Bedfordshire's website recently presented information about science weeks held in different schools. This information was placed on the website for others to learn from (see Figure 26.1). One of the science coordinators provided his contact details, offering help to others in the authority who wanted to run such a week. Informal networking of this kind is becoming more widespread as the Internet develops. It is also possible to set up, or join, online discussion groups with like-minded teachers.

Learning at a distance

Part of the problem with attending courses is the time it takes, and often the distance travelled. It can also be the case that courses are not set up at appropriate times, and certainly cannot reach all those primary teachers who might benefit. AstraZeneca Science Teaching Trust (AZSTT) funds a wide range of projects large and small, supporting and developing primary science (Bishop and Feasey 2006). Recognising that many teachers and science coordinators will not have the opportunity to attend a course, they have developed materials to support CPD, much of it online. They will send PowerPoint presentations to coordinators to help their work with colleagues.

Science Week
9th - 18th March 2007
King's Wood School – The Future is Wild

On the 9th to 18th March 2007 science week took place, providing people of all ages with an opportunity to take part in science and technology activities.

King's Wood School brought science week alive in a fun, interactive and exciting way by allowing all their pupils from Foundation stage to year 6 to carry out different investigations with regards to evolution, climate change and adaptation, called The Future is Wild. The concept originated from the Science Conference last year and the school has adapted their own ideas from the conference.

Pupils had the opportunity to create masks, pictures and models of space and creatures using materials with different textures. In their classrooms there are many wonderful displays of their work that was completed during the week. Pupils searched for worms on the field using the hoops, linking this to habitats and evolution, pouring over soapy water and counting how many came to the surface.

The week ended in spectacular style as children came to school in fancy dress and designed a future creature with modelling clay with pupils providing a very interesting scientific reason for their wonderful creations.

The school is already thinking of their theme for next year's science week. They recommend the science and space week to both Primary and Secondary schools in Buckinghamshire.

(http://bucksgfl.org.uk)

Figure 26.1 Sharing ideas on the Internet

Other, more or less formal, accredited and non-accredited courses are available. Such courses are in their infancy in this field, but will, no doubt grow in the coming years.

Teachers' TV, which we have mentioned several times in this book, is an excellent source of CPD, providing very useful reviews of resources as well as short (15 minute) videos which are broadcast on television and can be downloaded from the Internet. These can be used by teachers individually, or provide the basis of group work where the ideas can be discussed and ideas shared.

The Internet itself is a powerful source of information and so can be invaluable for teachers who identify a need, whether this is in terms of gaps in subject knowledge, or to develop pedagogy. It is difficult to sort out all the opportunities available. The key to making the most of these opportunities is to identify needs as clearly as possible. Indeed, selecting a course, collaborating with others, or joining a network are decisions that teachers need to make carefully. Planning CPD starts with identifying needs and then looking to ways in which these needs can be met. In the next section we focus on identifying needs and planning CPD.

What CPD?

Needs analysis

Making decisions about what training and development is needed for an individual is complicated. This is because there is a tension between the needs of the school and the needs of the individual. Schools have development plans which result from a mix of national and local priorities, school inspection reports, and school self-evaluation. Given that CPD is not currently seen simply as sending teachers on a course, decisions about what CPD cannot do must always be made at an individual level. We have, for example, argued that there is real value in teachers from a group of schools working together on a project. This implies the identification of a common need across schools, which would suggest an emphasis on local priorities rather than on individual need.

In a report on CPD in effective schools (Ofsted 2006), it was argued that, in primary schools, staff development had tended to focus on general issues such as 'learning to learn' and on numeracy and literacy to the detriment of other subject areas. They also pointed out that mentoring and coaching, which would be appropriate at the level of individual development needs, is under-used. In a more recent report (Ofsted 2008b) the lack of science staff development in primary schools was identified as a particular area of concern.

Ofsted (2006) indicated that some schools have good systems in place to identify school level needs and to take this forward into appropriate training. This is done through systems of performance management, or appraisal, and through staff self-assessment of needs using questionnaire type instruments set against national standards or the school development plan. Specific subject-focused needs analysis is less common. There are systems in schools for monitoring teaching through peer observation. Teaching subject coordinators can use peer observation as a means to establish non threatening conversations about learning and can help individuals to identify needs that could be addressed through mentoring and coaching, through working with others, course attendance or a combination of these. There is currently no framework for development in science teaching available that might help in needs identification. However, this may emerge as the Association for Science Education, working with science learning centres, develops guidance or systems for science teacher development and accreditation.

Sources of support for CPD in science

Science learning centres

There are ten science learning centres in England (SLCs): nine situated in regions and one in the national centre in York (which serves the whole of the UK). They are generally custom-built with excellent facilities and staffed by experts. The SLCs offer a range of courses tailored as far as possible to the needs of the area they serve. These include long and short courses across the full range of ages and types of schools including technicians and teaching assistants. The core courses normally involve whole day sessions with pre and post session readings and activities and often materials to take away. The teacher quoted in Box 26.1 had attended a local SLC course.

In addition bespoke CPD can be provided and sessions are also offered in venues other than the main centre for ease of transport.

Although the science learning centres have provided courses for significant numbers of educators, meeting the targets set for them, Ofsted (2008b) has reported that most of the primary schools they visited were unaware of them, and those that were had not been able to use them. This seems to be due to a combination of cost, distance and a lack of focus on science in schools. However, some of this looks set to change with additional funds now going into SLCs to support staff in attending short and more extended programmes at the National Science Learning Centre in York. The Enthuse project based at the York Centre (http://www.sciencelearningcentres.org.uk/WebPortal.aspx?page=2) has funds to cover course fees, residential costs, replacement costs and small grants to help attendees to implement their new ideas back in school. This may not reach all schools, but it is a clear recognition of the need for support in the vital area of science education.

The Association for Science Education (ASE)

The Association for Science Education (ASE) offers support, research and resources at UK level and at regional level. As well as *Primary Science*, one of its main journals, it organises regular conferences and training courses in regional centres, with a large annual conference taking place in early January in England and another one in Scotland in March. These conferences provide a wealth of up-to-date information, ideas and resources and are highly valued by participants, especially 'primary day'. ASE is a key source of knowledge for science educators. It has close links with the science learning centres, with international bodies, and also acts to lobby for reforms and support for science education. ASE has recently developed CSciTeach (see below) and is working to support further developments in CPD in science.

Funding CPD

The system for general support of CPD in England is one of funding devolved to schools. However, there are plans being developed to require teachers to continue to study at master's level after qualification, having possibly obtained some M-level credits during postgraduate training, as mentioned earlier. The system is not, at the time of writing, fully worked out, so it remains to be seen as to what its impact will be.

Wales (GTCW 2008) has a CPD funding programme that invites teachers to bid for funds, for individual or group bursaries, for action research projects, travel for visits and for sabbaticals. This approach focuses more on CPD by collaborative projects and learning visits than on formal courses. The criteria for judging the applications are that they will have an impact on teachers and on pupils, that there are appropriate means of evaluation in place and that the project is value for money.

The system recently set up in Northern Ireland is similar to that in Wales in that it has bursaries available, but here the funds provide support to cover attendance at courses or conferences, or absence from schools to undertake other professional development (GTCNI 2008).

Using the available support

It is important for teachers and school managers to know what training and development is needed, how to identify the best approach to addressing needs and to be able to find out what resources are available to help meet those needs. This information needs to be considered by the science subject leader in a school working with a CPD coordinator or senior manager to ensure that appropriate training for the school and the individual teachers is available.

Recognising professional development

The status of chartered science teacher (CSciTeach) has recently been established and is awarded by the ASE under the terms of its royal charter. Like chartered engineer or chartered scientist it is intended to offer recognition of the 'unique and demanding combination of skills, knowledge, understanding and expertise that are required by individuals that are involved in practising and advancing science teaching and learning' (Bell and Lawrence 2006). To register as a CSciTeach a teacher needs to present evidence of achievement under a number of headings. These are:

- evidence of qualification at master's level or equivalent in pedagogy/education together with an honours-level qualification where at least half of the degree content was science;

- at least four years teaching experience, of which two should have involved an appropriate level of responsibility;

- having engaged in and reflected on appropriate professional development;

- work with colleagues and others to develop science education beyond the classroom;

- demonstrate a commitment to personal CPD;

- work within the professional code of conduct of CSciTeach;

- be able to provide evidence of professional expertise and competence in relation to professional knowledge and understanding, professional practice and professional attributes.

The approach allows for a range of different routes to be taken by individual teachers as they build a portfolio of evidence.

In Scotland there is a focus on the provision of funding for experienced teachers who wish to continue and validate their professional development and expertise (SEED 2002a). Although the Chartered Teacher scheme, which is open to all teachers at the top of the main scale, is not subject specific, it involves teachers either taking a number of study modules with recognised providers (universities) in order to develop the evidence base needed, or to gain some exemption through the provision of a portfolio of evidence. The basic assumption is that the chartered teacher is characterised by four central professional values and personal commitments:

1. effectiveness in promoting learning in the classroom;

2. critical self-evaluation and development;

3. collaboration and influence;

4. educational and social values.

Summary

We have discussed in this chapter the importance of continuing professional development for teachers, the forms this can take, sources of support and recognition of achievement. The main points have been:

- continuing professional development is both a right and a responsibility for teachers who, as professionals, need space and time to reflect on their own practice to keep learning and developing in an ever-changing context in order to enhance the learning experience of pupils;

- there are many forms of CPD, from mentoring and coaching through collaborating networks or online learning to full-time master's programmes – no one form alone is likely to support adequately professional development that has an impact on the classroom; a combination is likely to be of most benefit;

- strategies for assessing CPD needs in primary science are not well developed; however, peer observation and dialogue between subject coordinators and colleagues can lead to the identification of forms of CPD most likely to be effective in particular cases;

- there is a range of sources of CPD for primary science teaching which are less well known at present than they might be; membership of ASE (or appropriate national bodies) by schools would go some way to addressing this problem;

- the science coordinator has an important role in identifying CPD needs and gathering information about funding and local support available and using information freely available on Teachers' TV and the Internet.

Further reading

Bishop, K. and Feasey, R. (2006) Supporting in-school opportunities for professional development, *Primary Science Review* 95: 37–8.

Eraut, M. (1994) *Developing Professional Knowledge and Competence*, London: Taylor and Francis.

Liyambo, R. (2005) Planning a creative science curriculum, *Primary Science Review* 88: 16–19.

References

AAAS (American Association for Advancement of Science) (1989) *Science for All Americans. A Project 2061 Report on Literacy Goals in Science, Mathematics and Technology,* Washington DC: AAAS.

AAAS (American Association for Advancement of Science) (1993) *Benchmarks for Scientific Literacy*, New York: Oxford University Press.

Abelson, R.P. (1988) Beliefs are like possessions, *Journal for the Theory of Social Behavior* 16: 223–50.

ACTS project website http://www.sustainablethinkingclassrooms.qub.ac.uk/ (Accessed July 2008).

Adams, J. (2006) Starting out in your own backyard, *Primary Science Review* 91: 7–10.

Adey, P. and Shayer, M. (1994) *Really Raising Standards: Cognitive Intervention and Academic Achievement,* London: Routledge.

Aldrich, F. and Sheppard, L. (2000) 'Graphicacy' the fourth 'R'?, *Primary Science Review* 64: 8–11.

Alexander, R. (1995) *Versions of Primary Education*, London: Routledge.

Alexander, R. (2004) *Towards Dialogic Teaching: Rethinking Classroom Talk,* Cambridge: Dialogos.

Archambault, L. and Crippen, K. (2007) The sites teachers choose: a gauge of classroom web use, *Contemporary Issues in Technology and Teacher Education* 7 (2): 59–74.

ARG (Assessment Reform Group) (2002) *Testing, Motivation and Learning,* Cambridge: Faculty of Education. Available for download from the ARG website http://www.assessment-reform-group. org/ (Accessed August 2008).

ASE (Association for Science Education) (1999) *Science and the Literacy Hour,* Hatfield: ASE.

ASE (2001) *Be Safe*, 3rd edn, Hatfield: ASE.

ASE (2002) *Be Safe! INSET pack,* 2nd edn, Hatfield: Association for Science Education.

Asoko, H. and de Bóo, M. (2001) *Analogies and Illustrations: Representing Ideas in Primary Science*, Hatfield: Association for Science Education.

Asoko, H. and Scott, P. (2006) Talk in science classrooms, in W. Harlen (ed.) A*SE Guide to Primary Science Education*, Hatfield: Association for Science Education.

Bamberger, Y. and Tal, T. (2007) Learning in a personal context: levels of choice in a free choice learning environment in science and natural history museums, *Science Education* 91 (1): 75–95.

Baraclough, H. and Bracey, B. (2005) Cannonballs, scabs and vomit (ugh!!), *Primary Science Review* 87: 26–7.

Barker, S. and Buckle, S. (2002) Bringing birds into the classroom, *Primary Science Review* 75: 8–10.

Barnes, D. (1976) *From Communication to Curriculum,* Harmondsworth: Penguin.

Barnes, D. and Todd, F. (1995) *Communication and Learning Revisited,* London: Heinemann.

Barr, K. (2003) Managing science and technology, *Primary Science Review* 79: 4–6.

Battro, A.M. (2000) *Half a Brain is Enough: The Story of Nico*, Cambridge: Cambridge University Press.

Becta (2003). What the research says about interactive whiteboards. Coventry: Becta. www.becta.org. uk/page_documents/research/wtrs_whiteboards.pdf (Accessed August 2008).

Becta (2007) Virtual learning environments http://partners.becta.org.uk/index.php?section=rh&rid=13640 (Accessed August 2008).

Becta (2008) schools.becta.org.uk/index.php?section=re&&catcode=&rid=12892&rr=0 (Accessed August 2008).

Bell, D. and Lawrence, J. (2006) Recognising professional expertise: an invitation to apply to become a chartered science teacher, *Education in Science* 217, April: 12–13.

Bianchi, L. (2003) Better learners, *Primary Science Review*, 80: 22–4.

Bishop, K. and Feasey, R. (2006) Supporting in-school opportunities for professional development, *Primary Science Review* 95: 37–8.

Black, P. and Wiliam, D. (1998a) Assessment and classroom learning, *Assessment in Education* 5 (1): 7–74.

Black, P. and Wiliam, D. (1998b) *Inside the Black Box,* London: School of Education, King's College London.

Black, P., Harrison, C., Lee, C., Marshall, B. and Wiliam, D. (2002) *Working inside the Black Box,* London: King's College London.

Black, P., Harrison, C., Lee, C., Marshall, B. and Wiliam, D. (2003) *Assessment for Learning: Putting it into Practice,* Maidenhead: Open University Press.

Boctor, S. and Rowell, P. (2004) Why do bees sting? Reflecting on talk in science lessons, *Primary Science Review* 82: 15–17.

Bowker, R. (2004) Children's perceptions of plants following their visit to the Eden Project, *Research in Science and Technology Education* 22 (2): 227–43.

Bowker, R. and Jasper, A. (2007) Don't forget your leech socks! Children's learning during an Eden education officers' workshop, *Research in Science and Technology Education* 25 (1): 135 50.

Braund, M. (2003) Staying the course: one year on, *Education in Science*, Association for Science Education, April 202: 11–13.

Braund, M. (2004) Bridging work in science: what's in it for primary schools? *Primary Science Review* 82, 24–7.

Braund, M and Driver, M (2002) Moving to the big school: what do pupils think about science practical work pre- and post-transfer? Paper presented at the Annual Conference of the British Educational Research Association, University of Exeter, 12–14 September.

Budd-Rowe, M. (1974) Relation of wait-time and rewards to the development of language, logic and fate control: part II, *Journal of Research in Science Teaching* 11 (4): 291–308.

Burr, S. and Simpson, F. (2006) Swing through with science: a project to support transition from primary to secondary school through science; the primary perspective, paper presented at the Scottish Educational Research Association (SERA) Conference, Perth, 23–25 November 2006.

Burrows, D. (2004) Tidying the cupboard: the role of subject leaders in primary schools, NCSL Autumn 2004 www.ncsl.or.uk.

Burrows, P (2003) Managing health and safety in primary science, *Primary Science Review* 79: 18–20.

Butler, R. (1988) Enhancing and undermining intrinsic motivation: the effects of task-involving and ego-involving evaluation on interest and performance, *British Journal of Educational Psychology* 58: 1–14.

Byrne, J. and Sharp, J (2002) *Using ICT in Primary Science Teaching,* Exeter: Learning Matters.

CACE (1967) *Children and their Primary Schools* (Plowden Report), London: HMSO.

Cassop Primary School Co. Durham (2007) Harnessing wind and sun: using energy wisely, *Primary Science Review* 100: 35–7.

Cavendish, J., Stopps, B. and Ryan, C. (2006) Involving young children through stories as starting points, *Primary Science Review* 92: 18–20.

CCEA (Council for Curriculum, Examinations and Assessment) (nd) Northern Ireland Curriculum *Ideas for Connected Learning* http://www.nicurriculum.org.uk/connected_learning/icl/index.asp (Accessed August 2008).

CIEA (Chartered Institute of Educational Assessors) (2008) http://www.ciea.org.uk/.

CLEAPSS (2006) A guide for primary science coordinators (L255), Brunel University.

Conroy, J., Hulme, M. and Menter I. (2008) *Primary Curriculum and Assessment: Primary Curriculum Futures Primary Review Research Survey 3/3*, Cambridge: University of Cambridge Faculty of Education. Available from http://www.primaryreview.org.uk/,

Cordingley, P., Bell, M., Evans, D. and Firth, A. (2005) The impact of collaborative CPD on classroom teaching and learning. Review: what do teacher impact data tell us about collaborative CPD? *Research Evidence in Education Library*, London: EPPI-Centre, Social Science Research Unit, Institute of Education, University of London.

Dabell, J., Keogh, B., Naylor, S. (2006) Planning with goals in mind, in W. Harlen, (ed.) *ASE Guide to Primary Science Education,* Hatfield: ASE: 135–41.

Davids, S. (2008) Growing faster than their sunflowers, *Primary Science* 101: 5–8.

Dawes, L. (2004) Talk and reasoning in classroom science, *International Journal of Science Education* 26 (6): 677–95.

DCELLS (2008) *Science in the National Curriculum for Wales,* Cardiff: DCELLS http://new.wales.gov.uk/topics/educationandskills/curriculum_and_assessment/arevisedcurriculumforwales/nationalcurriculum/sciencenc/?lang=en (Accessed August 2008).

DCSF (Department for Children, Schools and Families) (2008) *The Assessment for Learning Strategy,* Nottingham: DCSF Publications.

DES (1989) *Aspects of Primary Education: The Teaching and Learning of Science,* London: HMSO.

DES/WO (1983) *Science at Age 11: APU Science Report for Teachers No. 1,* London: DES and Welsh Office.

DeWitt, J. and Osborne, J. (2007) Supporting teachers on science focused school trips: towards an integrated framework of theory and practice, *International Journal of Science Education* 29 (6): 685–710.

DfEE (Department for Education and Employment) and QCA (1998) *Science Teacher's Guide: A Scheme of Work for Key Stages 1 and 2,* London: DfEE and QCA.

DfEE (1999) *The National Curriculum: Handbook for Primary Schools,* London: DfEE,

DfEE/QCA (2000) *Curriculum Guidance for the Foundation Stage.* London: DfEE and QCA.

DfES (Department for Education and Skills) (2003) *Excellence and Enjoyment: A Strategy for Primary Schools,* London: DFES. Available at www.dfes.gov.uk/primarydocument.

DfES (2004) *Every Child Matters: Change for Children,* London: The Stationery Office.

DfES (2005) *The Social and Emotional Aspects of Learning Toolkit,* London: DfES.

DfES (2006) *Learning Outside the Classroom Manifesto,* London: HMSO. http://www.teachernet.gov.uk/teachingandlearning/resourcematerials/outsideclassroom/ (Accessed July 2008).

DfES (2007) *Making Good Progress.* Consultation, London: Department for Education and Skills.

DfES/Ofsted (2004) *A New Relationship with Schools,* London: DfES and Ofsted.

Digizen (2008) *Young People and Social Networking Services: A Childnet International Research Report* Childnet www.digizen.org.

Dillon, J., Morris, M., O'Donnell, L., Rickinson, M. and Scott, M. (2005) *Engaging and Learning with the Outdoors: The Final Report of the Outdoor Classroom in a Rural Context Action Research Project,* Slough: NFER.

Earl, L. and Katz, S. (2008) Getting to the core of learning: using assessment for self-monitoring and self-regulation, in S. Swaffield (ed.) *Unlocking Assessment: Understanding for Reflection and Application,* London: David Fulton.

East Sussex School Improvement Service (2005) *Developing the Role of Subject Leaders in Primary, Secondary and Special Schools,* East Sussex School Improvement Service.

Edmonds, J. (2002) Inclusive science: supporting the EAL child, *Primary Science Review* 74: 4–6.

Elstgeest, J. (2001) The right question at the right time, in W. Harlen, (ed.) *Primary Science: Taking the Plunge,* 2nd edn, Portsmouth, NH: Heinemann.

Eraut, M. (1994) *Developing Professional Knowledge and Competence,* London: Taylor & Francis.

Ergo Computing (2007) Using tablet PCs to take a closer look, http://www.ergo.co.uk/pdf/case_studies/fairfield.pdf (Accessed August 2008).

Estyn (2004) *Guidance on the Inspection of Primary and Nursery Schools,* Cardiff: Estyn.

European Commission (2006) *Science Education Now: A Renewed Pedagogy for the Future of Europe,* (The Rocard report), Brussels: European Commission.

Evans, N. (2001) Thoughts on assessment and marking, *Primary Science Review,* 68: 24–6.

Evans, S., and Dunne, M. (2006) The digital microscope: that belongs in Key Stage 2 doesn't it?, *Primary Science Review* 93: 4–7.

Fairbrother, R. (1995) Pupils as learners, in R. Fairbrother, R. Black and P. Gill (eds), *Teachers Assessing Pupils,* Hatfield: ASE.

Feasey, R. (1998) Scientific investigations in context, in R. Sherrington (ed.) *ASE Guide to Primary Science Education,* Hatfield: ASE/Stanley Thornes.

Feasey, R. (1999) *Primary Science and Literacy,* Hatfield: Association for Science Education.

Feasey, R. (2003) Creative Futures, *Primary Science Review* 78: 21–3.

Feasey, R. and Gallear, R. (2000) *Primary Science and Numeracy,* Hatfield: Association for Science Education.

Fisher, J.A. (2001) The demise of fieldwork as an integral part of science education in schools: a victim of cultural change and political pressure, *Pedagogy, Culture and Society* 9 (1): 75–96.

Foxman, D., Hutchinson, D. and Bloomfield, B. (1991) *The APU Experience, 1977–1990,* London: Schools Examination and Assessment Council.

Fradley, C. (2006) Welly walks for science learning, *Primary Science Review* 91: 14–16.

Frand, J. (2000) The information-age mindset; changes in students and implications for Higher Education, *Educause review*: 15–24. http://connect.educause.edu/Library/EDUCAUSE+Review/TheInformationAgeMindsetC/40216?time=1204296604.

Galton, M.J., Simon, B. and Croll, P. (1980) *Inside the Primary Classroom,* London: Routledge and Kegan Paul.

Galton, M, Gray, J. and Ruddock, J. (1999a) *The Impact of School Transitions and Transfers on Pupil Progress and Attainment,* Research report RR131, London: DfEE.

Galton, M.J., Hargreaves, L., Comber, C., Wall, D. and Pell, T. (1999b) Changes in patterns of teacher interaction in the primary classroom: 1976–96, *British Educational Research Journal* 25 (1): 23–37.

Gardner, J. (ed.) (2006) *Assessment and Learning,* London: Sage.

Garet, M.S., Porter, A.C., Desimone, L., Birman, B.F. and Yoon, K.S. (2001) What makes professional development effective? Results from a national sample of teachers, *American Educational Research Journal* 38 (4): 915–45.

Gillard, L. and Whitby, V. (2007) Managing the primary curriculum: policy into practice in England, *Research in Science & Technological Education*, 25(2): 211–26.

Gipps, C.V. (1994) *Beyond Testing*, London: Falmer.

Goldsworthy, A. (2003) *Raising Attainment in Primary Science: Assessment, Monitoring and Evaluation*. Oxford: GHPD.

Goldsworthy, A., Watson, R. and Wood-Robinson, V. (1998) Sometimes it's not fair, *Primary Science Review* 53: 15–17.

Goldsworthy, A., Watson, R. and Wood-Robinson, V. (2000) *Investigations: Developing Understanding*, Hatfield: Association for Science Education.

Goswami, U. and Bryant, P. (2007) *Children's Cognitive Development and Learning*. Primary Review Research Survey 2/1a. Available at www.primaryreview.org.uk.

Greenfield, S. (1997) *The Human Brain: A Guided Tour*, London: Phoenix.

GTCNI (General Teaching Council for Northern Ireland) (2008) *Professional Development Bursary Programme* (Accessed July 2008) http://www.gtcni.org.uk/uploads/docs/Bursary%20 Application%20%20form%20and%20Information%20for%20Teachers.doc.

GTCW (General Teaching Council of Wales), CPD Funding Information Booklet April 2008–March 2011. http://www.gtcw.org.uk/cpd/information.html (Accessed July 2008).

Guichard, J. (1995) Designing tools to develop conceptions of learners, *International Journal of Science Education* 17(1): 243–53.

Hall, I. and Higgins, S. (2007) Primary pupils' perceptions of interactive whiteboards, *Journal of Computer Assisted Learning* 21:102–17.

Hall, J. (2005) *Neuroscience and Education: What can Brain Science Contribute to Teaching and Learning?* Spotlight 92, Glasgow: The SCRE Centre, University of Glasgow.

Harlen, W. (ed.) (2001) *Primary Science: Taking the Plunge*, 2nd edn, Portsmouth, NH: Heinemann.

Harlen, W. (2005) Teachers' summative practices and assessment for learning – tensions and synergies, *The Curriculum Journal* 16 (2): 207–23.

Harlen, W. (2006a) *Teaching, Learning and Assessing Science 5–12*, 4th edn, London: Sage.

Harlen, W. (2006b) On the relationship between assessment for formative and summative purposes, in J. Gardner (ed.) *Assessment and Learning*, London: Sage.

Harlen, W. (2007a) The SPACE legacy, *Primary Science Review* 97: 13–15.

Harlen, W. (2007b) *Assessment of Learning*, London: Sage.

Harlen, W (2007c) Holding up a mirror to classroom practice, *Primary Science Review* 100: 29–31.

Harlen, W. (2008) *Science as a Key Component of the Primary Curriculum: A Rationale with Policy Implications*, London: Wellcome Trust.

Harlen, W. and Deakin Crick, R. (2003) Testing and motivation for learning, *Assessment in Education* 10 (2): 169–207.

Harlen, W. and Holroyd, C. (1995) Primary teachers' understanding of concepts in science and technology. *Interchange* No 35 Edinburgh: SOED.

Harlen, W., Macro, C., Reed, K. and Schilling, M. (2003) *Making Progress in Primary Science: Study Book*, London: Routledge Falmer.

Harrison, C., Comber, C., Fisher, T., Haw, K., Lewin, C., Linzer, E., McFarlane, A., Mavers, D., Scrimshaw, P., Somekh, B. and Watling, R. (2002) *Impact2: the Impact of Information and Communication Technologies on Pupil Learning and Attainment*, Coventry: Becta.

Hawking, S.W. (1988) *A Brief History of Time*, London: Bantam Press.

Haworth, C., Dale, P. and Plomin, R. (2008) A twin study into the genetic and environmental influences on academic performance in science in nine-year-old boys and girls, *International Journal of Science Education* 30 (8): 1003–25.

Hickey, I., Murphy, C., Beggs, J. and Carlisle, K. (2005) Murder in the classroom, *Primary Science Review* 90: 6–8.

Hickey, I., Robson, D., Flanagan, M. and Campbell, P. (2008) Leonardo flies again: integrating science and art, *Primary Science* 103: 9–13.

Higgins, S., Beauchamp, G. and Miller, D. (2007) Reviewing the literature on interactive whiteboards, *Learning, Media and Technology* 32 (3): 213–35.

Hodson, D. (1993) Re-thinking old ways: towards a more critical approach to practical work in school science, *Studies in Science Education* 22: 85–142.

Hodson, D. (1998) *Teaching and Learning Science,* Buckingham: Open University Press.

Howard-Jones, P., Pollard, A., Blakemore, S-J., Rogers, P. Goshwami, U., Butterworkth, B., Taylor, E., Williamon, A., Morton, J. and Kaufmann, L. (2007) *Neuroscience and Education: Issues and Opportunities,* London: TLRP/ESRC.

Howe, C. (1990) Grouping children for effective learning in science, *Primary Science Review* (13): 26–7.

Howe, C., Rodgers, C. and Tolmie, A. (1992) The acquisition of conceptual understanding of science in primary school children: group interaction and the understanding of motion down an incline, *British Journal of Developmental Psychology* 10: 113–30.

Howe, C., Tolmie, A., Thurston, A., Topping, K., Christie, D., Livingston, K., Jessiman, E. and Donaldson, C. (2007) Group work in elementary science: towards organisational principles for supporting pupil learning, *Learning and Instruction* 17: 549–63.

Hoyle, E. and Megarry, J. (eds) (1980) *Professional Development of Teachers,* London: Kogan Page.

IAP (Interacademy Panel) (2006) Report of the working group on international collaboration in the evaluation of enquiry-based science education (IBSE) programs, Santiago, Chile: University of Chile, Faculty of Medicine.

The Independent (2008) Green tax revolt: Britons will not foot the bill to save planet, 2 June 2008.

Isaacs, N. (1962) The case for bringing science into the primary school, in *The Place of Science in Primary Education,* London: The British Association for the Advancement of Science.

Jabin, Z. and Smith, R. (1994) Using analogies of electricity flow in circuits to improve understanding, *Primary Science Review* 35: 23–6.

James, M., McCormick, R., Black, P., Carmichael, P., Drummond, M-J., Fox, A., MacBeath, J., Marshall, B., Pedder, D., Proctor, R., Swaffield, S., Swann, J. and Wiliam, D. (2007) *Improving Learning How to Learn,* London: Routledge.

Jannikos, M. (1995) Are the stereotyped views of scientists being brought into the 90s?, *Primary Science Review* (37): 27–9.

Jarvis, T. and Pell, A. (2005) Factors influencing elementary school children's attitude towards science before, during and after a visit to the UK National Space Centre, *Journal of Research in Science Teaching* 42 (1): 53–83.

Jelly, S.J. (2001) Helping children to raise questions – and answering them, in W. Harlen (ed.) *Primary Science: Taking the Plunge,* 2nd edn, Portsmouth, New Hampshire: Heinemann.

Jewitt, C., Moss, G. and Cardini, A., (2007) Pace, interactivity and multimodality in teachers' design of texts for interactive whiteboards in the secondary school classroom, *Learning, Media and Technology* 32 (3): 303–17.

Johnson, C. (2007) Whole school collaborative sustained science teacher professional development and science teacher change: signs of progress, *Journal of Science Teacher Education* 18: 629–61.

Johnston, J. (2005) *Early Explorations in Science,* Maidenhead: Open University Press.

Kennwell, S., Tanner, H., Jones, S. and Beauchamp, G. (2007) Analysing the use of interactive technology to implement interactive teaching, *Journal of Computer Assisted Learning* 24: 61–73.

Keogh, B. and Naylor, S. (1998) Teaching and learning science using Concept Cartoons, *Primary Science Review,* 51, 14–16.

Keogh, B. and Naylor, S. (2000) *Concept Cartoons in Science Education*, Sandbach: Millgate House Publishers.

Keogh, B and Naylor, S. (2004) Children's ideas, children's feelings, *Primary Science Review* 82: 18–20.

Keogh, B. and Naylor, S, (2006) Access and engagement for all, in W. Harlen (ed.) *ASE Guide to Primary Science Education,* Hatfield: ASE.

Keogh, B., Naylor, S., Downing, B., Maloney, J. and Simon S. (2006) Puppets bringing stories to life in science, *Primary Science Review* 92: 26–8.

Kibble, B. (2006) Teaching for progression in conceptual understanding, in W. Harlen, (ed.) *ASE Guide to Primary Science Education*, Hatfield: Association for Science Education.

Kiseil, J.F. (2007) Examining teacher choices for science museum worksheets, *Journal of Science Teacher Education* 18: 29–43.

Kluger, A.N. and DeNisi, A. (1996) The effects of feedback interventions on performance: a historical review, a meta-analysis, and a preliminary intervention theory, *Psychological Bulletin* 119: 254–84.

Kohn, A. (1993) *Punished by Rewards*, Boston, MA: Houghton Mifflin.

Lawrence, L. (2006) The science subject leader's role, in W. Harlen (ed.) *ASE Guide to Primary Science Education*, Hatfield: ASE, 83–9.

Layton, D. (1990) *Inarticulate Science.* Occasional Paper No. 17. Department of Education, University of Liverpool.

Layton, D. (1993) *Technology's Challenge to Science Education,* Buckingham: Open University Press.

Leadbeater, C. (2004) *Personalisation through Participation: A New Script for Public Services*, London: Demos.

Lemon, N.S. (2007) Take a photograph: teacher reflection through narrative, *Reflective Practice* 8 (2): 177–91.

Lias, S. and Thomas, C. (2003) Using digital photographs to improve learning in science, *Primary Science Review* 76: 17–19.

Ligorio, M.B. and Van der Meijden, H. (2007) Teacher guidelines for cross-national virtual communities in primary education, *Journal of Computer Assisted Learning* (2008) 24: 11–25.

Liyambo, R. (2005) Planning a creative science curriculum, *Primary Science Review* 88: 16–19.

Lowe, G. (2006) Goldilocks and the three variables, *Primary Science Review* 92: 11–13.

Luckin, R., du Boulay, B., Smith, H., Underwood, J., Fitzpatrick, G., Holmberg, J., Kerawalla, L., Tunley, H., Brewster, D and Pearce, D. (2005). Using mobile technology to create flexible learning contexts, *Journal of Interactive Media in Education* 22, Special Issue on portable learning – Experiences with Mobile Devices.

McCrory, P. (2008) Getting them emotional about science, *Education in Science*, 229: 26–7.

McFall, D. and Macro, C. (2004) Creativity and science in the nursery, *Primary Science Review* 81: 7–10.

McGuinness, C. (1999) *From Thinking Skills to Thinking Classrooms: A Review and Evaluation of Approaches for Developing Pupils' Thinking. Research Report RR115*. Nottingham: DfEE.

McGuinness, C. (2000) ACTS (Activating Children's Thinking Skills): a methodology for enhancing thinking skills across the curriculum. Paper presented at the ESRC TLRP conference 9/10 November, 2000.

McGuinness, C., Curry, C., Eakin, A. and Sheehy, N. (2005) Metacognition in primary classrooms: a pro-ACTive learning effect for children. Paper presented at the TLRP Annual Conference, University of Warwick, 28–30 November, 2005.

McMahon, K. and Davies, D. (2003) Building bridges between primary and secondary science for children and teachers, *Primary Science Review* 80: 7–9.

McMeniman, M. (1989) Motivation to learn, in P. Langford (ed.) *Educational Psychology: An Australian Perspective*, Cheshire: Longman.

Mant, J., Wilson, H. and Coates, D. (2007) The effect of increasing conceptual challenge in primary science lessons on pupils' achievement and engagement, *International Journal of Science Education* 29 (14): 1707–19.

Massey, A., Green, S., Dexter, T. and Hammet, L.(2003) *Comparability of National Tests over Time: KS1, KS2 and KS3 Standards Between 1996 and 2001. Final Report to the QCA of the Comparability over Time Project*, Cambridge: Research and Evaluation Division of the University of Cambridge Local Examinations Syndicate.

Mercer, N., Dawes, R., Wegerif, R. and Sams, C. (2004) Reasoning as a scientist: ways of helping children to use language to learn science, *British Educational Research Journal* 30 (3): 367–85.

Millar, R. and Osborne, J. (1998) *Beyond 2000: Science Education for the Future,* London: King's College London, School of Education.

Morgan, M. (ed.) (nd) *Art in the First Years of Schooling*, Suffolk County Council.

Moss, G., Jewitt, C., Levaãiç, R., Armstrong, V., Cardini. A. and Castle, F. (2007) *The Interactive Whiteboard, Pedagogy and Pupil Performance Evaluation: An Evaluation of the Schools Whiteboard Expansion (SWE) Project: London Challenge,* London: Institute of Education, University of London/DfES.

Murphy, C. and Beggs, J. (2003) Children's perceptions of school science, *School Science Review* 84 (308): 109–16.

Murphy, P., Davidson, M., Qualter, A., Simon, S. and Watt, D. (2000) Effective practice in primary science. A report of an exploratory study funded by the Nuffield Curriculum Projects Centre.

NACCCE (National Advisory Committee on Creative and Cultural Education) (1999) *All Our Futures: Creativity, Culture and Education,* London: DfEE. Available from www.artscampaigne.org.uk/campaigns/education/report.html.

Naylor, C., Erickson, G., Clarke, T., Lim-Fong, B., Brook, D., Cassie, L., Cyr, H., Fong, M., Robins, R., Watkins, D., Wong, G. and Zubke, S. (2008) My teaching took off sideways: the unexpected impact of Smartboards and the emergence of a professional learning community within an elementary school. Paper presented at the Canadian Society for Studies in Education (CSSE), University of British Columbia, Vancouver, May 31–June 2, 2008.

Naylor, S and Keogh, B (2000) *Concept Cartoons in Science Education*, Sandbach, Cheshire: Millgate House Publishers.

Naylor, S., Keogh, B. and Downing, B. (2007) Argumentation in primary science, *Research in Science Education* 37: 177–9.

NEF (New Economics Foundation) (2003) Forest Schools Evaluation Project: a study in Wales April to November
http://www.neweconomics.org/gen/uploads/bheolf55nxgesmexvhdh0v4529072004140937.pdf.

New Standards (1997) *Performance Standards: Volume 1 Elementary School, English, Language Arts, Mathematics, Science, Applied Learning,* Pittsburgh, PA: National Centre on Education and the Economy.

Newton, D.P. and Newton, L.D. (2001) Subject content knowledge and teacher talk in the primary science classroom, *European Journal of Teacher Education*, 24 (3): 369–79.

Newton, L.D., Newton, D.P., Blake, A. and Brown, K. (2002) Do primary school science books for children show a concern for explanatory enderstanding?, *Research in Science and Technological Education* 20 (2): 228–39.

Nimmons, F. (2003) Tracking Pupils' Progress, *Primary Science Review* 80: 13–15.

Northern Ireland Curriculum (2008) Ideas for connecting learning, www.nicurriculum.org.uk/connected_learning/id/index.asp.

NRC (National Research Council) (1996) *National Science Education Standards,* Washington DC: National Academy Press.

Nuffield Primary Science Teachers' Guides (1995) *Various Topics,* London: Collins Educational.

OECD (Organization for Economic Cooperation and Development) (1999) *Measuring Student Knowledge and Skills, a New Framework for Assessment,* Paris: OECD.

OECD (Organization for Economic Cooperation and Development) (2003) *The PISA 2003 Assessment Framework,* Paris: OECD.

OECD (Organization for Economic Cooperation and Development) (2007) *Understanding the Brain: The Birth of a Learning Science,* Paris: OECD.

Ofsted (2004) *Ofsted Science Subject Reports 2002/3. Science in the Primary School,* London: DfEE.

Ofsted (2006) *The Logical Chain: CPD in Effective Schools,* Reference HMI 2639. http://www.ofsted.gov.uk/portal/site/Internet/menuitem.eace3f09a603f6d9c3172a8a08c08a0c/?vgnextoid=86988f564353d010VgnVCM1000003507640aRCRD.

Ofsted (2008a) *Schools and Sustainability: A Climate for Change,* Ofsted May 2008.

Ofsted (2008b) *Success in Science,* Ref HMI 070195, http://www.ofsted.gov.uk/assets/Internet_Content/Shared_Content/Files/2008/june/sucinsci.pdf (Accessed August 2008).

Ormerod, M.B. and Duckworth, D. (1975) *Pupils' Attitudes to Science,* Windsor: NFER.

Osborne, R.J. and Freyberg, P. (1985) *Learning in Science: The Implications of 'Children's Science',* Auckland: Heinemann.

Osborne, J., Wadsworth, P. and Black, P. (1992) *Processes of Life,* SPACE Project Research Report, Liverpool: Liverpool University Press.

Owen, D., Baskerville, S. and Evans, W. (2008) From source to sea, *Primary Science* 101: 25–7.

Paterson, V. (1987) What might be learnt from children's writing in primary science? *Primary Science Review* 4: 17–20.

Peacock, A. (2006a) Editorial, *Primary Science Review* 91: 2–3.

Peacock, A. (2006b) *Changing Minds: The Lasting Impact of School Trips: A Study of the Long Term Impact of Sustained Relationships between Schools and the National Trust via The Guardianship Scheme.* http://www.nationaltrust.org.uk/main/w-schools-guardianships-changing_minds.pdf (Accessed July 2008).

Peacock, A. and Weedon, H. (2002) Children working with text in science: disparities with 'literacy hour' practice, *Research in Science and Technological Education* 20 (2): 185–97.

Popper, K. R. (1968) *The Logic of Scientific Discovery,* London: Hutchinson.

PricewaterhouseCoopers (2001) *Teacher Workload Study,* London: DfES.

PSR Editorial Board (2007) All change or small change? *Primary Science Review* 100: 9–13.

QCA (Qualifications and Curriculum Authority) (2003) *Foundation Stage Profile Handbook,* London: QCA.

QCA (2004) *Key Stage 2, Years 3 to 6, Assessment and Reporting Arrangements,* London: QCA.

QCA (2007a) *Science. Programme of Study for Key Stage 3 and Attainment Targets,* London: QCA.

QCA (2007b) *Foundation Stage Profile Optional Booklet,* London: QCA.

QCA (2007c) *Assessment and Reporting Arrangements.* London: QCA.

Qualter, A. (1996) *Differentiated Primary Science,* Buckingham: Open University Press.

Qualter, A. (2005) Role play boxes: taking science home, *Primary Science Review,* 90: 21–3.

Redmore, A. Teacher Expertise website: (Accessed August 2008) http://www.teachingexpertise.com/articles/cpd-for-science-teachers-2335.

Richardson, I. (2005) The baker did it! *Primary Science Review* 90: 4–5.

Richardson, I. (2006) What is good science education? in W. Harlen (ed.) *ASE Guide to Primary Science,* Hatfield: ASE.

Ritchie, R. (1998) From science coordinator to science subject leader, in R. Sherrington (ed.) *ASE Guide to Primary Science Education,* Hatfield: ASE.

Robertson, A. (2004) Let's think! Two years on! *Primary Science Review* 82: 4–7.

Royal Society (2006) *Taking a Leading Role,* London: The Royal Society.

Rudd, T. (2007) Future lab whiteboards report http://www.futurelab.org.uk/resources/documents/other/whiteboards_report.pdf.

Russell, T. and Harlen, W. (1990) *Assessing Science in the Primary Classroom: Practical Tasks,* London: Paul Chapman Publishing.

Russell, T. and Watt, D. (1990) *Primary SPACE Project Report: Growth,* Liverpool: Liverpool University Press.

Russell, T., Longden, K. and McGuigan, L (1991) *Primary SPACE Project Report: Materials,* Liverpool: Liverpool University Press.

Schilling, M., Hargreaves, L., Harlen, W. and Russell, T. (1990) *Assessing Science in the Primary Classroom: Written Tasks,* London: Paul Chapman Publishing.

Science 5/13 (1972) *Working with Wood,* Unit for Teachers, London: Macdonald.

SEED (Scottish Executive Education Department) (2002a) *Standards for Chartered Teacher,* Edinburgh: The Stationery Office.

SEED (2002b) *How Good is our School? Self-Evaluation Using Quality Indicators,* Edinburgh: HMIE.

SEED (2003) *Assessment of Achievement Programme, Report of the Sixth AAP Survey of Science,* Edinburgh: SEED.

SEED (Scottish Executive Education Department) (2005) *Circular 02,* June, Edinburgh: SEED.

Select Committee on Science and Technology (2007) Submission from the V&A Museum of Childhood Written Evidence, Memorandum 7 June 2007.

Serret, N. (2004) Leaping into the unknown: developing thinking in the primary science classroom, *Primary Science Review* 82: 8–11.

Sharp, J.G. and Hopkin, R.C. (2008) *National Primary Science Survey (England): In-service Training Audit; A Report Prepared for the Wellcome Trust,* Bishop Grosseteste University College Lincoln and the Wellcome Trust.

Shulman, L.S. (1987) Knowledge and teaching: foundations of the new reform, *Harvard Educational Review* 7, 1–22.

Shulman, L.S. (1991) Pedagogical ways of knowing, in *Improving the Quality of the Teaching Profession. International Yearbook on Teacher Education, 1990.* Singapore: ICET.

Simon, S., Black, P., Blondel, E. and Brown, M. (1994) *Forces in Balance,* Hatfield: ASE and King's College London

Skinner, B.F. (1950) Are theories of learning necessary? *Psychological Review* 57: 193–216.

Skinner, B.F. (1974) *About Behaviourism,* New York: Alfred A. Knopf.

Smith, F., Hardman, F. and Higgins, S. (2006) The impact of interactive whiteboards on teacher–pupil interaction in the national literacy and numeracy strategies, *British Educational Research Journal* 32 (3): 443–57.

SPACE (Science Processes and Concepts Exploration) Research Reports. *Evaporation and Condensation* (1990), *Growth* (1990), *Light* (1990), *Sound* (1990), *Electricity* (1991), *Materials* (1991), *Processes of Life* (1992), *Rocks, Soil and Weather* (1992), Liverpool: Liverpool University Press.

Sutherland, R., Armstrong, V., Barnes, S., Brawn, R., Breeze, N., Gall, M., Matthewson, S., Olivero, F., Taylor, A., Triggs, P., Wishart, J. and John, P. (2004) Transforming teaching and learning: embedding ICT into everyday classroom practices, *Journal of Computer Assisted Learning* 20: 413–25.

Sutton, N. (2001) The literacy hour and science: towards a clearer picture, *Primary Science Review* 69: 28–9.

Swaffield, S. (2008) Feedback: the central process in assessment for learning, in S. Swaffield (ed.) *Unlocking Assessment,* London: David Fulton.

TDA (Training and Development Agency for Schools) (2007) TDA Board, October 17.

Teachernet health and safety website http://www.teachernet.gov.uk/wholeschool/healthandsafety/visits/.

Teachers'TV (March 2008) Getting out of the classroom – a day with the RSPB, www.teacherstv/.

Teachers'TV (March 2008) Getting out of the classroom – outdoor learning with Forrest School, www.teacherstv/.

Teachers'TV (April 2008) Need to know: safe school trips, www.teacherstv/.

Teacher Training Agency (2001) *Qualifying to Teach: Professional Standards for Qualified Teacher Status and Requirements for Initial Teacher Training,* London: TTA, http://www.tta.gov.uk/php/read.php?sectionid=108.

Teaching and Learning Research Programme (2005) *Briefing No 11: Improving Pupil Group Work in Classrooms, A New Approach to Increasing Engagement in Everyday Classroom Settings at Key Stages 1, 2 and 3,* London: TLRPn, http://www.groupworkscotland.org/ (Accessed July 2008).

TERU (Technical Education Research Unit) (2007) The Leonardo Effect: A research report for NESTA, http://gtcni.openrepository.com/gtcni/bitstream/2428/15217/1/Leonardo%20final%20report%20for%20NESTA.pdf.

Thornton, L. and Brunton, P (2003) All about the Reggio Approach, *Nursery World,* January 2003, 15.

Tondeur, J., van Braak, J. and Valcke, M. (2007) Towards a typology of computer use in primary education, *Journal of Computer Assisted Learning* 23 (3): 197–206.

Tunnicliffe, S.D. (2001) Talking about plants: comments of primary school groups looking at plants exhibits in a botanical garden, *Journal of Biological Education* 36 (1): 27–34.

Tunnicliffe, S.D. and Litson, S. (2002) Observation or imagination, *Primary Science Review* 71: 25–7.

Tymms, P. (2004) Are standards rising in English primary school? *British Educational Research Journal* 30 (4): 477–94.

Varga-Atkins, T., Qualter, A. and O'Brien, M. (2008) From 'believers' to 'sceptics': school professionals' attitudes to professional development in learning networks, paper presented at the 10th International Conference on Education in Athens, 26–29 May 2008.

Vygotsky, L.S. (1962) *Thought and Language,* Massachusetts: MIT Press.

Wardle, C. (2000) Literacy links to light and dark, *Primary Science Review,* 64, 26–7.

Warwick, P., Wilson, E. and Winterbottom, M. (eds) (2006) *Teaching and Learning Primary Science with ICT*, Maidenhead: Open University Press.

Watt, D. and Russell, T. (1990) *Primary SPACE Project Report: Sound,* Liverpool: Liverpool University Press.

Wegerif, R. (2006) Literature review in thinking skills technology and learning futurelab, www.futurelab.org.uk/research/lit_reviews.htm.

Wellcome Trust (2005) *Primary Horizons: Starting Out in Science,* available from www.wellcome.ac.uk/primaryhorizons.

West Sussex Grid for Learning (2004) http://wsgfl.westsussex.gov.uk/ccm/content/curriculum/ict/teach-and-learn/interesting-tools/pc-tablets---st-philips-catholic-primary-school-arundel.en?page=1 (Accessed July 2008).

Wiliam, D. (2008) Quality in assessment, in S. Swaffield (ed.) *Unlocking Assessment,* London: David Fulton.

Williamson, B. (2006) Elephants can't jump: creativity, new technology and concept exploration in primary science, in P. Warwick, E. Wilson and M. Winterbottom (eds) *Teaching and Learning Primary Science with ICT,* Maidenhead: Open University Press.

Winter, S. (1998) International comparisons of student achievement, *Education 3–13,* 26 (2): 26–33.

Wright, L. (2006) School self-evaluation of teaching and learning science, in W. Harlen (ed.) *ASE Guide to Primary Science Education,* Hatfield: ASE, 73–9.

Zull, J.E. (2004) The art of changing the brain, *Educational Leadership* 62 (1): 68–72.

Index